THE FUNDAMENTALS OF RISK MEASUREMENT

THE FUNDAMENTALS OF RISK MEASUREMENT

CHRIS MARRISON, PH.D

Boston, Massachusetts   Burr Ridge, Illinois
Dubuque, Iowa   Madison, Wisconsin   New York, New York
San Francisco, California   St. Louis, Missouri

McGraw-Hill

*A Division of The **McGraw·Hill** Companies*

3 4 5 6 7 8 9 BKM BKM   0 9 8 7 6 5 4 3

ISBN 0-07-138627-0

This publication is designed to provide accurate and authoritative information in regard to the subject matter covered. It is sold with the understanding that the publisher is not engaged in rendering legal, accounting, or other professional service. If legal advice or other expert assistance is required, the services of a competent professional person should be sought.

> —*From a declaration of principles jointly adopted by a committee of the American Bar Association and a committee of publishers.*

McGraw-Hill books are available at special quantity discounts to use as premiums and sales promotions, or for use in corporate training programs. For more information, please write to the Director of Special Sales, Professional Publishing, McGraw-Hill, Two Penn Plaza, New York, NY 10121. Or contact your local bookstore.

CONTENTS

PREFACE

Over the last decade, the understanding of risk measurement has become increasingly important as most international banks have adopted Value-at-Risk, economic capital, and risk-adjusted return on capital (RAROC) to control and price their risks. They use these tools to find the loans, trades, and deals that are most profitable, leaving the unprofitable ones for their less sophisticated competitors. The understanding of risk measurement is therefore vital to those who want to manage a bank safely and profitably.

The importance of these risk measurement tools has been greatly magnified by regulators, such as the Federal Reserve and the Bank of England, who plan to start using these concepts to calculate the minimum amount of capital that banks must hold. For competitive and regulatory reasons, it is now necessary for all banks to have a sound risk-measurement framework.

This book was written to address the growing need for easy-to-understand information about how banks can apply effective risk measurement techniques. The goals of this book are the following:

- Provide quick access to the whys and hows of risk measurement.
- Provide easy-to-understand information, including equations and examples, that can be quickly applied to most risk measurement problems.
- Provide information about how risk measurement is used in the management of risk and profitability.

This is a textbook to teach you how to measure risk. The book assumes that you have a general background in science, economics, or finance, and now have a need to quickly understand the field of financial risk analysis. Alternatively you may already have a good understanding of one area of risk but now seek to have an integrated understanding across all types.

The book is deliberately compact so it can be read and understood quickly. It includes background chapters for those unfamiliar with finance and statistics, and includes descriptions of the many techniques that are commonly used in risk measurement. It applies these techniques to the four major risks faced by banks: market risk, credit risk, asset liability mismatch, and operating risk.

The book begins with chapters describing how banks make, and often lose, money. It then describes the two fundamental building blocks of integrated risk measurement: economic capital and RAROC. Chapter 3 reviews the statistical relationships that are commonly used in risk measurement and provides reference material for the rest of the book. It is useful for those readers who do not have a recent working knowledge of statistics.

Market risks arise when the perceived value of an investment falls and is most closely associated with trading operations. The measurement of market risks is covered in Chapters 4 to 11. Chapter 4 gives an overview of the main traded instruments and how they can be valued. This chapter is useful for those readers who are new to the finance industry.

Chapter 5 describes the most common ways to measure market risks: sensitivity analysis (including duration and the Greeks), stress testing, scenario testing, the Sharpe ratio and Value at Risk (VaR). It gives detailed examples using each of the metrics. Of these metrics, VaR has become the standard approach for measuring market risk. Chapter 6 is devoted to explaining the details of the three common approaches to calculating VaR: parametric VaR, historical VaR, and Monte Carlo VaR. We work through increasingly complex examples and compare the strengths of each approach. In Chapter 7 the VaR contribution methodology is used to pinpoint the source of a portfolio's risk.

Regulators allow banks to use their VaR caculators to set the amount of capital that they hold against market risks. Chapter 8 discusses the procedures required by regulators to test VaR calculators, and Chapter 9 shows how VaR can be used to calculate the economic capital for market risks. Chapter 9 also extends VaR to measure the risk of asset management operations.

Although VaR is the best single metric for market risks, it has several limitations. These limitations, and typical solutions, are discussed in Chapter 10. In Chapter 11 the market risk section concludes by describing how the results of risk measurement are used in risk management, including the procedure for setting VaR limits.

Chapter 12 introduces asset liability management (ALM). ALM is primarily concerned with the interest rate and liquidity risks that are created when commercial banks take in short-term deposits from customers and give out long-term loans. Chapter 12 describes how those risks arise and the risk characteristics of different types of deposits and loans.

The measurement of interest rate risk and liquidity risk for ALM is discussed in Chapters 13 and 14, including gap reports, rate shift scenarios, simulations, and models of customer behaviour.

Chapter 15 uses the ALM concepts to explain funds transfer pricing. This is one of the keys to integrated risk measurement and is a crucial component in measuring risk-adjusted profitability and setting prices to customers. A typical balance sheet is used to illustrate in detail how transfer pricing works.

Credit risk is the possibility of losses due to a counterparty or customer failing to make promised payments. It is covered in Chapters 16 to 23. Chapter 16 discusses the sources of credit risk and how measurement can be used to manage the risks. For readers who are unfamiliar with lending operations, Chapter 17 discusses the ways that credit exposures are structured in commercial and retail lending. It also describes the calculation of credit exposure for derivatives trading operations and gives an introduction to credit derivatives. Chapter 18 shows how the expected loss and unexpected loss for a single loan can be calculated from the probability of default, loss in the event of default, exposure at default and the grade migration matrix. These are the basic building blocks for both economic capital and the New Capital Accords from the Basel Committee.

Chapter 19 discusses the techniques that are used to estimate values for probability of default, loss given default, and exposure at default, including discriminant analysis and the Merton model. It also gives parameter values that can be used as the basis for the reader's own models. The parameter values are used in examples to demonstrate how the credit risk calculations are used.

Chapters 20 and 21 describe the common methods used to estimate the overall risk for a portfolio, including the covariance approach, the actuarial model, the Merton-based simulation model, the macro economic default model, and the macro economic cash-flow model are used for structured and project finance. The chapters also discuss the different approaches available for estimating default correlations and how the correlations can be used to estimate the unexpected loss contribution and the economic capital for a single facility within a portfolio. The chapters conclude with a section describing how the different models can be combined in a unified framework to create an integrated simulation of all the bank's risks.

The results for the credit portfolio models are used in Chapter 22 to give risk adjusted performance and pricing for loans. This chapter shows how to calculate the minimum price that should be charged to a loan customer. The analysis also shows how to include multiyear effects such as grade migration. Chapter 23 explains the New Capital Accords being introduced by the Basel Committee on Banking Supervision. This chapter summarizes the history of the Capital Accords, explains Tier I and Tier II capital, and details the three alternative capital calculations that will be allowed under the new accords. The chapter discusses the advantages and disadvantages of adopting each approach and the steps that a bank must take to comply with the new requirements.

Chapter 24 gives an introduction to the different types of operating risk and the approaches being developed to manage and measure these risks. The approaches are categorized as either qualitative, structural, or actuarial. Each approach is described, including key risk indicators and the approaches suggested in the Basel Accords.

The final chapter returns to the bank level and describes how all the models can be linked together to calculate economic capital and risk-adjusted profitability for the bank as a whole, including alternative methods for calculating inter-risk diversification. It concludes with the steps normally required to implement the bankwide measurement of economic capital and RAROC.

ACKNOWLEDGMENTS

This book and its author greatly benefited from the experience and insights of Jean Eske, Hans Helbekkmo, Yusuf Jafry, Liesl Leach, Pierre Medelsohn, Til Schuermann, and Maria Stein.

I look forward to your comments at CMarrison@RiskIntegrated.com

THE FUNDAMENTALS OF RISK MEASUREMENT

CHAPTER 1

The Basics of Risk Management

INTRODUCTION

Banks make money in one of two ways: providing services to customers and taking risks. For example, retail banks take in customers' deposits and provide them with the services of check clearance and safe storage. Retail banks also take risks by giving out personal loans and taking the risk that some of the loans may not be repaid. The bank is willing to take that risk if it is able to charge the customers a high rate of interest.

In this book we address the business of making money by taking risk. In general, if a bank takes more risk it can expect to make more money, but greater risk also increases the danger that the bank could lose badly and be forced out of business. Banks must run their operations with two goals in mind: to generate profit and to stay in business. Banks therefore try to ensure that their risk taking is informed and prudent. The control of that gambling is the business of risk management. The primary function of risk management is to ensure that the total risk being taken is matched to the bank's capacity for absorbing losses in case things go wrong. A second reason for understanding risk is to help the CEO direct the scarce resource of capital to the opportunities that are expected to create the maximum return with the minimum risk.

Proper risk management is essential for bank survival, and it enables management to allocate resources to various risk units based on a trade-off between risk and revenue potential. These risk-management decisions should be supported by quantitative risk measurement. Risk measurement attempts to answer the following four questions:

- How much could we lose?
- Can we absorb a significant loss without going bankrupt?
- Is the return high enough for us to take that risk?
- How can we reduce the risk without significantly reducing the return?

1

The goal of this book is to provide a detailed guide to the modern techniques for quantifying risk within a bank.

Before going into the mathematics of risk, it is very useful to have an idea of how banks are organized, how they make money, and especially how they can lose money. This chapter therefore describes bank operations and the way that risks are managed at the highest levels of the bank.

THE ORGANIZATIONAL STRUCTURE OF A TYPICAL BANK AND HOW EACH UNIT GENERATES REVENUE

Large, international banks are typically organized into five divisions: corporate banking, retail banking, asset management, insurance, and support. Figure 1-1 shows the typical organization of a universal bank.

The corporate banking division deals with other financial institutions and corporate clients such as large, industrial corporations. There are typically five primary groups: underwriting, mergers and acquisitions, sales and trading, commercial lending, and research.

The underwriting group creates new securities, such as stocks and bonds. For example, if a corporation wanted to raise money, it could go to a bank and ask it to underwrite an issuance of bonds. The bank would structure the bond contract then give the corporation cash. The bank would then sell the bonds to investors, and the corporation would be responsible for making the required payments on the bonds. The bank

FIGURE 1-1

Typical Organization of a Universal Bank

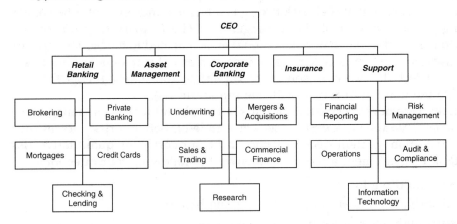

The above graphic details the organizational structure of a universal bank. Note that the majority of the book will focus on risk-management techniques for the corporate and retail banking divisions of the bank.

can make money as a fee from the corporation for structuring the contracts and can also make money by selling the bonds for a higher price than the amount given to the corporation. There is also a risk that the bank could lose money if the value of the bonds falls significantly before the bank can sell them.

The mergers and acquisitions (M&A) group advises corporations on how they can structure the finances of merged companies so as to minimize the funding cost and maximize the tax credits. The M&A group typically receives a fee from the client and uses some of the services of the underwriting group.

The sales and trading group sells securities to investors, trades securities with other banks, and manages the bank's asset and liability mismatch. As we will see, most of the bank's market risk resides in the sales and trading group. Within the trading group there is also the funding desk, which borrows and lends funds with other financial institutions whenever the bank has an overall deficit or surplus of funds.

The commercial finance group provides structured products to corporations, including loans. It also advises companies on their financial structures. For example, if a company wanted to fund a new venture, the commercial finance group would advise it on whether to use debt or equity to raise money. The group makes money largely by lending money to corporations at a moderately high interest rate. Due to the risk of default, a large portion of the credit risk in a bank arises from loans given by the commercial finance group.

The research group produces economic and company-specific reports that are used by the sales and trading group, used by the brokerage group, and sold to clients of the bank.

The retail division deals with the mass of personal customers. The main function is to take deposits from customers in the form of checking accounts, savings, and fixed deposits, then lend funds to other customers in the form of mortgages, credit cards, and personal loans. The division makes a profit by giving low interest rates to depositors and charging high interest rates to borrowers. This profit pays for the cost of processing all the accounts and should cover losses from defaults on loans.

Private banking and brokerage services may also be in the retail division, or they may be in the corporate division. Private banking provides tailored loans and investment to high-net-worth individuals. The brokerage group allows individuals access to the sales and trading group so that for a fee they can trade their securities.

The asset management division administers funds such as mutual funds or unit trusts in which individuals can invest. The asset management division is managing money that belongs not to the bank, but rather to the individuals or institutions. Therefore, if the value of the assets falls, the bank does not lose money directly, but may lose money in the form of reduced fee income.

Some banks also have an insurance division. The insurance division takes fees (or premiums) from its clients and promises to pay the clients if a specific incident happens. To be sure of having enough money to make the required payments, the insurance group holds a large amount of capital in the form of investments in securities such as stocks and bonds. The lines of business include property and casualty insurance, life insurance, and carefully tailored commercial insurance.

The support division has the crucial task of making sure everything works for the other divisions. The operations group ensures that all payments are processed, received, and recorded correctly. Audit and compliance ensures that all the policies and procedures are being followed, and also ensures that the bank complies with all government regulations. The financial reporting group produces information on the profit, loss, and the current amount of assets and liabilities. The risk management group also resides within the support division, where it can be independent from the groups that are taking the risks.

HOW BANKS CAN LOSE MONEY

In the section above we noted that banks often hope to make money by taking risks. However, banks can, and often do, lose money when they take these risks. Banking risks can be put in three categories: market risk, credit risk, and operating risk. Examples of losses occur daily and even hourly. To give an intuitive understanding of how money is lost, consider the following sample of case studies.

Market Risk

Market risk arises from the possibility of losses resulting from unfavorable market movements. It is the risk of losing money because the perceived value of an instrument has changed: for example, when investors are no longer willing to pay such a high price for a stock.

The classic market-risk example comes from losses in the stock market:

- The Nasdaq stock index lost 65% between March 2000 and March 2001.
- The Dow Jones index lost 31% in one week in 1987, 23% on Black Monday, October 19.
- The Dow Jones index lost 89% between 1929–1932, and it did not recover until 1954.

In each of these crises, banks made losses, and some went bankrupt. The ones who made the least losses were those who realized that they were vulnerable and reduced their positions before the crisis. For example, when Chase realized that it was overexposed to Russia at the beginning of 1998, it started to shed its Russian holdings; it was then able to carry on business as usual during the ensuing crisis as Russia defaulted.

On the other hand, Long Term Capital Management (LTCM) was a hedge fund that had bet heavily that any Russian default would have a correlated currency devaluation, which LTCM could use as a hedge. The default happened but the devaluation did not. The result was that LTCM lost $3 billion and was taken over.

Losses can also occur due to long-term market trends.

- In the 1980s many U.S. savings and loans (S&L) institutions went bankrupt because they had been lending out long-term fixed-rate mortgages and borrowing short-term deposits. This strategy was safe while interest rates were stable, but rates suddenly rose in the 1980s. The S&Ls were then left receiving low interest-payments from long-term mortgages but paying high interest rates to get deposits. After a few years of paying more than they received, many of these institutions went bankrupt. The management of these long-term interest-rate risks is typically called asset liability management (ALM).

Credit Risk

Credit risk arises from defaults, when an individual, company, or government fails to honor a promise to make a payment. There is a gray area between market risk and credit risk. The price of corporate bonds fluctuates relative to treasury bonds due to the market's perception of the probability of a corporate default. The aspect of risk before the default happens, is generally considered to be market risk. The actual default is considered credit risk.

Credit risk arises in many forms. The most obvious form is default on a loan, i.e., failure to repay an amount that has been lent. The same risk occurs when the issuer of a bond fails to make the payments promised by the bond. More subtle forms of credit risk arise in trading operations. *Counterparty risk* refers to the possibility that a trading counterparty will fail to pay if it loses money on a deal. *Settlement risk* occurs if a bank fails to settle its side of a trade; this is also known as *Herstatt risk*, after the famous default described below.

Loan Credit Risk

- In January of 1999, Guangdong International Trust and Investment Corporation defaulted on the repayment of $4.5 billion, half of which was owed to overseas banks.
- In August of 1999, Iridium, the satellite telecommunications company, defaulted on two syndicated loans of $1.5 billion that it had borrowed to launch the satellites but could not repay due to unexpectedly low earnings.

Issuer Credit Risk

- On August 17, 1998, Russia unilaterally rescheduled repayments on $43 billion of bonds that had been sold to western banks and investors. The investors eventually recovered only a fraction of the $43 billion.

- In February of 2001, PG&E, a Californian electric utility, defaulted on $726 million of short-term bonds that it had issued. However, its default was selective, and it continued to pay interest on $8 billion of other debt.

Counterparty Credit Risk

- In 1998, the Moscow Interbank Currency Exchange and several Russian banks defaulted on currency derivatives with Credit Suisse First Boston (CSFB). The exchange rate had moved such that the banks owed $600 million to CSFB.

Settlement Credit Risk

- In 1974, a small German bank, Bankhaus Herstatt, had a string of losses in foreign exchange dealings. It went bankrupt at the end of a trading day in Germany. Because it was the end of the trading day in Germany, it had already received $620 million worth of FX payments from its U.S. trading counterparties, but because the U.S. markets were still open, Herstatt had not yet been required to deliver $620 million for its side of the trades. At the time that it went bankrupt, it stopped all payments, and the U.S. banks lost virtually all of the $620 million.

Operating Risk

Operating risk encompasses all the other ways in which banks can lose money. The Basel Committee on Banking defines *operational risk* as "the risk of direct or indirect losses resulting from inadequate or failed internal processes, people and systems or from external events." Operating risk includes fraud and the possibility of a mistake being made.

- A U.S. government bond trader at the New York branch of a Japanese bank was able to switch securities out of customers' accounts to cover trading losses, which mounted to over $1 billion over 10 years.
- In 1997, NatWest lost $127 million and had to greatly reduce its trading operations because its options traders had been using the wrong data for implied volatility in their pricing models, and were therefore taking risks that they did not see.

Blends of Risks

Often banks will lose money from an incident that involves several forms of risk. This is well-illustrated in the collapse of Barings bank.

- Nick Leeson was a trader in the Singapore branch of Barings bank. He had seemingly generated 20% of Barings' profits in 1994. In fact, he had been making losses and hiding them in a fictitious account. To recover the losses he tried a large, risky gamble with derivatives on the Nikkei 225. In 1995, he lost $1 billion and wiped out Barings' capital. He was able to hide the original losses because he was in charge of both trading and accounting in the Singapore office. He was able to take the final gamble because senior management had no effective measurement of the risks being taken.

Banks try to minimize their losses by managing risk at three levels: at the transaction level, the business-unit level, and the corporate level. Most of this book will concern risk management and measurement at the transaction and business-unit levels. We will first look at the management and measurement of trading risks, followed by sections on asset/liability management, credit risk, and operating risk. Finally, we will show how each of the bank's risks can be brought together to estimate the total risk for the bank.

We will often refer to the contribution that the transaction or unit is making to the bank's overall risk. The next section will therefore describe the management of risk at the highest corporate levels and discuss the macro objectives of risk management.

MANAGING RISK AT THE MACRO LEVEL

Ultimately, risk, and all other bank functions, are overseen by the bank's board of directors. The board is urged to take risk by the shareholders who want high returns. Balancing the shareholders, the board is limited in its risk taking by debt holders, rating agencies, regulators, and the bank's own desire to stay in business. The result can be seen as a constrained maximization in which the institution is allowed to take a limited amount of risk and tries to maximize the returns on that risk.

The board oversees three key risk-management functions: deciding the target debt rating, determining the amount of available capital, and allocating risk limits to each business unit within the bank.

Determining the Target Debt Rating

The debt rating is a measure of the bank's creditworthiness and corresponds to the bank's probability of default. A high debt rating corresponds to a low probability of default. The bank's creditworthiness is determined by the amount of risks it takes compared to the amount of capital held. *Capital* is the difference in value between the bank's assets and liabilities. It can be viewed as the current net worth of the bank.

If the bank has a small amount of capital and takes a large amount of risk, there is a high probability that the losses will be greater than the capital, and the bank will go bankrupt. If the bank wants a high rating, it must hold a large amount of capital in relation to its risks.

Although the board sets the credit-rating goal, the actual ratings are granted by independent agencies that use quantitative and qualitative tools to assess a bank's strengths. These agencies include Standard & Poor's (S&P), Moody's, and Fitch.

A low target debt rating has the advantage that the bank can take on many risks and expect to earn a high rate of return for the shareholders. However, a low debt rating means that debt holders will charge higher interest rates to lend to the more risky bank.

The debt rating is also important to the bank's customers. For example, retail customers do not want to give their savings to a bank that is likely to go bankrupt. Similarly, corporations who are considering buying derivatives want to modify their market-risk positions and do not want to be exposed to the credit risk of a lowly rated counterparty. Therefore, corporations buying derivatives would not deal with lowly rated banks.

The highest S&P rating is "AAA," most international banks are rated "AA," and national and regional banks tend to be rated "A" or "BBB."

Once the board has decided the target debt rating, it must align the risks that it allows the bank to take with the amount of capital available.

Determining the Amount of Available Capital

In this discussion we will refer to liabilities, debt, assets, and shares. Readers unfamiliar with these concepts should refer to the appendix to this chapter. The *available capital* is the current value of the assets minus the current value of the liabilities. If all the assets and liabilities are traded, their values are simply the prices at which they trade. However, many assets such as personal loans are not frequently traded. Management must then determine a reasonable value for the assets. This is done by taking the nominal value of the assets and subtracting specific and general provisions. The *nominal value* is the total amount owed to the bank. The *specific provisions* is the amount that is expected to be unpaid by customers who are already in financial trouble. The *general provisions* is the amount that is expected to be unpaid by other customers who get in trouble over the next year. The *capital* is then the nominal amount, minus the provisions, minus the expected value of the liabilities:

$$\text{Capital} = \text{Nominal Asset Value} - \text{Provisions} - \text{Liabilities}$$

If the board wishes to increase the capital quickly, it can do so by issuing more bank shares. This gives the bank more cash without increasing the liabilities that must be paid to avoid default. Alternatively, the capital can be increased over several years by retaining earnings and not paying dividends to shareholders.

Allocating Risk Limits

Once the target debt rating is set and the amount of available capital has been calculated, the bank's total risk capacity is fixed. Conceptually, the relationship can be simplified to the following equation:

$$\text{Risk Capacity} = \text{Probability of Default} \times \text{Available Capital}$$

The board then decides how to allocate the total risk capacity to the different business units, e.g., trading, credit cards, and corporate lending. In doing this it must consider the expected return from each unit and the diversification of the risk between units. We will deal extensively with diversification later. In general, the board will allocate most of the risk capacity to the units that are expected to make the highest returns. The risk capacity is allocated by giving each business unit a limit on the amount of risk it can take. This limit may be in terms of risk capital or in more familiar terms, such as the total amount of loans it can give.

Having allocated a block of capital to a business unit, the board will expect the unit to make a profit on the risks it takes. The target rate of profit is called the *hurdle rate*.

These policy decisions are typically made by the board on an annual or quarterly basis. The day-to-day management of risk is delegated to the CEO, the chief risk officer, and the risk management group, who create risk reports and advise the board and the business units as to how they can maximize the bank's return with a limited amount of risk.

Importantly, for the risk-management function to be credible to shareholders, regulators, and senior management, it must be independent of line management interference. For example, risk managers should not report to the heads of the business units who are taking the risks, because in some circumstances, they may be tempted to "massage" the numbers to make the profitability of their own business units look good. Instead, risk managers should report to senior executives, such as CEOs and CFOs, who will recognize and reward accurate reporting.

SUMMARY

This chapter has given a qualitative overview of how banks make money and how they manage the risk of losing money. In the next chapter, we will start to build the quantitative framework of risk measurement.

APPENDIX: DEFINITION OF ASSETS, LIABILITIES, AND SHARES

Liabilities

In general, the term *liabilites* refers to all transactions for which the bank owes money to another party, however in common usage, the term liabilities may not include the equity owed to the shareholders, and would therefore only include the debt.

The debt may be in the form of bonds that the bank issues for itself, it may be in the form of loans given to the bank by other banks, or it may be in the form of deposits taken from corporations and retail customers. Debt holders expect to be paid a relatively small interest rate, but they also expect to get back the full amount of the principle that they lent to the bank.

Assets

Banks use the money that they have raised from debt and shares to buy assets. Generally, *assets* are any securities or transactions for which the bank is owed money by another party. The assets may, for example, be loans that they grant or equities they buy. In granting a loan, the bank gives cash to an individual or corporation. In return, the individual or corporation commits to making a series of future payments to the bank. This commitment of future payments is an asset to the bank, and a liability to the individual or corporation.

Shares and Equity

The *shareholders* are the owners of the bank and expect to get a share in the profits after the debt is paid. Most of the bank's profit and loss is reflected in the return that the shareholders receive. If the bank is profitable, it will pay dividends to the shareholders; if it is unprofitable, the shareholders will lose the money that they invested when they bought shares in the bank. Shares are also called *equities*. The value of the equity is close to the net value of the bank, i.e., the assets minus the liabilities. The net value of the bank is also called *capital*. There are several definitions for different types of capital, depending on how the value of the assets and liabilities are measured; therefore, it is not always true that the equity equals the capital, but often the terms are used interchangeably.

Risk Measurement at the Corporate Level: Economic Capital and RAROC

INTRODUCTION

This chapter discusses two concepts that will be used throughout this book and that are critical to the integrated measurement of risk: economic capital and risk-adjusted return on capital (RAROC). Economic capital gives us a common framework for quantifying the risk arising from many diverse sources. It also allows us to calculate the amount of equity capital that the bank should hold. RAROC has become the industry's standard way of measuring risk-adjusted profitability. It allows us to compare the profitability of different transactions. A variation on RAROC is shareholder value added (SVA), which we will describe at the end of the chapter. As an introduction to economic capital, let us first look more closely at the relationship between capital, risk, and the probability of default.

CAPITAL, RISK, AND THE PROBABILITY OF DEFAULT

The difference between the value of assets minus the value of liabilities is called capital. While the concept of assets and liabilities is fairly straightforward, the real-life interplay between the two is somewhat complex, as the value of each can change daily. This affects available capital, which impacts the bank's ability to pay its debts. There is therefore a tight relationship between the amount of capital a bank holds, the amount of risk it takes, and the probability of the bank's defaulting. Let us illustrate this with an example.

Illustration of the Relationship between Capital, Risk, and Default

Consider setting up a new bank. You get $5 million of capital from investors who want a share of the profits (shareholders). You borrow $95 million of debt from people who want a relatively safe return on their money (e.g., savings accounts, banks, or corporations with spare cash). You promise to pay back the $95 million in one year, plus 5% interest. You then buy $100 million of corporate bonds from companies like IBM or British Airways. These companies promise to pay you back $106 million in one year's time. These bonds are the assets of the bank. If none of the companies default, then in one year you will receive $106 million. You will then pay $99.8 million to the debt holders and pay $6.2 million to the shareholders. This gives a 25% return on equity (ROE) to the shareholders, which is a reasonable profit.

However, what happens if some of the bond issuers default on their promises? If at the end of the year 4% of the bonds default (with no recoveries) then the bond portfolio will pay only $102 million. The debt holders still get $99.8 million, but the shareholders absorb the loss, getting only $2.2 million. If at the end of the year the losses are even worse, and 8% of the bonds have defaulted, the bonds will be worth $98 million. This forces the bank to default on its obligation to the debt holders and only give them $98 million instead of the $99.8 million that they were promised. In this case, the bank goes out of business and the shareholders get nothing. These three possible outcomes are given in Table 2-1. The columns give the initial amount of assets, debt, and equity at the beginning of the year, and the amount at the end of the year, under the three different scenarios. The bottom row shows the return on equity, which is calculated by the following formula:

$$ROE = \frac{\text{Final Equity} - \text{Initial Equity}}{\text{Initial Equity}}$$

Now let us consider the same situation with the same assets but assuming that the bank had been set up with 10% equity at the start of the year and only 90% debt. Now there is a much better chance that the remaining assets will be sufficient to pay back the debt. The results in Table 2-2 show that under the three scenarios the percentage return on

TABLE 2-1

Capital Example: Basecase Results

Basecase	Initial	End of the year		
Default Rate		0%	4%	8%
Assets	$100.0	$106.0	$101.8	$97.5
Debt	$95.0	$99.8	$99.8	$97.5
Equity	$5.0	$6.3	$2.0	$ –
ROE		25%	−60%	−100%

This table shows the interplay between capital, risk, and the probability of default, demonstrating the close relationship between each variable.

TABLE 2-2

Capital Example: Results with Extra Capital

High Capital	Initial	End of the year		
Default Rate		0%	4%	8%
Assets	$100.0	$106.0	$101.8	$97.5
Debt	$90.0	$94.5	$94.5	$94.5
Equity	$10.0	$11.5	$7.3	$3.0
ROE		15%	−27%	−70%

This table shows that holding more equity increases the chances that the remaining assets will be sufficient to pay back the remaining debt.

equity is lower because the profits are diluted amongst $10 of shareholders rather than $5. But with $10 of initial capital, even in the worst case, at the end of the year the asset value is greater than the debt, and the bank does not fail.

Finally, consider the original case with 5% of equity, but with assets whose values could drop much further.[1] In this case let us say that up to 16% of the assets could default. Table 2-3 shows that for the same amount of capital, higher uncertainty in the asset value increases the probability of defaulting on the debt. In this case, the bank fails in two out of the three cases.

In the example above there were three scenarios for asset value. As a step closer to reality, let us now assume that there are ten possible scenarios and that each one could

TABLE 2-3

Capital Example: Results with Extra Risk

High Capital	Initial	End of the year		
Default Rate		0%	8%	16%
Assets	$100.0	$106.0	$97.5	$89.0
Debt	$95.0	$99.8	$97.5	$89.0
Equity	$5.0	$6.3	$ −	$ −
ROE		25%	−100%	−100%

This table demonstrates that with the same amount of capital, an increase in the uncertainty in the asset value increases the default probability.

TABLE 2-4

Results of 10 Possible
Credit-Loss Scenarios

Scenario	Asset Value
1	96.5
2	98.4
3	100.6
4	101.7
5	102.3
6	103.2
7	103.9
8	104.4
9	104.7
10	105.2

occur with equal probability. The results are shown in Table 2-4 and plotted in the histogram of Figure 2-1. The histogram gives us a crude indication of the probability distribution for the asset value. For example, it shows us that there is a 20% chance that the asset value will be less than $100.

FIGURE 2-1

Histogram of 10 Credit-Loss Scenarios

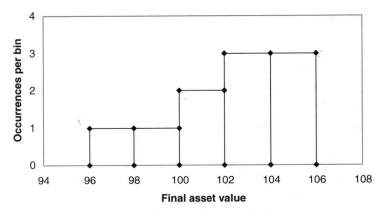

This histogram gives an indication of the probability distribution for the asset value.

INTRODUCTION TO PROBABILITY DISTRIBUTIONS

In reality, there are an infinite number of possible outcomes for the asset value. We represent the distribution of these possible outcomes with a probability density function. (The link between the histogram and the probability density function is discussed further in Chapter 3.) Figure 2-2 shows a typical probability density function for credit losses. Along the x-axis is the value of the assets. The height of the function in the y-axis gives the probability of any given loss occurring. From this distribution we can see the probability of the asset value falling below the debt value. The probability of this happening is the area in the tail. The probability distribution for the second case, with extra equity, looks like Figure 2-3, with very low probability of default. The probability distribution for the third case, with extra risk, looks like Figure 2-4. Notice that the shape of the distribution in Figure 2-4 has changed as the risk of the assets changes.

FIGURE 2-2

Probability Distribution for the Example's Base Case

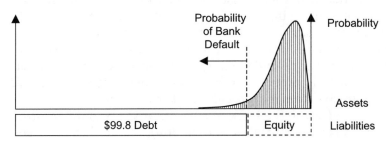

This is a typical probability density function for credit losses enabling us to see the probability of the asset value falling below the debt value.

FIGURE 2-3

Probability Distribution for Example with Extra Equity

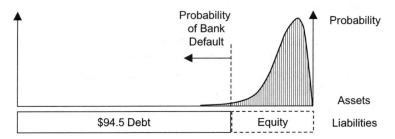

Extra equity increases the probability of default.

FIGURE 2-4

Probability Distribution for Extra Risk

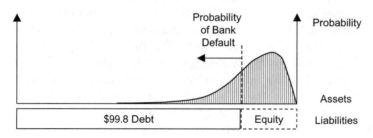

Extra uncertainty increases the probability of default.

ECONOMIC CAPITAL

The examples above illustrated that a triangle exists between initial capital, the risk taken, and the probability of the bank being forced to default. In this book we will discuss many ways to measure the risks taken. Economic capital is one of the most important risk metrics because it provides us with a unifying framework to translate all the risks into a single metric. For market risks we will first compute the daily value-at-risk and then translate it into economic capital. For credit and operating risks we will estimate the economic capital directly from the probability distribution of losses.

The economic capital is the net value the bank must have at the beginning of the year to ensure that there is only a small probability of defaulting within that year. The *net value* is the value of the assets minus liabilities. The *small probability* is the probability that corresponds to the bank's target credit rating. For example, an A-rated bank assumes a default rate of around 0.1% over the next year. Of course, it is impossible to actually observe the probability of default of a single bank. Any single bank will either default or not default, but by looking at the average default rate of all banks in a given grade, it is possible to link credit ratings to the probability of default. This is illustrated in Table 2-5. (100 basis points equals 1%.)[2]

By defining capital in this way we are viewing the shareholder's equity as being a cushion against default. It is equivalent to saying that the economic capital is the amount that shareholders must pay into the bank at the beginning of the year so that the bank can carry out its planned investments and maintain its target credit rating. Now that we have qualitatively explored the concept of economic capital, let us get down to the business of defining it mathematically.

TABLE 2-5

Correspondence between Debt Rating
and Annual Probability of Default

S&P Rating	Probability (basis points)
AAA	1
AA	4
A	12
BBB	50
BB	300
B	1100
CCC	2800
Default	10000

Table showing the link between credit rating and probability of default.
Derived from "Corporate Defaults: Will things get worse before they
get better?" Leo Brand, Reza Bahar, Standard & Poor's Credit Week,
January 31, 2001.

Economic Capital for Credit Risks

For the credit risk of lending operations,[3] the required economic capital (EC) depends on the probability distribution of the losses. A typical probability distribution for credit losses is sketched in Figure 2-5. This sketch shows the distribution of the value of the

FIGURE 2-5

The Relationship between EL, UL, MPL, and the Probability of Default

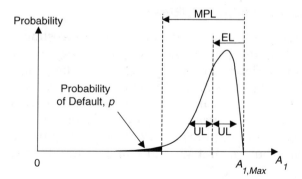

A typical probability distribution for credit losses showing the distribution of the value of the
asset portfolio at the end of the year and the descriptive statistics: EL, UL, and MPL.

asset portfolio at the end of one year. We will use the term A_0 to denote the value of the assets at the beginning of the year and A_1 to denote the actual value of the assets that occurs at the end of the year. The maximum value for A_1 is denoted by $A_{1,\max}$ and is attained if none of the loans default.

Three key statistics are used to describe the distribution: the expected loss (EL), the unexpected loss (UL), and the maximum probable loss (MPL). Calculating the shape of the distribution and the values for the associated statistics is a difficult task that we will leave until the chapters on credit risk. The EL is the mean of the losses and UL is the standard deviation. The bank should expect to lose EL on average each year. The MPL is a confidence level such that there is only a small probability (p) that the losses could be worse than the MPL.

The required value of the probability corresponds to the bank's target debt rating. For a single-A rated bank p is around 0.1%, and the MPL is the level of loss that is so bad that there is only a one-in-one-thousand chance of the loss being greater than the MPL.

The economic capital is closely approximated as MPL minus EL, i.e., it is the additional amount that could be lost beyond EL with probability p:

$$EC \approx MPL - EL$$

A careful analysis (shown in the appendix) finds that the amount of economic capital to be held at the beginning of the year for a loan portfolio depends on the interest rate to be received from the loans (r_A) and the rate that the bank must pay on its debt (r_D)

$$EC_0 = MPL \frac{(1 + r_A)}{(1 + r_D)} - A_0 \frac{(r_A - r_D)}{(1 + r_D)}$$

If we assume that the rate on the loans, r_A is such that it will equal the costs of the debt, r_D, plus the expected loss on the portfolio, we find that the economic capital closely matches the simple definition of MPL minus EL.

Economic Capital for Market Risks

For market risks we assume that the trading group will carry out a set of investment strategies within predefined limits, and that the profitability of this strategy has a probability distribution. This is illustrated in Figure 2-6. It is possible that the profitability could be negative, in which case the trading group would not be able to pay back all of the liabilities that it had incurred during the year unless it had a reserve. This reserve is the required economic capital. The *required economic capital* can be considered to be the amount of money that the shareholders put in reserve at the beginning of the year so that the trading operation can carry out its strategy and maintain the desired debt rating.

In the later market-risk chapters we will show how the loss distribution is calculated for a given trading strategy. This allows us to calculate a maximum probable loss,

FIGURE 2-6

Illustration of the Maximum Probable Loss for Market Risks

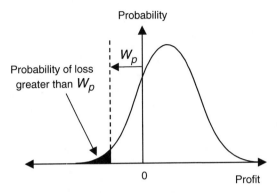

Probability distribution of market risk profits showing the shape
of the distribution and the maximum probable loss.

W_p, such that there is only probability p that the profitability over a year will be worse
than W_p.

$$p = \text{Probability}[\text{Profit} < W_p]$$

The economic capital to be held at the beginning of the year is then the maximum
probable loss, discounted back at the risk-free rate (r_f) to give the amount that must
be put in reserve to maintain the required target debt rating.[4]

$$EC = \frac{W_p}{(1 + r_f)}$$

Economic Capital for Operating Risks

Conceptually, the calculation of economic capital for operating risks is the same as for
market risks, except that the probability distribution has a different shape, as illustrated
in Figure 2-7. The difficulty is in finding accurate data to characterize this distribution.
This is one of the industry's main challenges in risk management and the current
progress will be described in the later chapters.

RISK-ADJUSTED PERFORMANCE

Up to this point we have discussed methods for describing risk in terms of required
economic capital. Economic capital is useful for identifying large risks and setting the
total amount of capital to be held by the bank. However, when deciding whether to

FIGURE 2-7

Illustration of the Maximum Probable Loss for Operating Risks

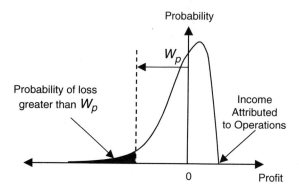

The probability distribution for operating risks, including income derived from operations.

carry out a transaction, the bank is not only concerned about the risk; it is also interested in profitability relative to that risk. By measuring risk-adjusted performance (RAP), a bank can integrate risk measurement into the daily profitability management of the business.

Using Risk-Adjusted Performance to Make Business Decisions

Risk-adjusted performance can be used to support the following business decisions:

- At the product level, to decide which products are profitable and how products must be priced to ensure that they are profitable.
- At the relationship level, to show which customer relationships are profitable.
- At the transaction level, to decide whether to enter into a transaction, and if so, at what price.
- At the individual or group level, to compensate staff based on the profit they generate compared with the amount of the bank's capital they consume.
- At the business-unit level, to decide which units are adding the greatest profit relative to the risks they are taking. Given this information, senior management can decide which business should grow and which should shrink. A typical finding is that high-risk, high-return businesses, such as trading and commercial lending, are less profitable on a risk-adjusted basis than less glamorous businesses, such as retail lending.

Traditionally, the banking industry relied on measurements that gave an incomplete picture of performance and its relation to risk. The two most common measurements were return on assets (ROA) and return on equity (ROE). *ROA* is the profit divided by the dollar value of the portfolio. *ROE* is the profitability divided by either book capital or the regulatory capital. The *book capital* is the net value of the bank as measured by accounting methods. The *regulatory capital* is the minimum amount of capital that must be held by the bank according to regulators such as the Bank of England and the Federal Reserve. The return on assets takes no account of the risk of the assets, and until the adoption of new methods for regulatory capital, the regulatory capital will be very insensitive to risk. As an alternative, over the last decade the industry has developed two metrics for risk-adjusted performance that are based on economic capital: RAROC and SVA. RAROC is the risk-adjusted return on capital, and SVA is shareholder value added.

Risk-Adjusted Return on Capital (RAROC)

RAROC is the *expected net* risk-adjusted *profit* (ENP) divided by the economic capital that is required to support the transaction.

$$\text{RAROC} = \frac{\text{ENP}}{\text{EC}}$$

RAROC treats all transactions as if they are the buying and selling of securities for an investment portfolio. The "price" of the security is the amount of economic capital that the shareholder must put aside for the transaction to happen. The return on the transaction is the net increase in value. For a loan transaction, this is the interest income on the loan, plus any fees (*F*), minus interest to be paid on debt, minus operating costs (*OC*), and minus any losses (*L*).

The interest income on the loan asset is the initial loan amount (A_0) multiplied by the interest rate on the loan (r_A). The interest to be paid on the debt is the amount of debt (D_0) multiplied by the interest rate on the debt (r_D). The amount of debt required is the loan amount minus the economic capital. The RAROC equation for a loan is therefore as follows:

$$\text{RAROC} = \frac{\overbrace{A_0 r_A + F}^{\text{Int + Fees}} - \overbrace{D_0 r_D}^{\text{Int Cost}} - \overbrace{OC}^{\text{Ops}} - \overbrace{L}^{\text{Loss}}}{EC}$$

$$= \frac{A_0 r_A + F - (A_0 - EC) r_D - OC - L}{EC}$$

For a trading transaction, the RAROC is the net change in the value (ΔV) of the position, minus operating costs (in this case, any debt costs are counted as part of the change in the value of the position). The RAROC equation for a trading position is as follows:

$$\text{RAROC} = \frac{\Delta V - OC}{EC}$$

RAROC can be calculated on a retrospective or prospective basis. If it is used on a retrospective basis (e.g., to calculate the previous year's profitability) the actual loss or change in value is used. If it is being used on a prospective basis (e.g., to predict the profitability of a future deal) we use the expected loss or change in value. For a loan, the expected RAROC profitability is given by the following:

$$RAROC = \frac{A_0 r_A + F - (A_0 - EC)r_D - OC - EL}{EC}$$

For a trading transaction, it is given by:

$$RAROC = \frac{E(\Delta V) - OC}{EC}$$

where $E(\Delta V)$ is the expected change in value.

Expected Returns

Senior management normally sets a target for the return it expects business units to make for using capital. This minimum value for RAROC is called the *hurdle rate* (*H*). All transactions should be expected to pass over this hurdle to be considered viable. The rate is typically set as a single number for the whole bank. The actual value chosen is around 12 to 20% and depends on the return that the shareholders expect for investing their capital in the bank. The rate that shareholders expect depends on the riskiness of the bank, and the correlation between losses that the bank suffers and changes in the level of the general market. More formally, the rate is set according to the theory of the Capital Asset Pricing Model, which is discussed later.

Once the hurdle has been set, it determines how much the bank must expect to make on each transaction for it to be viable. If we replace RAROC with the minimum value for RAROC (*H*), we can calculate the minimum return required on a loan transaction:

$$H = \frac{A_0 r_A + F - (A_0 - EC)r_D - OC - EL}{EC}$$

Therefore, the minimum expected return for a loan transaction should be at least the amount shown below.

$$A_0 r_A + F = (A_0 - EC)r_D + OC + EL + H \times EC$$

This is the amount that the bank must charge the loan customer.

Similarly, we can calculate the minimum expected change in value for a trading transaction:

$$E(\Delta V) = H \times EC + OC$$

This discussion of RAROC gives us a measure of the percentage return that we expect to make for each unit of risk (as defined by economic capital). It is also useful to have an absolute measure of the return in dollars.

Shareholder Value Added (SVA)

Shareholder value added (SVA) gives a dollar-based measure of performance. It is simply the actual or expected profitability minus the required profitability to meet the hurdle rate. The required profitability is the hurdle rate multiplied by the economic capital required. Based on the RAROC equations, the expected SVA for a loan is as follows:

$$SVA = [A_o r_A + F - (A_0 - EC)r_D - OC - EL] - H \times EC$$

Similarly, for a trading transaction, SVA is the expected return minus the hurdle return:

$$SVA = [E(\Delta V) - OC] - H \times EC$$

SUMMARY

This chapter has covered many concepts that are the fundamental building blocks for modern risk measurement. We started by discussing the relationship between risk, capital, and the probability of default. This allowed us to define the amount of capital needed to support a given level of risk and maintain a target credit rating for the bank. Finally, we used the economic capital as a measure of risk and defined RAROC and SVA to be measures of risk-adjusted profitability.

This discussion assumed that we could obtain the economic capital from loss-probability distributions. We will now spend many chapters discussing how those distributions can be calculated. Along the way, we will also develop a better understanding for how banks control risk and some of the other tools used to complement economic capital.

APPENDIX: DETAILED DERIVATION OF THE ECONOMIC CAPITAL FOR A LOAN PORTFOLIO

We wish to determine the amount of economic capital that should be held at the beginning of the year such that there is a very small probability of the bank's defaulting by the end of the year. The economic capital is the value of the assets minus the value of the debt. It can be considered to be the amount that must be raised from the shareholders to allow the bank to buy a risky portfolio of loans and maintain its debt rating. At the beginning of the year, the value of the assets bought will equal the debt plus the economic capital:

$$A_0 = D_0 + EC_0$$

The amount of debt to be paid back at the end of the year depends on the debt interest rate (r_D):

$$D_1 = (1 + r_D)D_0$$

The value of the loans at the end of the year will depend on the rate being charged on the assets (r_A), and on the percentage of the assets that default. Let us define λ to be the loss rate that is experienced. We can then calculate the final asset value to be as follows:

$$A_1 = (1 + r_A)(1 - \lambda)A_0$$

The economic capital remaining at the end of the year is the value of the assets minus the debt:

$$EC_1 = A_1 - D_1$$
$$= (1 - r_A)(1 - \lambda)A_0 - (1 + r_D)D_0$$

If the assets equal the debt at the end of the year, the available capital will be zero, and the bank will be on the verge of default. This could occur if the loss rate (λ) is large. Given the bank's target debt rating and its corresponding probability of default, the available economic capital is allowed to drop to zero only if the losses equal λ_p, where λ_p is the MPL as a percentage of A_1. If λ equals λ_p, the available economic capital at the end of the year equals zero:

$$0 = (1 + r_A)(1 - \lambda_p)A_0 - (1 + r_D)D_0$$

We can solve this equation for D_0, then substitute it into the equation for the initial required economic capital:

$$EC_0 = A_0 - D_0$$
$$= A_0 - A_0 \frac{(1 + r_A)(1 - \lambda_p)}{(1 + r_D)}$$
$$= A_0 \left(\frac{(r_D - r_A) + \lambda_p + \lambda_p r_A}{(1 + r_D)} \right)$$

In this expression, λ_p represents the "worst-case" loss of principal; r_D represents the debt-interest costs that must be paid; r_A is the interest earned from the assets that is expected if there are no defaults, and it reduces the required initial amount of capital. $\lambda_p r_A$ is the "worst-case" loss of interest earned from the assets. The factor of $(1 + r_D)$ in the denominator enters because there is no need to make debt-interest payments on the economic capital.

This expression for EC is quite complex but if we make some simplifying assumptions we can get back to the simple definition for EC. Remember that the required rate for r_A is as follows:

$$r_A = \frac{(A_0 - EC)r_D + OC + EL + H \times EC - F}{A_0}$$

Assume that the fees and operating costs are zero (or equal). Further, assume that $(A_0 - EC)$ approximately equals A_0. Finally, let us neglect the return on capital, $H \times EC$. We now have the following:

$$r_A = r_D + \frac{EL}{A_0}$$

$$= r_D + \mu$$

Here, μ is the expected loss as a percentage of the initial asset value. If we substitute this value for r_A, we find that the economic capital closely matches the simple definition of MPL minus EL:

$$EC_0 = A_0 \left(\lambda_p \frac{(1 + r_D + \mu)}{(1 + r_D)} - \mu \right)$$

$$\approx A_0 (\lambda_p - \mu) \text{ because } \frac{(1 + r_D + \mu)}{(1 + r_D)} \approx 1$$

NOTES

1 Typically, when the bank invests in more risky assets, it will expect that they will pay the bank a higher rate of interest, which in turn will modify the bank's probability of default. This factor is included in the later discussion on economic capital, but for simplicity, it is not included in this example.

2 As discussed in the credit section, the rate of default changes over time. The probabilities shown here are the annual rate of default averaged over three years from the date of rating the company.

3 Lending operations may also have market risk, but this risk is treated separately, as explained in the section on asset and liability management.

4 This assumes that at the beginning of the year, the capital is invested at the risk-free rate. Alternative investment assumptions could be made and included in the analysis to calculate W_p.

Review of Statistics

INTRODUCTION

In the previous chapter, we gave a qualitative overview of the measurement of risk, and we started to build a quantitative framework. We quantified risk as the amount of economic capital consumed, and this capital was shown to depend on the probability distribution of potential losses. This quantification according to the probability distribution of potential losses is at the core of modern risk measurement, and we will spend many chapters discussing how the distribution can be obtained for different types of risks. In this chapter, we will give a deeper explanation of probability distributions and discuss other statistical techniques that are commonly used in risk measurement. This chapter is intended to gather together the core statistical techniques that will be used in the rest of the book. It gives a single place for reference so in the later chapters we will not need to digress from finance each time we need to apply a statistical technique.

As a reader, you can treat this chapter in one of two ways: read it all now and get the pain over with, or skip to the chapters that are of particular interest to you and refer back to this chapter when needed. If you are fortunate enough to be familiar with statistics already, you can just read the section headers to make sure that there is nothing that you have missed, and then go on to the market-risk chapters.

We will cover the following topics in this chapter:
- The creation of histograms and probability distributions from empirical data.
- The statistical parameters used to describe the distribution of losses: mean, standard deviation, skew, and kurtosis.
- Examples of market-risk and credit-risk loss distributions to give an understanding of the practical problems that we face.
- The idealized distributions that are used to describe risk: the Normal, Log-Normal, and Beta probability distributions.

- The use of confidence intervals, confidence levels, and percentiles.
- How to include correlations between random losses.
- The statistics for a sum of separate losses.
- The equations that can be used to describe a random time series, such as the evolution of interest rates.
- A brief reminder of addition and multiplication for matrices. Matrices will be used later to make complex equations more readable.

PROBABILITY DENSITIES

The primary use of probability densities in risk measurement is to show us the likelihood of any given level of losses. For example, we can use them to show us the probability of losses from a given portfolio being greater than a million dollars in one day.

We will introduce probability densities by describing how they can be empirically constructed from raw data. The first step will be to create histograms of the data. We will then modify the histogram to become a graph of probability and further modify it to become a graph of probability density.

Construction of Probability Densities from Historical Data

Let us return to the example in Chapter 2, in which we had 10 possible scenarios for asset value at the end of the year. In Chapter 2, we quickly went from the sample distribution to probability distributions. Here we will do the same, but more thoroughly. The possible values are shown again in Table 3-1. We can define ranges of possible asset values and count how many samples fall within each range. These ranges are also called *bins* or *buckets* because we place each sample into one of the bins. For our example, we define the ranges to be $2 increments, from $96 to $106, which gives the results of Table 3-2. We can plot these results as the histogram in Figure 3-1.

The histogram displays how many occurrences or samples fall within each range or bin. We can restate this in terms of the probability of one random sample falling in any given bin. The probability is calculated by dividing the number of samples in each bin by the total number of samples. If we define n_i to be the number of samples falling in bin number i (as in Table 3-2), and N to be the total number of samples (in this case, 10), then we can calculate the probability P_i of a sample falling in bin i. The probability is given by the simple equation:

$$P_i = \frac{n_i}{N}$$

In many cases, it will be easier to work with probability densities rather than raw probabilities. The *probability density* is defined to be the probability of a sample falling in a given range divided by the width of the range (w). In the example above, we chose the width of the range to be $2. The probability density is signified by a lowercased p:

TABLE 3-1

Results of 10 Credit-Loss Scenarios

Scenario	Asset Value
1	96.5
2	98.4
3	100.6
4	101.7
5	102.3
6	103.2
7	103.9
8	104.4
9	104.7
10	105.2

Examples of 10 possible scenarios for asset values at the end of a year.

TABLE 3-2

Number of Occurrences in Each Range

Range	Number of Occurrences
96–98	1
98–100	1
100–102	2
102–104	3
104–106	3

Table showing the number of results that fall in each range of possible asset values.

$$p_i = \frac{P_i}{w}$$

The probability density for this example is plotted in Figure 3-2, which looks very similar to the histogram of Figure 3-1. In the histogram, the y-axis showed the number of samples per bin. In the probability density, the y-axis shows the number of samples per bin divided by the total number of samples and the bin width:

$$p_i = \frac{n_i}{Nw}$$

[handwritten annotations:]
n_i = number of samples in the bin
N = total # of samples
w = width of samples

FIGURE 3-1

Histogram of 10 Credit-Loss Scenarios

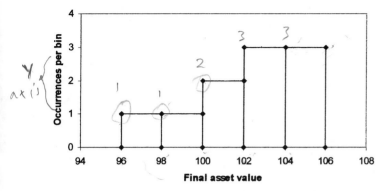

Histogram showing how many results fall in each range.

FIGURE 3-2

Probability Density for the Credit-Loss Example

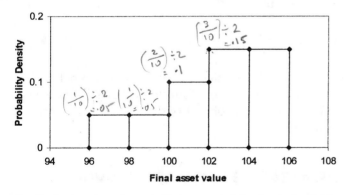

so, given a set of results, we can show the probability of each of those occurring, compared to each other.

The distribution of results scaled to be a probability density by dividing the number of results in each range by the width of the range, which in this case is $2.

Cumulative Probabilities

The probability density can be used to tell us the probability of a variable falling in a given range. From this we can also calculate the *cumulative probability*. This is the probability of the random variable falling below a given number. The cumulative probability can be estimated by multiplying the probability density by the bin width to get probabilities for each bin, and by summing up all the probabilities for values less than or

FIGURE 3-3

Cumulative Probability for the Credit-Loss Example

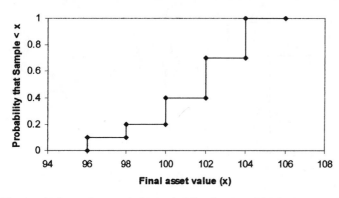

The graph shows the cumulative probability density, which is the sum of all the results falling in or below the given range.

equal to the given number. The cumulative probability (CP) up to the given number (x_i) can be expressed by the following summation:

$$CP(x_i) = w \sum_{k=1}^{i} p_k$$

Here $\sum_{k=1}^{i} p_k$ means the sum of the probability densities for all the bins from 1 to i.

For our example, the graph of the cumulative probability constructed this way is shown in Figure 3-3, in which the y-axis shows the probability that the random variable will be less than the value shown in the x-axis.

DESCRIPTIVE STATISTICS: MEAN, STANDARD DEVIATION, SKEW, AND KURTOSIS

In the discussion above, we described the random variable of asset value in graphical form. The properties of the variable can also be quantified in terms of mean, standard deviation, skew, and kurtosis. In calculating these statistics, we need to bear in mind that there are two tightly related but subtly different sets of statistics. The first set is the mean, standard deviation, skew, and kurtosis that describe the actual underlying process that produces the random results. The second set is the mean, standard deviation, skew, and kurtosis of the results that we observe. This second set is called the set of the sample statistics.

In general, we cannot know the true statistics of a process; we can only observe the individual results, calculate the sample statistics, and then use these as the best

estimates of the statistics of the underlying process. Here we shall use an apostrophe (')
to denote the statistics of the underlying process.

Mean

= average

The *mean* is typically denoted by the Greek letter μ or by a bar over the symbol for the
random variable, e.g., $\bar{x}$. The mean value of a variable produced by a random process is
the sum of the possible results, each weighted by the probability of the result. If the
process can only produce a discrete number of results, the mean is the weighted sum of
the results:

$$\mu' = \sum_{i=1}^{N} x_i P(x_i)$$

Here, N is the total number of possible results, and $P(x_i)$ is the probability of result x_i. If
the underlying process is continuous, then there is an infinite number of possible
results, and we use integration to calculate the mean:

$$\mu' = \int_{x=-\infty}^{\infty} x p(x) dx$$

Here, $p(x)$ is the probability density function for x, and $p(x)dx$ is the probability of x
falling in the range dx. The mean value of the underlying process is also called the
expected value, denoted by $E(x)$.

The sample mean of a set of random results is simply the sum of the results
divided by the number of results (N):

$$\mu = \frac{1}{N} \sum_{i=1}^{N} x_i$$

Here, x_i represents the individual results. The probability function, $p(x)$ is implied by
the distribution of the values that were observed. For the 10-sample example of asset
values we calculate the mean as follows:

total 1020·9

mean

$$\mu = \frac{1}{10} \sum_{i=1}^{10} x_i$$

= $\frac{1}{10}$[96.5 + 98.4 + 100.6 + 101.7 + 102.3 + 103.2 + 103.9 + 104.4 + 104.7 + 105.2]

= 102.1   ∴ average

Standard Deviation

The *standard deviation* gives a measure of the degree to which the random results vary
away from the mean. This is a key statistic in risk measurement because it gives a

measure of how different the results could be from the desired result of making a profit. The standard deviation is generally denoted by σ. The standard deviation squared is called the *variance*:

$$\text{Variance} = \sigma^2$$

The variance for a random process is the probability-weighted sum of the square of the differences between the result and the mean. For a process giving discrete results, the standard deviation is given by the following:

$$\sigma'^2 = \sum_{i=1}^{N} \left[(x_i - \mu')^2 P(x_i) \right]$$

For a continuous variable, it is given by the integral:

$$\sigma'^2 = \int_{x=-\infty}^{\infty} \left[(x - \mu')^2 p(x) \right] dx$$

The sample variance is given by the sum of the squared deviations from the sample mean divided by $N - 1$.

$$\sigma^2 = \frac{1}{N-1} \sum_{i=1}^{N} (x_i - \mu)^2$$

The division by $N - 1$ ensures that the expected value of the sample variance equals the variance of the underlying distribution. The derivation of the factor $N - 1$ is a little complex, but depends on the fact that the sample mean is not necessarily the same as the true mean. For our example, the variance is 8.2, and the standard deviation is 2.9:

$$\sigma^2 = \frac{1}{9} \sum_{i=1}^{10} (x_i - 102.1)^2$$

$$= \frac{1}{9} \left[(-5.6)^2 + (-3.7)^2 + (-1.5)^2 + (-0.4)^2 + 0.2^2 + 1.1^2 + 1.8^2 + 2.3^2 + 2.6^2 + 3.1^2 \right]$$

$$= 8.2$$

Skew

The *skew* is a measure of the asymmetry of the distribution. In risk measurement, it tells us whether the probability of winning is similar to the probability of losing.

The skew for discrete and continuous process are calculated as follows:

$$s' = \sum_{i=1}^{N} \left[\left(\frac{x_i - \mu'}{\sigma'} \right)^3 p[x_i] \right]$$

$$s' = \int_{-\infty}^{\infty} \left[\left(\frac{x - \mu'}{\sigma'} \right)^3 p[x] \right] dx$$

The sample skew includes terms to ensure that the expected value of the sample skew equals the skew of the underlying process:

$$s = \frac{N}{(N-1)(N-2)} \sum_{i=1}^{N} \left[\left(\frac{x_i - \mu}{\sigma} \right)^3 p[x_i] \right]$$

For our example, the sample skew is calculated as follows:

$$s = \frac{10}{9 \times 8} \sum_{i=1}^{10} \left[\left(\frac{x_i - 102.1}{2.9} \right)^3 \right]$$

$$= \frac{10}{72} \left[(-2)^3 + (-1.3)^3 + (-0.5)^3 + (-0.1)^3 + 0.1^3 + 0.4^3 + 0.6^3 + 0.8^3 + 0.9^3 + 1.1^3 \right]$$

$$= -0.95$$

Kurtosis

Kurtosis is useful in describing extreme events, e.g., losses that are so bad that they only have a 1 in 1000 chance of happening. Consider two different trading portfolios whose values have the same mean, standard deviation, and skew, but different kurtosis. Every 1000 days, the portfolios could be expected to suffer a "bad" loss. In these extreme events, the portfolio with the higher kurtosis would suffer worse losses than the portfolio with lower kurtosis. We will illustrate this later with actual market data.

The kurtosis for discrete and continuous process are calculated as follows:

$$k' = \sum_{i=1}^{N} \left[\left(\frac{x_i - \mu'}{\sigma'} \right)^4 p[x_i] \right]$$

$$k' = \int_{-\infty}^{\infty} \left[\left(\frac{x - \mu'}{\sigma'} \right)^4 p[x] \right] dx$$

The kurtosis of a sample is calculated as follows:

$$k = \frac{N(N+1)}{(N-1)(N-2)(N-3)} \sum_{i=1}^{N} \left[\left(\frac{x_i - \mu}{\sigma} \right)^4 \right]$$

For our example, the kurtosis is 4.4:

$$k = \frac{10 \times 11}{9 \times 8 \times 7} \sum_{i=1}^{10} \left[\left(\frac{x_i - 102.1}{2.9} \right)^4 \right]$$

$$= \frac{110}{504} \left[(-2)^4 + (-1.3)^4 + (-0.5)^4 + (-0.1)^4 + 0.1^4 + 0.4^4 + 0.6^4 + 0.8^4 + 0.9^4 + 1.1^4 \right]$$

$$= 4.4$$

Later in this chapter, we will discuss the Normal probability distribution. The kurtosis for the Normal distribution is three, and this distribution is so commonly used that some researchers define the "excess kurtosis" as being the calculations above minus three, i.e.:

$$k' = \sum_{i=1}^{N} \left[\left(\frac{x_i - \mu'}{\sigma'} \right)^4 p[x_i] \right] - 3$$

$$k' = \int_{-\infty}^{\infty} \left[\left(\frac{x - \mu'}{\sigma'} \right)^4 p[x] \right] dx - 3$$

$$k = \frac{N(N+1)}{(N-1)(N-2)(N-3)} \sum_{i=1}^{N} \left[\left(\frac{x_i - \mu}{\sigma} \right)^4 \right] - 3 \frac{(N-1)^2}{(N-2)(N-3)}$$

Distributions with a kurtosis greater than the Normal distribution are said to have *leptokurtosis*.

ANALYSIS OF HISTORICAL LOSS STATISTICS

Up to this point we have illustrated probability distributions, probability densities, and statistics using the simple example with 10 different outcomes for asset values. Now let us apply this language and theory to examine real, historical financial data.

Credit Risk Example

Table 3-3 shows the annual rate of default over the last 19 years on bonds rated by Standard & Poor's. The data is plotted as a histogram in Figure 3-4. Along the x-axis is the proportion of bonds that defaulted. (100 basis points equals 1%.) The y-axis shows the number of years in which the loss rate fell within each of the 50 basis-point ranges from 0 to 400.

Let us now discuss the information that we can obtain from this data. In 7 of the 19 years, the loss rate was between 50 and 100 basis points. The worst annual loss was 297 basis points. The mean loss rate was 127 basis points, with a standard deviation of 72 basis points. The skew was 0.9 (reflecting the asymmetry), and the excess kurtosis was 0.24 (reflecting the extreme event of a 297-basis-point loss).

Market Risk Example

Figure 3-5 gives the histogram of daily relative changes in the S&P 500 equity index over 10 years, from January of 1990 to December of 2000. The relative change for day T is calculated as the change in the level of the index divided by the level one day previously:

TABLE 3-3

Bond-Default Rates over 19 Years

Year	Bond-Default Rate (basis points)
1982	125
1983	68
1984	84
1985	99
1986	175
1987	93
1988	146
1989	151
1990	256
1991	297
1992	121
1993	47
1994	52
1995	91
1996	43
1997	52
1998	116
1999	198
2000	212

From "Corporate Defaults: Will Things Get Worse Before They Get Better?"
Leo Brand & Reza Bahar, Standard & Poor's Credit Week, January 31, 2001.

$$\text{Relative Change } (T) = \frac{\text{Level}(T) - \text{Level}(T-1)}{\text{Level}(T-1)}$$

The maximum change in one day was 5%, the minimum was −7%, the mean daily change was 0.05% (14%/year), the standard deviation was 0.9%, and the skew and kurtosis were −0.2 and 7.5 respectively. From this data we can make several observations. The standard deviation of daily returns is much higher than the mean. The shape of the probability distribution is close to being symmetric and has a familiar bell shape, but it has a kurtosis that is significantly greater than 3, and therefore is not a Normal distribution.

The size of the bins along the x-axis is in 0.5% increments from −7.5% to +7.5%. The y-axis shows the number of results falling in each bin, but it is not very useful to say that with 2800 samples, around 700 will fall within the bin between 0 and 0.5%. An alternative is to divide each result by the total number of samples and the bin width, to

FIGURE 3-4

Histogram of Bond Losses over 19 Years

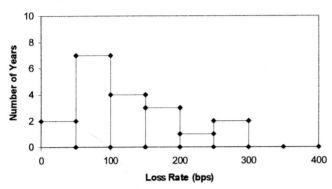

Histogram of bond-default rates over 19 years. The *X*-axis shows proportion of bonds that defaulted in basis points, with 100 basis points equaling 1%. The *Y*-axis shows number of years the loss rate fell within each of the 50 basis point ranges, from 0 to 400.

FIGURE 3-5

Histogram of Daily Returns for the S&P 500

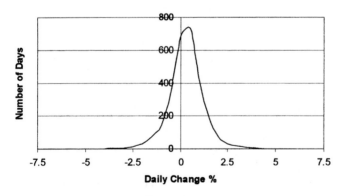

Histogram of daily relative changes in the S&P equity index over a 10-year period.

produce the probability density. This gives us a result that is independent of the number of samples and the sizes of the bins. The sample probability-density function for the S&P 500 is shown in Figure 3-6. The only change compared with Figure 3-5 is the scale on the *y*-axis.

FIGURE 3-6

Probability Density of Daily Returns for the S&P 500

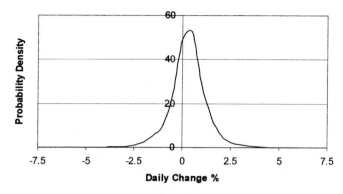

Daily returns on the S&P 500 index presented as a probability-density function.

STANDARD PROBABILITY-DENSITY FUNCTIONS

In the examples above, we simply plotted the observed data in histograms and calculated their statistics. An alternative is to use an equation to describe the probability-density function. A *probability-density function* is an equation that gives a value for the probability density as a function of the possible value of the random variable and parameters such as the mean, standard deviation, skew, and kurtosis. This allows us to know the complete probability distribution without collecting vast amounts of data. Here we will discuss three distributions that are commonly used in risk measurement: the Normal distribution, the Log-normal distribution, and the Beta distribution.

The Normal Distribution

The *Normal distribution* is also known as the *Gaussian distribution* or *Bell curve*. It is the distribution most commonly used to describe the random changes in market-risk factors, such as exchange rates, interest rates, and equity prices. This distribution is very common in nature because of the Central Limit Theorem, which states that if a large amount of independent, identically distributed, random numbers are added together, the outcome will tend to be Normally distributed. The equation for the Normal distribution is as follows:

$$p[x] = \frac{1}{\sqrt{2\pi}\sigma} e^{-\left(\frac{(x-\mu)^2}{2\sigma^2}\right)}$$

Here, $p[x]$ is the probability density for the variable taking the value x. $p[x]$ depends on three variables: the value of x, the mean of the distribution, μ, and the standard deviation, σ. The skew of the Normal distribution is always zero, and the kurtosis is always three. Figure 3-7 shows $p[x]$ for different values of x with a mean of one and a standard deviation of two.

Earlier, we summed the sample results to estimate the cumulative probability. With a probability-density function, we use integration rather than summation to obtain the cumulative-probability function:

$$CPF(x) = \int_{-\infty}^{x} p(y)dy$$

Here, y is the symbol that we use for integration, and x is the upper limit of the integration interval. The cumulative probability for x tells us the probability of a random sample having a value that is less than x. Figure 3-8 shows the cumulative-probability function for the Normal function with a mean of one and standard deviation of two.

You may have noticed the similarity between the Normal function and the distribution of the S&P returns (Figure 3-6). Figure 3-9 shows the S&P 500 returns with a Normal distribution of the same mean (0.05%) and standard deviation (0.9%) imposed upon it. The Normal distribution is the dotted line. The curves are reasonably similar, but notice that the peak for the raw data is higher and to the right. This is because there are a few extreme negative days (of losses up to −7%), which drag down the mean of the Normal function and make the standard deviation quite high. This can be seen in Figure 3-10 that expands the y-axis to show the detail of the low-probability events. Notice that the curve obtained directly from the S&P data has a greater probability density out in the tails, especially the few days of losses around −7%. This is reflected in the high kurtosis of 7.5. Notice also that there are more extreme losses than gains, reflected in the negative

FIGURE 3-7

The Normal Probability-Density Function

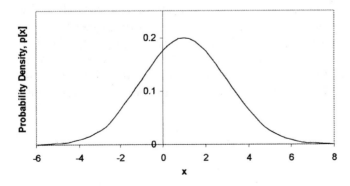

FIGURE 3-8

The Normal Cumulative-Probability Function

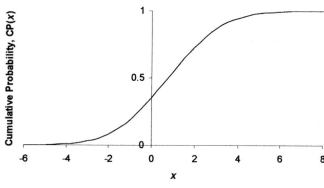

FIGURE 3-9

Comparison of Normal Distribution with Actual S&P Data

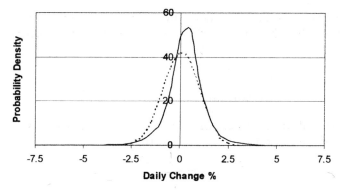

This figure shows the S&P 500 returns compared with a Normal distribution of the same mean (0.05%) and standard deviation (0.9%) imposed on it.

skew of −0.7. This is a common problem when using the Normal distribution to represent market data, and one that we will return to in the chapters on market risk.

The Log-Normal Distribution

The *Log-normal distribution* is useful for describing variables which cannot have a negative value, such as interest rates and stock prices. If the variable has a Log-normal distribution, then the log of the variable will have a Normal distribution:

$$\text{If} \quad x \sim \text{LogNormal}$$

$$\text{Then} \quad \text{Log}(x) \sim \text{Normal}$$

FIGURE 3-10

Comparison of Normal Distribution with Actual S&P Data—Detail

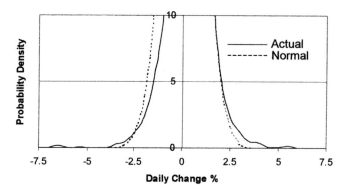

An expanded *Y*-axis showing the detail of the low-probability events.

Conversely, if you have a variable that is Normally distributed, and you want to produce a variable that has a Log-normal distribution, take the exponential of the Normal variable:

$$\text{If} \qquad z \sim \text{Normal}$$
$$\text{Then} \quad e^z \sim \text{LogNormal}$$

Figure 3-11 shows the Log-normal distribution corresponding to a Normal distribution with a mean of zero and a standard deviation of one. Notice that the distribution is highly skewed.

FIGURE 3-11

Illustration of the Log-Normal Distribution

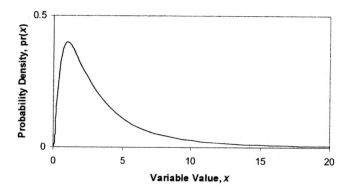

FIGURE 3-12

Comparison of Beta Distribution with Actual Credit-Loss Data

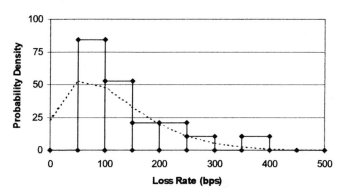

The Beta Distribution

The *Beta distribution* is useful in describing credit-risk losses, which are typically highly skewed, as we saw in the bond-default rates in Figure 3-4.

The formula for the Beta distribution is quite complex; however, it is available in most spreadsheet applications. As with the Normal distribution, it only requires two parameters (in this case called α and β) to define the shape. α and β are functions of the desired mean and standard deviation of the distribution; they are calculated as follows:

$$\alpha = \frac{\mu^2(1-\mu)}{\sigma^2} - \mu$$

$$\beta = \frac{\mu(1-\mu)^2}{\sigma^2} + (\mu - 1)$$

For the bond-default data that we examined earlier, the mean is 1.27%, and the standard deviation is 0.62%. The value of α and β is therefore 4.15 and 322, respectively. With these values, the Beta distribution has the shape shown in Figure 3-12. Figure 3-12 compares the Beta distribution with the histogram obtained by binning the raw data. (The probability density was obtained from the histogram by dividing by the number of samples, 19, and the bin width, 50bps, or 0.005.) The figures show that the Beta distribution effectively smoothes the empirical data.

CONFIDENCE INTERVALS, CONFIDENCE LEVELS, AND PERCENTILES

Confidence intervals are one of the ways that we can use probability distributions to make statements about the probabilities of future events. Confidence intervals allow us to state with a given level of certainty the range of values that a variable is likely to take. For example, the probability that x will fall between a and b is given by:

$$P[a < x < b] = \int_a^b p[x]dx$$

Here, a is the lower end of the interval, b is the upper end, and $p[x]$ is the probability-density function. For example, consider a Normal distribution with a mean of 0 and standard deviation of 1. This is called a *Standard Normal distribution*. There is a 68% confidence that a random variable from a Standard Normal distribution will fall between -1 and $+1$. For this variable, a 68% confidence interval is therefore $+/-1$. Table 3-4 shows a range of confidence intervals and the associate probabilities for the Standard Normal distribution.

In risk management, *confidence levels* are often more useful than confidence intervals because we are usually concerned with the downside risk or worst-case level. The confidence level is a single number rather than a range. It is the level that will not be exceeded, with a given probability. For example, there is only a 5% chance that a variable drawn from a Standard Normal distribution will have a value greater than 1.64. We can therefore say that the 95% confidence level for this variable is 1.64. Table 3-5 gives several confidence levels for the Standard Normal distribution.

The inverse of the confidence levels is the *percentile*. For example, the 99 percentile (or "99%ile") is the level such that 99% of the results fall below that level. For a Normal distribution, the 99%ile is at the mean, plus 2.32 times the standard deviation. When dealing with empirical data, the 99%ile is the result that is 99% from the start of the data series after the series has been ordered. If, for example, there were 300 variables in a series, the 99%ile would be the third from the end of the ordered series.

TABLE 3-4

Confidence Intervals for the Standard Normal Distribution

Confidence Interval	Probability (%)
$+/-1.00$	68.2
$+/-1.64$	90.0
$+/-1.96$	95.0
$+/-2.00$	95.4
$+/-2.32$	98.0
$+/-2.50$	98.8
$+/-3.00$	99.7

TABLE 3-5

Confidence Levels for the Standard Normal Distribution

Confidence Level	Probability (%)
1.00	84.1
1.64	95.0
1.96	97.5
2.00	97.7
2.32	99.0
2.50	99.4
3.00	99.9

CORRELATION AND COVARIANCE

So far, we have been discussing the statistics of isolated variables, such as the change in the equity prices. We also need to describe the extent to which two variables move together, e.g., the changes in equity prices and changes in interest rates.

If two random variables show a pattern of tending to increase at the same time, then they are said to have a *positive correlation*. If one tends to decrease when the other increases, they have a *negative correlation*; and if they are completely independent, and there is no relationship between the movement of x and y, they are said to have *zero correlation*.

The quantification of correlation starts with *covariance*. The covariance of two variables can be thought of as an extension from calculating the variance for a single variable. Earlier, we defined the variance as follows:

$$\sigma^2 = \frac{1}{N-1} \sum_{i=1}^{N} \left[(x_i - \bar{x})^2 \right]$$

The variance for each of two separate variables, x and y, can therefore be calculated as:

$$\sigma_x^2 = \frac{1}{N-1} \sum_{i=1}^{N} [(x_i - \bar{x})(x_i - \bar{x})]$$

$$\sigma_y^2 = \frac{1}{N-1} \sum_{i=1}^{N} [(y_i - \bar{y})(y_i - \bar{y})]$$

The covariance between the variables is calculated by multiplying the variables together at each observation:

$$\sigma_{xy}^2 = \frac{1}{N-1} \sum_{i=1}^{N} [(x_i - \bar{x})(y_i - \bar{y})]$$

If the change in x is always positive when the change in y is positive, the covariance will come out to be a large number. If when the change in x is positive, the change in y is sometimes positive and sometimes negative, the terms will cancel each other out, and the covariance will tend towards zero.

The correlation is defined by normalizing the covariance with respect to the individual variances:

$$\rho_{xy} \equiv \frac{\sigma_{xy}^2}{\sigma_x \sigma_y}$$

The maximum possible value for a correlation is one, and the minimum is negative one. The correlation of a variable with itself is simply the variance divided by the variance, and is therefore always equal to one.

THE STATISTICS FOR A SUM OF NUMBERS

In risk measurement, we are often interested in finding the statistics for a result which is the sum of many variables. For example, the loss on a portfolio is the sum of the losses on the individual instruments. Similarly, the trading loss over a year is the sum of the losses on the individual days. Let us consider an example in which y is the sum of two random numbers, x_1 and x_2.

The mean of the sum of two random numbers is simply the sum of the means of the individual numbers:

$$\bar{y} = \bar{x}_1 + \bar{x}_2$$

The variance of a sum of random variables is the sum of the variances of the individual variables, plus the covariances:

$$\sigma_y^2 = \sigma_{x_1}^2 + \sigma_{x_2}^2 + 2\rho_{x_1,x_2}\sigma_{x_1}\sigma_{x_2}$$

This relationship is used in many places in risk measurement, and for those who are interested, can be derived as follows:

$$\sigma_y^2 = \frac{1}{N-1}\sum_{i=1}^{N}(y_i - \bar{y})^2$$

$$= \frac{1}{N-1}\sum_{i=1}^{N}\left((x_{1,i} + x_{2,i}) - (\bar{x}_1 + \bar{x}_2)\right)^2$$

$$= \frac{1}{N-1}\sum_{i=1}^{N}\left((x_{1,i} - \bar{x}_1)^2 + (x_{2,i} - \bar{x}_2)^2 + 2(x_{1,i} - \bar{x}_1)(x_{2,i} - \bar{x}_2)\right)$$

$$= \sigma_{x_1}^2 + \sigma_{x_2}^2 + 2\sigma_{x_1,x_2}^2$$

$$= \sigma_{x_1}^2 + \sigma_{x_2}^2 + 2\rho_{x_1,x_2}\sigma_{x_1}\sigma_{x_2}$$

The examples above were for two variables. In general, if y is a sum of q variables, then:

$$y = x_1 + x_2 + \cdots + x_q$$

$$= \sum_{j=1}^{q} x_j$$

$$\bar{y} = \bar{x}_1 + \bar{x}_2 + \cdots + \bar{x}_q$$

$$= \sum_{j=1}^{q} \bar{x}_j$$

$$\sigma_y^2 = \sigma_1 \sigma_1 + \rho_{1,2} \sigma_1 \sigma_2 + \cdots + \rho_{1,q} \sigma_1 \sigma_q + \cdots + \sigma_q \sigma_q$$

$$= \sum_{j=1}^{q} \sum_{k=1}^{q} \rho_{j,k} \sigma_j \sigma_k$$

It is worth noting that the correlation between variables a and b is the same as the correlation between b and a, i.e.,

$$\rho_{a,b} = \rho_{b,a}$$

One particularly useful application of this equation is when the correlation between the variables is zero. This assumption is commonly made for day-to-day changes in market variables. If we make this assumption, then the variance of the loss over multiple days is simply the sum of the variances for each day:

$$\sigma_{T\,days}^2 = \sigma_{Day\,1}^2 + \sigma_{Day\,2}^2 + \cdots + \sigma_{Day\,T}^2$$

If we further assume that the variance of the loss on each day is the same, then the variance over T days is simply T times the variance over one day:

$$\sigma_{T\,days}^2 = T\sigma_{Day\,1}^2$$

By taking the square root of each side, we can show that the standard deviation of the loss over T days is the standard deviation of the loss over one day, multiplied by the square root of T:

$$\sigma_{T\,days} = \sigma_{Day\,1}\sqrt{T}$$

This relationship is commonly used in the analysis of market risk to predict how bad the cumulative losses could be over multiple days.

RANDOM PROCESSES

For many random phenomena, such as equity prices and interest rates, the value in one time period will depend on the value in previous periods. For example, a very simple model for stock prices would be to say that the price is a random walk in which the stock price, S, on any given day is equal to the previous day's price plus a random number, x_t:

$$S_t = S_{t-1} + x_t$$

A typical assumption is that the random number is drawn from a Standard Normal distribution, multiplied by the required standard deviation:

$$S_{t+1} = S_t + \sigma\sqrt{\Delta T}z_t, \quad z_t \sim N(0,1)$$

Here, S_t is the stock price at time t, σ is the standard deviation of the stock price over one period, and ΔT is the number of time steps between each period. $N(0,1)$ signifies a Normal distribution with a mean of zero and standard deviation of one. If σ was the daily standard deviation, and the time steps were days, then ΔT would equal 1. If σ was the daily standard deviation, and the time steps were years, then ΔT would equal 250 (the number of trading days in a year). In practice, the random walk of equities is closer to being a geometric process, i.e., as the stock price increases, the size of the random changes also increases. This geometric process is included in the model below:

$$S_{t+1} = S_t + S_t\sigma\sqrt{\Delta T}z_t$$

We can further complicate the model by adding a mean expected growth rate, μ:

$$S_{t+1} = S_t + S_t\mu\Delta T + S_t\sigma\sqrt{\Delta T}z_t$$

This describes the evolution of stock prices reasonably well but is not good for describing interest rates. Interest rates do not have a long-term expected growth, but instead, over long periods they tend to return to a set level called the *long-term average*.

There are many models for random interest-rate processes. One of the most straightforward is the Cox-Ingersoll-Ross (CIR) model. The CIR model is as follows:

$$r_{t+1} = r_t + c(r_m - r_t) + \sigma_r\sqrt{r_t}z_{r,t}$$

Here, r_t is the rate at time t, c is the rate of decay towards r_m, and r_m is the long-term mean for the rate. Whenever r_t is greater than r_m, the term $c(r_m - r_t)$ becomes negative and tends to move the rates back down. The square root of r in the last term scales the random disturbance so when rates are low, the disturbance will be low, and there is a low possibility of creating negative interest rates.

BASIC MATRIX OPERATIONS

When there are many variables, the normal algebraic expressions become cumbersome. An alternative way of writing these expressions is in matrix form.

Matrices are just representations of the parameters in an equation. You may have used matrices in physics to represent distances in multiple dimensions, e.g., in the x, y, and z coordinates. In risk, matrices are commonly used to represent weights on different risk factors, such as interest rates, equities, FX, and commodity prices.

For example, we could say that the value of an equity portfolio was the sum of the number (n) of each equity held multiplied by the value (v) of each:

$$V_{Portfolio} = n_a v_a + n_b v_b + n_c v_c$$

This can also be written in matrix notation as follows:

$$V_{Portfolio} = N \times V^T$$

$$N = \begin{bmatrix} n_a & n_b & n_c \end{bmatrix}$$

$$V = \begin{bmatrix} v_a & v_b & v_c \end{bmatrix}$$

Notice that matrices and vectors are typically represented by capital letters and scalars by lowercased letters.

In this section, we give a quick reminder of the basic matrix operations. Consider a row vector, A. The transpose of A is a column vector:

$$A = \begin{bmatrix} a & b \end{bmatrix}$$

$$A^T = \begin{bmatrix} a \\ b \end{bmatrix}$$

Consider a matrix, M, with two rows and three columns. The transpose is a matrix with three rows and two columns:

$$M = \begin{bmatrix} a & c & e \\ b & d & f \end{bmatrix}$$

$$M^T = \begin{bmatrix} a & b \\ c & d \\ e & f \end{bmatrix}$$

Matrices can be summed by separately adding the individual elements, i.e., the first element of one vector is added to the first element of the other vector. Consider two row vectors, A and B. The sum of two row vectors is another row vector:

$$A = \begin{bmatrix} a & b \end{bmatrix}$$

$$B = \begin{bmatrix} c & d \end{bmatrix}$$

$$A + B = \begin{bmatrix} a & b \end{bmatrix} + \begin{bmatrix} c & d \end{bmatrix}$$

$$= \begin{bmatrix} a + c & b + d \end{bmatrix}$$

Matrices are multiplied together by multiplying the rows of the first vector with the columns of the second vector. Consider a row vector, A, and a column vector, B. The product of these is a scalar:

$$A = \begin{bmatrix} a & b \end{bmatrix}$$

$$B = \begin{bmatrix} c \\ d \end{bmatrix}$$

$$A \times B = \begin{bmatrix} a & b \end{bmatrix} \begin{bmatrix} c \\ d \end{bmatrix}$$

$$= ac + bd$$

Now consider a row vector, A, and a matrix, C. The product is a row vector:

$$A = \begin{bmatrix} a & b \end{bmatrix}$$

$$C = \begin{bmatrix} c & d \\ e & f \end{bmatrix}$$

$$A \times C = \begin{bmatrix} a & b \end{bmatrix} \begin{bmatrix} c & d \\ e & f \end{bmatrix}$$

$$= \begin{bmatrix} ac + be & ad + bf \end{bmatrix}$$

As further illustration, consider A and C with numerical values:

$$A = \begin{bmatrix} 1 & 2 \end{bmatrix}$$

$$C = \begin{bmatrix} 4 & 7 \\ 5 & 3 \end{bmatrix}$$

$$A \times C = \begin{bmatrix} 14 & 13 \end{bmatrix}$$

By following the rules for matrix operations, we can find matrices that represent the answers to systems of equations. We will use matrices on a couple of occasions in this book, notably in calculating Parametric Value at Risk (VaR). In Parametric VaR, we will use matrices to replace summations of products. For example, we earlier defined the variance for a sum of correlated variables to be as follows:

$$\sigma_y^2 = \sigma_1 \sigma_2 + \rho_{1,2} \sigma_1 \sigma_2 + \cdots + \rho_{1,q} \sigma_1 \sigma_q + \cdots + \sigma_q \sigma_q$$

$$= \sum_{j=1}^{q} \sum_{k=1}^{q} \rho_{j,k} \sigma_j \sigma_k$$

This can be written in matrix form simply as:

$$\sigma_y^2 = SRS^T$$

Here, S and R are defined as follows:

$$S = \begin{bmatrix} \sigma_1 & \sigma_2 & \cdots & \sigma_q \end{bmatrix}$$

$$R = \begin{bmatrix} 1 & \rho_{1,2} & & \rho_{1,q} \\ \rho_{1,2} & 1 & & \rho_{2,q} \\ & & \ddots & \\ \rho_{t,q} & \rho_{2,q} & & 1 \end{bmatrix}$$

If we only had two risk factors, the calculation would be as follows:

$$\sigma_y^2 = SRS^T$$

$$S = \begin{bmatrix} \sigma_1 & \sigma_2 \end{bmatrix}$$

$$R = \begin{bmatrix} 1 & \rho_{1,2} \\ \rho_{1,2} & 1 \end{bmatrix}$$

$$SR = \begin{bmatrix} \sigma_1 & \sigma_2 \end{bmatrix} \begin{bmatrix} 1 & \rho_{1,2} \\ \rho_{1,2} & 1 \end{bmatrix}$$

$$= \begin{bmatrix} \sigma_1 + \rho_{1,2}\sigma_2 & \rho_{1,2}\sigma_1 + \sigma_2 \end{bmatrix}$$

$$(SR)S^T = \begin{bmatrix} \sigma_1 + \rho_{1,2}\sigma_2 & \rho_{1,2}\sigma_1 + \sigma_2 \end{bmatrix} \begin{bmatrix} \sigma_1 \\ \sigma_2 \end{bmatrix}$$

$$= \sigma_1\sigma_1 + \rho_{1,2}\sigma_2\sigma_1 + \rho_{1,2}\sigma_1\sigma_2 + \sigma_2\sigma_2$$

$$= \sigma_1^2 + 2\rho_{1,2}\sigma_1\sigma_2 + \sigma_2^2$$

which gets us back to the algebraic expression for variance.

SUMMARY

In this chapter, we gathered together the core statistical techniques that are used in the balance of the book to measure various forms of risk. Next, we will look at the main instruments that banks trade and why they trade them. We will also explore how each instrument can be valued to manage risk effectively.

Background on Traded Instruments

INTRODUCTION

The previous chapters provided a macro view of risk management, including its relationship to risk measurement, the definition of key concepts such as economic capital, and descriptions of the core risk-measurement techniques. Having built that foundation, we can now move our discussion to a micro level—namely, a detailed discussion of specific risk-measurement tools and techniques for each type of risk.

We will first spend several chapters discussing the measurement of market risk for traded instruments. We will then move on to asset/liability management, credit risk, operating risk, and finally the approaches that can be used to pull all the risks together to measure the total risk to the bank.

Market risk arises from the possibility of losses resulting from unfavorable market movements. It is the risk of losing money because the perceived value of an instrument has changed. The difference between credit risk and market risk is that in credit risk there needs to be a default or failure by a counterparty to fulfill an obligation. In market risk, we deal simply with changes in the prices that investors are prepared to pay.

Over the next few chapters, we will describe the types of transactions that cause market risk, several ways of measuring the risk, and how banks organize themselves to manage the risk.

Before launching into the mathematics of risk measurement, it is necessary to have a reasonable understanding of the types of trades and instruments that give rise to the risk. This chapter will detail the main instruments that banks trade and why they trade them—along with an explanation of how to value each of the instruments. Valuation is very important in risk measurement because risk is all about potential changes in value. Typically, a bank trades the following instruments:

- Debt instruments, also known as fixed income or bonds
- Forward rate agreements

- Equities, also known as stocks
- Foreign exchange, also known as FX or currency
- Forwards and futures
- Swaps
- Options

Futures, swaps, and options are different types of derivatives contracts. They are called derivatives because their value is derived from other instruments, such as bonds. We will look at each of these instruments in detail.

In valuing instruments, one of the principal techniques is to decompose a complex instrument into a set of simple instruments with the same payments. The technical term for this is *arbitrage pricing theory*. An arbitrage is a trade in which a set of securities are bought and sold such that the combination provides a profit but has no risk. Such a riskless profit is attractive, and once the combination is well-known in the market, many investors will buy and sell the components of the arbitrage until their buying causes prices to adjust and the arbitrage opportunity goes away. In describing these equivalent arbitrage portfolios, we will use the terms *long* and *short*. Being long roughly corresponds to having an asset, and being short roughly corresponds to having a liability. If a bank is long an instrument, it owns the rights to the instrument. If it is short, it has promised to give the rights to another party. For example, if the bank is short a bond, it means that they have promised to give the bond to another party.

DEBT INSTRUMENTS

For debt instruments, we will look at their general structure, their valuation, and how changes in their values can be related to changes in interest rates.

Debt instruments are securities that provide interest payments but no ownership claim on the issuer. *Debt* is a liability or an obligation on a company or government agency to make specified payments. Debt and fixed-income securities are synonymous. Until recently, all debt contracts had fixed-interest payments, and the term "fixed income" continues to be used even though many debt securities now have interest payments that change depending on market conditions. Debt instruments include bonds, notes, commercial paper, syndicated loans, and 144a issues. These are described further in the introduction to the credit-risk section.

From a market-risk manager's perspective, there are four important features for debt instruments:

- Maturity
- Issuer credit rating
- Payment structure
- Currency

Let's look at each instrument in more detail.

Bond Structures

Maturity

Maturity is the time left until final payment. Although the time to final payment is a continuous variable, market convention has different names for different levels of maturity. Instruments with a maturity of over five years are called *bonds*. Those with a maturity of one to five years are called *notes*, and those with a maturity of less than a year are called *bills* or *money market instruments*. The money market is used by corporations and banks for short-term funding. The short-term interest rates are driven by immediate supply and demand, and are relatively insensitive to the long-term economic conditions. Because of their short maturity, the value of a money market instrument is quite insensitive to the prevailing interest rates, and therefore has relatively low market risk.

Issuer Credit Ratings

As discussed earlier, the credit risk of most bonds is rated by a third-party company called a *rating agency*, such as Standard & Poor's. These ratings are very important for three reasons:

- The ratings generally correspond to probabilities of default. Bonds with high probabilities of default trade at lower prices than risk-free bonds. As we discuss later in the chapter, a lower price implies a higher interest rate. The difference between the interest rate for a risky bond and the interest rate for a risk-free bond of the same maturity is called the *credit spread*.
- Many institutional investors, such as pension funds, must adhere to fund restrictions that require them to buy only bonds of "investment grade." To be investment grade, a bond must be rated BBB or better.
- The Basel Committee on Banking Supervision is prompting bank regulators, such as the Federal Reserve and the Bank of England, to set bank capital requirements according to the credit quality of the bonds they hold. Table 4-1 below shows one of the options for the amount of capital to be set aside for corporate loans.

T A B L E 4-1

The Effect of Credit Rating on
Regulatory Capital to be Held

AAA to AA	A	BBB to BB	Below BB
1.6%	4.0%	8.0%	12.0%

("Consultative Document, The Standardized Approach to Credit Risk, The New Basel Accord," January, 2001, The Basel Committee on Banking Supervision, The Bank for International Settlements.)

Payment Structure

The payments of interest on a bond are called *coupons* and are either fixed or floating. *Fixed-rate bonds* pay the same percentage every time, and the rate is fixed when the bond is first issued. *Floating-rate* bonds pay a variable percentage and the interest rate is reset periodically to a prevailing market rate. For example, a five-year floating-rate bond would make payments every six months. At each time of payment, the amount for the next payment will be set according to the prevailing six-month, interbank borrowing rate. A small additional spread would be added to compensate for the relatively illiquid nature of a five-year bond, compared to reinvesting in a series of six-month bonds.

Currency

Debt instruments can be denominated in any currency. The probability of default tends to be less if the currency of the bond is the same as the base currency of the entity issuing the bond. This is especially true of governments who always have the option of printing more money to repay bonds denominated in their own currencies. This makes domestic government bonds almost risk free; therefore, bonds of a given currency have their interest rates set relative to the bonds of the government that issues that currency.

The Valuation of Bonds

Now that we have a better understanding of the various characteristics of debt instruments and how they are classified, it is time to explain how they are actually valued. This is the foundation for measuring the risk of changes in bond values. We will first explain how to value a bond with a single known payment. Then we will discuss how bonds with multiple payments can be valued using a yield curve. The discussion may at first seem a little circular because we use observed prices to get a yield curve, then use the yield curve to estimate prices. However, the utility of the yield curve is that by observing the price of a few bonds, we can create a yield curve and thereby predict the price for all bonds.

Valuing a Single Payment

It is important to understand how single payments are valued so we can value complex bonds by decomposing them into single payments.

Any bond promising to pay a certain amount at a future point in time has a value. The value is the price that investors are prepared to pay today to own that bond, and therefore own the right to the future cashflow. If we consider a bond that promises to make a single payment, at time t, then the current value of the bond and the future payment amount can be used to define a discount factor (DF):

$$DF_t = \frac{\text{Value}}{\text{Payment}_t}$$

The discount factor will be less than one, as it is almost always better to have cash now than the same amount promised in the future. The *discount factor* includes all the effects that cause the value to be less than the promised amount, including the effects of inflation and the possibility of default. If the cash flow is certain (e.g., a fixed-rate government bond), then the discount is called the *risk-free discount*. If the cash flow is risky, e.g., if there is a possibility of default, the value will be less, and therefore, the discount factor will be smaller. The discount factor for a given maturity, t, can be used to define a discount rate, r_t, which is more familiarly known as an *interest rate*. The usual expression for the discount rate is as follows:

$$DF_t = \frac{1}{(1 + r_t)^t}$$

This expression uses discrete compounding. For continuous compounding, the rate is defined by using the exponential function:

$$DF_t = e^{-t \times r_t}$$

e is approximated by 2.7. Discrete compounding is more intuitive for most people, but continuous discounting is easier to use in the mathematics of finance, e.g., in option pricing. The value for r_t will be slightly different depending on which convention is used.

Valuing Bonds with Multiple Payments

Zero-coupon bonds are bonds that do not pay interest explicitly. They have only a single "bullet" payment, and are therefore also known as *bullet bonds*. The bond is sold at a discount to face value, with the difference between the face value and the sale price implicitly being the interest payment. The value of a risk-free zero-coupon bond is simply the amount of the payment multiplied by the risk-free discount factor:

$$\text{Value} = \text{Payment}_t \times DF_t$$

$$= \frac{\text{Payment}_t}{(1 + r_t)^t}$$

If there were many zero-coupon bonds being traded with different maturities, we could use the above equation to construct a graph with t in the x-axis and r_t in the y-axis. Such a graph is called a *yield curve* and is illustrated in Figure 4-1. The terms yield and discount rate are often used synonymously.

Figure 4-1 shows the average yield curve for the U.S. dollar over the last 10 years. The curve generally, but not always, slopes up because of the additional cost of liquidity for long-dated cashflows, and because long-dated cashflows have a greater risk of their values being eroded through inflation.

Using the current yield curve we can closely estimate the current value of any bond. Coupon-paying bonds have a series of fixed-intermediate-interest payments. The value of a coupon-paying bond is the sum of the value of the individual payments.

FIGURE 4-1

The Average U.S. Yield Curve over the Last 10 Years

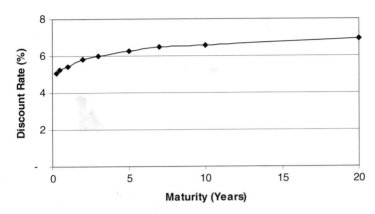

Using the rates from the yield curve, the bond can be valued as the discounted sum of the payments or cashflows:

$$\text{Price} = \sum_t \frac{C_t}{(1 + r_t)^t}$$

Here, C_t is the cash flow at time t, and the price is the price at which the bond can currently be bought.

Construction of the Yield Curve

It would be relatively easy to value all bonds if there were many traded zero-coupon bonds whose price could be observed. However, there are many zero-coupon bonds traded for short maturities up to about a year, but bonds with longer maturities typically have coupons, and therefore, it is not possible to directly observe the zero-coupon yield for long maturities.

As an alternative to direct observation, traders synthetically create the implied zero-coupon yield curve using "bootstrapping." In bootstrapping, we first observe the price of a zero-coupon bond and calculate the discount rate for that maturity. We then observe the price of a coupon bond of a slightly longer maturity, and we subtract the value of the short-term coupons using the discount rate that we observed from the zero-coupon bond. The remaining value must be the price that the market is willing to pay for the longer-maturity cashflow, and we can therefore define a discount rate for this longer maturity. We then repeat the process, steadily observing bonds with longer maturities, and subtracting the value of the earlier payments using the discount rates we found as we progressed up the yield curve.

As an example of bootstrapping, consider two simple bonds with the payments and prices shown in Table 4-2. Bond A has 1 cashflow in 6 months. Bond B has a

TABLE 4-2

Two Bonds Used for the
Bootstrapping Example

	Bond A	Bond B
Cashflow at 6 months	$100	$3
Cashflow at 12 months		$100
Observed Market Price	$98	$98

The data in the table helps us to construct an equation to find the
discount rate for the cashflow at 12 months.

cashflow at 6 months and one at 12 months. We will use these to find the discount rate
for payments in 12 months.

From the price of Bond A, we calculate that the 6-month discount rate is 4.1%:

$$\text{Value} = \frac{\text{Payment}_t}{(1+r_t)^t}$$

$$\$98 = \frac{\$100}{(1+r_{0.5})^{0.5}}$$

$$r_{0.5} = \left(\frac{100}{98}\right)^2 - 1 = 4.1\%$$

The $3 coupon on Bond B at 6 months is therefore worth $2.94:

$$\text{Value}_{B,6\,\text{month}} = \frac{\$3}{(1+4.1\%)^{0.5}} = \$2.94$$

The remaining cashflow of $100 at one year must therefore be worth $95.06. This allows
us to calculate the one-year discount rate to be 5.2%:

$$\$95.06 = \frac{\$100}{(1+r_1)^1}$$

$$r_1 = \frac{\$100}{\$95.06} - 1 = 5.2\%$$

In summary, bonds are valued by decomposing them into a series of single payments
and discounting each payment according to the yield curve:

$$\text{Price} = \sum_T \frac{C_t}{(1+r_t)^t}$$

The yield curve may be constructed by directly observing the price of zero-coupon bonds or by using bootstrapping to isolate individual cashflows within a bond of multiple payments.

Yield to Maturity

The yield-curve process described above is the one used in risk measurement. But you may also hear of bond values being described in terms of their "yield to maturity." The yield to maturity (y) is the internal rate of return for a bond, given the current market price and the future cashflows. It is the single value of y that satisfies this equation:

$$\text{Price} = \sum_t \frac{C_t}{(1+y)^t}$$

The yield to maturity is continually changing as market prices change. Notice that there is an inverse relationship between price and yield: as the price increases, the yield drops. A coupon-paying bond is said to be at Par if the yield to maturity equals the coupon rate. This is equivalent to saying that the price equals the face value. It is said to be at a Premium if the coupon rate is greater than the yield, and it is at a Discount if the coupon is below yield.

Measuring Interest Rate Sensitivity Using Duration

Duration is a measure of the interest rate sensitivity of the value of a bond or loan. This is useful because once we know the duration and the possible movement of interest rates, we have a measure of how much value the bank could lose in its bond portfolio.

As an example, if a bond had a duration of seven, it would mean that that value of the instrument would decline by seven percent if interest rates rose one percent. Duration is calculated based on changes in the present value of the bond. As discussed in the previous section, the price or value (V) is the sum of the discounted cash flows (C):

$$V = \sum_t \frac{C_t}{(1+r)^t}$$

For convenience, we will define V_t as the present value of the single cash flow that occurs at time t:

$$V_t = \frac{C_t}{(1+r)^t}$$

The present value for the whole bond is then given by:

$$V = \sum_t V_t$$

There are two types of duration: Macauley duration and modified duration. Macauley duration is easier to calculate, but modified duration is more accurate. *Macauley duration* is simply the average time for cash flows, weighted by their present values:

$$\text{Macauley Duration} \equiv \frac{1}{V}\sum_t tV_t$$

Macauley duration was useful when only slide rules were available, but computers allow us to use the more accurate modified duration. *Modified duration* is based on the derivative of the value with respect to interest rates:

$$\frac{dV}{dr} = \sum_t \frac{-tC_t}{(1+r)^{t+1}} = \sum_t \frac{-tV_t}{(1+r)}$$

Modified duration is found by dividing this derivative by the initial value and multiplying by negative one. The multiplication by negative one is used to make modified duration compatible with Macauley duration:

$$\text{Modified Duration} \equiv \frac{1}{V}\left(-\frac{dV}{dr}\right)$$

$$= \frac{1}{(1+r)}\frac{1}{V}\sum_t tV_t$$

If we had not divided by V we would have had the absolute price sensitivity, which is called *duration dollars*:

$$\text{Duration \$} = -\frac{dV}{dr}$$

The change in the value of a bond is closely approximated by the derivative of value with respect to rates, multiplied by the change in rates:

$$\Delta V \approx \frac{dV}{dr} \times \Delta r$$

From here, the link to duration is obvious:

$$\Delta V \approx -1 \times \text{Duration \$} \times \Delta r$$

$$= -1 \times \text{Modified Duration} \times V \times \Delta r$$

You may have noticed that the unit of duration is time. This may seem strange, but it is because duration is the sensitivity with respect to interest rates, and interest rates are in units of increase per time period. Therefore, since duration is change in percentage value per change in interest rate, the unit of duration is time.

Having come this far, you may wonder why we bother with duration rather than just using the derivative directly. The simple answer is that it is market custom. Many bank financial reports will give "duration," but few will give "the derivative of value with respect to interest rates." Therefore, it is necessary to understand the meaning of duration.

Duration has significant limitations as a measure of risk. It is the first derivative of value with respect to rates. As such, it is a linear measure and only describes changes in the value of a bond based on small parallel shifts in the yield curve. It does not describe the value changes that could result from the convexity of bond prices or complex shifts in the yield curve.

Convexity is the nonlinear relationship between the price of a bond and its yield, as illustrated in Figure 4-2. As duration is a linear description of value changes, it becomes increasingly inaccurate as the rate change becomes larger.

Most yield curve movements can be broken down as combinations of shift, twist, and flex, as illustrated in Figure 4-3. The yield curve is said to shift if rates of all maturities move by the same amount. The curve twists if long-term rates move a different amount compared to short-term rates. Flex occurs if long- and short-term rates move in the opposite direction of medium rates.

In later chapters, when we come to measuring the Value at Risk for bonds, we will find that shift, twist, and flex can be accounted for relatively easily by letting rates at different maturities move by different amounts. However, to account for

FIGURE 4-2

Illustration of Bond-Price Convexity

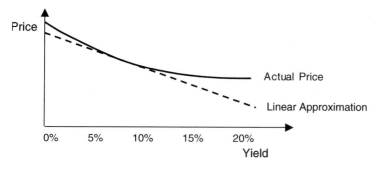

FIGURE 4-3

Illustration of Yield-Curve Shift, Twist, and Flex

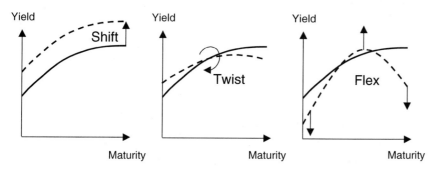

convexity, we need to give up the linear approximation of duration and use full bond valuation.

The discussion above assumed that the bond had coupons that were fixed. If the coupons are floating, the duration will be much less because if rates move, the coupon payments will move to compensate. Each time the rates are reset, the value of the bond comes back to par, i.e., the value of the bond equals the principle amount. This means that the value is insensitive to changes in the interest rates and the duration is close to zero. In practice, most floating-rate bonds reset the rate for the next payment a few months in advance. You know that on the date of that next reset, you will get the specified cashflow plus you will own a bond that you can sell for the full principal amount. This is equivalent to having a fixed-rate bond that matures on the next reset date. The duration, then, is equal to the time remaining until that next reset, which is typically much less than the time to maturity.

FORWARD RATE AGREEMENTS

A *forward rate agreement* (FRA) is a contract to give a loan at a fixed rate starting at some point in the future. For example, the agreement could be that in 2 years' time the bank will lend $100 to the customer. The customer will then pay 8% per year for 5 years, and in 7 years' time the customer will pay back the principal of $100. Customers would want such agreements if they had projects for which they expected to start construction in 2 years, and they wanted to fix the borrowing costs now.

Using arbitrage arguments, a forward rate agreement can be decomposed into being long a fixed-rate bond, with the first coupon being paid at some starting point in the future, and short a zero-coupon bond corresponding to the bank's initial payment to the company. This is illustrated in Table 4-3 for the example above.

Often, the FRA does not entail an actual loan with all of its associated covenants and payments. Instead, at the date on which the loan would have commenced, the

TABLE 4-3

Representation of a Forward Rate
Agreement as Two Bonds

Year	2	3	4	5	6	7
FRA	-$100	$8	$8	$8	$8	$108
Long a Bond	–	$8	$8	$8	$8	$108
Short a Zero	-$100	–	–	–	–	–

Table showing how a forward rate agreement can be decomposed into being long a fixed-rate bond, and short a zero-coupon bond.

parties pay the difference in net present value (NPV) of the cashflows. The calculation of the NPV uses the market rate on the commencement date to discount the cash flow. For the previous example, the calculation of the payment from the bank would be as follows:

$$\text{NPV} = 100 - \left[\frac{\$8}{(1+r_1)^1} + \frac{\$8}{(1+r_2)^2} + \frac{\$8}{(1+r_3)^3} + \frac{\$8}{(1+r_4)^4} + \frac{\$108}{(1+r_5)^5} \right]$$

The discount rates, r_1 to r_5, are those existing on commencement date. For example, r_5 is the 5-year discount rate that will be observed 2 years from now. If rates had risen to be higher than 8%, the term in brackets will be less than \$100, and the bank will owe money to the company. The company can then take this money and use it as compensation to offset the increased cost of borrowing that it would experience if it now went into the market and obtained a loan at the prevailing rates.

Up to this point, we have discussed how to value an FRA once the forward lending rate has been set; now we will discuss how that rate is set. When initiating a forward rate agreement, a bank will set the borrowing rate according to the forward rates currently observed in the market.

Forward rates are obtained from the current yield curve using arbitrage arguments. The argument is that if an investor wants to invest money until some distant time, t_2, she has two choices:

1. Buy a bond that matures at t_2.
2. Buy a bond that matures at an intermediate time, t_1, and buy a forward rate agreement that locks in an interest rate from t_1 to t_2.

Let us use the symbol r_1 for the interest rate currently available for bonds maturing at t_1, and r_2 for those maturing at t_2. We will use $f_{1,2}$ to represent the forward rate that can be locked in from t_1 to t_2.

If the amount to be invested is \$100, the first investment strategy will yield the following result:

$$\text{Cash}_{t2} = \$100(1+r_2)^{t_2}$$

The second strategy will yield the following:

$$\text{Cash}_{t2} = \$100(1+r_1)^{t_1}(1+f_{1,2})^{t_2-t_1}$$

If either of these strategies provided better results, all investors would move to that strategy, increasing the demand for the given product and changing the rates until both strategies gave the same result. The forward rate is therefore related to the two rates from the yield curve as follows:

$$(1+r_2)^{t_2} = (1+r_1)^{t_1}(1+f_{1,2})^{t_2-t_1}$$

$$f_{1,2} = \left[\frac{(1+r_2)^{t_2}}{(1+r_1)^{t_1}} \right]^{\frac{1}{t_2-t_1}} - 1$$

EQUITIES

Equities are also known as shares or stocks. Equities represent ownership in a company for the holder, and a right to the profits once all of the debts have been paid. Equity values reflect all of the factors associated with the business risks, and as a result, are very volatile compared with bonds.

In addition to stocks that give direct ownership in a company, there are also synthetic instruments such as American Depository Receipts (ADRs) that are not equities, but are contracts designed to mirror the cash flow of an underlying equity and therefore have the same risk. It is also possible to invest in an instrument that pays the same return as an equity market index, and also has equity-like risk. These include swaps in which one side pays a fixed rate and receives an amount proportional to the level of the stock market.

Investors use many techniques to value equities, but most of these include a large amount of intuition and "art." The best way to learn about market risk for equities is to open an Internet brokerage account, invest $1000, and watch it disappear. From a risk-measurement perspective, equities are so complex as to be simple. There are so many factors that affect equity values that they are generally considered simply to be instruments whose future value is random. The future changes in value are typically considered to have a Normal or Log-normal distribution with the same standard deviation as the historical changes in the equity price.

The value changes can be further broken down into systemic and idiosyncratic risks. The *systemic* risk is the movement in the equity price that occurs because of a general movement in the stock market. The amount by which the stock tends to move with the market is called the beta (β). The *idiosyncratic risk* (ϵ), describes price movements that are uncorrelated with the market and are due solely to the performance of the individual company. This can be summarized in the following equation for the change in value:

$$\Delta V = V_0(\beta \Delta M + \epsilon)$$

Here, V_o is the current value, ΔM is the change in the market index, and ϵ is the uncorrelated idiosyncratic change. For a diversified portfolio of many equities, the idiosyncratic risks tend to cancel each other out, leaving the trader or investor exposed to the sum of the systemic risks of all the stocks:

$$\Delta V_{Portfolio} = \left[\sum_{k=1}^{N} V_{o,k} \beta_k \right] \Delta M$$

Here, N is the number of equities, β_k is the beta for equity k, and $V_{o,k}$ is the current value of equity k. This is the approach most commonly used when assessing the overall risk of a portfolio.

FOREIGN EXCHANGE

Foreign exchange (FX) trading is also known as currency trading. Generally, FX markets are the most liquid of all of the markets; i.e., large volumes are traded, and it is easy to find someone to buy or sell at a price close to the current market value. There are many ways that currencies can be traded, including spot, forwards, foreign securities, and derivatives.

Spot FX trades are simply an exchange of currencies, and the settlement of the exchange typically happens within a day. *Forward trades* are agreements to exchange specified amounts of each currency at a specified date in the future. Securities with payments denominated in a foreign currency carry both the risk of changes in value of the security (e.g., a drop in the value of a foreign equity), plus the risk of a change in the exchange rates. As an example, consider a U.S. bank holding a bond issued by a Mexican company. The bank could lose money if the company defaults, if the peso interest rates increase, or if the peso devalues compared with the dollar.

The value of an instrument denominated in a foreign currency is simply found by calculating the current value of the instrument in the foreign currency, then exchanging to the local currency at the prevailing rate.

FORWARDS

Most trading is conducted in the spot market (also known as the cash market). In the spot market, trades are settled as soon as operationally possible after the trade agreement has been made, typically within a couple of days. In contrast to spot trades, a *forward contract* is an agreement to buy a security or commodity at a point in the future. At the time of agreeing to the forward contract, the amounts are fixed for the quantity of the security or commodity to be delivered, the delivery price to be paid, and the delivery date. Typically, the delivery date is several months into the future. Here are some examples of forward contracts:

- A *bond forward* is an obligation to buy or sell a bond at a predetermined price and time.
- An *equity forward* is an obligation to buy or sell a specific equity at a predetermined price and time.
- An *FX forward* is an obligation to buy or sell a currency on a future date for a predetermined exchange rate. On that date, there will be simultaneous exchange of the full amount of each currency.
- A *gold forward* is an obligation to deliver a specified quantity of gold on a fixed date and receive a fixed delivery price.

Forwards are one of the types of derivative contracts because the value of the forward is derived from the value of the current or future spot prices of the underlying security or commodity. After the contract has been agreed, but before the delivery takes place, the value of the contract will change. This change occurs because new contracts are being signed with different delivery prices. As an example, consider entering into a contract to buy 100 ounces of gold in 3 months' time with a delivery price of $250 per ounce. One month later, assume that a crisis occurs, people want gold, and are willing to pay $300 for an ounce of gold to be delivered in 2 months. In this case, you could guarantee to deliver 100 ounces in 2 months for $300/ounce. In 2 months, you would be certain to make a net profit of $5000. The current value of the contract is therefore worth $5000 discounted at the risk-free rate for 2 months. If the discount rate was 5%, the contract would be worth $4959.

$$\$4959 = \frac{100}{(1+5\%)^{1/6}}(300-250)$$

In general, the value of a forward agreement is the number of items to be delivered (N), times the difference between current market delivery price (D_C) and the originally agreed delivery price (D_0), discounted by the risk-free rate (r_f) from the time of delivery (t):

$$\text{Contract Value} = \frac{N}{(1+r_f)^t}(D_C - D_0)$$

As a slightly more complex example, let us consider a contract to deliver 100 British pounds and buy 150 U.S dollars in 3 months' time. The value of that contract in U.S. dollars is 150 dollars discounted at the 3-month U.S. interest rate, minus 100 pounds discounted at the 3-month U.K. rate, then exchanged into dollars at the current spot FX rate. This is summarized in the equation below:

$$\text{Contract Value} = \frac{150}{\left(1+r_{US,3\,mo}\right)^{3/12}} - FX_{US/UK,Spot}\frac{100}{\left(1+r_{UK,3mo}\right)^{3/12}}$$

The value of this contract will change if either of the interest rates or the FX rate changes.

An alternative way of doing this analysis is to consider entering into a forward exchange from pounds to dollars at the current FX forward rate, then discounting the result according to U.S. interest rates:

$$\text{Contract Value} = \left(1+r_{US,3mo}\right)^{3/12} \times \left(150 - 100 \times FX_{US/UK,3moForward}\right)$$

Here, 150 is the agreed delivery price, and $100 \times FX_{US/UK,3moForward}$ is the current market price for 3-month delivery. For there to be no arbitrage opportunities, the forward rate must be related to the current spot rate and interest rates as follows:

$$FX_{US/UK,3moForward} = FX_{US/UK,Spot}\left[\frac{(1+r_{US.3mo})}{(1+r_{UK,3mo})}\right]^{3/12}$$

FUTURES

Futures are the same as forwards contracts except that they are traded on exchanges. The market risk for futures is essentially the same as forwards, but there are three practical differences:

- Futures are for standardized amounts and standardized delivery dates, and forwards can be for any amount and date.
- The credit risk for futures is reduced because they are exchange traded. If counterparties fail to honor their agreements to make deliveries, the exchange will make the deliveries in their place.
- The credit of risk futures is reduced because the change in the value of the futures contract is offset by compensatory daily payments, so the value of the contract minus the value of the cash you have received is always close to zero.

The value and the market risk for futures are evaluated in the same ways as for forwards.

SWAPS

A *swaps contract* is an agreement between two counterparties to exchange payments at several specified points in the future. The amount of the payments is determined by a formula in the contract. The formula will typically specify the payments as a function of market factors, such as the short-term interest rates, FX rates, or commodity prices.

Swaps are derivatives because their values are derived from the current and future values of underlying securities. Swaps were first developed in the 1980s, and now there are many types, including the following:

Interest-Rate Swap

In an interest-rate swap, a regular fixed amount is paid by one counterparty, and a floating amount is paid by the other counterparty. The floating amount is the prevailing short-term interest rates multiplied by a notional loan amount. The *notional amount* can be thought of as the size of an imaginary loan or bond.

For example, Party A agrees to pay Party B cash flows every 6 months for 5 years. The amount of the cashflow is 4% (annual 8%) times a notional amount of $100 million (i.e., $4 million every 6 months). In return, every 6 months Party B will make a payment equal to $100 million times the LIBOR divided by 2 (to account for the payments being semiannual). *LIBOR* is the London Interbank Offer Rate; it is the rate at which banks lend to each other. The lending can be in any currency, and London is chosen rather than any other market because of the liquidity of the market. As an example, 6-month U.S. dollar LIBOR is the rate at which banks will lend U.S. dollars to each other for 6 months.

In practice, each time a payment is made, the 6-month LIBOR will be observed and used to fix the payment to be made in 6 months' time. The counterparties exchange the difference between the cashflows rather than the whole amount. For example, if a payment had just been made, and 6-month LIBOR was 10%, the payment at the end of the next 6-month period from counterparty B to A would be $1 million: (5%–4%) × $100 million.

The value of such a swap can be determined by considering the swap to be the combination of a fixed-rate bond and a floating-rate bond. In the example above, counterparty A has the same cashflows as if it was short a fixed-rate bond and long a floating-rate bond. The value of the swap to counterparty A is therefore the value of a floating-rate bond of $100 million minus an 8% fixed-rate 5-year bond of $100 million.

Typically, the swap payments are modified slightly to reflect any difference in the creditworthiness of the 2 parties. This credit spread is much less than would be used for a full loan of the same notional value because the actual exposure amount is much less than the notional amount. For example, on an interest-rate swap with a $100 million notional amount, the interest payments due will be just a few percent of the $100 million. If the counterparty defaults, the bank will lose the interest payments, not the full $100 million.

Currency Swap

A *currency swap* is a combination of an FX spot and FX forward transaction with principal amounts exchanged at the beginning and end of the transaction. Thus, risk measurement of currency swaps is accomplished by simply disaggregating the swap into a spot and a forward.

Basis Swap

A *basis swap* is the regular payment of one floating amount against a different floating amount. For example, the U.S. Treasury rate against LIBOR.

Equity Swap

An *equity swap* is the regular payment of equity index or an equity value against a floating interest rate, such as LIBOR.

In general, the valuation of a swap can be accomplished by deconstructing the swap into the two underlying instruments on each side of the swap, and then valuing those instruments.

OPTIONS

An *option* is a type of derivative contract. An option gives the holder the right but not the obligation to buy or sell an underlying asset at a future time, at a predetermined price. The predetermined price is called the *strike price*. The party holding the right to choose is said to be long the option, and the counterparty who sold or wrote the option is said to be short the option.

Options are similar to futures, but with one important difference: the holder can choose whether to exercise the option at the time of contract expiration. Options carry an "aura of mystery" because they can be difficult to value. Adding to this mystery is the fact that there are many option classifications. Therefore, this section will focus on explaining the different types of options and approaches used to price them and to assess the risk. The goal of this section is to give the reader an intuitive feel for the factors that drive pricing and risk.

Options can be classified as one of the following:

- *Vanilla options* (so called because traders consider them to be as plain as vanilla ice cream). These have very simple contract terms for payments and are relatively easy to value.
- *Packages of vanilla options* are simply the sum of several vanilla options put together into one deal.
- *Exotic options* are nonvanilla options that are complex and typically tailored for an individual customer. It is possible to write virtually any form of option contract depending on any observable market factor, such as equity prices, exchange rates, or even the weather.

Options can be categorized according to the rights given to the holder:

- *Puts*: A put option gives the holder the right to sell the underlying security and receive a predetermined strike price.
- *Calls*: A call option gives the holder the right to buy the underlying security by paying a predetermined strike price.

The strike price is agreed on at the beginning of the option contract, and is the cash amount to be paid for the underlying security. At the beginning of the contract, the counterparties also agree on the ultimate maturity (or expiration date) and alternatives to exercising the option, including:

- *European-style*, which can only be exercised at the end date.
- *American-style*, which can be exercised on any date until maturity.
- *Bermudan-style* which can only be exercised on certain dates. (The option is so called because Bermuda is partway between Europe and America.)
- *Asian-style*, which bases payments on an average price over a period. This technique is useful for shallow markets that are highly volatile or exposed to the risk of price manipulation.

Each option style can now be traded in any geography. When the option is exercised, there are two possibilities for settlement: physical delivery and cash settlement. Physical delivery requires that the strike price be paid, and the underlying security should be delivered. Cash settlement requires only that the difference in the value of the security at the time of exercise and the strike price of the option should be delivered.

To give a more intuitive understanding of how options work, let us look at examples of a call and put option.

Call-Option Example

Consider a European-style call-option contract on IBM stock with maturity on August 21, 2002, and a strike price of $75. If you own this option, then you may *buy* 100 IBM shares—100 shares being a contract norm—on August 21, 2002, and pay a strike price of $75 each. If, on that day, the stock is worth $82, the option is "in the money," and you will receive $700 as determined by the following equation:

$$\text{Call payoff} = \text{number of shares} \times (\text{value} - \text{strike})$$

$$\$700 = 100 \times (82 - 75)$$

If the stock is worth $72 (out of the money), then the option would expire worthless because you would not want to buy the stock for $75.

Put-Option Example

Consider a European-style put-option contract on IBM stock with maturity on August 21, 2002, and a strike price of $75. If you own this option, then you may *sell* 100 IBM shares on August 21, 2002 and receive a strike price of $75 each. If, on that day, the stock is worth $72, you would sell the shares for $75 and receive $300. The payoff would be $300:

$$\text{Put payoff} = \text{number of shares} \times (\text{strike} - \text{value})$$

$$\$300 = 100 \times (75 - 72)$$

If the stock is worth $82, the option would expire worthless because you would not want to sell the stock for $75.

Option Valuation at Time of Expiration

As we have seen in the example above, there can be great value in holding an option, and therefore, a price has to be paid to obtain an option. The first step in determining what price to pay for an option is understanding the potential payoff at the expiration date. The payoff is the value of the option contract at the time of maturity. It depends on the structure of the contract and the value of the underlying security.

Let's use the symbol V for the value of the payoff, X for the strike price, and S for the value of the underlying stock that is bought or sold.

In general, on the expiration date the value of a call is the maximum of 0 or $S - X$:

$$\text{Call: } V = \max(0, S - X)$$

If S is more than X, the call is said to be in the money. Otherwise, it is said to be out of the money.

The value of a put at expiration is the maximum of 0 or $X - S$. If S is less than X, the put is in the money.

$$\text{Put: } V = \max(0, X - S)$$

The logic for the call and put is summarized in Table 4-4.

Figure 4-4 illustrates the payoff as a function of the stock price at the time of the exercise. As the stock price on the x-axis changes, the stock price on the y-axis also changes, but the strike price stays fixed. The payoff is shown in terms of what you have to give to exercise the option and what you get in return. If you exercise the option, the difference between what you get and what you give is the payoff.

Option Valuation before Expiration

In the discussion above, we established the value of the payoff at the time when the option expires, but what is the value of an option at some time before expiration? As an example, consider a call option that has a strike price that is higher than the current stock price. If the call was about to expire, it would have zero value. However if there were several months before expiration, there is a possibility that by the time of expiration, the stock price will move to become greater than the strike price. If that were to occur, the option would be valuable at expiration. If we were given the chance to buy this option several months before expiration, how much should we be prepared to pay for the possibility of it becoming valuable? The answer to this question is provided by option valuation.

TABLE 4-4

Logic and Payoff for Exercising Options

	Stock Price Less than Strike	Stock Price More than Strike
Call	"Out of the money"	"In the money"
	Do not buy the stock	Buy stock at the strike price
	Make no profit	Make profit
Put	"In the money"	"Out of the money"
	Sell stock for strike price	Do not sell the stock
	Make profit	Make no profit

FIGURE 4-4

Option Payoff as a Function of the Price of the Underlying

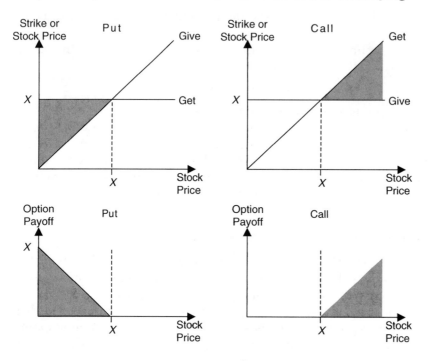

There are three primary ways to find the value of an option:

- Formulas based on the Black-Scholes equation
- Binomial trees
- Monte Carlo simulations

The Black-Scholes Equation

The *Black-Scholes equation* was developed by two professors who were later awarded a Nobel Prize for their accomplishment. The equation is relatively easy and fast compared with other pricing approaches because it has several simplifying assumptions. Because of the simplifications, it is only accurate for vanilla puts and calls. However, it is often used as a first approximation to the value for many other types of options.

In its basic form, the Black-Scholes equation calculates the current value of holding an option on a stock. The equation assumes that the option can only be exercised at maturity, and that there are no dividends or transaction costs. It also assumes that the percentage change in the stock price has Normal distribution.

With these restrictions, the value of a call option on a stock is a function of the following five variables:

S = Spot price of the underlying security

T = Time left to maturity of the option

X = Strike price of option

r = Risk-free interest rate to the time of option expiration

σ = Annual volatility for the underlying security.

(Volatility is the standard deviation of the price change as a percentage of the initial price.) Given these definitions, the Black-Scholes equation for the price of a call option (C) is as follows:

$$C = SN(d_1) - Xe^{-rT}N(d_2)$$

where

$$d_1 = \frac{ln\left(\frac{S}{X}\right) + \left(r + \frac{\sigma^2}{2}\right)T}{\sigma\sqrt{T}}$$

$$d_2 = \frac{ln\left(\frac{S}{X}\right) + \left(r - \frac{\sigma^2}{2}\right)T}{\sigma\sqrt{T}}$$

$N(d)$ is the value of the standard cumulative Normal distribution function for d. In other words, $N(d)$ is the probability of a random number having a value equal to or less than d. The cumulative Normal distribution function is illustrated in Figure 4-5. Notice that as d goes to negative infinity, the probability of the outcome being less than d goes to zero. As d goes to positive infinity, the probability of the outcome being less than d goes to one.

Understanding the cumulative Normal function allows us to understand how changes in the variables affect the value of the call. We stated that the Black-Scholes equation is as follows:

$$C = SN(d_1) - Xe^{-rT}N(d_2)$$

FIGURE 4-5

Cumulative Normal Probability Distribution

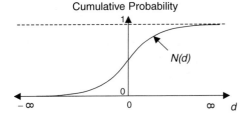

The first term, $SN(d_1)$, says that value of a call increases with the value of the underlying stock, S. The second term $Xe^{-rT}N(d_2)$ says the value of the option is less if the strike price, X, is high, and the value is greater if the time, T, or discount rate, r, is high. The effect of high T or r is to reduce the NPV of the strike price that would need to be paid if the option were exercised.

Let us now consider d_1 and d_2. Notice that the difference between d_1 and d_2 is that in d_1 the volatility is added, and in d_2 it is subtracted. You could roughly think of d_1 as being the extent to which the price could move up and d_2 the extent to which it could move down. If the volatility, σ, or time, T, increases, d_1 becomes larger and d_2, becomes smaller; therefore, the difference between $N(d_1)$ and $N(d_2)$ becomes larger, and the value of the call increases. In general, holding an option becomes more valuable with an increase in uncertainty in the outcome. This increase in value occurs because the payoff is asymmetric. If uncertainty increases, it is more likely that there will be a large change in the stock price, up or down. If the stock price moves up a large amount; we gain a large amount; if the stock price falls, we do not lose as much because the value of the option has a floor of zero.

As the option reaches expiration and T goes to zero, d_1 and d_2 both become equal to the following:

$$d_1 = d_2 = \frac{ln\left(\frac{S}{X}\right)}{0}$$

If S is greater than X, the logarithm will be positive, d_1 and d_2 will equal positive infinity, and $N(d_1)$ and $N(d_2)$ will equal one. The value of the call at expiration is then simply:

$$C_{T=0} = S - X$$

If S is less than X, the logarithm will be negative, and $N(d_1)$, $N(d_2)$, and the call value equal at expiration equals zero. This corresponds with our earlier analysis of the value of an option at expiration.

As a numerical example, consider a call option on a stock that has a current price of $100 and an annual variance of 2.5%. Assume that the risk-free rate is 5%, the call option has a strike price of $100, and the time to expiration is 6 months. The values for these parameters are given in Table 4-5.

To give an appreciation of the effect of parameter changes on option values, Figures 4-6 to 4-10 show how the price of the example option changes when there are changes in the stock price, strike price, risk-free rate, volatility, and time to maturity.

Note in Figure 4-6 that when the stock price becomes low, there is little probability of it ever rising above the strike price, and the option value drops toward zero. However, when the stock price is high, there is little chance of it dropping below the strike price, and the option will almost certainly be exercised. In this case, the value of the option is the stock value minus the net present value of the strike price.

The opposite effect happens if we keep the stock price fixed and move the strike price, as illustrated in Figure 4-7.

TABLE 4-5

Parameter Values for Option Example

Parameter	Value
S ($)	100
X ($)	100
r (/year)	5%
σ^2 (/year)	2.5%
T (years)	0.50
$\ln(s/x)$	0
$\sigma\sqrt{T}$	0.111
d_1	0.28
d_2	0.17
$N(d_1)$	0.61
$N(d_2)$	0.57
$SN(d_1)$	61.0
$Xe^{-rT}N(d_2)$	55.3
C ($)	5.7

FIGURE 4-6

Effect of Stock Price on the Value of a Call Option

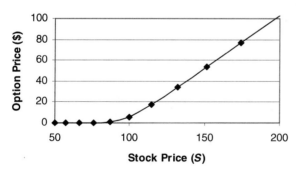

Figure 4-8 shows that changes in interest rates have little direct effect on this option. This would not be the case if the underlying for the option was an interest-rate-sensitive instrument, such as a bond.

Figure 4-9 shows that the option value drops as the volatility of the stock price decreases. Ultimately, if the volatility drops to 0, the stock becomes a risk-free investment. In this case, the value of the stock should grow steadily at the risk-free rate to

FIGURE 4-7

Effect of Strike Price on the Value of a Call Option

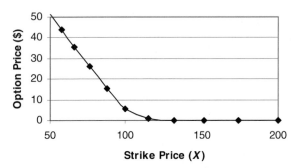

FIGURE 4-8

Effect of Interest Rate on the Value of a Call Option

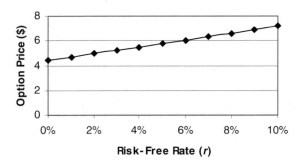

FIGURE 4-9

Effect of Stock-Price Volatility on the Value of a Call Option

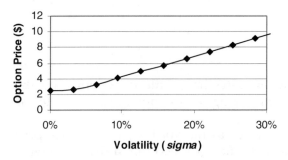

FIGURE 4-10

Effect of Change in Time to Expiration on the Value of a Call Option

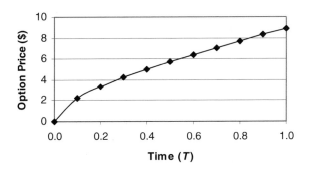

equal $102.53 at the expiration date. With no volatility, the option is therefore certain to be in the money by $2.53. The NPV of $2.53 is $2.47, which is the current value of holding the option with no volatility.

Figure 4-10 shows that as the time to maturity increases, the uncertainty increases, and the option becomes more valuable. If there was no time to maturity left, the option would be worthless because for this option we set the strike equal to the stock price.

The Time Value of an Option

The *time value* of an option is defined as the actual option value minus the intrinsic value. The *intrinsic value* is the value that would be realized if the option was about to expire. For a call, the intrinsic value is the maximum of zero or $(S - X)$. The time value for a call option is summarized in the following equation:

$$\text{Call Time Value} = C - \max[0, (S - X)]$$

For a put, the intrinsic value is the maximum of zero or $(X - S)$.

Figure 4-11 shows the value of an option for different possible values of the stock price. Three lines are shown, the value of an option with six months to expiration, the value with three months to expiration, and the value if the option had to be exercised immediately. As the time decreases, the time value drops to zero, and the option price falls to the intrinsic price.

The time value is a function of both the time to expiration and the volatility of the stock. The time value increases with uncertainty, and is therefore large if the volatility of the underlying is high and the time to maturity is long. With increased uncertainty, it is more valuable to have a choice between the stock and the strike.

Implied Volatility

In the discussion above, we used values for S, T, r, X, and σ to find the price of the call, C. Alternatively, if we observed options being traded in the market at a given price, we

FIGURE 4-11

Time Value of an Option

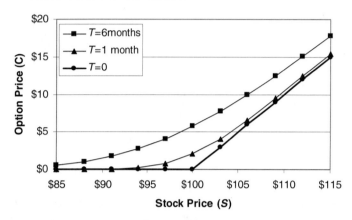

could use the Black-Scholes equation in reverse to find what value of σ would be needed to cause this price. This value is the implied volatility. It is the expected volatility of the stock that is implied by the current trading price of the option. It is interesting to know this implied volatility because it tells us how much volatility the traders are expecting in the stock price. It is therefore a measure of future expectations. Consider pricing an option the day after a crisis has occurred in the market. If we looked at historical data for prices, we would find that the volatility was relatively low; however, the implied volatility would be high. This is because historical volatility describes what has happened, but implied volatility describes what is expected to happen.

In using the Black-Scholes equation to price an option, we mentioned several simplifying assumptions, such as the assumption that relative changes in stock prices have a Normal distribution. These assumptions mean that the estimated value of the option will not be quite equal to the true value of the option, as shown in Figure 4-12. Similarly, when we use the Black-Scholes equation in reverse to find the implied volatility, the simplifying assumptions cause slight distortions. The two most important distortions are the "volatility smile" and the "volatility skew."

The *volatility smile* is the phenomenon that the implied volatility for options that are deep in or deep out of the money is significantly higher than for options at the money. This occurs because true stock-price movements do not have the Normal distribution assumed in the Black-Scholes equation. In reality, extreme movements are more common than would be predicted by the Normal distribution. Therefore, options that are deep out of the money have a higher chance of moving into the money than would be predicted using the Normal distribution, so the true price is higher than that predicted by the Black-Scholes equation. If we were to maintain the assumption that stock prices move Normally, this higher price could only be accounted for by assuming

FIGURE 4-12

Difference between the Actual Option Price and the Theoretical Price

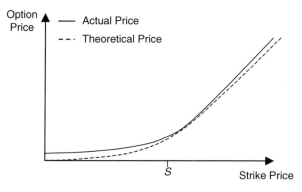

that the volatility was higher. The same mechanism also applies to stocks that are deep in the money.

There is a slight difference between options that are in or out of the money, and this produces the *volatility skew*. The volatility skew is most strongly observed for options on equities. In this case, options that are out of the money appear to have a higher volatility than those in the money. This is because of supply-and-demand effects in the market that tend to increase the value of out of the money options relative to in the money options. Figure 4-13 illustrates the volatility smile and skew. The smile is represented by the fact that a and b are greater than zero; the skew is represented by a being greater than b.

Alternative Approaches to Valuing Options

So far, we have discussed the properties of the analytical approaches based on the Black-Scholes equation. As we have seen, these approaches make significant assumptions about the nature of the market and the structure of the option. However, there are two approaches that reduce the number of required assumptions: namely, binomial trees and Monte Carlo evaluation. These approaches are used by traders in cases where the Black-Scholes approaches would be inaccurate, e.g., for exotic options.

Binomial Trees

Binomial trees use a tree of possible future values for the underlying and the associated option values. The base of the binomial tree is the current market condition. From that base, the tree takes a small step forward in time and has two possible branches for the stock price: it can either go up or down. The required amount of up or down movement in the price and the associated probabilities are tied together using reasoning similar to

FIGURE 4-13

Illustration of the Smile and Skew for Implied Volatility

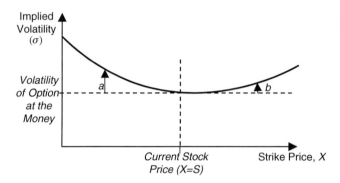

that used in the Black-Scholes equation. From the end of each branch, another two branches step forward in time. This is repeated until the branches reach the option's expiration date. At this point, the result is a tree of possible future stock prices.

Having established the range of possible stock prices, a typical valuation process is as follows. The payoff for the option is valued for all the possible stock prices at the end time, and the process then moves back through the tree towards the current date. At each time step, the option is valued based on its possible future value along each of the branches and the probability of taking each branch. Figure 4-14 illustrates a simple binomial tree to value the call option in our previous example.

Monte Carlo Evaluation

Although *Monte Carlo evaluation* can be easier to construct than a binomial tree, and more accurate, it does require a large amount of computer time because it typically uses many more possible future values than the binomial tree.

In essence, Monte Carlo evaluation randomly simulates future price paths for the underlying and evaluates the option along each path. The option value is then the NPV of the average option value for each path. Figure 4-15 gives an example of 5 random simulations. Figure 4-16 gives the outcome distribution of 1000 simulations for the stock price on the expiration date, and Figure 4-17 gives the corresponding outcome distribution of the option value. As we would expect, the distribution for the option value is the same as for the stock except that it is shifted by the value of the strike price ($100), and all of the results in which the stock price was less than the strike price are piled onto $0.

Packages of Vanilla Options

With this new understanding of the factors affecting option prices, let us look at how options are used in trading. If a trader has a specific idea about the way the stock price will

FIGURE 4-14

Illustration of a Two-Step Binomial Tree

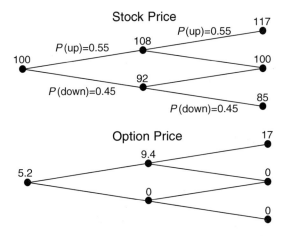

The upper tree shows stock-price movements and their associated probabilities starting at the left with a stock price of 100, a 55% chance of moving up to 108, and 45% chance of moving down to 92. The lower tree shows the value of holding the option given the possible future movements of the stock. The value of the option at one point is the probability-weighted value of the option at the next two points, discounted according to the time difference.

FIGURE 4-15

Example of Five Monte Carlo Simulations for Stock Prices

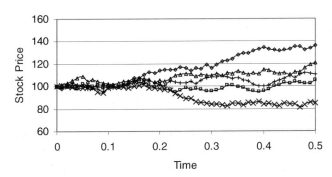

change, a mixture of the stock plus puts and calls can be used to create a payoff structure that is tailored to profit in the expected market. Many different forms of payoff can be formed by combining options and the underlying instrument. The most common combinations are the addition of an option and the underlying as illustrated in Figure 4-18.

Being long the stock and long a put means the trader benefits if the value of the stock increases. But if the stock value decreases, the trader is protected from any loss

FIGURE 4-16

Distribution of Outcomes for Stock Prices

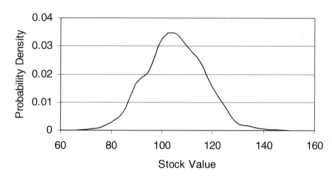

FIGURE 4-17

Distribution of Outcomes for Option Prices

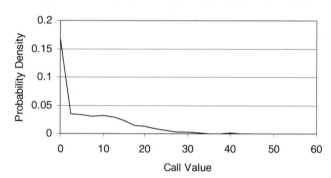

because the put can be exercised to give away the stock and receive the strike price. This combination is known as a *protection put*.

Being long the stock and short a call means that if the stock rose above the strike price, the trader would expect the holder of the call option to exercise the option and take the stock in return for giving the strike. If the stock remained or fell below the strike, the option would be worthless, and the trader would have gained the initial income for having sold the call. This combination of owning the stock and being short the call option is known as a *covered call*.

Other common packages of options are described below. These combinations are called *spreads* because their value depends on the difference, or the spread, in the price between different options. The total price of the package is simply the sum of the prices of the individual options.

FIGURE 4-18

FIGURE 4-18

Payoff for Options Combined with the Stock

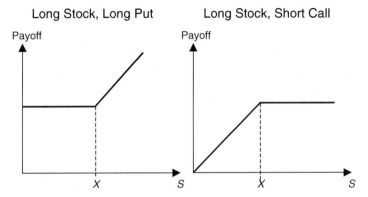

The Bull Spread

This spread is created by buying a call with a strike price, X_1, below the current price of the underlying, and selling a call with a strike price, X_2, above the current level. The cost of the call option with the low strike price will be greater than the profit made by selling the call with a high strike price. Figure 4-19 illustrates the profit from a bull spread as a function of the price of the underlying. Note that we have subtracted the cost of initially buying the option so you can see the overall profit rather than just the final payoff.

For a *bull spread*, if the stock price is low, the options expire worthless, and the investor loses the initial cost of the options. If the stock is high, both options are in the money, but the option struck at X_1 is worth more than the option struck at X_2, so the investor makes a profit. It is therefore called a bull spread because it is bought by investors who expect the market to rise.

It may seem odd to have sold the upper call because by selling this call the trader has limited the potential profit. However, by selling the upper call, some income is generated to offset the cost of buying the lower option.

The Bear Spread

The *bear spread* is made by going short a call option with a low strike price, X_1, and long a call with a high strike price, X_2, as in Figure 4-20. It works in the opposite way of the bull spread, and is profitable if the price of the underlying drops.

The investor initially makes a profit because the call with a low strike price is more valuable than the call with a high strike price. If the price of the stock drops below X_1, both options expire worthless, and the investor keeps the profit. If the final price of the stock is high, both options are in the money. However, the option struck at X_1 is worth more than the option struck at X_2, so the investor has to pay out more on the short position than is received on the long position, creating a loss.

The Butterfly Spread

The *butterfly spread* consists of four options: long a call option struck at X_1, short two call options struck at X_2, and long a call option struck at X_3, as illustrated in Figure 4-21. It can be viewed as the sum of the bull and bear spreads. The butterfly spread is profitable if the underlying does not move significantly. However, if there is a significant movement, the investor loses the premium and receives no payoff.

The Calendar Spread

The *calendar spread* uses two call options with identical strike prices but different maturity dates. The strike prices are chosen to be close to the current price of the stock to maximize the difference in time value. The spread is made by going long a long-term call and short a short-term call. By having identical strike prices, the investor is largely protected from changes in the stock price. The investor will have to pay more for the long-term call than the short-term call because of the difference in the time values. The time value of the short-term call will decay faster than that of the long-term call, increasing the difference in the prices. If the volatility of the stock does not change, the investor will be able to sell the combination after a few weeks for more than the initial purchase price. If the volatility increases, the difference will be even greater, and the investor will make more of a profit. If the volatility decreases, the investor could make a loss. Figure 4-22 illustrates the three cases.

FIGURE 4-19

A Bull Spread

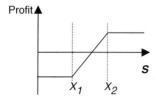

A bull spread made by buying a call option with a low strike price and selling a call with a high strike price. The x-axis shows possible values for the stock. The y-axis shows the corresponding profit from the option.

FIGURE 4-20

A Bear Spread

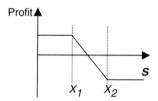

A bear spread made by selling a call option with a low strike price and buying a call with a high strike price.

FIGURE 4-21

A Butterfly Spread

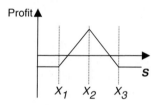

A butterfly spread made by buying a call option with a low strike price, selling two calls at the money, and buying a fourth call with a high strike price.

FIGURE 4-22

A Calendar Spread

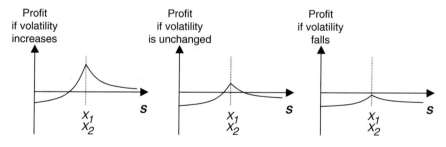

The profitability of the calendar spread is shown as a function of the stock price. If the stock price moves far from the strike price, the time value of both options falls towards zero, and the investor makes a loss. Three cases are shown; if volatility increases, the investor makes an additional profit. If volatility decreases, the investor could make a loss.

Exotic Options

The set of *exotic options* is comprised of any options other than vanilla options. They are tailor-made for specific profit or hedging opportunities, and the payoffs cannot be decomposed into the payoffs from vanilla options; i.e., you cannot recreate the pattern of payoffs from an exotic option by combining a set of vanilla options. Although exotic options are relatively rare, they have an infinite number of possible forms. The more common ones are described below.

Forward starts have a strike price that is to be fixed at a future date. For example, the option may give the right to buy a stock within a year, for whatever the stock price is in six months' time.

Binary options have discontinuous payouts. For example, the option might be structured to pay $20 if the final stock price is anywhere above $110, but $0 otherwise.

Look-back options pay the maximum (or minimum) price of the underlying over a certain period of time, minus the strike price. The payment is made on the expiration date. At that time, the participants "look back" to see the highest price of the underlying between the initial date of the option contract and the expiration date. These options do not depend on the final price of the underlying (unless the final value also happens to be the peak value). The value of the options is therefore path dependent, meaning that the history of the stock price determines the value of the option, not just the final price.

Barrier options are also path dependent, and have a clause that determines what will happen when the price of the underlying hits a certain barrier. For example, a *knock-out barrier option* has a clause that says the option pays out and ceases to exist as soon as the stock hits a certain level. A *knock-in option* says that the option does not exist until the stock hits a certain level. The barrier may be either higher or lower than the current stock price. If the barrier is higher, the options are called "up and out" or "up and in." If the barriers are lower, the options are called "down and out" or "down and in."

Compound options are options on options. They give the right to buy an option in the future.

Chooser options allow the holder to specify whether the option should be a call or a put at some point in the future. For example, the contract may say that in 6 months' time, the owner of the option must choose whether the option should be a put or a call, and that put or call will expire in 18 months' time. Chooser options are also known as "As You Like It" options.

Common Option "Jargon"

Before we go on to the mathematics risk for options, it is useful to know some of the common words and terminology used when trading options:

- An *outright* or *naked position* means having an unhedged position, such as selling a call option without owning the stock.

- Having a *covered call* is being short the call and long the stock. This is a useful technique because it limits the risk for the writer of the option. If the stock becomes very valuable, the writer will be able to deliver the stock without first having to find cash to buy the stock.
- A *back-to-back position* is one that is fully hedged, e.g., being long an option with one counterparty and short the same option with a different counterparty. This eliminates the market risk because any losses on one option are offset by gains on the other. Each option is priced slightly differently to enable the trader to make a profit. Typically, this difference in price is possible because one of the options is being provided to a corporate customer who does not have full access to the market.

Now that we have discussed the different options and their valuation techniques, we can begin to discuss risk measurement for options.

Risk Measurement for Options

As we discussed above, the value of options is sensitive to changes in the value of the underlying, interest rates, and volatility. This means that changes in market conditions can lead to the risk of losses for banks that hold options. The sensitivity of options to these market changes is described by what is known as the *Greeks*. They are called Greeks because they are symbolized by the Greek letters delta, gamma, vega, theta, and rho. The Greeks are similar to duration in that they estimate the change in the value of the option if one of the market variables changes. Each of the Greeks is described below.

Delta
Delta is the first derivative of the option price (P) with respect to the value of the underlying stock (S):

$$\Delta = \frac{\partial P}{\partial S}$$

Delta is the linear approximation of how much the value of the option will change if the value of the underlying changes by $1.00. For example, if delta is 0.5, then a $1.00 move in the stock will cause a 50-cent change in the option value. Often, traders will describe a position as being "delta-hedged." This means the trader has bought a combination of options and the underlying such that the overall position has a delta equal to 0. This removes most of the exposure to the underlying, but leaves the gamma, vega, rho, and theta risks.

　　Delta is not an exact description of the change in the value of the option because, as we have seen, the option value is not a simple linear function of the stock price; therefore, the change in the option value is not proportional to the change in the underlying. For example, if the underlying moves up by $1, the option value may increase by 55 cents; but if it falls by $1, the option value may decrease by 45 cents. The difference between the true value change and the change predicted by delta is called *gamma risk*, and is illustrated in Figure 4-23.

Gamma
Gamma is the second derivative of value with respect to the price of the underlying, and it describes how much more the price of the option will change beyond the linear approximation of delta:

$$\Gamma = \frac{\partial^2 P}{\partial S^2}$$

Gamma helps to describe the nonlinear risk of the option by using the *Taylor Series Expansion*, as shown below:

$$dP = \Delta(dS) + \frac{1}{2}\Gamma(dS)^2$$

Vega
Vega describes the option value's sensitivity to changes in the volatility (σ). It is the first derivative of the option price with respect to implied volatility. It represents how much the option value will change if the volatility of the stock price changes by 100% per year. If vega equals 0.6, the value of the option will increase by 60% if volatility increased by 100%:

$$\upsilon = \frac{\partial P}{\partial \sigma}$$

FIGURE 4-23

Illustration of Gamma Risk

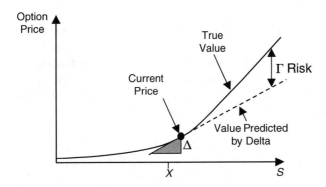

Rho

Rho is the first derivative of the option price in relation to interest rates. It represents how much the option value changes when interest rates change:

$$\rho = \frac{\partial P}{\partial r}$$

Theta

Theta is the first derivative of the option in relation to time. It represents how much the option value changes as it moves toward maturity:

$$\theta = \frac{\partial P}{\partial T}$$

The Greeks can be calculated analytically by using calculus to differentiate a pricing equation, such as the Black-Scholes equation. Alternatively, the Greeks can be calculated by pricing the option with one value of the risk factor and then slightly moving the risk factor and pricing again.

For example, delta would be calculated from the following equation, where ϵ is a small addition to S. Typically, ϵ would be chosen to be approximately equal to the volatility of the risk factor:

$$\Delta = \frac{P(S + \epsilon) - P(S)}{\epsilon}$$

Notice that the Greeks give linear approximations to changes due to one risk factor. If several factors change, the total value change can be estimated by summing the Greeks:

$$\delta V \approx \Delta \times \delta S + \frac{1}{2} \Gamma \times \delta S^2 + v \times \delta \sigma + \rho \times \delta r + \theta \times \delta T$$

While many trading rooms use the Greeks as a primary measure of risk, most trading rooms also use the Value at Risk tool to measure option risk, and this will be discussed in the next chapter.

SUMMARY

In this chapter, we detailed the main instruments that banks trade and why they trade them. We also explained how to value each instrument so that its risk can be managed effectively. Next, we will explain how to measure their changes in value and their market risk.

CHAPTER 5

Market-Risk Measurement

The previous chapter described the major types of traded instruments and how to value them. This gives us the foundation to measure changes in the values of traded instruments, i.e., to measure the risk. The five common approaches to measuring market risk are the following:

- Sensitivity analysis
- Stress testing
- Scenario testing
- Capital Asset Pricing Model (CAPM)
- Value at Risk (VaR)

This chapter will look at each in more detail.

SENSITIVITY ANALYSIS

In the previous chapter, we have already touched on sensitivity analysis in our discussion on bond duration and option Greeks. Sensitivity analysis is a useful measure to quickly show how changes in the market could affect the value of the portfolio. The potential change in the portfolio's value depends on the bank's position. *Position* is a general term used to describe the composition of the assets and liabilities in the portfolio.

Sensitivity analysis is a description of how much the portfolio's value (V) is expected to change if there is a small change in one of the market-risk factors (f). The market-risk factors are the market variables from which the value of all other instruments can be derived. The main risk factors are interest rates, credit spreads, equity prices, exchange rates, implied volatility, commodity prices (e.g., gold & oil), and forward prices for each of these factors. There are three alternative but equivalent ways of thinking about sensitivity: it is the relative change, the first derivative, or the best linear approximation.

The *relative change* is the change in value of the portfolio when a risk factor changes by a small amount (ϵ), divided by the change in the risk factor:

$$\text{Sensitivity} = \frac{V(f + \epsilon) - V(f)}{\epsilon}$$

The *first derivative* is the calculus extreme of the relative change when ϵ tends to zero:

$$\text{Sensitivity} = \left[\frac{V(f + \epsilon) - V(f)}{\epsilon} \right]_{\epsilon \to 0} = \frac{\partial V}{\partial f}$$

The *linear approximation* is the sensitivity that best satisfies the following equation:

$$V(f + \epsilon) = V(f) + \epsilon \times \text{Sensitivity}$$

Sensitivity Analysis for Bonds

For any given portfolio, we calculate the sensitivity to each of the market-risk factors. For bonds, the only risk factors are interest rates and credit spreads. As we discussed in the previous chapter, the sensitivity to interest rates is the negative of the duration dollars as described in the equation below:

$$V = \sum \frac{C_t}{(1 + r)^t}$$

$$\frac{dV}{dr} = \sum \frac{-tC_t}{(1 + r)^{t+1}}$$

$$= -\text{Duration\$}$$

The sensitivity to credit spreads is also equal to duration dollars. To see this, consider the rate, r, to be the sum of the risk-free rate (r_f) and the credit spread (s). Changes in r can therefore be caused by changes in the risk-free rate or the credit spread.

$$r = r_f + s$$

$$V = \sum \frac{C_t}{(1 + r_f + s)^t}$$

$$\frac{dV}{dr_f} = \sum \frac{-tC_t}{(1 + r_f + s)^{t+1}}$$

$$= -\text{Duration\$}$$

$$\frac{dV}{ds} = \sum \frac{-tC_t}{(1 + r_f + s)^{t+1}}$$

$$= -\text{Duration\$}$$

Changes in the value of the bond (δV) can then be estimated as the sum of changes due to the risk-free rate (δr_f) and changes due to the credit spread (δs):

$$\delta V = \frac{dV}{dr_f}\delta r_f + \frac{dV}{ds}\delta s$$

As noted in the previous chapter, duration does not measure changes in value due to bond-price convexity or due to twisting and flexing of the yield curve. It cannot describe twist and flex risk because it assumes parallel shifts in the yield curve, i.e., that the change in the rate is equal for all maturities.

Duration is also sometimes called PVBP or DV01. These both mean the same thing. PVBP is the present value of a basis-point change in interest rates, and DV01 is the delta value for a 1-basis point change ($\delta r = 1\,\mathrm{bp} = 0.01\%$).

$$PVBP = DV01 = -Duration\$ \times 0.0001$$

$$= \frac{dV}{dr} \times 0.0001$$

Sensitivity Analysis for Equities

The sensitivity to equity prices of a portfolio containing an equity from a single company is simply the number of equities being held (N): if you hold 1000 IBM shares, and the price of IBM increases by \$1, you gain \$1000. More formally, the sensitivity can be derived from the share price as follows:

$$V = N \times S$$

$$\frac{\delta V}{\delta S} = N \times \frac{\partial S}{\partial S}$$

$$= N$$

$$\delta V = N\delta S$$

If you have a portfolio of many equities, you could calculate the sensitivity with respect to each company's share price, but this creates too much data to be analyzed easily. A commonly used alternative is to look at how the value of the portfolio changes with a general market change. This analysis has three steps. The first is to describe each equity's value in terms of its beta, i.e., the extent to which its price tends to change when the general market changes. This is found from the historical covariance between the stock price and market price. The equity's value is then described as being the current value (S_0), plus beta times the market change, plus a random idiosyncratic change (ϵ):

$$S = S_0[1 + \beta m + \epsilon]$$

Here, m is the relative change from the current market level (M_0):

$$m = \frac{M - M_0}{M_0}$$

The second step is to differentiate the equation for value with respect to the market level.

$$\frac{\partial S}{\partial m} = S_0 \beta$$

The final step is to sum the sensitivity to the market for all the equities in the portfolio.

$$\frac{\partial V_P}{\partial m} = \sum_{k=1}^{P} N_k S_{k,0} \beta_k$$

Here, P is the total number of different equities in the portfolio, and V_p is the value of the portfolio. This equation gives us the expected dollar change in the value of the portfolio if the general market changes. For example, if the market fell by 1%, we would expect to lose the following amount on the portfolio:

$$\delta V = \frac{\partial V_P}{\partial m} \times \delta m$$

$$= \left(\sum_{k=1}^{P} N_k S_{k,0} \beta_k \right) \times 1\%$$

Sensitivity Analysis for Foreign Exchange

Sensitivity analysis for FX positions is very similar to equities in that the change in value of the position equals the amount of currency held times the change in the exchange rate. It is also possible to do a correlation analysis similar to the beta analysis to show how the value of the whole portfolio would change if the major currency changed, but normally the number of currencies being traded is sufficiently low that banks just look at each currency separately.

Sensitivity Analysis for Forwards and Futures

The value of a forward agreement is the number of items to be delivered (N) times the difference between current price that the market will accept for delivery (D_C), and the originally agreed delivery price in the forward contract (D_0) discounted by the risk-free rate (r_f) from the time of delivery (t):

$$\text{Contract Value} = \frac{N}{(1 + r_f)^t} (D_C - D_0)$$

In this equation, there are two factors that can vary with the market: the current price (D_C) and the discount rate (r_f). The sensitivities and changes are given simply by the derivatives:

$$\frac{\partial V}{\partial D_C} = \frac{N}{(1 + r_f)^t}$$

$$\frac{\partial V}{\partial r_f} = \frac{-tN}{(1 + r_f)^{t+1}}(D_C - D_0)$$

$$\delta V = \frac{\partial V}{\partial D_C}\delta D_C + \frac{\partial V}{\partial r_f}\delta r_f$$

Sensitivity Analysis for Options

For options, the sensitivity is described by the Greeks. These were discussed in the previous chapter, but are so widely used that you will want to get to know them by heart, and it is worth quickly reviewing them here.

Delta is the first derivative of the option price with respect to the price of the underlying:

$$\Delta = \frac{\partial P}{\partial S}$$

Gamma is the second derivative of price with respect to the price of the underlying. Unlike most of the other sensitivity measures, gamma is the second derivative rather than the first, and therefore captures some of the nonlinearity:

$$\Gamma = \frac{\partial^2 P}{\partial S^2}$$

Vega is the first derivative of price with respect to implied volatility, as seen below:

$$\upsilon = \frac{\partial P}{\partial \sigma}$$

Rho is the first derivative of price with respect to interest rates:

$$\rho = \frac{\partial P}{\partial r}$$

Theta is the first derivative of price with respect to time, as seen below:

$$\theta = \frac{\partial P}{\partial T}$$

The change in the value of an option can be approximated from the Greeks and the change in the value of the market-risk factors:

$$\delta V \approx \Delta \times \delta S + \frac{1}{2}\Gamma \times \delta S^2 + \upsilon \times \delta \sigma + \rho \times \delta r + \theta \times \delta T$$

STRESS TESTING

The sensitivity analyses discussed above give decent approximations for the change in the value of the portfolio when the change in the market-risk factors is small. However, if the change in a risk factor is large (e.g., in a crisis), the linear sensitivity will not give a good estimate to the change in the value of a portfolio.

In stress testing, large changes are made in the risk factors, and full, nonlinear pricing is used to revalue the portfolio and estimate the loss. The purpose of stress testing is to provide a clear, objective measure of risk that is easily understood and everyone buys into. For stress testing, a standard set of changes in the risk factors is set, and the subsequent change in portfolio value is calculated. For example, a typical stress statement would be "If interest rates move up by 2%, we would lose \$15 million; if they move by 4%, we would lose \$28 million."

Typically, the movements are standardized in order to communicate them easily throughout the organization. For example, the changes in all equity values may be set at -20%, -10%, and $+10\%$ and $+20\%$. It also makes sense to decide which factors should be moved together to analyze the results more easily. This is called "blocking."

One example of blocking is to move all Latin American exchange rates at the same time rather than having one result for each currency. However, one downside of exchange-rate blocking is that the gains from one currency would perfectly offset losses from another. Therefore, there is no indication of the loss that would occur if the rates moved differently.

Here are the steps to construct a stress test:

1. Determine the complete set of market factors that could affect the value of the portfolio.
2. Decide which factors should be blocked together or moved independently; e.g., a Latin American bank would probably block together all its exposures to Asian currencies because they would be a small part of the portfolio, and analyzing them individually would distract management from the main sources of risk.
3. Decide what approximate change is a reasonable test for each factor. Four or six times the standard deviation of daily movements for each factor would be reasonable.
4. Apply the price movements.
5. Revalue all positions affected by the risk factor. For example, a change in FX will affect FX spots, forwards, swap options, and the value of the holdings of foreign equities. Use full, nonlinear pricing models to revalue the portfolio. For example, changes in option values should be calculated using a full option pricing model—not just the Greeks.
6. Report the change in present value.

The results may be presented in a table or graph. An example of a graph is shown in Figure 5-1, and a table is shown in Figure 5-2. The table shows just 20 representative risk

FIGURE 5-1

Graphical Display of Stress-Test Results

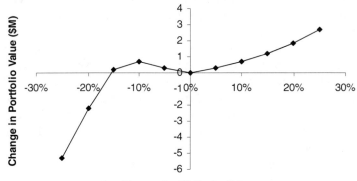

Change in All Equity Prices

Equity-price changes are shown in the *x*-axis; portfolio-value changes are shown in the *y*-axis. As equity prices rise, the overall value of the portfolio rises. As equity prices fall, the portfolio value initially rises, then falls sharply. Such a result could be produced by a portfolio containing equities and bear spreads.

FIGURE 5-2

Illustration of Stress-Testing Report

Risk Factor	Risk-Factor Change (%)				Portfolio-Value Change ($M)			
U.S. Yield-Curve Shift	-20	-10	10	20	12.6	6.2	-5.9	-11.7
U.S. Yield-Curve Twist	-20	-10	10	20	6.3	3.1	-2.9	-5.6
U.S. Yield-Curve Flex	-20	-10	10	20	8.4	3.2	-3.1	-5.9
U.K. Yield-Curve Shift	-20	-10	10	20	1.9	1.2	-0.7	-1.1
Yen Yield-Curve Shift	-20	-10	10	20	1.9	1.1	-0.6	-1.5
Euro Yield-Curve Shift	-20	-10	10	20	-1.6	-1.1	1.1	1.3
Emerging-Markets Shift	-40	-20	20	40	0.9	0.5	-0.5	-0.9
U.K. FX	-20	-10	10	20	-4.3	-1.9	2.7	5.4
Yen FX	-20	-10	10	20	-2.5	-1.1	1.6	3.3
Euro FX	-20	-10	10	20	2.3	3.0	-3.7	-7.4
Emerging-Markets FX	-40	-20	20	40	-3.4	-1.2	3.5	6.4
All U.S. Equities	-20	-10	10	20	-23.2	-9.6	9.6	19.2
All U.K. Equities	-20	-10	10	20	-14.6	-7.3	7.3	8.9
All Euro Equities	-20	-10	10	20	3.4	1.7	-1.7	-3.4
All other Equities	-40	-20	20	40	-2.8	-1.4	1.4	2.8
Change in Credit Spreads	-20	-10	10	20	0.8	0.4	-0.3	-0.7
All Interest-Rate Volatilities	-40	-20	20	40	0.9	0.4	-0.4	-0.9
All FX Volatilities	-40	-20	20	40	0.4	0.2	-0.2	-0.4
All Equity Volatilities	-40	-20	20	40	2.3	1.1	-1.1	-2.3
Oil Price Change	-40	-20	20	40	-0.1	0.0	0.0	0.1

Note: a 10% twist in the yield curve represents a 10% drop in the overnight rate and a 10% increase in the 10-year rate, with intermediate rates shifted proportionally. A 10% flex represents a 10% drop in the overnight rate, a 10% drop in the 10-year rate, and no change in the 4-year rate. Intermediate rates are shifted proportionally.

This table shows stress tests for 20 representative risk factors.

factors; banks will typically use around 100 factors. The sharp, nonlinear fall in value would typically be caused by holding options and would not have been shown by the Greeks.

While stress testing is generally helpful, there are three drawbacks:

1. The test can yield many reams of data without directly indicating which result represents the most significant problem.

2. The chosen moves in the risk factors are not tightly related to a probability of movement.

3. The test makes the simple assumption that the correlation between the movement in different risk factors is zero or one; i.e., they move independently or in lockstep. This can mask potentially serious losses that could occur if one rate moved slightly differently from another rate. For example, consider the case of a U.S. bank holding an FX forward in which it was to pay U.S. dollars and receive pounds sterling and another swap in which it was to receive the same amount of U.S. dollars and pay euros. If sterling and the euro were blocked together, then when different rates were tested, any estimated loss on one trade would be offset by gains on the other, and it would appear that the overall portfolio had no risk. However, if the sterling and euro rates were to move separately, there could be considerable losses.

Scenario testing is one approach to avoid these drawbacks.

SCENARIO TESTING

Stress testing and scenario testing are similar in that both use specified changes in the market-risk factors and reprice the portfolio with full, nonlinear pricing models. However, in stress testing, the changes in risk factors are very uniform and objective. In scenario testing, the changes are tailored and subjectively chosen. In scenario testing, informed opinion is used to create a limited set of worst-case scenarios. Each scenario corresponds to a specific type of market crisis, such as U.K. equities market crashes, a default by China, or the raising of oil prices by OPEC.

Typically, 5 to 10 "worst-case" scenarios are chosen. The scenarios are typically derived from one of three sources: previous crises, the bank's current portfolio, and the opinion of the bank's experts such as the head trader, bank economists, and the risk management group.

In using previous crises, the risk management group looks at historical data from many markets and asks: what if those events were to happen here and now? For example, if a 20% one-day drop in the U.S. market happened in 1987, one scenario could be that the same happens for all the euro markets.

In basing the scenarios on the current portfolio, the bank's experts look at the current state of the portfolio and ask: what event would be most damaging to us given this portfolio?

Basing the scenarios on the bank's expert opinion allows the bank's staff to test their greatest worries given their knowledge of the current economy and market.

Once each scenario has been chosen, it is then necessary to estimate how all of the risk factors would change in that scenario. For example, a crash in the U.K. equities market would affect U.K. interest rates, U.S. equity markets, exchange rates, and all the other factors. By moving all the risk factors, the scenario implicitly includes all the correlations between risk factors.

Here are the steps to create and use a scenario analysis:

1. Choose 5–10 scenarios that would upset the markets in which the bank trades. Estimate the changes in each risk factor based on the crisis scenarios you have identified. This estimation can be based on expert opinion and historical data from previous crises.
2. Value the portfolio under the given scenario using full, nonlinear pricing models.
3. Test the portfolio each day to see how much could be lost under each scenario.
4. Review and update the scenarios quarterly, or more often if events dictate.

While scenario analysis is generally helpful, there are four drawbacks:

1. It is time-consuming to do it properly.
2. Only a limited number of scenarios can be tested.
3. The values chosen are very subjective.
4. There is the potential for conflict of interest, as the person taking the risk and making the trade is often the expert who is asked to provide the worst-case scenario.

THE CAPITAL ASSET PRICING MODEL

Several metrics have been developed by asset managers to measure the risk and performance of investment portfolios. Most are based on the Capital Asset Pricing Model (CAPM).[1] CAPM specifies that the expected return on an asset (r_a) is a function of the risk-free rate, the average market return, and the correlation between the asset and the market as shown in the following equation:

$$r_a = r_f + \beta(r_m - r_f)$$

where

$$\beta = \frac{\rho_{a,m}\sigma_a}{\sigma_m}$$

Here, r_f is the risk-free rate of return; typically the interest rate paid by government bonds. Any return above the risk-free rate is known as the excess return. r_m is the average expected return for the market as a whole. σ_a is the volatility of the value of the asset, σ_m is the volatility of the value of the market, and $\rho_{a,m}$ is the correlation between changes in the value of the asset and changes in the value of the market.

The underlying idea is that in an efficient market, an investor can buy a well-diversified portfolio that removes all the risks except the systemic risk of the market as a whole. Therefore, the investor should only be concerned with the amount of systemic risk being taken. Similarly, the performance and risk metrics traditionally used to assess investments seek to show how the investment is performing compared with a simple investment in the diversified market. The most popular of these metrics are the Sharpe Ratio and Treynor Ratio.

The Sharpe Ratio

The Sharpe Ratio for a portfolio is a measure of the excess return divided by the risk. It is defined as the portfolio return minus the risk-free rate, divided by the standard deviation of the excess return:

$$S = \frac{r_p - r_f}{\sigma_{(r_p - r_f)}}$$

The Treynor Ratio

The Treynor Ratio is defined as the portfolio return minus the risk-free rate, divided by portfolio beta:

$$T = \frac{r_p - r_f}{\beta}$$

where β measures how much the portfolio value changes when the market changes:

$$\beta = \rho_{p,m} \frac{\sigma_{(r_p - r_f)}}{\sigma_{(r_m - r_f)}}$$

$\rho_{p,m}$ is the correlation between the market and the portfolio, $\sigma_{r_p - r_f}$ is the percentage volatility of the portfolio's excess return, and $\sigma_{r_m - r_f}$ is the percentage volatility of the market's excess return.

VALUE AT RISK

Value at Risk (VaR) is a measure of market risk that tries objectively to combine the sensitivity of the portfolio to market changes and the probability of a given market change. As we will discuss over the next few chapters, VaR has some significant limitations that require the continued use of stress and scenario tests as a backup, but overall, VaR is the best single risk-measurement technique available. As such, VaR has been adopted by the Basel Committee to set the standard for the minimum amount of capital to be held against market risks.

Value at Risk is defined as the value that can be expected to be lost during severe, adverse market fluctuations. Typically, a severe loss is defined as a loss that has a 1% chance of occurring on any given day. If we are measuring daily losses, this is equivalent to saying, "On average, we will lose VaR *or more* on two to three days per year." VaR can be calculated at any roll-up level, including the instrument level, portfolio level, or bank level.

A common assumption is that movements in the market have a Normal probability distribution, meaning there is a 1% chance that losses will be greater than 2.32 standard deviations. Assuming a Normal distribution, 99% VaR can be defined as follows:

$$VaR_T = 2.32\sigma_T$$

where σ is the standard deviation of the portfolio's value. This is illustrated in Figure 5-3.

The subscript T in the VaR expression refers to the time period over which the standard deviation of returns is calculated. VaR can be calculated for any time horizon. For trading operations, a one-day horizon is typically used. VaR for a one-day horizon is occasionally called DEaR: Daily Earnings at Risk.

For an example of a VaR statement, consider an equity portfolio with a daily standard deviation of $10 million. Using the assumption of a Normal distribution, the 99% confidence interval VaR is $23 million. We would expect that the losses would be greater than $23 million on 1% of trading days, or 2 to 3 days per year. Senior management should clearly understand that VaR is not the worst possible loss. Losses equal to the size of VaR are expected to happen several times per year; VaR is therefore not equal to capital. We will discuss the relationship between VaR and capital in great depth in

FIGURE 5-3

Illustration of the Relationship between VaR and Standard Deviation

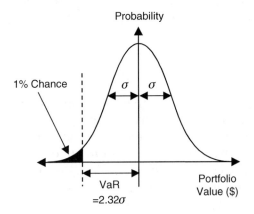

later chapters, but a very rough rule of thumb is that the capital should be 10 times VaR. In the next few chapters, we will go into great detail on how VaR can be calculated, but here we will give an intuitive feeling for VaR by showing how it can be approximated for some instruments.

VaR for Bonds

For a bond, VaR can be approximated by multiplying the dollar duration by the "worst-case" daily interest move. This gives the value change in the "worst case."

$$VaR \approx \text{Duration Dollars} \times \delta r_{worst\ case}$$

$$= \left(-\frac{dV}{dr}\right) \times \delta r_{worst\ case}$$

We chose worst-case interest-rate moves such that there is a probability of only 1% that the change could be more than this worst case. If we assume that interest-rate movements have a Normal probability distribution, then the 1% worst case will correspond to 2.32 standard deviations of the daily rate movements (σ_r); the VaR for a bond is approximately equal to the duration dollars times 2.32 standard deviations:

$$VaR \approx \left(-\frac{dV}{dr}\right) 2.32\sigma_r$$

As an example. If the duration is 7 years, the current price is $100, and the daily standard deviation in the absolute level of interest rates is 0.2%, then the VaR is approximately $3.24:

$$VaR \approx \$100 \times 7 \times 0.2\% \times 2.32 = \$3.24$$

The approximations that we made here were as follows: the changes in the rate is Normally distributed, the rates for every tenor move by the same amount, and the change in the price can be well-approximated by the linear measure of duration.

VaR for Equities

The VaR for an equity is easy to calculate if we assume that equity prices have a Normal distribution. The VaR is then the number of shares held (N), multiplied by 2.32 and the standard deviation of the equity price (σ_E):

$$VaR = 2.32\sigma_E \times N$$

So, for example, if we held 100 shares of IBM, and the daily standard deviation of the price was 10 cents, the VaR would be $23.2:

$$VaR = 2.32 \times \$0.1 \times 100 = \$23.2$$

VaR for Options

A simple approximation of the VaR to an option can be obtained using the linear sensitivities, i.e., the Greeks. The standard deviation of the option price caused by changes in the stock price is simply the standard deviation of the stock price multiplied by delta. The VaR for the option is then approximated as being 2.32 times the standard deviation of the option price:

$$VaR \approx 2.32 \times \Delta \times \sigma_S$$

Here, σ_S is the daily absolute volatility of the stock price. A closer approximation including some of the nonlinear risk may be given using gamma and the Taylor series:

$$VaR \approx \left[2.32 \times \Delta \times \sigma_S + \frac{1}{2}\Gamma(2.32 \times \sigma_S)^2 \right]$$

However, this approximation using gamma can be misleading for options that are near expiration and close to the money (i.e., S close to X). In this case, gamma becomes very large because it is measuring the curvature at the corner where the strike price and option price are equal. The only reliable way of assessing option risk is to go to the full computational expense of fully recalculating the change in the option price given a change in the market. For being long a call option, the VaR would be as shown below:

$$VaR = C(S) - C(S - 2.32 \times \sigma_S)$$

Here, $C(S)$ represents the pricing function, e.g., the Black-Scholes equation.

In the approaches outlined above for measuring risk for options, we focused on changes in value arising from movements in the stock price, or S. Similar value changes can be calculated using the other Greeks. For example, using the vega and the 2.32 standard-deviation change in implied volatility to determine the VaR due to changes in implied volatility and interest rates. However, we have not yet explored the more complex problem of including the possibility of several risk factors moving at once. We will tackle this problem in the next chapter.

General Considerations in Using VaR

In the discussion above, we gave approximations for calculating the one-day 99% VaR. However, there are several conventions in use for the VaR probability, which implies a different multiplication factor for the standard deviation. The most common alternative is to set the tail probability at 2.5%. If a Normal distribution is assumed, this implies a multiplier of 1.96 rather than 2.32.

In some cases, we may wish to know the VaR for the potential losses over multiple days. A reasonable approximation to the multiday VaR is that it is equal to the one-day VaR multiplied by the square root of the number of days:

$$VaR_T = VaR_1 \sqrt{T} = DEaR\sqrt{T}$$

This relationship requires the following assumptions:

1. Changes in market factors are Normally distributed.
2. The one-day VaR is constant over the time period.
3. There is no serial correlation. Serial correlation is present if the results on one day are not independent of the results on a previous day.

The derivation of this relationship was explained fully in the statistics chapter; it comes from the variance of the sum of T uncorrelated random numbers.

In general, for trading operations it is safe to assume that if the term VaR is used without a specified time, it means one-day VaR. Occasionally, the term VaR is also used to refer to the potential loss from asset liability management—in which case a monthly or yearly horizon is used. Also, the term "credit VaR" is sometimes used to describe the loss distribution from a credit portfolio. This is quite different from the VaR used for trading portfolios.

The major limitation of VaR is that it describes what happens on bad days (e.g., twice a year) rather than terrible days (e.g., once every 10 years). VaR is therefore good for avoiding bad days, but to avoid terrible days you still need stress and scenario tests.

SUMMARY

In this chapter, we detailed the five common approaches to measuring market risk, including sensitivity analysis, stress testing, scenario testing, the Capital Asset Pricing Model, and Value at Risk. Next, we will explain how to calculate VaR using the three key methods in common use.

NOTE

1 "Capital Asset Prices: A Theory of Market Equilibrium under Conditions of Risk," W. F. Sharpe, *Journal of Finance*, vol. 19, pp. 425–442, September, 1964.

CHAPTER 6

The Three Common Approaches for Calculating Value at Risk

INTRODUCTION

The previous chapter explained the importance of Value at Risk (VaR); namely, it is the best single measure to assess market risk. It is a good measure of risk because it combines information on the sensitivity of the value to changes in market-risk factors with information on the probable amount of change in those factors. VaR tries to answer the question, "How much could we lose today given our current position and the possible changes in the market?" VaR formalizes that question into the calculation of the level of loss that is so bad that there is only a 1 in 100 chance of there being a loss worse than the calculated VaR. VaR estimates this level by knowing the current value of the portfolio and calculating the probability distribution of changes in the value over the next trading day. From the probability distribution we can read the confidence level for the 99-percentile loss.

To estimate the value's probability distribution, we use two sets of information: the current position, or holdings, in the bank's trading portfolio, and an estimate of the probability distribution of the price changes over the next day. The estimate of the probability distribution of the price changes is based on the distribution of price changes over the last few weeks or months.

The goal of this chapter is to explain how to calculate VaR using the three methods that are in common use: Parametric VaR, Historical Simulation, and Monte Carlo Simulation.

ATTRIBUTES AND LIMITATIONS SHARED BY ALL THREE METHODS

It is important to note that while the three calculation methods differ, they do share common attributes and limitations. For example, each approach uses market-risk factors. Risk factors are fundamental market rates that can be derived from the prices of securities being traded. Typically, the main risk factors used are interest rates, foreign exchange rates, equity indices, commodity prices, forward prices, and implied volatilities. By observing this small number of risk factors, we are able to calculate the price of all the thousands of different securities held by the bank. For example, it is possible to price all government bonds by knowing the risk-free interest rates for just a dozen points on the yield curve. This risk-factor approach uses less data than would be required if we tried to collect historical price information for every security.

Each approach uses the distribution of historical price changes to estimate the probability distributions. This requires a choice of historical horizon for the market data; e.g., how far back should we go in using historical data to calculate standard deviations? This is a trade-off between having large amounts of information or fresh information.

Because VaR attempts to predict the future probability distribution, it should use the latest market data with the latest market structure and sentiment. However, with a limited amount of data, the estimates become less accurate, and there is less chance of having data that contains those extreme, rare market movements which are the ones that cause the greatest losses.

Each approach has the disadvantage of assuming that past relationships between the risk factors will be repeated; e.g., it assumes that factors that have tended to move together in the past will move together in the future.

Each approach uses binning (also known as mapping) to put cash flows into a finite number of buckets. To understand the need for binning, consider a bond portfolio which will have coupons and principal payments due almost daily for several years. It would be possible to calculate the duration for every cash flow, then calculate the statistics of the rate movements for each day, but this requires a very large amount of data. As an alternative, we can bin (or map) all the cash flows onto a limited number of time points, and just deal with the statistics of those time points. Typically, approximately 10 time points are used, including 3 months, 6 months, 12 months, 18 months, 2 years, 5 years, and 10 years. To understand the process of mapping, consider a cash flow of $100 falling due in 6 years. This could be mapped onto the 5- and 10-year points as $75 at 5 years and $25 at 10 years. The mapping will try to preserve some combination of cash flow, present value, duration, or stand-alone VaR amounts. The process of binning is discussed in Appendix A to this chapter.

Each approach has strengths and weaknesses when compared to the others, as summarized in Figure 6-1. The degree to which the circles are shaded corresponds to the strength of the approach. The factors evaluated in the table are the speed of computation, the ability to capture nonlinearity, the ability to capture non-Normality, and the independence from historical data. *Nonlinearity* refers to the price change not being a linear function of the change in the risk factors. This is especially important for options. *Non-Normality* refers to the ability to calculate the potential changes in risk factors without assuming that they have a Normal distribution. Note, for example, that

FIGURE 6-1

Summary of VaR Techniques

	Parametric VaR	Monte Carlo Simulation	Historical Simulation
Speed of computation	●	○	◑
Ability to capture nonlinearity	○	●	●
Ability to capture nonnormality	○	◑	●
Independence from historical data	◑	◑	○

The relative strengths of the VaR calculation methods are shown by the extent of the shading.

Parametric VaR is fast, but does not capture non-Normality and nonlinearity. Monte Carlo captures nonlinearity, but does not capture non-Normality and can be slow. Historical simulation captures non-Normality and nonlinearity, but the resuts are heavily influenced by the exact form of historical market movements; e.g., if there was a significant crisis in the past, historical simulation will keep reliving that crisis in exactly the same form.

PARAMETRIC VaR

Parametric VaR is also known as Linear VaR, Variance-Covariance VaR, Greek-Normal VaR, Delta Normal VaR, or Delta-Gamma Normal VaR. The approach is parametric in that it assumes that the probability distribution is Normal and then requires calculation of the variance and covariance parameters. The approach is linear in that changes in instrument values are assumed to be linear with respect to changes in risk factors. For example, for bonds the sensitivity is described by duration, and for options it is described by the Greeks.

The overall Parametric VaR approach is as follows:

- Define the set of risk factors that will be sufficient to calculate the value of the bank's portfolio.
- Find the sensitivity of each instrument in the portfolio to each risk factor.
- Get historical data on the risk factors to calculate the standard deviation of the changes and the correlations between them.
- Estimate the standard deviation of the value of the portfolio by multiplying the sensitivities by the standard deviations, taking into account all correlations.
- Finally, assume that the loss distribution is Normally distributed, and therefore, approximate the 99% VaR as 2.32 times the standard deviation of the value of the portfolio.

Parametric VaR has two advantages:

- It is typically 100 to 1000 times faster to calculate Parametric VaR compared with Monte Carlo or Historical Simulation.
- Parametric VaR allows the calculation of VaR contribution, as explained in the next chapter.

It also has significant limitations:

- It gives a poor description of nonlinear risks.
- It gives a poor description of extreme tail events, such as crises, because it assumes that the risk factors have a Normal distribution. In reality, as we found in the statistics chapter, the risk-factor distributions have a high kurtosis with more extreme events than would be predicted by the Normal distribution.
- Parametric VaR uses a covariance matrix, and this implicitly assumes that the correlations between risk factors is stable and constant over time.

To give an intuitive understanding of Parametric VaR, we have provided three worked-out examples. The examples are fundamentally quite simple, but they introduce the method of calculating Parametric VaR. There are a lot of equations, but the underlying math is mostly algebra rather than complex statistics or calculus.

The main statistical relationship that will be used is taken from Chapter 3: the variance of the sum of two numbers is a function of the variance of the individual numbers and the correlation between them. If we have a portfolio of two instruments, the loss on the portfolio (L_P) will be the sum of the losses on each instrument:

$$L_P = L_1 + L_2$$

The standard deviation of the loss on the portfolio (σ_P) will be as follows:

$$\sigma_P^2 = \sigma_1^2 + \sigma_2^2 + 2\rho_{1,2}\sigma_1\sigma_2$$

Here, σ_1 is the standard deviation of losses from instrument 1, and $\rho_{1,2}$ is the correlation between losses from 1 and 2.

Three different notations are used in this chapter: algebraic, summation, and matrix. Algebraic notation is used for most of the equations because it is easiest to understand if there are just a few variables; however, it becomes cumbersome with many variables. It then becomes easier to use summation or matrix notation. As an example, consider the following equation in algebraic notation:

$$\sigma_P^2 = \sigma_1^2 + \sigma_2^2 + 2\rho_{1,2}\sigma_1\sigma_2$$

This can be written in summation notation as follows:

$$\sigma_P^2 = \sum_{i=1}^{2}\sum_{j=1}^{2} \rho_{i,j}\sigma_i\sigma_j$$

This means first sum over j from 1 to 2 then sum over i from 1 to 2:

$$\sigma_P^2 = \sum_{i=1}^{2}\left(\rho_{i,1}\sigma_i\sigma_1 + \rho_{i,2}\sigma_i\sigma_2\right)$$

$$= \rho_{1,1}\sigma_1\sigma_1 + \rho_{1,2}\sigma_1\sigma_2 + \rho_{2,1}\sigma_2\sigma_1 + \rho_{2,2}\sigma_2\sigma_2$$

$$= \sigma_1^2 + \sigma_2^2 + 2\rho_{1,2}\sigma_1\sigma_2$$

The matrix notation for the same equation is as follows:

$$\sigma_P^2 = SRS^T$$

$$S = [\sigma_1 \quad \sigma_1]$$

$$R = \begin{bmatrix} 1 & \rho_{1,2} \\ \rho_{1,2} & 1 \end{bmatrix}$$

$$S^T = \begin{bmatrix} \sigma_1 \\ \sigma_2 \end{bmatrix}$$

If we carry out the usual matrix multiplications we get back to the same original equation:

$$RS^T = \begin{bmatrix} \sigma_1 + \rho_{1,2}\sigma_2 \\ \rho_{1,2}\sigma_1 + \sigma_2 \end{bmatrix}$$

$$SRS^T = [\sigma_1\sigma_1 + \rho_{1,2}\sigma_2\sigma_1 + \rho_{1,2}\sigma_1\sigma_2 + \sigma_2\sigma_2]$$

$$= \sigma_1^2 + \sigma_2^2 + 2\rho_{1,2}\sigma_1\sigma_2$$

Notice that all three notations give the same result. The choice of the notation to use is not terribly important and is generally dictated by convention and convenience.

Calculating VaR using the Parametric Approach: Example One

The examples worked out below use absolute changes in risk factors. In practice, relative changes are often used because the distribution of relative changes is closer to Normal. However, working out the equations with relative changes is more complicated, and adds little intuitive understanding. Therefore, the relative changes are relegated to Appendix B.

The first example calculates the stand-alone VaR for a bank holding a long position in an equity. The *stand-alone VaR* is the VaR for the position on its own without considering correlation and diversification effects from other positions. The present value of the position is simply the number of shares (N) times the value per share, V_S.

$$PV_\$ = N \times V_S$$

The change in the value of the position is simply the number of shares multiplied by the change in the value of each share:

$$\Delta PV_\$ = N \times \Delta V_S$$

The standard deviation of the value is the number of shares multiplied by the standard deviation of the value of each share. (This step is explained more thoroughly in the statistics chapter.)

$$\sigma_V = N \times \sigma_S$$

As we have assumed that the value changes are Normally distributed, there will be a 1% chance that the loss is more than 2.32 standard deviations; therefore, we can calculate the 99% VaR as follows

$$VaR = 2.32 \times N \times \sigma_S$$

In this very simple example, notice that there are two elements: N, which describes the sensitivity of the position to changes in the risk factor, and σ_S, which describes the volatility of the risk factor.

Calculating VaR using the Parametric Approach: Example Two

As a slightly more complex example, consider a government bond held by a U.K. bank denominated in British pounds with a single payment. The present value in pounds (PV_p) is simply the value of the cash flow in pounds (C_p) at time t discounted according to sterling interest rates for that maturity, r_p:

$$PV_p = \frac{C_p}{\left(1 + r_p\right)^t}$$

The sensitivity of the value to changes in interest rates is the derivative with respect to r_p:

$$\frac{\partial PV_p}{\partial r_p} = \left[\frac{-tC_p}{\left(1 + r_p\right)^{t+1}} \right]$$

Notice that this is the same as duration but without the minus sign. For simplicity in this example, let us represent the derivative by d_r:

$$d_r = \left[\frac{-tC_p}{(1 + r_p)^{t+1}} \right]$$

The change in the value is the sensitivity multiplied by the change in interest rates:

$$\Delta PV_p = d_r \times \Delta r_p$$

The standard deviation of PV_p is then the standard deviation of the rate times d_r, and the 99% VaR is 2.32 times the result:

$$VaR = 2.32 \times d_r \times \sigma_{r_p}$$

To make this example more concrete, consider a bond paying 100 pounds (C_p) in 5 years' time (t), with the 5-year discount rate at 6% (r_p), and a standard deviation in the rate of 0.5% (σ_{r_p}). The present value is then 74 pounds, the sensitivity (d_r) is -352 pounds per 100% increase in rates, and the VaR is 4.1 pounds:

$$PV_p = \frac{100}{(1.06)^5} = 74$$

$$d_r = \frac{-5 \times 100}{(1.06)^6} = -352$$

$$VaR = \left| 2.32 \times \frac{-5 \times 100}{(1.06)^6} \times 0.5\% \right| = 4.1$$

The bars on each side of the equation indicate that we take the absolute value; i.e., we drop the minus sign. We need to use the absolute value because we have taken a short-cut in this calculation. As we will discover in the next example, Parametric VaR is actually 2.32 times the standard deviation of value, i.e., the square root of the variance, and is therefore always positive. When dealing with one risk factor, as above, we can skip the step of squaring then taking the square root, but if we skip this step, we need to make sure that the result is not negative.

Calculating VaR Using the Parametric Approach: Example Three

The two examples above were simple because they had only one risk factor. Now let us consider a multidimensional case: the same simple bond as before, but now held by a U.S. bank. The U.S. bank is exposed to two risks: changes due to sterling interest rates and changes due to the pound-dollar exchange rate. The value of the bond in dollars is the value in pounds multiplied by the FX rate:

$$PV_\$ = FX \times PV_p$$

$$= FX \frac{C_p}{(1 + r_p)^t}$$

The change in value due to changes in interest rates is as before, but translated into dollars:

$$\frac{\partial PV_\$}{\partial r_p} = FX \frac{-tC_p}{(1 + r_p)^{t+1}}$$

$$\Delta PV_\$ = FX \frac{-tC_p}{(1 + r_p)^{t+1}} \Delta r_p$$

The linear change in value due to a change in FX rates is simply given by the derivative with respect to FX:

$$\frac{\partial PV_\$}{\partial FX} = \frac{C_p}{(1+r_p)^t}$$

Therefore, the change in value due to a change in FX is given by the following:

$$\Delta PV_\$ = \Delta FX \frac{C_p}{(1+r_p)^t}$$

The change in value due to both a change in rates and a change in FX is given by the sum of individual changes:

$$\Delta PV_\$ = \frac{C_p}{(1+r_p)^t} \Delta FX + FX \frac{-tC_p}{(1+r_p)^{t+1}} \Delta r_p$$

For simplicity, let us define the derivative with respect to FX to be d_{FX} and the derivative with respect to sterling interest rates to be d_{r_p}:

$$d_{FX} = \frac{C_p}{(1+r_p)^t}$$

$$d_{r_p} = FX \frac{-tC_p}{(1+r_p)^{t+1}}$$

(Notice that d_{r_p} is different than the one used in the previous example because it is now for a U.S. bank, and therefore is in dollars.) We can now rewrite the equation for change in value in a simpler form:

$$\Delta PV_\$ = d_{FX} \Delta FX + d_{r_p} \Delta r_p$$

Now we want to get an expression for the variance of PV. The main complication is that changes in FX are correlated with changes in interest rates. To get from deltas to variances for correlated variables, we need to use the relationship we discussed earlier for the sum of losses:

$$L_P = L_1 + L_2$$

$$\sigma_P^2 = \sigma_1^2 + \sigma_2^2 + 2\rho_{1,2}\sigma_1\sigma_2$$

We can use this equation to find the standard deviation of the bond value by making the following substitutions:

$$L_1 = d_{FX} \Delta FX$$

$$L_2 = d_{r_p} \Delta r_p$$

$$L_P = \Delta PV_\$$$

Here, d_{FX} and d_{r_p} are fixed multipliers, but ΔFX and Δr_p are random values. The variances of ΔFX and Δr_p are estimated from the historical data. The variance for FX rates is as follows (where FX_t is the FX historical rate on day t):

$$\Delta FX_t = FX_t - FX_{t-1}$$

$$\sigma_{FX}^2 = \frac{1}{N-1} \sum_{t=1}^{N} (\Delta FX_t)^2$$

(Assuming the mean is zero.) The variance for interest rates is calculated similarly:

$$\Delta r_{p,t} = r_{p,t} - r_{p,t-1}$$

$$\sigma_{r_p}^2 = \frac{1}{N-1} \sum_{t=1}^{N} \left(\Delta r_{p,t}\right)^2$$

The correlation is estimated from the cross-multiplication of the changes:

$$\rho_{FX,r_p} = \frac{1}{N-1} \left(\frac{\sum_{t=1}^{N} \Delta r_{p,t} \Delta FX_t}{\sigma_{r_p} \sigma_{FX}} \right)$$

These values can be substituted for σ_1, σ_2, and $\rho_{1,2}$:

$$\sigma_1 = d_{FX} \sigma_{FX}$$

$$\sigma_2 = d_{r_p} \sigma_{r_p}$$

$$\rho_{1,2} = \rho_{FX,r_p}$$

Substituting this back in the equation for σ_P gives us the variance for the bond's value:

$$\sigma_P^2 = (d_{FX}\sigma_{FX})^2 + 2\rho_{FX,r_p}(d_{FX}\sigma_{FX})\left(d_{r_p}\sigma_{r_p}\right) + \left(d_{r_p}\sigma_{r_p}\right)^2$$

Standard deviation is the square root of variance, and VaR is 2.32 times the standard deviation; therefore, VaR is as follows:

$$VaR = 2.32\, \sigma_P$$

$$= 2.32\sqrt{(d_{FX}\sigma_{FX})^2 + 2\rho_{FX,r_p}(d_{FX}\sigma_{FX})\left(d_{r_p}\sigma_{r_p}\right) + \left(d_{r_p}\sigma_{r_p}\right)^2}$$

To put numerical values to this, assume that the bond is the same as before: paying 100 million pounds in 5 years' time, with the 5-year discount rate at 6%, and a standard deviation in the rate of 0.5%. Also assume that the exchange rate is 1.6 dollars per pound, the volatility of the rate is 0.02, and the correlation between FX rates and interest rates is −0.6. We will use this example several times in the following chapter, and the parameter values are therefore shown in Table 6-1.

With these values we obtain the current value, the sensitivities, and the VaR result of $9.05:

TABLE 6-1

Parameter Values for the Example of a
Sterling Bond

Parameter	Value
Cashflow (C_p)	100 pounds
Maturity (t)	5 years
Interest rate (r_p)	6%
Interest-rate standard deviation (σ_{r_p})	0.5%
Exchange rate (FX)	1.6 dollars/pound
Exchange-rate standard deviation (σ_{FX})	0.02 dollars/pound
Correlation (ρ_{FX,r_p})	−0.6

Parameter values needed to calculate the VaR for a foreign-currency bond.

$$PV_\$ = \$119$$

$$d_{FX} = 74.7$$

$$d_r = -564.0$$

$$VaR = \$9.05$$

In the example above we had only two risk factors. We can generalize the VaR equation relationship to give VaR for a position with many risk factors:

$$VaR = 2.32\sqrt{(d_1\sigma_1)^2 + 2\rho_{1,2}(d_1\sigma_1)(d_2\sigma_2) + (d_2\sigma_2)^2 + \cdots + 2\rho_{N-1,N}(d_{N-1}\sigma_{N-1})(d_N\sigma_N) + (d_N\sigma_N)^2}$$

Here, N is the total number of risk factors being used, and d_N is the derivative of the portfolio's value with respect to the Nth risk factor:

$$d_N = \frac{\partial V}{\partial f_N}$$

The equation above can become cumbersome and can be written more compactly in summation notation:

$$VaR = 2.32\sqrt{\sum_{i=1}^{N}\sum_{j=1}^{N}\left[\rho_{i,j}(d_i\sigma_i)\left(d_j\sigma_j\right)\right]}$$

Alternatively, we can use matrix notation. Using matrix notation, we can put the derivatives into a vector and the statistics into a covariance matrix:

$$D = \begin{bmatrix} d_{FX} & d_{r_p} \end{bmatrix}$$

$$C = \begin{bmatrix} \sigma_{FX}^2 & \sigma_{FX}\sigma_{r_p}\rho_{FX,r_p} \\ \sigma_{FX}\sigma_{r_p}\rho_{FX,r_p} & \sigma_{r_p}^2 \end{bmatrix}$$

The covariance matrix has the variances of the risk factors along the main diagonal and has the covariances off the diagonal. Notice that the covariance matrix is symmetric. Appendix C describes the covariance matrix in more detail. We obtain the variance of the portfolio, σ_{PV}^2, by multiplying the derivative vector with the covariance matrix:

$$\sigma_{PV}^2 = DCD^T$$

where D^T is the transpose of D. (In a transpose, the rows and columns are switched.) VaR is then given by a simple expression:

$$VaR = 2.32\sqrt{DCD^T}$$

In our numerical example D, C, D^T and VaR are as follows:

$$D = \begin{bmatrix} 74.7 & -563 \end{bmatrix}$$

$$C = \begin{bmatrix} 0.0004 & -0.00006 \\ -0.00006 & 0.000025 \end{bmatrix}$$

$$D^T = \begin{bmatrix} 74.7 \\ -563 \end{bmatrix}$$

VaR is obtained by matrix multiplication:

$$VaR = 2.32\sqrt{DCD^T}$$

$$= \$9.05$$

In general, if we have many risk factors, we can extend the vector of sensitivities and the covariance matrix:

$$D = [d_1, d_2, \ldots, d_N]$$

$$C = \begin{bmatrix} \sigma_1\sigma_1 & \rho_{1,2}\sigma_1\sigma_2 & & \rho_{1,N}\sigma_1\sigma_N \\ \rho_{2,1}\sigma_2\sigma_1 & \sigma_2\sigma_2 & & \rho_{2,N}\sigma_2\sigma_N \\ & & \ddots & \\ \rho_{N,1}\sigma_N\sigma_1 & \rho_{N,2}\sigma_N\sigma_2 & & \sigma_N\sigma_N \end{bmatrix}$$

Using Parametric VaR to Calculate Risk Sensitivity for Several Positions

In the example above, we had one security that was sensitive to two different risk factors. If the portfolio is made up of several securities, each of which is affected by the same risk factor, then the sensitivity of the portfolio to the risk factor is simply the sum of the sensitivities for the individual positions. For example, consider a portfolio holding our example 100-pound five-year bond and 100 pounds of cash. The value of the bond in dollars was given as:

$$Value_{Bond} = FX \frac{100}{(1 + 6\%)^5}$$

The value of the cash position is simply 100 pounds translated into dollars:

$$Value_{Cash} = FX \times 100$$

The present value of the portfolio is simply the sum of the value of the two securities:

$$PV_P = FX \frac{100}{(1 + 6\%)^5} + FX \times 100$$

The sensitivity of the value to changes in the FX rate is given by the derivative with respect to FX rates:

$$d_{FX} = \frac{100}{(1 + 6\%)^5} + 100$$

The sensitivity to interest rates is unchanged from the previous example. In matrix notation, we have one vector for the bond, one for the cash, and then the sum for the portfolio. The VaR in this case is $13.11.

$$D_{Bond} = \begin{bmatrix} 74.7 & -563 \end{bmatrix}$$

$$D_{Cash} = \begin{bmatrix} 100 & 0 \end{bmatrix}$$

$$D_{Position} = D_{Bond} + D_{Cash}$$

$$= \begin{bmatrix} 174.7 & -563 \end{bmatrix}$$

In general, if we have multiple risk factors, 1 to N, and have multiple securities, A through Z, the vector for the portfolio will be the sum of the vectors for the individual securities:

$$D_A = \begin{bmatrix} d_{A,1}, d_{A,2}, d_{A,3}, \cdots d_{A,N} \end{bmatrix}$$

$$D_B = \begin{bmatrix} d_{B,1}, d_{B,2}, d_{B,3}, \cdots d_{B,N} \end{bmatrix}$$

$$\vdots$$

$$D_Z = \begin{bmatrix} d_{Z,1}, d_{Z,2}, d_{Z,3}, \cdots, d_{Z,N} \end{bmatrix}$$

$$D_{Portfolio} = D_A + D_B + \cdots + D_Z$$

$$D_{Portfolio} = \begin{bmatrix} (d_{A,1} + d_{B,1} + \cdots + d_{Z,1}), \cdots, (d_{A,N} + d_{B,N} + \cdots + d_{Z,N}) \end{bmatrix}$$

The *VaR* for the portfolio is calculated as before, but using the sensitivity vector for the chosen portfolio:

$$VaR_{Portfolio} = 2.32\sqrt{D_{Portfolio}C\,D_{Portfolio}^{T}}$$

The Structure of Parametric VaR Calculators

The section above discussed the methodologies for calculating parametric VaR. Many vendors have incorporated these methodologies into "industrial-strength" calculators that can be run daily to calculate VaR for all the thousands of securities in a bank's trading operation. Figure 6-2 gives a typical layout for a Parametric VaR calculator.

These calculators work in the following manner:

- The calculator is fed market data and position data. The market data comes from data vendors such as Telerate, Bloomberg, and Reuters. The position data comes from the trader's deal capture or position-keeping system, i.e., the systems that the traders use to record their purchases and sales.
- The position and market data must then be cleaned to remove gross errors, such as rates that are entered in decimals instead of percentages. There must also be

FIGURE 6-2

The Modules within a Parametric VaR Calculator

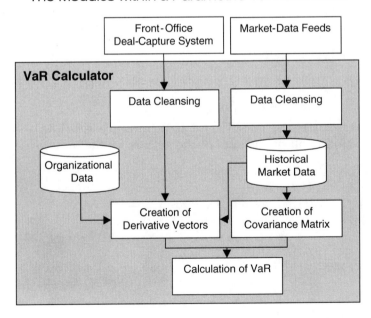

algorithms to fill in any missing data, including data for markets that had local holidays.
- The market data is used to calculate the covariance matrix and is fed into the calculation of the derivative vectors.
- The derivative vectors for each type of security are calculated using analytic formulas or by perturbing pricing calculators by small amounts to get the delta.
- VaR is then calculated by multiplying the derivative vectors with the covariance matrix.

Typically, VaR will be reported both for the institution as a whole and for individual desks and traders as if they were stand-alone units. Organizational data for the bank is stored and used to determine which derivative vectors should be added together for each business unit.

The VaR calculator is typically run overnight in a batch process with the intention of showing management the risk profile at the start of the next day. Ideally, at the start of the day, senior management should get a report showing the current position of the bank, how much could be lost in the coming day, and the main causes of such a loss. Management can then act to hedge or reduce any positions that it considers to be too dangerous.

Intraday Calculation of VaR

As noted above, the VaR calculator is typically run overnight in a batch process. Intraday calculations are also desirable for two reasons:

- Some fast-moving positions can build up significant risks very quickly, and management would like early warning.
- As discussed later, some banks limit the maximum amount of VaR that a trader can have. If this is the case, traders must have some way of knowing whether the next trade would cause these limits to be violated.

The industry is still grappling with the problems of quickly calculating intraday VaR, but the most common approach is to use an incremental calculation. In an incremental calculation, the overnight batch process produces the covariance matrix and the derivative vectors for all the bank's existing positions. Traders are then given VaR calculators on their desks that have sufficient functionality to create derivative vectors for any new trades that they are considering. These vectors are added to their existing derivative vector to calculate the new VaR. This is illustrated in Figure 6-3. The intraday calculator is similar to the full, overnight calculator except the intraday calculator stores the market data and derivative data from the previous night's batch.

FIGURE 6-3

Calculation of Intra-Day Parametric VaR

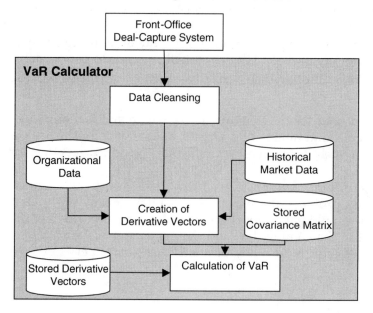

Diagram of how an intraday VaR calculator operates. Traders use this VaR calculator to calculate the VaR for potential trades by creating a derivative vector for the new trade and adding it to the vectors for their existing trades.

HISTORICAL-SIMULATION VaR

Conceptually, historical simulation is the most simple VaR technique, but it takes significantly more time to run than parametric VaR. The historical-simulation approach takes the market data for the last 250 days and calculates the percent change for each risk factor on each day. Each percentage change is then multiplied by today's market values to present 250 scenarios for tomorrow's values. For each of these scenarios, the portfolio is valued using full, nonlinear pricing models. The third-worst day is then selected as being the 99% VaR.

As an example, let's consider calculating the VaR for a five-year, zero-coupon bond paying $100. We start by looking back at the previous trading days and noting the five-year rate on each day. We then calculate the proportion by which the rate changed from one day to the next:

$$\Delta_t = \frac{r_{t+1} - r_t}{r_t}$$

Scenarios are then created for tomorrow's rate by applying the proportional change to today's rate:

$$r_{Scenario,k} = r_{Today}(1 + \Delta_t)$$

We shift from a subscript of t to k because there is a conceptual shift. We use data from the past days to create scenarios of what could happen tomorrow. The scenarios therefore do not represent what has happened, but what could happen in the next day. Using these scenarios, we value the bond using the usual formula:

$$Value_{Scenario,k} = \frac{100}{(1 + r_{Scenario,k})^5}$$

and then calculate the change in value:

$$\Delta V_k = Value_{Scenario,k} - Value_{Today}$$

Table 6-2 gives an example of 10 days of data (rather than 250 days). The "Rate" column shows the rate observed at the end of each day. The next columns show the proportional change and the scenario that would occur if that change were to happen starting from today's rate. The final columns show the bond value and loss in each scenario. In this example, the worst-case change is a loss of 39 cents, which is a rough estimate of the 10-percentile loss.

TABLE 6-2

Example of Historical VaR Calculation

Data	Rate (%)	Proportional change	Scenario rate	Bond Value ($)	Change in Value ($)
9-Jul	5.02	0.6%	5.03	78.25	−0.10
10-Jul	5.05	−0.9%	4.96	78.52	0.17
11-Jul	5.01	1.9%	5.09	78.00	−0.35
12-Jul	5.10	0.2%	5.01	78.32	−0.03
13-Jul	5.11	−0.8%	4.96	78.50	0.14
16-Jul	5.07	2.1%	5.11	77.96	**−0.39**
17-Jul	5.18	1.0%	5.05	78.17	−0.19
18-Jul	5.23	−0.2%	4.99	78.40	0.05
19-Jul	5.22	−0.2%	4.99	78.39	0.04
20-Jul	5.21	−4.0%	4.80	79.10	0.75
23-Jul	5.00			78.35	

There are two main advantages of using historical simulation:

- It is easy to communicate the results throughout the organization because the concepts are easily explained.
- There is no need to assume that the changes in the risk factors have a structured parametric probability distribution (e.g., no need to assume they are Joint-Normal with stable correlation).

The disadvantages are due to using the historical data in such a raw form:

- The result is often dominated by a single, recent, specific crisis, and it is very difficult to test other assumptions. The effect of this is that Historical VaR is strongly backward-looking, meaning the bank is, in effect, protecting itself from the last crisis, but not necessarily preparing itself for the next.
- There can also be an unpleasant "window effect." When 250 days have passed since the crisis, the crisis observation drops out of our window for historical data, and the reported VaR suddenly drops from one day to the next. This often causes traders to mistrust the VaR because they know there has been no significant change in the risk of the trading operation, and yet the quantification of the risk has changed dramatically.

MONTE CARLO SIMULATION VaR

Monte Carlo simulation is also known as Monte Carlo evaluation (MCE). It estimates VaR by randomly creating many scenarios for future rates, using nonlinear pricing models to estimate the change in value for each scenario, and then calculating VaR according to the worst losses.

Monte Carlo simulation has two significant advantages:

- Unlike Parametric VaR, it uses full pricing models and can therefore capture the effects of nonlinearities.
- Unlike Historical VaR, it can generate an infinite number of scenarios and therefore test many possible future outcomes.

Monte Carlo has two important disadvantages:

- The calculation of Monte Carlo VaR can take 1000 times longer than Parametric VaR because the potential price of the portfolio has to be calculated thousands of times.
- Unlike Historical VaR, it typically requires the assumption that the risk factors have a Normal or Log-Normal distribution.

The Monte Carlo approach assumes that there is a known probability distribution for the risk factors. The usual implementation of Monte Carlo assumes a stable, Joint-Normal distribution for the risk factors. This is the same assumption used for Parametric VaR. The analysis calculates the covariance matrix for the risk factors in the same way as Parametric VaR but unlike Parametric VaR, it then decomposes the matrix as described below. The decomposition ensures that the risk factors are correlated in each scenario. The scenarios start from today's market condition and go one day forward to give possible values at the end of the day. Full, nonlinear pricing models are then used to value the portfolio under each of the end-of-day scenarios. For bonds, nonlinear pricing means using the bond-pricing formula rather than duration, and for options, it means using a pricing formula such as Black-Scholes rather than just using the Greeks.

From the scenarios, VaR is selected to be the 1-percentile worst loss. For example, if 1000 scenarios were created, the 99% VaR would be the tenth-worst result. Figure 6-4 summarizes the Monte Carlo approach:

Most of the Monte Carlo approach is conceptually simple. The one mathematically difficult step is to decompose the covariance matrix in such a way as to allow us to create random scenarios with the same correlation as the historical market data. For example, in the previous example of a Sterling bond held by a U.S. bank, we assumed a correlation of −0.6 between the interest rate and exchange rate. In other words, when the interest rate increases, we would expect that the exchange rate would tend to decrease. One way to think of this is that 60% of the change in the exchange rate is driven by changes in the interest rate. The other 40% is driven by independent, random factors. The trick is to create random scenarios that properly capture such relationships.

If we just have two factors, we can easily create correlated random numbers in the following way:

FIGURE 6-4

Illustration of the Process for Monte Carlo VaR

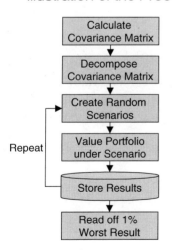

- Draw a random number, z_1, from a Standard Normal distribution.
- Multiply z_1 by the standard deviation of the first risk factor (σ_A) to create the first risk factor for that scenario, f_A:

$$f_A = \sigma_A z_1, \quad z_1 \sim N(0,1)$$

- Multiply z_1 by the correlation, $\rho_{A,B}$.
- Draw a second independent random number, z_2.
- Multiply z_2 by the root of one minus the correlation squared $\left(\sqrt{1 - \rho_{A,B}^2}\right)$.
- Add the two results together to create a random number (y) that has a standard deviation of one and correlation $\rho_{A,B}$ with f_A:

$$y = z_1 \rho_{A,B} + z_2 \sqrt{1 - \rho_{A,B}^2}, \quad z_2 \sim N(0,1)$$

- Multiply y by the standard deviation of the second risk factor, σ_B, to create the second risk factor for that scenario, f_B:

$$f_B = \sigma_B y$$

This process can be summarized in the following equations:

$$f_A = \sigma_A z_1, \quad z_1 \sim N(0,1)$$

$$f_B = \sigma_B \left(z_1 \rho_{A,B} + z_2 \sqrt{1 - \rho_{A,B}^2} \right), \quad z_2 \sim N(0,1)$$

For the previous bond example, we would create changes in the risk factors r_p and FX by using the following equations:

$$\sigma_{r_p} = 0.5\%$$

$$\sigma_{FX} = 0.02$$

$$\rho_{FX,r_p} = -0.6$$

$$\delta FX = 0.02 \times z_1, \quad z_1 \sim N(0,1)$$

$$\delta r_p = 0.005 \left(-0.6 z_1 + z_2 \sqrt{1 - 0.36} \right), \quad z_2 \sim N(0,1)$$

Unfortunately, this simple approach does not work if there are more than two risk factors. If there are many risk factors, we need to create the correlation by decomposing the covariance matrix using either Cholesky decomposition or Eigen-value decomposition. We will give an overview of each approach.

Cholesky Decomposition

Cholesky decomposition finds a new matrix, A, such that the transpose of A times A equals the covariance matrix, C:

$$C = A^T A$$

A is also required to be upper triangular, i.e., all the elements below the main diagonal are zero; e.g.:

$$A = \begin{bmatrix} \alpha & \beta \\ 0 & \phi \end{bmatrix}$$

$$A^T = \begin{bmatrix} \alpha & 0 \\ \beta & \phi \end{bmatrix}$$

As a two-dimensional example, assume that we have a covariance matrix with known covariances a, b, and c:

$$C = \begin{bmatrix} \sigma_A^2 & \rho_{AB}\sigma_A\sigma_B \\ \rho_{AB}\sigma_A\sigma_B & \sigma_B^2 \end{bmatrix} = \begin{bmatrix} a & b \\ b & c \end{bmatrix}$$

We now wish to find the elements of A to satisfy the following equation:

$$C = A^T A$$

$$\begin{bmatrix} a & b \\ b & c \end{bmatrix} = \begin{bmatrix} \alpha^2 & \alpha\beta \\ \alpha\beta & \beta^2 + \phi^2 \end{bmatrix}$$

A will be as required if we define its elements as follows:

$$\alpha^2 = a$$

$$\alpha\beta = b$$

$$\beta^2 + \phi^2 = c$$

This can be solved as follows:

$$\alpha = \sqrt{a}$$

$$\beta = \frac{b}{\sqrt{a}}$$

$$\phi = \sqrt{c - \frac{b^2}{a}}$$

Now we take two random numbers, z_1 and z_2, drawn independently from Normal distributions with a mean of zero and standard deviation of one to create a vector Z:

$$Z = \begin{bmatrix} z_1 & z_2 \end{bmatrix}$$

If we multiply A by Z, we get a vector, F, of two random risk factors that are correlated according to the original covariance matrix:

$$F = ZA$$

$$[\delta f_A \quad \delta f_B] = [z_1 \quad z_2] \begin{bmatrix} \sqrt{a} & \dfrac{b}{\sqrt{a}} \\ 0 & \sqrt{c - \dfrac{b^2}{a}} \end{bmatrix}$$

$$\delta f_A = z_1 \sqrt{a}$$

$$\delta f_B = \sqrt{c} \left(z_1 \frac{b}{\sqrt{ac}} + z_2 \sqrt{1 - \frac{b^2}{ac}} \right)$$

If you recognize that $\frac{b}{\sqrt{ac}}$ is the correlation between the risk factors, you will see that in this two-dimensional example, the result comes out to be the same as our previous simple approach for getting correlated random numbers.

As a further example, recall the statistics of the risk factors for our example of the 100-pound bond:

$$\sigma_{r_p} = 0.5\%$$

$$\sigma_{FX} = 0.02$$

$$\rho_{FX,r_p} = -0.6$$

For this example, the covariance and Cholesky matrices are as follows:

$$C = \begin{bmatrix} 0.0004 & -0.00006 \\ -0.00006 & 0.000025 \end{bmatrix}$$

$$A = \begin{bmatrix} 0.02 & -0.003 \\ 0 & 0.004 \end{bmatrix}$$

This gives us the following equations for changes in the risk factors:

$$\delta FX = 0.02 \times z_1$$

$$\delta r_p = -0.003 \times z_1 + 0.004 \times z_2$$

In the two-dimensional example above, we had two risk factors and could easily calculate the Cholesky decomposition by hand. For a larger number of risk factors, the equations become more tedious, but many software packages include Cholesky decomposition. If you need to program a Cholesky decomposition, you can find suitable algorithms in Numerical Recipes.[1]

Cholesky decomposition is relatively straightforward to program, but the algorithm used to find the Cholesky matrix does not work if the matrix is not positive definite. To be positive definite, all the Eigenvalues (see below) of the covariance matrix must be positive. In practical terms, this means that none of the risk factors can have a perfect correlation with another factor. This condition often breaks down when constructing covariance matrices, either because there is not enough historical data to show that variables are independent, or because of small errors in the data. In practice, Cholesky decomposition tends to fail if there are more than 10 to 20 risk factors in the covariance matrix.

Eigenvalue Decomposition

The alternative to Cholesky decomposition is Eigenvalue decomposition, which is also known as Principal Components analysis. It is more difficult to program than Cholesky decomposition, but it will work for covariance matrices that are not positive definite. This means that it will work for covariance matrices with hundreds of risk factors. Eigenvalue decomposition only fails if different parts of the matrix were built with data from different time periods (because inconsistencies in the data may cause negative variances for some of the principal components). Eigenvalue decomposition also has the advantage that it can give intuitive insights into the structure of the random risk factors, allowing us to identify the main drivers of risk. This can help us reduce the number of simulations needed.

Eigenvalue decomposition works by looking for two matrices, Λ and E, to satisfy the following equation:

$$C = E^T \Lambda E$$

C is the covariance matrix. Λ is a square matrix in which all the elements other than the main diagonal are zero:

$$\Lambda = \begin{bmatrix} \lambda_1 & 0 & 0 & 0 \\ 0 & \lambda_2 & 0 & 0 \\ 0 & 0 & \ddots & 0 \\ 0 & 0 & 0 & \lambda_N \end{bmatrix}$$

E is such that when it is multiplied by its transpose, the result is the identity matrix:

$$I = E^T E$$

Because Λ is diagonal, it can easily be broken into two parts. This allows us to decompose the covariance matrix:

$$C = B^T B$$

$$B = \Lambda^{1/2} E$$

$$\Lambda^{1/2} = \begin{bmatrix} \sqrt{\lambda_1} & 0 & & 0 \\ 0 & \sqrt{\lambda_2} & & 0 \\ & & \ddots & \\ 0 & 0 & & \sqrt{\lambda_N} \end{bmatrix}$$

$$E = \begin{bmatrix} e_{11} & e_{12} & & e_{1N} \\ e_{21} & e_{22} & & e_{2N} \\ & & \ddots & \\ e_{N1} & e_{N2} & & e_{NN} \end{bmatrix}$$

To generate correlated random numbers, we use the matrix B from Eigenvalue decomposition in the same way as the A matrix obtained from Cholesky decomposition:

$$F = ZB$$

$$[\delta f_A \quad \delta f_B] = [z_1 \quad z_2] \begin{bmatrix} e_{11}\sqrt{\lambda_1} & e_{12}\sqrt{\lambda_1} \\ e_{21}\sqrt{\lambda_2} & e_{22}\sqrt{\lambda_2} \end{bmatrix}$$

As an example, for our two-dimensional bond example, the results are as follows:

$$[\delta FX \quad \delta r_p] = [z_1 \quad z_2] \begin{bmatrix} 0.004 & 0 \\ 0 & 0.02 \end{bmatrix} \begin{bmatrix} 0.154 & 0.988 \\ 0.988 & -0.154 \end{bmatrix}$$

Which gives this result after multiplying out the matrices:

$$\delta FX = -0.154 \times 0.004 \times z_1 + 0.02 \times 0.988 \times z_2$$

$$\delta r_p = 0.004 \times 0.988 \times z_1 - 0.02 \times 0.154 \times z_2$$

For those with some experience with matrix math, Appendix D digs deeper into why it should be that Eigenvalue decomposition produces properly correlated numbers.

The Eigen vectors also have special properties that are useful for speeding up Monte Carlo evaluations. Each Eigen vector defines a market movement that is by definition independent of the other movements (due to the requirement that $I = E^T E$). The best illustration of the special properties of Eigen vectors is the Eigenvalue decomposition of a yield curve.

Let us consider the U.S. government yield curve. Below, there is the standard deviation (S), correlation (R) and covariance (C) matrices for absolute changes in the 3-month, 1-year, 5-year and 20-year interest rates. This is followed by the calculation of the B matrix, which is very interesting:

$$S = \begin{bmatrix} 0.051 & 0.052 & 0.061 & 0.054 \end{bmatrix}$$

$$R = \begin{bmatrix} 1 & 0.61 & 0.42 & 0.31 \\ 0.61 & 1 & 0.83 & 0.67 \\ 0.42 & 0.83 & 1 & 0.88 \\ 0.31 & 0.67 & 0.88 & 1 \end{bmatrix}$$

$$C = S^T R S$$

$$= \begin{bmatrix} 0.0026 & 0.0016 & 0.0013 & 0.0008 \\ 0.0016 & 0.0027 & 0.0026 & 0.0019 \\ 0.0013 & 0.0026 & 0.0038 & 0.0029 \\ 0.0008 & 0.0019 & 0.0029 & 0.0029 \end{bmatrix}$$

The Eigenvalue decomposition of C is as follows:

$$\Lambda^{1/2} = \begin{bmatrix} 0.016 & 0 & 0 & 0 \\ 0 & 0.025 & 0 & 0 \\ 0 & 0 & 0.046 & 0 \\ 0 & 0 & 0 & 0.094 \end{bmatrix}$$

$$E = \begin{bmatrix} 0.097 & -0.480 & 0.724 & -0.486 \\ 0.407 & -0.694 & -0.124 & 0.581 \\ -0.847 & -0.195 & 0.264 & 0.417 \\ 0.327 & 0.500 & 0.625 & 0.502 \end{bmatrix}$$

$$B = \Lambda^{1/2} E$$

$$= \begin{bmatrix} 0.00 & -0.01 & 0.01 & -0.008 \\ 0.01 & -0.02 & 0.00 & 0.01 \\ -0.04 & -0.01 & 0.01 & 0.02 \\ 0.03 & 0.06 & 0.06 & 0.05 \end{bmatrix}$$

Let us look at how B would be used to create random scenarios:

$$\begin{bmatrix} \delta r_{3mo} & \delta r_{1yr} & \delta r_{5yr} & \delta r_{20yr} \end{bmatrix} = \begin{bmatrix} z_1 & z_2 & z_3 & z_4 \end{bmatrix} \begin{bmatrix} 0.00 & -0.01 & 0.01 & -0.01 \\ 0.01 & -0.02 & 0.00 & 0.01 \\ -0.04 & -0.01 & 0.01 & 0.02 \\ 0.03 & 0.05 & 0.06 & 0.05 \end{bmatrix}$$

Notice that the rows of B describe changes in the rates that are a shift, twist, flex, and wiggle:

$$\text{Wiggle} = z_1 \begin{bmatrix} 0.01 & -0.01 & 0.01 & -0.01 \end{bmatrix}$$

$$\text{Flex} = z_2 \begin{bmatrix} 0.01 & -0.02 & 0.00 & 0.01 \end{bmatrix}$$

$$\text{Twist} = z_3 \begin{bmatrix} -0.04 & -0.01 & 0.01 & 0.02 \end{bmatrix}$$

$$\text{Shift} = z_4 \begin{bmatrix} 0.03 & 0.05 & 0.06 & 0.05 \end{bmatrix}$$

For a given change in the random factor (z), the shift has the strongest effect, and the wiggle is the weakest.

   If z_4 increases by 1, all the rates shift up by the amount shown on the bottom row of the B matrix; i.e., the 3-month rate will shift up by 3bps, the 1-year rate will shift up by 5bps, the 5-year rate will shift up by 6bps, and the 20-year rate will shift up by 5bps. When z_3 increases by 1, the 3-month and 1-year rates twist down, but the 5-year and 20-year rates twist up, according to the third row of the matrix. When z_2 increases by 1, the 1-year rate flexes down a little, but the other rates stay the same or increase slightly, as in the second row of B. When z_1 increases by 1, there is a small wiggle down of the 1- and 20-year rates, and a wiggle up of the 3-month and 5-year rates. In summary, this matrix shows us the extent to which changes in the yield curve can be regarded as independent movements of shift, twist, flex, and wiggle.

   Figure 6-5 plots the 4 rows of the B matrix for U.S. interest rates; these are the principal components of any rate shift. Notice that for a 1-unit change in the random z factor, the shift has the highest impact, and the wiggle has very little influence on the final shape. If we kept z_1, and z_2 constant, and just let z_3 and z_4 be random, we would capture most of the uncertainty in rates because the flex and wiggle are comparatively small.

Improving the Speed of Monte Carlo Computation

Monte Carlo evaluation is generally considered to be computationally intensive; i.e., it takes a long time to compute the results, compared with Parametric VaR. Creating the random scenarios for the risk factors takes relatively little time to run once it is programmed. The slow part of running Monte Carlo VaR is doing the pricing of all instruments under each scenario. Several techniques have been developed to reduce the computation time. Here, we will discuss four of the most popular:

  • Parallel processing
  • Stabilization of results
  • Variance-reduction techniques
  • Approximate pricing

Let's look at each in more detail:

FIGURE 6-5

Principal Component Analysis of the U.S. Yield Curve

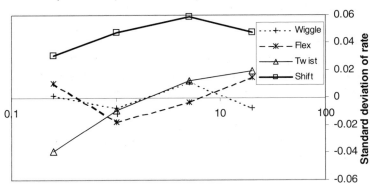

Maturity point in the yield curve (years)

This figure plots the four rows of the B matrix for the U.S. interest rates. In a Monte Carlo simulation, each row is multiplied by a separate random number drawn from a Standard Normal distribution. And then the rows are added together. The result is a set of scenarios which tend to have large shifts, moderate twists, small flexing, and even smaller wiggle.

Parallel Processing

Parallel processing simply uses several computers and simultaneously evaluates different groups of scenarios or instruments on each. Some care has to be taken to distribute the processes and collate the results, but this is relatively easy. The main drawback is the cost of hardware.

Stabilization of Results

Stabilization of results reduces the number of scenarios that need to be run. If we allow the scenarios to be completely different on one day compared with the next, it is quite likely that the results will change not because there has been any fundamental change in the risk, but because different random scenarios have been tested. The common approach to reducing this problem is to run many scenarios each day to "average out" the random fluctuations.

An alternative approach is to run fewer scenarios but fix the Normally distributed, independent, random numbers that are used to create the scenarios and only allow the correlation matrix and portfolio composition to change from day to day. The consequence is that the results only change due to real market and portfolio changes.

The random numbers can be fixed either by generating the numbers once and storing them, or by using the same seed number to start the random sequence each day. Although fixing the random numbers sounds straightforward, it does require discipline when writing the program to ensure that the same random number will be used in the same place for every run.

There is a slight disadvantage to fixing the random numbers because there is less opportunity to test obscure scenarios that may cause unusual losses. As a compromise, you may allow a proportion of the random numbers to change each day.

Variance-Reduction Techniques

Variance-reduction techniques choose the numbers to be more evenly distributed than in the pure random case. This reduces the randomness in the results and allows us to use fewer scenarios. In some cases, the number of scenarios may be reduced by a factor of 10 to 100 while still maintaining the same accuracy.

There are a number of techniques that do this. The most easily implemented techniques are Antithetic sampling, Stratification, Importance sampling, and the Latin Hypercube. They are briefly outlined below.

Antithetic sampling is the easiest variance reduction technique. If we wanted to create N random scenarios, we would first create $N/2$ random, normally distributed numbers as usual, then take the negative of all those random numbers to be the second set of scenarios. This guarantees that the overall set of random numbers will be perfectly balanced about the mean.

For Stratification, we divide the sample space into N cells and randomly take a single sample from within each cell. This ensures that the samples will be well-spread throughout the sample space.

As an example, consider two risk factors, f_A and f_B, whose possible values are uniformly distributed between zero and one. Here we have a two-dimensional sample space. Assume that we want to take four samples from this space. In this case, we would cut each dimension in two and create our four samples as follows:

Sample 1

$$f_{A,1} = 0.5 \times u, \quad u \sim U(0,1)$$
$$f_{B,1} = 0.5 \times u, \quad u \sim U(0,1)$$

Sample 2

$$f_{A,2} = 0.5 + 0.5 \times u, \quad u \sim U(0,1)$$
$$f_{B,2} = 0.5 \times u, \quad u \sim U(0,1)$$

Sample 3

$$f_{A,3} = 0.5 \times u, \quad u \sim U(0,1)$$
$$f_{B,3} = 0.5 + 0.5 \times u, \quad u \sim U(0,1)$$

Sample 4

$$f_{A,4} = 0.5 + 0.5 \times u, \quad u \sim U(0,1)$$
$$f_{B,4} = 0.5 + 0.5 \times u, \quad u \sim U(0,1)$$

Here, $u \sim U(0,1)$ means that u is a random number sampled from a uniform distribution between zero and one. Figure 6-6 sketches typical resulting samples.

In general, it is necessary to ensure that there is an equal probability of a sample occurring in each cell. If we wanted to create variables with a distribution other than uniform, we first create uniform, stratified, random numbers as above and then transform them to have the distribution that we need. The transformation is done by using the inverse of the cumulative probability function to map from a uniform distribution to the required distribution. For a Normal distribution, this mapping is sketched in Figure 6-7. The symbol $N()$ denotes a Normal distribution, and Φ denotes a Standard Normal distribution with a mean of zero and standard deviation of one.

In a spreadsheet application, such as Microsoft's Excel, uniformly distributed, random numbers can be created using the command "rand()". These can be converted into having a standard Normal distribution using the command "Norminv(rand(),0,1)". If we were stratifying one random factor into four strata, we could create four stratified, random numbers from the following commands:

$$Z1 = \text{Norminv}(0.00 + 0.25 * \text{rand}(), 0, 1)$$
$$Z2 = \text{Norminv}(0.25 + 0.25 * \text{rand}(), 0, 1)$$
$$Z3 = \text{Norminv}(0.50 + 0.25 * \text{rand}(), 0, 1)$$
$$Z4 = \text{Norminv}(0.75 + 0.25 * \text{rand}(), 0, 1)$$

Let us move on to Importance sampling. Importance sampling biases the selection of random numbers towards the places that are of most importance to us, e.g., crises in the tails of the distribution. This can be done by creating random numbers that have a higher standard deviation than the true risk factors. Once the results have been calculated, their probability is adjusted according to the relative probabilities of the true distribution and the sample distribution.

The Latin Hypercube is most useful if there are only one or two risk factors that are particularly important in causing losses. The Latin Hypercube technique starts in a

FIGURE 6-6

Results from Stratified Sampling

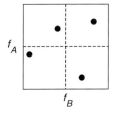

f_A

f_B

Stratified sampling is a variance-reduction technique enabling selected numbers to be more evenly distributed than those in the pure random case.

FIGURE 6-7

Creation of a Normally Distributed Variable from a Uniformly Distributed
Variable

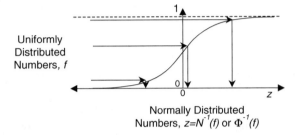

Uniformly
Distributed
Numbers, f

Normally Distributed
Numbers, $z=N^{-1}(f)$ or $\Phi^{-1}(f)$

Here, the set of uniformly distributed, random numbers (f) are put into the inverse of the Normal distribution to
create a set of Normally distributed numbers (z). If a number in the uniform set is close to zero, it will produce
a number close to negative infinity in the Normal set. A uniform number close to 0.5 becomes close to zero,
and a uniform number close to one becomes close to infinity.

similar way to Stratified sampling in that we divide each dimension into a number of
segments. However, we then take only one sample from each segment. The result is
illustrated in Figure 6-8. Notice that each dimension is very finely covered, but not all
combinations of the two variables are explored.

In using Variance reduction, it is important to note that as the number of risk
factors increases, it becomes more difficult to create well-balanced pseudorandom numbers. A common technique, therefore, is to concentrate the random numbers on the most
important risk factors and let the lesser factors be purely random. If Eigen-value decomposition has been used, the most important risk factors are the ones corresponding to
the largest element in the Λ matrix.

FIGURE 6-8

Results from a Latin Hypercube

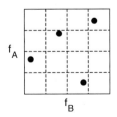

f_A

f_B

The Latin Hypercube ensures that samples do not overlap in any dimension.

Approximate Pricing

Approximate pricing reduces the computation time for each instrument by simply taking less time to evaluate each scenario. This is done by using simple models that are not as accurate, but can be run quickly. A typical example would be to use the Black-Scholes equation to approximate the value of an option that would be more accurately priced by binomial trees.

SUMMARY

In this chapter, we explained how to calculate VaR using three methods that are in common use: Parametric VaR, Historical simulation, and Monte Carlo simulation. Next, we will explain how to attribute VaR to the source of each risk.

APPENDIX A: THE BINNING OF CASH FLOWS

As discussed earlier in the chapter, binning is important for discounting cash flows because it enables us to reduce the amount of data that we need to handle. Without binning, we would need to store the yield curve and rate volatilities for every day until the final cash flow in the portfolio was due, typically around 30 years. By binning, we group all future cash flows onto a limited number of points on the yield curve, e.g., overnight, 3 months, 6 months, 1 year, 2 years, 5 years, 10 years, and 30 years. A crude way of doing this would be to move every cash flow to the nearest point on the yield curve, e.g., a payment of $100 in 4 years would be considered to be a payment of $100 at 5 years; however, this would distort measures such as duration. An alternative is to represent a single, true cash flow as a series of fictitious cash flows spread over several points on the yield curve.

In binning the cash flows, we typically try to preserve some combination of the cash-flow amount, present value, and duration. If we want to meet all three conditions, we need to have three possible variables, i.e., cash flows at three different points on the yield curve. This is generally considered to be excessive. Instead, we just try to satisfy two of the conditions by altering the cash flows at the two points just before and after the true cash flow.

Let us consider mapping a cash flow, C_5, that is expected to occur five months from now. This will be represented by cash flows at the three-month and six-month points.

If we wish to preserve the cash flow and duration, we must choose the cash flows at the three-month and six-month points (C_3 and C_6) to set the following to be equal:

$$C_5 = C_3 + C_6$$

$$D_5 = D_3 + D_6$$

$$D_5 = \frac{-5/12C_5}{(1+r_5)^{17/12}}, \quad D_3 = \frac{-3/12C_5}{(1+r_5)^{15/12}}, \quad D_6 = \frac{-6/12C_5}{(1+r_5)^{18/12}}$$

As an example, assume that the cash flow at 5 months is $100, the 3-month rate is 5%, the 5-month rate is 5.1%, and the 6-month rate is 5.15%; then the equations become:

$$\text{Cash flow: } 100 = C_3 + C_6$$

$$\text{Duration: } -0.388 \times 100 = -0.235 \times C_3 - 0.464 \times C_6$$

This can be solved to obtain the required dummy cash flows:

$$C_3 = \$33.2$$

$$C_6 = \$66.8$$

APPENDIX B: EQUATIONS FOR PARAMETRIC VAR WORKED OUT IN TERMS OF RETURNS

In the introduction to Parametric VaR, the equations were worked out in terms of absolute changes in the risk factors. For example, if the exchange rate went from 1.5 to 1.6, we considered that to be a change of 0.1 rather than a relative change of 7%. Relative changes are also called "returns." Working out the equations in terms of relative changes is a little more complex, but makes the results more accurate because the relative changes typically have a more Normal distribution than the absolute changes. This appendix shows how our previous example would be modified to use relative changes.

Parametric VaR: Example 3

The example is a bond denominated in British pounds with a single payment and owned by a U.S. bank. As it is held by a U.S. bank, the value should be converted to dollars. The value of the bond in dollars is the value in pounds multiplied by the FX rate:

$$PV_\$ = FX \times PV_p$$

$$= FX \frac{C_p}{\left(1 + r_p\right)^t}$$

The change in value due to both a change in rates and a change in FX is given by the sum of individual changes:

$$\Delta PV_\$ = \frac{C_p}{\left(1 + r_p\right)^t} \Delta FX + FX \frac{-tC_p}{\left(1 + r_p\right)^{t+1}} \Delta r_p$$

We can divide and multiply this equation by the current rates to get an expression in terms of returns:

$$\Delta PV_\$ = \frac{C_p}{\left(1 + r_p\right)^t} FX \left(\frac{\Delta FX}{FX}\right) + FX \frac{-tC_p}{\left(1 + r_p\right)^{t+1}} r_p \left(\frac{\Delta r_p}{r_p}\right)$$

We now define the derivative vectors to include multiplication by the current rate:

$$d_{FX} = \frac{C_p}{\left(1 + r_p\right)^t} FX$$

$$d_{r_p} = FX \frac{-tC_p}{\left(1 + r_p\right)^{t+1}} r_p$$

The rest of the VaR calculation continues as before but now using the standard deviations of the historical returns rather than the absolute values:

$$\Delta r_{p,t} = r_{p,t} - r_{p,t-1}$$

$$\Delta FX_t = FX_t - FX_{t-1}$$

$$\sigma_{FX}^2 = \frac{1}{N-1} \sum_{t=1}^{N} \left(\frac{\Delta FX_t}{FX_t}\right)^2$$

$$\sigma_{r_p}^2 = \frac{1}{N-1} \sum_{t=1}^{N} \left(\frac{\Delta r_{p,t}}{r_{p,t}}\right)^2$$

$$\sigma_{FX,r_p}^2 = \frac{1}{N-1} \sum_{t=1}^{N} \left(\frac{\Delta r_{p,t}}{r_{p,t}} \frac{\Delta FX_t}{FX_t}\right)$$

Note that the variance and covariance equations neglect the subtraction of the small mean, which for daily rate changes is usually a reasonable assumption. If we wished to add the extra complication of subtracting the mean, we would use the following:

$$\sigma_{FX}^2 = \frac{1}{N-1} \sum_{t=1}^{N} \left[\frac{\Delta FX_t}{FX_t} - \overline{\left(\frac{\Delta FX_t}{FX_t}\right)}\right]^2$$

$$\sigma_{r_p}^2 = \frac{1}{N-1} \sum_{t=1}^{N} \left[\frac{\Delta r_{p,t}}{r_{p,t}} - \overline{\left(\frac{\Delta r_{p,t}}{r_{p,t}}\right)}\right]^2$$

$$\sigma_{FX,r_p}^2 = \frac{1}{N-1} \sum_{t=1}^{N} \left[\left(\frac{\Delta r_{p,t}}{r_{p,t}} - \overline{\left(\frac{\Delta r_{p,t}}{r_{p,t}}\right)}\right)\left(\frac{\Delta FX_t}{FX_t} - \overline{\left(\frac{\Delta FX_t}{FX_t}\right)}\right)\right]$$

APPENDIX C: CONSTRUCTION OF COVARIANCE MATRICES

The construction of a covariance matrix is central to both Parametric VaR and Monte Carlo VaR. There are two approaches to constructing the matrix that are in common use: the random walk and the exponentially weighted moving average.

The random-walk assumption for the Covariance Matrix is that the correlations and standard deviations are stable over time. This allows us to use the usual calculation for the variances and covariances:

$$\sigma_{i,j}^2 = \frac{1}{T-1} \sum_{t=1}^{T} \left(x_{i,t} - \overline{x_i} \right)^2$$

$$\sigma_{i,j}^2 = \frac{1}{T-1} \sum_{t=1}^{T} \left(x_{i,t} - \overline{x_i} \right) \left(x_{j,t} - \overline{x_j} \right)$$

Here, $x_{i,t}$ represents risk factor i at time t. If VaR is being calculated using absolute changes, then $x_{i,t}$ is simply the change in the factor f_i from day $t-1$ to day t:

$$x_{i,t} = f_{i,t} - f_{i,t-1}$$

If VaR is being calculated using relative changes, then $x_{i,t}$ is the relative change:

$$x_{i,t} = \left(\frac{f_{i,t} - f_{i,t-1}}{f_{i,t-1}} \right)$$

In practice, the mean change is much smaller than the standard deviation of the change and can be neglected with little loss of accuracy. Typically, between 180 and 250 days of historical data are used. Decreasing the number of days means that there are fewer samples for accurately estimating the parameters. However, increasing the number of days means including periods when market conditions could have been significantly different from today.

The Exponentially Weighted Moving Average (EWMA) is slightly more difficult to program but is better for estimating the latest covariances than the simple random walk, and has become an industry standard. The EWMA approach assumes that recent data gives better information about market conditions than past data. It therefore weights recent changes more heavily. The covariance is calculated recursively using yesterday's estimate of the covariance and today's market change, as follows:

$$\sigma_{i,j,T}^2 = (1 - \lambda) x_{i,T} x_{j,T} + \lambda \sigma_{i,j,T-1}^2$$

Here, λ is a decay factor, typically with a value between 0.9 and 0.99. $x_{i,T}$ is the market change for risk factor i on day t, and $\sigma_{i,j,T-1}^2$ is the previous day's estimate of the covariance between risk factors i and j. The above expression is equivalent to the weighted sum of the daily changes, as shown below:

$$\sigma_{i,j,T}^2 = (1 - \lambda) \sum_{t=0}^{N} \lambda^t x_{i,T-t} x_{j,T-t}$$

With λ equal to 0.9, today's data will have a weight of 0.1, and data from 20 days ago will have a weight of $(1 - \lambda)\lambda^{20}$, i.e., 0.012. With such a weighting, data from before 20 days has very little influence on the EWMA result, which means that the EWMA will be more responsive to changes in the market than the simple random-walk estimate.

APPENDIX D: PROOF THAT EIGENVALUE DECOMPOSITION GIVES THE REQUIRED COVARIANCE

If you want to dig deeper into why it should be that Eigenvalue decomposition produces properly correlated numbers, consider calculating the covariance of the random factors in F. The covariance of the random factors is given by the expected value of the outer product of F and its transpose:

$$C_F = E(F^T F)$$

We can now replace F with its value in terms of the results of the Eigenvalue decomposition, B, and the uncorrelated, random numbers, Z.

$$E(F^T F) = E(B^T Z^T Z B) = B^T E(Z^T Z)B$$

Z is a set of uncorrelated numbers with a standard deviation of one; therefore, $E(Z^T Z)$ is the identity matrix:

$$B^T E(Z^T Z)B = B^T IB = B^T B$$

$B^T B$ was constructed to equal the covariance matrix of historical changes in the original risk factors:

$$C = B^T B$$

Therefore, the covariance matrix of the newly generated, random numbers equals the covariance matrix of the historical data:

$$C_F = C$$

NOTE

1 *Numerical Recipes in C: The Art of Scientific Computing*, W. H. Press et al., Cambridge University Press, 1997.

Value-at-Risk Contribution

INTRODUCTION

In the previous chapter, we detailed alternative approaches for calculating the Value at Risk (VaR). It is now time to consider how the results can best be used to give management deep insights into the risks the bank is running. The output from a VaR calculation includes the following reports that can be used to identify the magnitude and source of each risk:

- Total VaR for the trading operation
- Stand-alone VaR for each subportfolio
- Stand-alone VaR for each risk factor
- Sensitivity to each risk factor
- VaR Contribution for each subportfolio
- VaR Contribution for each risk factor

The first four of these reports are generated easily from the analyses we discussed in the previous chapter. The total VaR is calculated by including all of the bank's instruments and risk factors. The stand-alone VaR for a subportfolio is the VaR that the portfolio would have if we ignored the rest of the bank. Similarly, the stand-alone VaR for each risk factor is calculated by setting the standard deviation on all the other risk factors equal to zero. The sensitivity of the value of the portfolio to changes in risk factors is given by the derivative vector that is used in Parametric VaR.

The main problem with the stand-alone VaR is that the sum of the stand-alone VaRs does not, in general, equal the total VaR. Also, the stand-alone VaR ignores the correlation with the rest of the portfolio. This is because the equation for the total VaR includes squaring all the stand-alone VaRs, including correlation, and later taking the square root. For clarity, consider the following Parametric VaR example for a portfolio with two subportfolios, A and B. Here, $SVaR$ represents the stand-alone VaR:

$$VaR_{Portfolio} = \sqrt{SVaR_A^2 + 2\rho_{AB}SVaR_A SVaR_B + SVaR_B^2}$$

The VaR Contribution (VaRC) technique is useful because it gives us a measure of risk for each individual subportfolio that includes the interportfolio correlation effects. Furthermore, VaRC is constructed so that the sum of VaRC for all the subportfolios equals the total VaR for the portfolio. This allows us to make straightforward statements such as, "The VaR for the bank is $8 million, caused by contributions of $2 million from the equities desk, $3 million from bonds, $2 million from FX, and $1 million from derivatives."

As explored in the following chapters, VaRC is also useful for allocating the bank's capital to those units causing the risk and for setting limits on the amount of risk that individual traders may take. The process used to define VaRC is the same as the process that is used later in the credit-risk chapters to define ULC, the Unexpected Loss Contribution.

This chapter will show the derivation of VaRC for individual risk factors and for individual subportfolios. We will show how VaRC can be calculated in algebraic, summation, and matrix forms. In each case, we will start with a portfolio of just two risks and then generalize to a portfolio of many risks.

Most of this analysis will be for VaRC derived from Parametric VaR. At the end of the chapter, we will also show how VaRC can be defined for Historical and Monte Carlo simulations.

DERIVATION OF VᴀRC IN ALGEBRAIC NOTATION

Consider a portfolio exposed to two sources of risk, A and B. The variance of the value of the portfolio will be equal to the sum of the variances caused by the two sources and the covariance between them:

$$\sigma_P^2 = \sigma_A^2 + 2\rho_{A,B}\sigma_A\sigma_B + \sigma_B^2$$

We can rearrange the terms in this equation to make them a sum of a factor multiplied by σ_A and one multiplied by σ_B:

$$\sigma_P^2 = \sigma_A(\sigma_A + \rho_{A,B}\sigma_B) + \sigma_B(\sigma_B + \rho_{A,B}\sigma_A)$$

If we divide both sides by the standard deviation of the portfolio, we get an additive equation for standard deviation:

$$\sigma_P = \sigma_A\left(\frac{\sigma_A + \rho_{A,B}\sigma_B}{\sigma_P}\right) + \sigma_B\left(\frac{\sigma_B + \rho_{A,B}\sigma_A}{\sigma_P}\right)$$

The terms within the brackets can be thought of as representing the average correlation between the given risk and the rest of the portfolio. In the Parametric approach, the 99% VaR is 2.32 times the standard deviation:

$$VaR_P = 2.32\sigma_P$$

$$= 2.32\sigma_A\left(\frac{\sigma_A + \rho_{A,B}\sigma_B}{\sigma_P}\right) + 2.32\sigma_B\left(\frac{\sigma_B + \rho_{A,B}\sigma_A}{\sigma_P}\right)$$

This allows us to define the VaR contributions for the two risks, A and B, such that they add up to the total VaR:

$$VaRC_A = 2.32\sigma_A\left(\frac{\sigma_A + \rho_{A,B}\sigma_B}{\sigma_P}\right)$$

$$VaRC_B = 2.32\sigma_B\left(\frac{\sigma_B + \rho_{A,B}\sigma_A}{\sigma_P}\right)$$

$$VaR_P = VaRC_A + VaRC_B$$

Note that each VaRC factor includes both the correlation with the other factors and the variance of the other factors. In Parametric VaR, consider that each variance is the sensitivity multiplied by the standard deviation of the risk factor:

$$\sigma_A = d_1\sigma_1$$

$$\sigma_B = d_2\sigma_2$$

With this substitution, the variance of the portfolio's value and VaRC are calculated as follows:

$$\sigma_P^2 = (d_1\sigma_1)^2 + 2\rho_{1,2}(d_1\sigma_1)(d_2\sigma_2) + (d_2\sigma_2)^2$$

$$VaRC_1 = 2.32 \times d_1\sigma_1\frac{[d_1\sigma_1 + \rho_{1,2}d_2\sigma_2]}{\sigma_P}$$

$$VaRC_2 = 2.32 \times d_2\sigma_2\frac{[d_2\sigma_2 + \rho_{1,2}d_1\sigma_1]}{\sigma_P}$$

In the bond example of the previous chapter, risk was caused by both the interest rate and FX rate, and we had the following values:

$$d_{FX} = 74.7$$

$$d_{r_p} = 563$$

$$\sigma_{FX} = 0.02$$

$$\sigma_{r_p} = 0.5\%$$

$$\rho_{FX,r_p} = -0.6$$

$$VaR = 9.05$$

$$\sigma_P = 3.09$$

With these values, you should find the following results for VaRC:

$$VaRC_{FX} = \$2.82$$

$$VaRC_{r_p} = \$6.21$$

These results show us that for this bond, there is twice as much risk caused by the interest-rate movements than by FX movements.

If we have more than two risk factors, we can go through the same process of grouping the terms to obtain the following result for VaRC:

$$VaRC_1 = 2.32d_1\sigma_1\left(\frac{d_1\sigma_1 + \rho_{1,2}d_2\sigma_2 + \cdots + \rho_{1,N}d_N\sigma_N}{\sigma_P}\right)$$

$$VaRC_N = 2.32d_N\sigma_N\left(\frac{\rho_{N,1}d_1\sigma_1 + \rho_{N,2}d_2\sigma_2 + \cdots + d_N\sigma_N}{\sigma_P}\right)$$

DERIVATION OF VaRC IN SUMMATION NOTATION

Summation notation can be useful if there are many risk factors because it can express long equations in a compact form. In many cases it is useful as a shorthand. In summation notation, VaR was previously written as follows:

$$\sigma_P^2 = \sum_{i=1}^{N}\sum_{j=1}^{N}\rho_{i,j}(d_j\sigma_j)(d_i\sigma_i)$$

We can again group and then divide by σ_P to get a series of terms that can be summed across i:

$$\sigma_P = \sum_{i=1}^{N}d_i\sigma_i \times \frac{\sum_{j=1}^{N}\rho_{ij}d_j\sigma_j}{\sigma_P}$$

For each i, the associated term defines the VaR contribution for factor i:

$$VaRC_i \equiv 2.32 \times d_i\sigma_i \times \frac{\sum_{j=1}^{N}\rho_{i,j}d_j\sigma_j}{\sigma_P}$$

DERIVATION OF VaRC IN MATRIX NOTATION

Matrix notation also gives a good shorthand way of writing equations. It also allows us to easily show how the VaRC can be calculated either for single risk factors affecting many positions or for single positions affected by many risk factors.

We can write the VaR equation for two risk factors in matrix notation as follows:

$$VaR = 2.32\sigma_P$$

$$\sigma_P^2 = DCD^T$$

$$D = [d_1 \quad d_2]$$

$$C = \begin{bmatrix} \sigma_1^2 & \rho_{1,2}\sigma_1\sigma_2 \\ \rho_{1,2}\sigma_1\sigma_2 & \sigma_1^2 \end{bmatrix}$$

To define VaRC, we can break D into two vectors corresponding to the sensitivity of the value to each of the risk factors:

$$D_1 = [d_1 \quad 0]$$

$$D_2 = [0 \quad d_2]$$

$$D = D_1 + D_2$$

The equation for variance can now be written as a sum:

$$\sigma_P^2 = DCD^T$$

$$\sigma_P^2 = (D_1 + D_2)CD^T$$

$$= D_1CD^T + D_2CD^T$$

The standard deviation can be defined as either the square root of the variance, or as the variance divided by the standard deviation:

$$\sigma_P = \sqrt{DCD^T}$$

$$\sigma_P = \frac{DCD^T}{\sigma_P}$$

By using both of these definitions, we can write the standard deviation in terms of D and C:

$$\sigma_P = \frac{DCD^T}{\sqrt{DCD^T}}$$

Now we can split apart the numerator to define VaRC:

$$\sigma_P = \frac{D_1CD^T}{\sqrt{DCD^T}} + \frac{D_2CD^T}{\sqrt{DCD^T}}$$

$$VaRC_1 \equiv 2.32\frac{D_1CD^T}{\sqrt{DCD^T}}$$

$$VaRC_2 \equiv 2.32\frac{D_2CD^T}{\sqrt{DCD^T}}$$

$$VaR = VaRC_1 + VaRC_2$$

In general, if we wish to calculate VaRC with respect to many risk factors, we do so by breaking down the sensitivity vector into a series of vectors with all the elements equal to zero other than the element corresponding to the risk factor of interest:

$$D = [d_1 \quad d_2 \quad \cdots \quad d_N]$$
$$D_1 = [d_1 \quad 0 \quad \cdots \quad 0]$$
$$D_2 = [0 \quad d_2 \quad \cdots \quad 0]$$
$$\vdots$$
$$D_N = [0 \quad 0 \quad \cdots \quad d_N]$$

Example of Calculating VaRC Using Matrix Notation

In the earlier chapter, we calculated VaR for a Sterling-denominated bond held by a U.S. bank. This bond has two risk factors: the exchange rate and the interest rate. In matrix notation, the VaRC for the bond is derived as follows. First, we break apart the sensitivity vector D:

$$D = [d_{FX} \quad d_{r_p}]$$
$$D_{FX} = [d_{FX} \quad 0]$$
$$D_{r_p} = [0 \quad d_{r_p}]$$
$$C = \begin{bmatrix} \sigma_{FX}^2 & \sigma_{FX}\sigma_{r_p}\rho_{FX,r_p} \\ \sigma_{FX}\sigma_{r_p}\rho_{FX,r_p} & \sigma_{r_p}^2 \end{bmatrix}$$

Then, put these vectors into our definitions for VaRC:

$$VaR = 2.32\frac{D_{FX}CD^T}{\sqrt{DCD^T}} + 2.32\frac{D_{r_p}CD^T}{\sqrt{DCD^T}}$$

From the previous chapter, the numerical values are as follows:

$$D = [74.7 \quad -563]$$
$$D_{FX} = [74.7 \quad 0]$$
$$D_{rp} = [0 \quad -563]$$
$$C = \begin{bmatrix} 0.0004 & -0.00006 \\ = -0.00006 & 0.000025 \end{bmatrix}$$
$$D^T = \begin{bmatrix} 74.7 \\ -563 \end{bmatrix}$$

After carrying out the matrix multiplications, we get the results for the total VaR and VaRC:

$$VaR = \$9.05$$

$$VaRC_{FX} = \$2.82$$

$$VaRC_{rp} = \$6.21$$

VᴀRC CALCULATED FOR SUBPORTFOLIOS

In the derivation above, we showed the VaR Contribution for different risk factors. VaRC can also be calculated for different business units or subportfolios, each of which may share some risk factors with the other desks. This is most easily shown in matrix notation. In this case, we break down the D vector into the sensitivity vector for each subportfolio. Consider the following bank consisting of a number of portfolios, a to z. The sensitivity vector for the bank as a whole has an element for each of the N risk factors:

$$D = \begin{bmatrix} d_1 & d_2 & \cdots & d_N \end{bmatrix}$$

Each sensitivity is the sum of the sensitivities of each of the subportfolios, a to z:

$$d_1 = d_{1,a} + d_{1,b} + \cdots + d_{1,z}$$

$$d_N = d_{N,a} + d_{N,b} + \cdots + d_{N,z}$$

Here, $d_{1,a}$ is the derivative of the value of subportfolio a with respect to risk factor 1. We can put the sensitivity of each subportfolio into separate vectors:

$$D_a = \begin{bmatrix} d_{1,a} & d_{2,a} & \cdots & d_{N,a} \end{bmatrix}$$

$$D_b = \begin{bmatrix} d_{1,b} & d_{2,b} & \cdots & d_{N,b} \end{bmatrix}$$

$$\vdots$$

$$D_z = \begin{bmatrix} d_{1,z} & d_{2,z} & \cdots & d_{N,z} \end{bmatrix}$$

The sensitivity vector for the whole bank will equal the sum of the sensitivity vectors for the subportfolios:

$$D = D_a + D_b + \cdots D_z$$

It is equivalent to calculate the portfolio variance in either of the following ways:

$$\sigma_P^2 = DCD^T$$

$$= (D_a + D_b + \cdots D_z)CD^T$$

From this, we can use the same process as we used for the risk factors to now define VaRC for the subportfolios:

$$VaRC_a = \frac{2.32 \times D_a CD^T}{\sqrt{DCD^T}}$$

As an example, consider a portfolio that is the sum of two positions: our usual sterling bond and 100 pounds of cash. The derivative vector for the bond position is:

$$D_{Bond} = \begin{bmatrix} d_{Bond,FX} & d_{Bond,r_p} \end{bmatrix}$$

And the vector for the cash is:

$$D_{Cash} = \begin{bmatrix} d_{Cash,FX} & 0 \end{bmatrix}$$

The vector for the combined position is the sum of the individual vectors:

$$D = \begin{bmatrix} d_{Bond,FX} + d_{Cash,FX} & d_{Bond,r_p} \end{bmatrix}$$

From this, we can calculate VaR and VaRC:

$$VaR = 2.32\sqrt{DCD^T}$$

$$VaRC_{Bond} = \frac{2.32 \times D_{Bond}CD^T}{\sqrt{DCD^T}}$$

$$VaRC_{Cash} = \frac{2.32 \times D_{Cash}CD^T}{\sqrt{DCD^T}}$$

For our example, the numerical values are as follows:

$$D = \begin{bmatrix} 174.7 & -563 \end{bmatrix}$$

$$D_{Bond} = \begin{bmatrix} 74.7 & -563 \end{bmatrix}$$

$$D_{Cash} = \begin{bmatrix} 100 & 0 \end{bmatrix}$$

$$C = \begin{bmatrix} 0.0004 & -0.00006 \\ -0.00006 & 0.000025 \end{bmatrix}$$

$$VaR = \$13.12$$

$$VaRC_{Bond} = \$8.86$$

$$VaRC_{Cash} = \$4.26$$

CALCULATING VaRC WHEN USING MONTE CARLO OR HISTORICAL SIMULATION

With the Monte Carlo and Historical simulation methods, we can calculate a VaRC by going through all the simulation results and examining all the scenarios in which the VaR is exceeded by the experienced losses. For example, if we run 5000 scenarios, the 99% VaR would be defined by the 50th-worst result. VaRC can be calculated using these 50 cases when the losses equal or exceed the VaR.

On each occasion when the VaR is exceeded, we record the losses from the individual position. This gives the percentage contribution of each position to the portfolio's loss in those particularly bad scenarios:

$$\%Contribution\ of\ Position_i = \frac{\sum[Loss_i|\left(Loss_p > VaR\right)]}{\sum\left[Loss_p|\left(Loss_p > VaR\right)\right]}$$

Where $[Loss_i|(Loss_p > VaR_p)]$ represents the loss from position i, given that the portfolio loss is greater than the portfolio VaR.

We then define the VaR Contribution in monetary terms for position i to be the total VaR for the portfolio (VaR_p) multiplied by the percentage contribution of the position:

$$VaRC_i = VaR_p \times \%Contribution\ of\ Position_i$$

SUMMARY

This chapter explained the derivation of VaRC for individual risk factors and individual subportfolios. It also showed how VaRC can be calculated in algebraic, summation, or matrix form. Next, we will explore the tests that should be carried out on VaR calculators to ensure their validity.

CHAPTER 8

Testing VaR Results to Ensure Proper Risk Measurement

INTRODUCTION

Up to this point, we have discussed how positions change value, and have used relatively complicated math to calculate the statistics of those changes. This has enabled us to construct estimates of the probability distributions of the future losses and therefore estimate VaR. Now testing is required to tie the results back to reality and give confidence that VaR is a true measure of the risks. This is especially important now that the Basel Committee allows banks to use their own VaR models to assess the amount of regulatory capital that they hold for market risks. The goal of this chapter is to detail the tests that should be carried out on VaR calculators to ensure their validity.

VaR-TESTING METHODOLOGIES

There are three different types of tests that should be carried out on the results generated from a VaR calculator:

- Software-installation test
- Profit-and-Loss (P&L) reconciliation test
- Modeled-probability-distribution back-test

Software Installation Test

Installation testing is carried out by the risk measurement group after the initial installation of the calculator, and whenever changes are made to the software. The purpose of the test is to ensure that the results coming from the software are in accordance with the equations that the risk management group thinks the software embodies, i.e., to make sure there are no mistakes in the code.

A typical approach is to calculate the VaR for different portfolios, covering all the traded-instrument types, and compare the results with a manual, spreadsheet calculation. Another approach is to set up a series of stress tests, changing a whole series of parameters and ensuring that the results change as expected.

P&L Reconciliation Test

The P&L test is carried out daily by the risk measurement group in conjunction with the finance and operations groups. As part of the VaR calculations, the software should value the current position. Changes in the value should closely match changes in the P&L that are reported in the accounting systems. This ensures that all the positions have been included, and the valuations are reasonably accurate.

This reconciliation is made difficult because discrepancies can arise from many sources, including:

- Positions that were recognized in the accounting system but missed by the VaR calculator.
- The VaR calculator's inability to capture intraday changes in market values and consequent changes in cash balances. For example, if a stock price rose during the day and the trader sold the stock, the amount of cash received by the accounting system would be more than would be expected by the calculator.
- Different sources of market data being fed to the calculator and accounting systems, e.g., the accounting system valuing the portfolio according to prices at mid-day and the calculator using prices at the end of the day.
- Inaccurate valuation models (e.g., using Black-Scholes for pricing complex options).

Significant discrepancies between the estimated P&L from the VaR calculator and the actual P&L from the accounting system indicate a problem. These problems are most often caused by faulty pricing models in the calculator or the mistake of loading only a few of the bank's positions into the VaR calculator. This can be caused by a broken data link to some of the position-reporting systems.

If the P&L can be well reconciled to the changes in value predicted by the calculator, we can be reasonably sure that the calculator is valuing the bank's positions correctly. However, the purpose of a VaR calculator is not only to assess the value, but also to assess the probability distribution of possible value *changes*. Checking this probability distribution requires a more complex test.

Back-Testing the Modeled Probability Distribution

Back-testing requires many days of data and is therefore only carried out monthly or quarterly. The purpose of this test is to make sure that the probability distribution (e.g., the VaR) is consistent with actual losses. This is checked through back-testing. Back-testing compares the loss on any given day with the VaR predicted for that day. Figure 8-1 illustrates VaR and the experienced losses over 100 days. The VaR changes slowly from day to day as positions change and as the market volatility changes. The P&L jumps about depending on the actual trading results each day.

Let us define an *exception* to mean any day in which the actual P&L fell below the calculated confidence interval for the daily VaR. In 100 trading days, we would expect 1 exception (as on day 73 in the figure). In a year of 250 trading days, we would expect 2 to 3 exceptions.

If it was the case that we always got a representative sample, then we could say that our VaR was a good representation of the actual distribution if we only experience exceptions 1% of the time. If we experience exceptions more or less often, we would conclude that the VaR was not an accurate representation of the distribution of losses.

Unfortunately, there is additional complication because the number of exceptions is in itself a random number. Even if the VaR perfectly represents the probability distribution of losses, sometimes the bank will be lucky and the random market movements will cause fewer losses than usual; sometimes they will be unlucky and suffer many losses. This uncertainty in sampling means that it is difficult to tell whether the experienced number of exceptions is due to a poor model or to bad luck.

Fortunately, there is a framework to calculate the probability of having a given number of exceptions. The exceptions are a binomial variable. Binomial variables are those that can have a value of zero or one. Exceptions are binomial because on any given day there either is or is not an exception. If the VaR calculator is correct, then on each day there is a 1% chance of an exception and a 99% chance of there being no exception.

FIGURE 8-1

A Comparison of VaR and Actual Losses over 100 Days

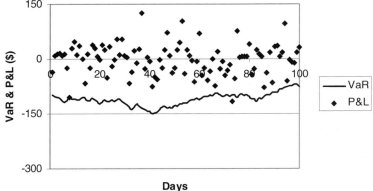

The number of exceptions over 250 days has a Bernoulli distribution. The *Bernoulli distribution* describes the probability of having a given number of outcomes that are equal to one if a binomial variable is sampled multiple times.

From the Bernoulli distribution, we can calculate the probability of a given number of exceptions occurring, as shown in Table 8-1. From this table, we can see that if the VaR calculator is correct, there is a 13% chance of having 4 exceptions in 250 trading days, and an 89% chance that there will be 0 to 4 exceptions. We can also see that there is only a 0.01% chance of there being 10 or more exceptions. We can interpret this by saying that it is very unlikely to get 10 or more exceptions if the VaR model is correct i.e., if 10 or more exceptions do occur, it is likely that the model is incorrect.

This principle is used by the Basel Committee to check that a bank's VaR calculator is performing well. If more than 4 exceptions have occurred in the last 250 trading days, the Capital Accords for market risk require that the bank should hold additional capital to compensate for the possible unreliability of the bank's calculator. Table 8-2 shows that each number of exceptions puts the calculator into a green, yellow, or red "zone." Corresponding to each number of exceptions, there is a multiplier by which the amount of market-risk capital must be increased. We investigate capital further in the next chapter.

Back-testing should not only be carried out for the whole portfolio, but also for subportfolios to test if they are being measured accurately. This avoids the possibility of

TABLE 8-1

Probability of Exceptions Experienced in
250 Days if the VaR Model is Correct

Exceptions	Probability	Cumulative Probability
0	8.1%	8.1%
1	20.5%	28.6%
2	25.7%	54.3%
3	21.5%	75.8%
4	13.4%	89.2%
5	6.7%	95.9%
6	2.7%	98.6%
7	1.0%	99.6%
8	0.3%	99.9%
9	0.1%	99.98%
10+	0.01%	99.99%

This table demonstrates that 10 or more exceptions are unlikely if the VaR model
is correct.

TABLE 8-2

Relationship between the Number of Exceptions in Back Testing and the Amount of Regulatory Capital to be Held for Market Risks

Exceptions	Zone	Multiplier
0	Green	1.00
1	Green	1.00
2	Green	1.00
3	Green	1.00
4	Green	1.00
5	Yellow	1.13
6	Yellow	1.17
7	Yellow	1.22
8	Yellow	1.25
9	Yellow	1.28
10+	Red	1.33

From: Amendment to Capital Accord to incorporate market risks, Basel Committee on Banking Supervision, January 1996.

inaccuracies in some subportfolios being undetected because they are masked by the rest of the portfolio.

SUMMARY

This chapter demonstrated how to conduct tests on VaR calculators to ensure their validity and to give us confidence that VaR is a true measurement of the risks. Next, we will describe how to use VaR to calculate the capital needed to withstand market risks.

Calculating Capital for Market Risk

INTRODUCTION

VaR gives a solid foundation for assessing the amount of capital that should be held by a bank to protect it in the case of losses arising from market risks. There are three reasons for analyzing the capital consumed by market risks:

- Complying with industry regulations
- Calculating economic capital to control the bank's default probability
- Measuring Risk-Adjusted Profitability

Each of these measures can be based on VaR, as we will describe below. At the end of this chapter, we also note that VaR can be used to manage the institutional-level risk, not only for banks, but also for asset managers.

COMPLYING WITH INDUSTRY REGULATIONS

In 1996, the Basel Committee on Banking Supervision recommended to national regulators that the minimum capital to be set aside for market risks should be based on VaR.[1] Under normal circumstances with a VaR Calculator that is functioning well, the regulatory capital should equal the 99% 1-day VaR, multiplied by 3, times the square root of 10:

$$Capital = 3 \times \sqrt{10} \times VaR_{99\%}$$

The square root of 10 represents the losses that could occur over a 10-day holding period, e.g., if there was a 10-day crisis in which the markets became illiquid. The factor of 3 allows 3 such events to happen each year. If the back-testing shows an unusual number of exceptions, the capital should be increased according to Table 8-2 in the previous chapter.

In calculating the VaR, each bank is allowed to use whatever method it thinks will best pass the back-test. However, the model selected must be used consistently, and it must be the primary model for reporting and managing risks within the bank.

CALCULATING ECONOMIC CAPITAL TO CONTROL THE BANK'S DEFAULT PROBABILITY

To be allowed to stay in business by the regulators, banks must hold at least the capital discussed above. However, if banks wish to maintain a high credit rating and a low probability of default, they may wish to hold more capital. This amount is calculated using the Economic Capital framework. Chapter 2 discussed the connection between a bank's economic capital and its default probability. In that chapter, the economic capital for market risks was given as:

$$EC = \frac{W_p}{(1 + r_f)}$$

Where r_f is the risk-free rate, and W_p is the maximum probable loss such that there is only probability p that the profitability over a year will be worse than W_p:

$$p = \text{probability}\left[\text{Profit} < W_p\right]$$

VaR gives us the maximum probable loss that could happen with a 1% probability over one day. To get the economic capital, we need to translate from 1% to the required confidence level and from one day to one year.

If banks only held enough capital to have a 1% chance of avoiding default, they would be rated around BB or BBB. If banks want to be more secure, they must increase the amount of capital.

If we assume that the losses are Normally distributed, then if a bank held capital equal to 2.32 times the standard deviation of the possible *annual* losses, there would be a 1% chance that the actual loss over 1 year would exceed the capital. If the bank held capital equal to 3.7 times the standard deviation of losses, there would only be a 0.01% chance that the actual loss would exceed the capital. The bank could therefore expect to be rated AA or AAA. Table 9-1 gives the relationship between the amount of capital that a bank holds against market risks and the consequent probability that the actual losses would be greater than the capital.

Typically, A-rated institutions have a default probability of around 0.1%. From Table 9-1, we can say that an A-rated institution should aim to hold capital equal to 3.1 times the standard deviation of the potential annual change in value (assuming a Normal distribution).

$$\textit{Economic Capital}_A = 3.1 \times \sigma_{1\,year}$$

TABLE 9-1

The Relationship between the Amount of
Capital Held against Market Risks and the
Associate Probability of the Banks
Defaulting

Capital divided by standard deviation of potential losses	Probability of default
2.3	1.00%
2.6	0.50%
3.1	0.10%
3.3	0.05%
3.7	0.01%

Now we need to find the standard deviation of the potential annual change in value. We already know that 99% VaR is 2.32 times the standard deviation of the potential daily change in value:

$$VaR = 2.32\sigma_{1\,day}$$

Now we need a way to scale from daily standard deviation to annual standard deviation. This can be crudely approximated by assuming that losses are uncorrelated from one day to the next, and that the VaR is constant during the year. With these assumptions, we can use the familiar "square-root-of-T"[2] approximation assuming 250 trading days per year:

$$\sigma_{Tdays} = \sqrt{T}\sigma_{1day}$$

$$\sigma_{250} = \sigma_{1year} = \sqrt{250}\sigma_1$$

Bringing these three equations together, we can estimate economic capital as a function of VaR:

$$Economic\ Capital_A \sim 3.1 \times \sigma_{1year}$$

$$= 3.1 \times \sqrt{250} \times \sigma_{1day}$$

$$= \sqrt{250} \times \frac{3.1}{2.32} VaR$$

$$= 6.68 \times \sqrt{10} \times VaR$$

This is more than twice as high as the regulatory capital. One reason for the discrepancy is that banks may wish to be more creditworthy than is implied by the minimum regulatory capital. Another reason is that the regulatory capital implicitly includes a reduction due to diversification between market risks and the other risks in the bank, e.g., credit risk (this is covered in Chapter 25). A further reason is that we assumed that the standard deviation of losses scales with the square root of time. This assumption breaks down for two reasons. The first is that over long periods, such as a year, effects such as mean reversions manifest themselves. The second reason is that it assumes that the trader holds a fixed position all year and takes whatever losses the market brings. With the trader's skill, and with bank's policies to stop losses, this should not be the case.

The only tractable solution to including the mean reversion and management effects is to use Monte Carlo simulation. This approach is explored in detail in an article entitled. "Changing Regulatory Capital to Include Liquidity and Management Intervention," Marrison, C.I., Schuermann, T.D., and Stroughair, J., *The Journal of Risk Finance*, August, 2000. The approach in this article creates many simulations of price changes for a year and the bank's response to these changes. By combining the market movements and the bank's expected response, we can relate the one-day VaR to the required economic capital. The scaling between the two is strongly dependent on the bank's stop-loss policies and the liquidity of the instruments, but in general, the required economic capital for an A rating was found to be between one and two times the minimum regulatory capital.

Once the capital has been established for the portfolio as a whole, it can be allocated to the individual traders, subportfolios, transactions, or desks, using the VaRC methodology. The capital allocated to an individual transaction is the VaRC for the transaction, divided by the VaR for the whole portfolio, and multiplied by the capital for the whole portfolio:

$$Allocated\ Capital_{Transaction} = Capital_{Portfolio} \frac{VaRC_{Transaction}}{VaR_{Portfolio}}$$

MEASURING RISK-ADJUSTED PROFITABILITY

Once we know the capital being consumed by a particular transaction, we can calculate the Risk-Adjusted Return on Capital (RAROC) and the Shareholder Value Added (SVA), as explained in Chapter 2. Knowing the risk-adjusted performance, we can properly decide on whether the profit from a transaction is worth the risk and whether a trader is performing well or just risking a lot of the bank's capital.

The RAROC is simply the net income from the transaction divided by the capital consumed:

$$RAROC = \frac{Net\ Income_{Transaction}}{Allocated\ Capital_{Transaction}}$$

If the transaction only lasts a few days (T) and only requires capital for that time, the calculated RAROC should be annualized so that it can be compared with the RAROC from other transactions:

$$RAROC_{Annual} = (1 + RAROC_T)^{\frac{250}{T}} - 1$$

The Shareholder Value Added is calculated by subtracting the hurdle income from the expected or actual income. The *hurdle income* is the amount of capital consumed multiplied by the hurdle rate that the shareholders require as a minimum return for risking their capital. The hurdle rate H_T, for a short-term transaction lasting T days can be calculated from annual hurdle rate, H_{Annual}:

$$H_T = (1 + H_{Annual})^{\frac{T}{250}} - 1$$

The required income is then the capital consumed multiplied by H_T:

$$Required\ Income = Allocated\ Capital \times H_T$$

The SVA is then the net income minus the required income:

$$SVA = Net\ Income - Allocated\ Capital \times H_T$$

Convincing traders that their bonuses should be reduced according to *Allocated Capital* $\times H_T$ is left as an exercise for the reader.

THE USE OF VaR BY ASSET MANAGERS

Asset managers, such as mutual funds, have two sets of risks to control: risks to their fund holders and risks to their shareholders. Their fund holders suffer losses directly if the value of the funds falls. VaR, as a measure of portfolio volatility, is perfectly suited to measuring this risk and can be used without any modification. The shareholders suffer losses if the net earnings of the asset management company fall. The earnings are typically partially tied to the performance of the funds, but also depend on costs and on the fees charged.

The volatility of the earnings, the source of earnings volatility, and the risk-adjusted profitability can be calculated by using VaR augmented with information on the structure of fees and costs. As this book is focused on risk measurement for banks, we will not spend any more time here discussing risk measurement for asset managers, but simply note that it can be done, and for further information see "Institution-Level Risk Measurement for Asset Managers," Marrison, C.I., *Risk*, pp. S26–S28, September, 2001.

SUMMARY

In this chapter, we showed how VaR can be used to calculate the amount of capital that should be held by a bank to protect it in the case of losses from market risk. Next, we will explore VaR's limitations and explain how to minimize them.

NOTES

1 Amendment to Capital Accord to incorporate market risks, Basel Committee on Banking Supervision, January 1996.

2 As discussed in Chapter 3.

CHAPTER 10

Overcoming VaR's Limitations

INTRODUCTION

While VaR is the single best way to measure risk, it does have several limitations. The most pressing limitations are the following:

- It assumes that the variances and correlations between the market-risk factors are stable.
- It does not give a good description of extreme losses beyond the 99% level.
- It does not account for the additional danger of holding instruments that are illiquid.

One approach to addressing VaR's limitations is to measure the risk both with VaR and with other, completely different methods, such as stress and scenario testing, as discussed in Chapter 5. However, in this chapter, we discuss approaches that can be used to augment the standard VaR methods. These methods allow the risk manager to improve the measurement of VaR, thereby improving the ability to set capital, measure performance, and identify excessive risks.

This chapter has three sections: an approach to letting variances change over time, several approaches for assessing extreme events, and finally, several approaches to quantify liquidity risk.

ALLOWING VARIANCE TO CHANGE OVER TIME

The usual approach to constructing the covariance matrix is to calculate the variance of the risk factors over the last few months and assume that tomorrow's changes in the risk factors will come from a distribution that has the same variance as experienced historically. We could write this as an equation by saying that the expected variance tomorrow (σ^2_{T+1}) is the variance of changes in the factor over the last few months:

$$\sigma^2_{T+1} = \frac{1}{N-1} \sum_{t=T-N}^{T} x_t^2$$

Here, x_t is the change on day t. We assume that the mean change is relatively small and therefore neglect it from the equation.

Although this approach is simple and robust, it is well known by practitioners that the volatility of the market changes over time: sometimes the market is relatively calm, then a crisis will happen, and the volatility will jump up.

GARCH is an approach that allows the estimation of σ^2_{T+1} to vary quickly with recent market moves. GARCH stands for Generalized Autoregressive Conditional Heteroskedasticity, which basically means that the variance on one day is a function of the variance on the previous day. GARCH assumes that the variance is equal to a constant, plus a portion of the previous day's change in the risk factor, plus a portion of the previous day's estimated variance:

$$\sigma^2_{T+1} = \omega + \alpha x_T^2 + \beta \sigma_T^2$$

ω, α, and β are constants. x_T is the latest change in the risk factor. To use this equation, we need to find values for ω, α, and β. The best value for these variables is the value that produces estimates of the future variance that are as close as possible to the variance that is later experienced. In practice, it is not possible to observe variance; all we can observe is the market change. Therefore, to find values for ω, α, and β, we estimate the "true" variance by looking at the market changes for a few days before and after the day in question. The equation above was for the variance of a single factor. We can also use GARCH to estimate the covariance between two factors, x and y:

$$\sigma^2_{xy,T+1} = \omega + \alpha x_T y_T + \beta \sigma^2_{xy,T}$$

In general, GARCH is difficult to use for more than a few risk factors because as the number of risk factors increases, it becomes difficult to find reliable values for the parameters ω, α, and β that need to be estimated for each variance and covariance.

One simple and practical version of GARCH is achieved by setting the variables as follows:

$$\omega = 0$$

$$\beta = \lambda$$

$$\alpha = 1 - \lambda$$

$$\sigma^2_{T+1} = (1 - \lambda)x_T^2 + \lambda \sigma_T^2$$

In this case, GARCH reduces to being the exponentially weighted moving average (EWMA), as discussed in Appendix C to Chapter 6.

APPROACHES FOR ASSESSING EXTREME EVENTS

The usual implementations of Parametric and Monte Carlo VaR assume that the risk factors have a Normal probability distribution. As discussed in the statistics chapter, most markets, especially poorly developed markets, exhibit many more extreme movements than would be predicted by a Normal distribution with the same standard deviation.

The term used to describe probability distributions that have a kurtosis greater than that of the Normal distribution is *leptokurtosis*. Leptokurtosis can be considered to be a measure of the fatness of the tails of the distribution. Measuring the effects of leptokurtosis is important because risk factors with a high kurtosis pose greater risks than factors with the same variance but a lower kurtosis. We will describe four techniques that are used to assess the additional risk caused by leptokurtosis:

- Jump Diffusion
- Historical Simulation
- Adjustments to Monte Carlo Simulation
- Extreme Value Theory

Jump Diffusion

The jump-diffusion model assumes that tomorrow's random change in the risk factor can come from one of two Normal distributions. One distribution describes the typical market movements; the other describes crisis movements. In simplified form, there is a probability of P that the sample will come from the typical distribution and a small probability of $(1 - P)$ that it will come from the crisis distribution:

$$x \sim N(\mu_t, \sigma_t) \quad \text{with Probability } P$$
$$x \sim N(\mu_c, \sigma_c) \quad \text{with Probability } 1 - P$$

Here, μ is the mean daily return, and σ is the daily standard deviation. μ_t and σ_t describe the typical distribution, and μ_c and σ_c describe the crisis distribution. The result is a combined distribution that has fatter tails than a pure Normal distribution.

The main problem to this approach is that it is difficult to determine the parameter values. In the model above, five parameters must be determined (μ_t, σ_t, μ_c, σ_c, and P).

Historical Simulation

Historical simulation does not require an assumption for the form of the probability distribution. It simply takes the price movements that have occurred and uses them to revalue the portfolio directly. This has the advantage of including the full richness of the complex interactions between risk factors. However, historical simulation is strongly backward looking because the changes in the risk factors are determined by the last crisis, not the next crisis.

Adjustments to Monte Carlo Simulation

Usually, Monte Carlo simulation uses Normal distributions. However, it is also possible to carry out Monte Carlo evaluation using leptokurtic distributions, such as jump diffusion or the Student's T distribution. It is relatively easy to create such distributions for single risk factors, but more difficult to ensure that the correlations between the factors are correct. This problem is reduced a little if Eigenvalue decomposition is used because Eigenvalue decomposition specifically isolates the few fundamental risk factors that drive most of the changes. This allows us to concentrate on ensuring that those principal risk factors have appropriate leptokurtic distributions.

Extreme Value Theory

Extreme Value Theory (EVT) takes a different approach to calculating VaR and is an alternative to the three common methods. EVT concentrates on estimating the shape of only the tail of a probability distribution. Given this shape, we can find estimates for losses associated with very small probabilities, such as the 99.9% VaR. A typical shape used is the Generalized Pareto Distribution that has the following form:[1]

$$Probability(Result \geq x) = (ax + b)^{-c}$$

Here, a, b, and c are variables that are chosen so the function fits the data in the tail. The main problem with the approach is that it is only easily applicable to single risk factors. It is also, by definition, difficult to parameterize because there are few observations of extreme events.

LIQUIDITY RISK

The Importance of Measuring Liquidity Risk

Liquidity risks can increase a bank's losses; therefore, they should be included in the calculation of VaR and economic capital.

There are two kinds of liquidity risk: liquidity risk in trading, and liquidity risk in funding (also known as funding risk). The *funding risk* is the possibility that the bank will run out of liquid cash to pay its debts. This funding risk is usually considered in the framework for asset liability management and will be discussed in later chapters. This chapter discusses liquidity risk in trading.

The *liquidity risk in trading* is the risk that a trader will be unable to quickly sell a security at a fair price. This could happen if few people normally trade the given security, e.g., if it was the equity for a small company. It could also happen if the general market is in crisis and few people are interested in buying new securities. This happened in the fall of 1998 after the Russian default, when even U.S. government bonds, normally the most liquid of securities, suddenly became illiquid.

Such a situation can cause losses in several ways. One way would be if the trader urgently needed to sell the position to get cash and repay a debt that was due. In this case, to find interested buyers, the trader would be forced to offer the security at a deep discount to its fair price. Losses due to illiquidity could also occur if the trader planned to sell any position that started making a loss, but then found that it took several days to sell the security at its fair price. This would expose the trader to the possibility of additional losses over that period.

We can view these two possible loss mechanisms as two extreme manifestations of the same problem. In one extreme, the trader sells immediately at an unusually low price. In the other extreme, the trader slowly sells at the current fair price, but risks suffering additional losses.

It is important to recognize the liquidity risk because it can add significantly to losses. Furthermore, if liquidity risk is not included in the risk measurement, it gives incentives to traders to buy illiquid securities. The incentives arise because in the market, illiquid securities offer a higher expected return to compensate for their higher liquidity risk. If this additional risk is not measured, traders will have an incentive to invest in these high-yielding assets, knowing that the bank will not charge them for the additional risk. Our problem now is to quantify that additional risk.

Quantifying Liquidity

The first step in quantifying the liquidity risk is to quantify the liquidity of any given instrument. One extreme approach to testing the liquidity of the market is for the risk manager to order a trader to close out a position and thereby directly observe how long it takes to clear the position, or how much of a discount must be made to close the position immediately. However, such an approach causes significant disruption to the trading operation and does not test the market in crisis conditions.

Another approach is to estimate the number of days required to close out the position. The *close-out time* is the time required to bring the position to a state where the bank can make no further loss from the position. It is the time taken to either sell or hedge the instrument. The number of days can be based on the size of the position held by the trader compared with the daily traded volume:

$$Close\ Out\ Days = T = \frac{Position\ Size}{F \times Daily\ Volume}$$

F is a factor that gives the percentage of the daily volume that can be sold into the market without significantly shifting the price. If F were set equal to 10%, it would imply that 10% of the daily volume can be sold each day without significantly shifting the market. The *Daily Volume* can be the average daily volume or the volume in a crisis period. The volume in a crisis period could be approximated as the average volume minus a number of standard deviations. This approach is quite crude but relatively objective, and it is easy to gather the required data.

Another alternative to quantifying the liquidity risk is to measure the average bid-ask spread relative to the mid price. The *bid* is the price that investors are willing to bid (or pay) to own the security. The *ask* is the price that owners of the security are asking to sell the security. The *mid* is halfway between the bid and ask. If the bid and ask are close to the mid, it implies that there are many market participants who agree on the fair value of the security and are willing to trade close to that price. If the bid-ask spread is wide, it means that few investors are willing to buy the security at the price the sellers think is fair. If a trader wanted to sell the security immediately, the trader would have to lower the ask price to equal the bid rather than wait for some investor to agree that the high ask price was fair.

Both the close-out time and the bid-ask spread can be used to quantify liquidity risk. We will explore how in the following sections.

Using Close-Out Time to Quantify Liquidity Risk

The most common approach to assessing the liquidity risk is to use the "square-root-of-T" adjustment for VaR. This is also known as "close-out-adjusted VaR." The result of the approach is that the VaR for a position that takes T days to close is assumed to equal the VaR for an equivalent liquid position that could be closed out in one day times the square root of T:

$$VaR_T = \sqrt{T} \ VaR_1$$

VaR_T is the 99th percentile cumulative loss that could be experienced over T days.

The approach assumes that the position will be held for T days, and then on the last day, it will be sold completely. It uses the reasoning that the losses over T days will be the sum of losses over the individual days:

$$L_T = \ell_1 + \ell_2 + \cdots + \ell_T$$

where L_T is the cumulative loss over T days and ℓ_t is the loss on day t. We can assume with reasonable accuracy that losses are *independent and identically distributed* (IID), meaning losses are not correlated day to day, and the standard deviation of losses is the same each day. The variance of the loss over T days is therefore the sum of the variance of the losses on the individual days:

$$\sigma^2_{L_T} = \sigma^2_{\ell_1} + \sigma^2_{\ell_2} + \cdots + \sigma^2_{\ell_T}$$

If we assume that the variance of the losses on each day is the same, then the sum equals T times the variance on the first day:

$$\sigma_{L_T}^2 = T\sigma_{\ell_1}^2$$

$$\sigma_{L_T} = \left(\sqrt{T}\right)\sigma_{\ell_1}$$

The 99th percentile cumulative loss over T days is therefore:

$$VaR_T = 2.32\sigma_{L_T}$$

$$= 2.32\sqrt{T}\sigma_{L_1}$$

$$= \sqrt{T} \times VaR_1$$

A slightly refined approach is to assume that the position is closed out linearly over T days. In this case, the variance of the loss decreases linearly each day:

$$\sigma_{L_T}^2 = \sigma_{\ell_1}^2 + \sigma_{\ell_2}^2 + \cdots + \sigma_{\ell_T}^2$$

$$\sigma_{L_T}^2 = \left(\frac{T}{T}\sigma_{\ell_1}\right)^2 + \left(\frac{T-1}{T}\sigma_{\ell_1}\right)^2 + \cdots + \left(\frac{1}{T}\sigma_{\ell_1}\right)^2$$

$$\sigma_{L_T}^2 = \sigma_{\ell_1}^2\left[\left(\frac{T}{T}\right)^2 + \left(\frac{T-1}{T}\right)^2 + \cdots + \left(\frac{1}{T}\right)^2\right]$$

$$VaR_T = 2.32\sqrt{\sigma_{\ell_1}^2\left[\left(\frac{T}{T}\right)^2 + \left(\frac{T-1}{T}\right)^2 + \cdots + \left(\frac{1}{T}\right)^2\right]}$$

$$VaR_T = Var_1\sqrt{\left[\left(\frac{T}{T}\right)^2 + \left(\frac{T-1}{T}\right)^2 + \cdots + \left(\frac{1}{T}\right)^2\right]}$$

To illustrate the difference between this and the simple square-root-of-T adjustment, consider a closeout period of 10 days. The square-root-of-T method gives:

$$VaR_{10} = VaR_1 \times \sqrt{10}$$

$$= VaR_1 \times 3.16$$

Whereas the linear close-out gives a measure of VaR that is significantly smaller:

$$VaR_{10} = VaR_1 \times \sqrt{1 + 0.9^2 + 0.8^2 + 0.7^2 + 0.6^2 + 0.5^2 + 0.4^2 + 0.3^2 + 0.2^2 + 0.1^2}$$

$$= VaR_1 \times 1.96$$

The problem with both of these closeout-adjusted VaR approaches is that it does not give an apples-to-apples comparison with other risks. It compares the amount that could be lost over one day for a liquid position with the amount that could be lost over T days for the illiquid position. However, it is not the case that a trader holding a position with a 10-day closeout period is taking 3 times as much risk as a trader holding an equivalent liquid position. This is because in a 10-day period, the trader with the liquid position gets to gamble, and possibly lose, 10 times, whereas the trader with the illiquid position simply has one long gamble. To properly measure the significance of liquidity, we need to include the trader's intended behavior.

The effects of trading and management styles can be assessed using simulations to produce a true apples-to-apples comparison of the additional risk caused by holding illiquid securities. An approach to this is discussed below.

Using Simulation-Based Techniques to Quantify Liquidity Risk

Consider two positions that are identical, except that one can be sold within a day, and the other cannot be sold for year. If the trader in charge of each position decides to hold it for a year, then the loss would be the same for each. However, if the trader in charge of the liquid position decides to sell on the first day, the potential loss would be significantly less. This illustrates that the impact of liquidity is a function of both the security's liquidity and the management style. Increased liquidity gives the trader greater options to buy and sell the instrument, but if these options are not exercised, they are worthless.

With this line of thinking, we can suggest an approach that simulates market movements and the trader's response. We can use this to quantify the amount that can be lost at the end of each year, and therefore the risk. We can then compare the loss suffered on a liquid position with the loss that would be suffered if the position was illiquid. This gives a measure of the relative risk.

This approach is taken in the paper "Changing Regulatory Capital to Include Liquidity and Management Intervention," Marrison, C.I., Schuermann, T.D., and Stroughair, J., *The Journal of Risk Finance*, August, 2000. In this paper, a simulation model is used. The model includes variability in market values and the bank's response to losses. The bank's response is to reduce its holdings of securities whenever it suffers large losses, and increase its holdings if it has gains. Specifically, the bank tries to keep its risks in line with its remaining capital. The speed with which the bank can adjust its holdings is dictated by the closeout time of the security. The paper shows that a security with a holding period of 250 days requires about twice as much capital as a completely liquid position.

Using the Bid-Ask Spread to Assess Liquidity Risk

The closeout adjustments discussed above assumed that the trader was taking one extreme course of action by gradually closing out the position at the mid price and refusing to give any discount. The other extreme is to assume that the trader will sell out immediately by giving a discount that brings the price down to the bid price. This discount is an additional loss.

This approach was explained in Bangia, A., Diebold, F.X., Schuermann, T. and Stroughair, J. "Liquidity on the Outside," *Risk*, vol. 12, pp. 68–73, June, 1999.

Bid-ask spreads change over time. Bangia et al. use the assumption that the additional drop in the price is half the usual bid-ask spread plus the 99th percentile movement in the spread as shown below:

$$Additional\ Drop_{99\%} = 0.5\bar{S} + 2.32\sigma_S$$

Where $\bar{S}$ is the average spread, and σ_S is the standard deviation of the spread. This additional drop is then added to the one-day liquid VaR:

$$Liquidity\ Adjusted\ VaR = VaR + Additional\ Drop$$

This approach is most directly applicable for stand-alone instruments or risk factors, but it is also possible to consider it as an adjustment to the variances used in the covariance matrix.

SUMMARY

As we learned in this chapter, VaR has various limitations; however, there are approaches that can be employed to mitigate these limitations and improve the measurement of VaR. In the next chapter, we will detail how market-risk measurement is used in market-risk management.

NOTE

1 "Steps in Applying Extreme Value Theory to Finance," Younes Bensalah, Working Paper 2000-20, Bank of Canada, ISSN 1192 5434, Nov. 2000.

CHAPTER 11

The Management of Market Risk

INTRODUCTION

In the previous chapters, we spent a large amount of time describing how risks can be measured. In this chapter, we discuss how risk measurement is used in risk management. A bank's risk-management function is typically headed by the chief risk officer (CRO). Reporting to the CRO will be the chief credit officer, the chief market risk officer, and the chief operating risk officer. Within the market-risk organization there are three groups: policies and procedures, risk measurement, and risk management (Figure 11-1). In this chapter, we describe the work of each of these groups, especially the business of setting and managing risk limits.

ESTABLISHING POLICIES AND PROCEDURES

The staff of the policies and procedures group typically has a background in audit, operations, and financial reporting. Their task is to establish and maintain a framework of policies and procedures to ensure that the trading operation is well controlled. The task can be broken into three components: defining responsibilities, ensuring disciplined risk measurement, and approving new operations.

Defining Responsibilities

Responsibilities should be established for the risk management group, the head of trading, accounting, information technology, operations, and the legal department. The distribution of responsibilities should ensure that for every risk the bank faces,

FIGURE 11-1

Typical Organization of a Market-Risk Management Group

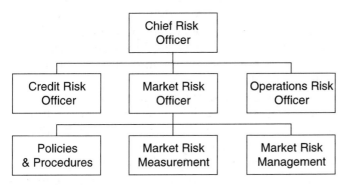

someone is responsible for reporting the amount of risk, and someone is responsible for acting to control the risk.

In establishing the responsibilities, it is very important that the risk management group does not report to the trading group. They must report directly to the CEO or senior risk committee. Their pay and promotion must not be dependent on the trading group. Similarly, the settlements and accounting groups must also be separate from the traders.

Before individuals are allowed to trade, they must receive a formal delegation of authority to trade. The delegation of authority to trade is a document signed on behalf of the CEO that specifies the individuals who are allowed to commit the bank to make a trade with a counterparty. The document should specify which products may be traded by each individual and desk. The document may also specify the pricing models that may be used.

Ensuring Disciplined Risk Measurement

The policy group should establish the procedures to be used for reporting risk-measurement results. The risk measurements are used to control the bank and report to external authorities, such as the regulators. It is therefore important that the measurements should be made in an approved fashion. The policy group will provide the rules for how new risk-measurement models get approved for use by the bank, when and how they should be tested, and who is allowed to use them. For example, it should not be the case that a trader is able to access and alter a system that is calculating the risk of his or her position.

Approving New Operations

In the natural push to remain competitive, the bank's operations and products are continually changing. Policies should be in place for approving new products, new pricing models, and new counterparties. The approval policy for new products should require that there be a business case for introducing the new product, clear specification of who may trade the product, and a plan for how the risk-monitoring and accounting systems will be changed to include the product.

The approval policy for new pricing models should include a parallel spreadsheet calculation made by the risk management group to verify the accuracy of the model. The approval should also specify which products are to be priced using each model.

The approval policy for new counterparties is typically created in conjunction with the settlements and credit groups. The settlements group will ensure that they are satisfied that the counterparty can reliably deliver and settle any trade that the counterparty makes. The credit group must verify that they are satisfied that the counterparty is unlikely to default. According to the creditworthiness, limits will be set on the amount of trading that can be done with the counterparty.

CREATING RISK-MEASUREMENT REPORTS

The risk-measurement group is typically staffed with "quants," i.e., people with strong quantitative skills. The group must also have information technology (IT) staff to operate the systems required to manage the large amounts of data that must be fed into the risk calculators.

The goal of the group is to produce frequent, timely, accurate risk reports both for internal and external constituencies. The main internal constituencies are risk management, senior management, and the traders.

Senior management uses the reports created by risk measurement to ensure that the risks match the amount of available capital, and to decide if they are comfortable with the risk profile of the bank. To do this, they need to know the total risk and the main sources of risk, both in terms of portfolio and risk factors.

The traders use the reports to better understand their risk, to let them see how their position is correlated with the rest of the bank, and to let them challenge any possible errors in the report before it is used to assess capital charges or gets reported to external constituencies.

The main external constituencies are the regulators, rating agencies, and investors. Regulators and rating agencies use risk reports to ensure that the bank has a low probability of failure and that the capital is adequate to cover the risks. Typically, the external reports are generated monthly or quarterly and include bank-level VaR, back-testing results, and available capital being held.

Investors use the risk section of the annual report to be sure that the bank has adequate risk controls and that the risk is commensurate with their expected return. All major banks now include a report from the risk management group including the average VaR for the bank's major operations. The section discloses the broad methodology used for risk measurement, a description of controls, and measures of the absolute level of risk, such as the average VaR.

The daily reports for internal management contain the following information:

- The absolute position showing the value of each security held and the net value of the trading operation, i.e., the available economic capital
- The P&L from the previous day according to accounting
- The P&L from the previous day according to the risk calculator
- Sensitivity, stress, and scenario reports for every portfolio and subportfolio
- The stand-alone VaR according to the Parametric, Historical, and Monte Carlo approaches
- VaRC by desk and risk factor
- The extent of limit utilization
- Required and available regulatory and economic capital
- Comments on any unusual risks or discrepancies

Wherever possible, graphics should be used to communicate this information so executives can quickly see the risk situation. Figure 11-2 illustrates the first page of a market-risk report. The subsequent pages would give the details for each portfolio, risk factor, and type of risk measurement. Figure 11-3 illustrates the contents of the first page of detailed analysis. From these reports, the risk management group should be able to identify any particularly dangerous situations quickly and take action to reduce the risk. In Figure 11-3, the most significant risk is revealed by the scenario test for a default in the emerging markets.

When reading risk reports, the main things to look for are the following:

- Significant discrepancies between the accounting P&L and the P&L predicted by the risk calculator.
- The absolute VaR relative to the net value of the operation.
- The distribution of VaR across different desks.
- Significant differences between Parametric and Monte Carlo VaR, which would indicate that the portfolio has a significant nonlinear sensitivity to price changes.
- Significant differences between Monte Carlo VaR and Historical VaR, which would indicate that the correlations assumed in the Monte Carlo VaR may not be stable or the kurtosis may be high.
- Significant nonlinearities in the results of the stress tests, which could indicate options that have the potential for creating unusually large losses if the market changes significantly.

FIGURE 11-2

Illustration of the First Page of a Market-Risk Report

Summary Market-Risk Report: 21 July 2001

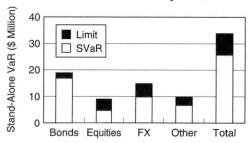

Stand-Alone VaR and Limits
The bond desk has the largest
Stand-Alone VaR. All desks are within
their limits. The bond desk has asked
for an increase. This could be done
by reducing the limits to FX & Equities.

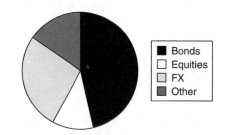

VaR Contribution
On a diversified basis, the bond desk is
causing almost half of the trading
operation's risk. We should be cautious
about increasing their limit.

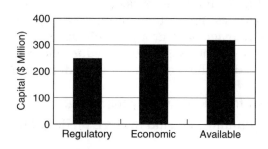

Capital Analysis
We have significantly more capital
available than required by the
regulators. However, the available
capital is not much more than the
economic capital required to maintain
our credit rating. We should not
significantly increase our total risk.

- Large differences between the results of the VaR and the results of the scenario
tests, which would indicate that the bank's experts can foresee a scenario which
is not reflected in the historical data used to calculate the VaR (this is the most
significant risk in Figure 11-3.)

Based on the reports, the market-risk management team will investigate any areas of
concern, and when necessary, act to reduce the risk to the bank.

Creation of the reports takes significant effort because of the short time available
and the number of systems that feed into the risk calculator. It is very common that
there will be data missing or corrupted in the market-data feeds or the bank's position

FIGURE 11-3

Illustration of the Details of a Market-Risk Report

$ Millions	Bonds	Equities	FX	Other	Total
Position					
Long	4661	254	413	242	5570
Short	4605	120	368	159	5252
Interdesk Assets	144	−107	5	−42	0
Net	200	27	50	41	318
Previous Day's P&L					
Accounting	−2.7	0.1	−7.0	1.5	−8.0
Risk Models	−2.5	0.1	−6.6	1.6	−7.3
Sensitivity					
+1% of Risk Factor	9	−2	−3	3	-
Stress					
−20%	190	−43	−79	-	-
−10.00%	94	−24	−20	-	-
10.00%	−90	25	48	-	-
20.00%	−220	73	62	-	-
Scenarios					
Gulf War	14	−22	−5	6	−7
Emerg. Mkt. Default	−53	−3	−18	−5	−78
Stand-Alone VaR					
Parametric	17	5	10	7	26
Historical	18	8	13	10	28
Monte Carlo	18	7	12	9	28
VaR Contibution					
Parametric	12	3	7	4	26
Historical	14	4	6	4	28
Monte Carlo	12	6	5	5	28
Limits					
Stand-Alone VaR	19	9	15	10	34
Capital					
Regulatory	114	28	66	38	247
Economic	136	29	80	54	299
Available	200	27	50	41	318

Conclusions from this report would be as follows: P&L from the accounting system and the risk models match moderately well. The stress tests show that there are no unusual nonlinearities in the changes in value. The scenarios show a worrying possibility of a significant loss if there is a default in the emerging markets. The results of the three different VaRs match reasonably well, so there is unlikely to be an unusual nonlinearity or sensitivity to an extreme market movement. The VaR contribution shows that almost half the risk comes from the bond desk, but all desks are well within their limits, and the available capital is in excess of the required capital.

information. It is good practice to get the relatively fast Parametric VaR results first and check them for gross errors before setting off the long Historical and Monte Carlo evaluations.

MANAGING MARKET RISK AND RISK LIMITS

The risk management group must be able both to understand the complexities of the risk reports, and to be able to discuss the results with traders. The group is therefore generally staffed with a mixture of quants and ex-traders.

It is rare that banks give their risk managers the authority to make trades to reduce the risk. Normally, risk managers have two avenues for taking action if they detect an excessive risk: they can bring the risk to the attention of the trader and senior management, or they can change the risk limits. The risk limits are set by senior management and the market-risk management group. If traders want to extend their limits, they must first obtain the approval of the market risk manager.

The setting and management of limits is both important and complex. We take the next few pages to explore limits in detail. We discuss the purpose of limits, the different types of limits, the general principles for setting limits, and how limits can be set using the VaR-contribution methodology.

A bank's framework of limits is the mechanism by which senior management controls the total risk that can be taken and the general nature of the risk. The limits tell each trader and trading group the maximum amount of risk that they can take. For senior management, the limits provide comfort in knowing that the total amount of risk will not be too high, and they provide a way of allocating the bank's risk capacity to the opportunities that are likely to give the greatest risk-adjusted return. Limits also allow a delegation of authority in that a trader or desk is allowed to take any position it sees fit, so long as it does not exceed the limits.

There are two overall types of risk limits used in trading operations: counterparty-credit limits and market-risk limits. Counterparty limits depend on the creditworthiness of the counterparty, and limit the total exposure of the bank to that counterparty. The measurement and management of credit exposure is treated in the later chapters. Here, we discuss only limits on market risks.

Limits on market risks can be classified into two groups: operational limits and limits on position size. Let us first look at three types of operational limits: inventory age, concentration, and stop-loss limits.

Inventory Age Limits

Inventory age limits set the time for which any security is held without being sold. This is to prevent traders from sitting on illiquid positions or positions with an unrecognized loss. The time allowed will depend on the overall purpose of the desk. If the desk is expected to trade in and out of positions quickly, the limit will be on the order of days. If the desk is expected to use long-term strategies, the limits can be on the order of weeks or months.

Concentration Limits

Concentration limits prevent traders from putting all their eggs in one basket. They ensure that a trader's risk is not concentrated in one instrument or market. For example, the FX desk may be limited to taking no more than 25% of its risk in any one currency, or the equities desk may be limited to a maximum of 10% in any one company. As protection against illiquidity, the risk managers may also limit the total percentage of a company's equity that may be held.

Stop-Loss Limits

Stop-loss limits act as a safety valve in case something starts to go wrong. Stop-loss limits state that specified action must take place if the loss exceeds a threshold amount. An example of a stop-loss limit would be to say that if a position loses more than 15%, it must be sold immediately to prevent further loss, and the trader should be suspended from trading for a "cooling-off" period of two weeks. Tight stop-loss limits reduce the maximum possible loss, and therefore reduce the capital required for the business. However, if the limits are too tight, they reduce the trader's ability to make a profit.

Limits on Position Size

Let us turn now to limits on position size. There are three common ways of limiting the position size: the nominal amount, the sensitivity, and the VaR. A limit on the nominal amount simply specifies the total amount of securities that a trader/desk or portfolio can hold. For example, the equities desk may be told that they may not own more than $500 million of equities. Sensitivity limits restrict measures such as the duration of a bond portfolio, the beta of an equities portfolio or the Greeks of an options portfolio.

For controlling risk, neither of these methods are as good as VaR limits, but they are still used for three reasons:

- They provide familiar, traditional risk metrics to the trader.
- They provide a safety net in case there is a problem in the VaR calculation.
- They are quickly and easily calculated, which is especially useful for positions that change rapidly within each day.

Although these methods provide a useful backstop, most banks have now adopted a VaR-limit system, at least for the major desks in the trading room, if not for the individual traders. VaR limits specify the maximum amount of VaR that each desk can cause. Before looking at the mechanics of setting the amounts for VaR limits, let us first look at the general characteristics of a good framework for limits.

Principles for Setting Limits

The main principles to be followed in setting limits are as follows:

- They should be risk based; i.e., the measurement of limit utilization should be directly proportional to the amount of risk taken. This is the case for VaR, and generally the case for sensitivities. However, nominal limits are not risk based because two securities with the same nominal value can have very different risk profiles.
- Limits should be fungible at lower levels. This means that a trader should be allowed to take risks to exploit the best opportunities available without being too tightly bound by a complex limit system. Similarly, a senior trader should be able to move limits from one subordinate desk to another.
- The limits should be aligned with the bank's competitive advantages. For example, a Norwegian bank could be expected to have large limits for trading Scandinavian equities but small limits for trading Asian equities.
- If a portfolio is to be managed within a given set of limits, it should not be possible for changes in another portfolio to cause the limits to be broken. Given this principle, limiting with stand-alone VaR is good, but limiting directly according to VaR contribution would not work well because the VaRC of one portfolio changes whenever there is a change in the composition of any of the other portfolios.
- Both hard and soft limits may be set. If the limit is hard, then traders know that they will be disciplined or fired for violating the limit. If the limit is soft, a violation simply leads to a conversation in which the trader is advised to reduce the position.

VaR can be used to create a limits framework that conforms to these principles.

Setting VaR Limits

The usual practical starting point for setting VaR limits is to measure the current stand-alone VaR for each desk and set the limits to be a little higher or lower depending on whether management wants the given desk to grow or shrink.

However, if you were starting from a blank sheet, the limits would be set by starting with the total capital available to the trading operation and relating that to the maximum amount of VaR that can be supported by that capital. For regulatory capital, the relationship is as follows:

$$Required\ Capital = 3 \times \sqrt{10} \times VaR_{99\%}$$

Therefore:

$$VaR_{99\%} \ Limit = \frac{Available \ Capital}{3 \times \sqrt{10}}$$

This sets the VaR limit for the trading operation as a whole. For the portfolios within the trading operation, the VaR limit (VaRL) should be set including the average correlation between each portfolio. If there were only two portfolios, this would be as follows:

$$VaRL^2_{All} = VaRL^2_1 + VaRL^2_2 + 2\rho_{1,2}VaRL_1 VaRL_2$$

In this equation, we know the limit for all trading ($VaRL_{All}$) and we know the average correlation between the two portfolios ($\rho_{1,2}$). We can therefore use the quadratic equation to get $VaRL_2$ in terms of $VaRL_1$:

$$VaRL_2 = \frac{-2\rho_{1,2}VaRL_1 + \sqrt{(2\rho_{1,2}VaRL_1)^2 - 4(VaRL^2_1 - VaRL^2_{All})}}{2}$$

The optimal amount to be allocated to each portfolio depends on the expected return per unit of stand-alone VaR. Consider an example in which one business unit is expected to return \$1.5 per dollar of VaR, and another is expected to return \$1.3 per dollar of VaR. Let us assume that the correlation between them ($\rho_{1,2}$) is 0.3, and that the VaR limit for the trading operation ($VaRL_{All}$) is \$100. Table 11-1 shows different values for $VaRL_1$ and the consequent values for $VaRL_2$ to ensure that the total VaR remains at \$100. It also shows the expected revenue from each desk and the total revenue. For this example, the total revenue is expected to be maximized if $VaRL_1$ equals \$70 and $VaRL_2$ equals \$53.

TABLE 11-1

Finding the Optimal Combination for VaR Limits

VaRL 1	VaRL 2	Revenue 1	Revenue 2	Total Return
100	0	150	0	150
90	24	135	32	167
80	41	120	53	173
70	53	105	69	**174**
60	64	90	83	173
50	73	75	95	170
40	80	60	105	165
30	87	45	113	158
20	92	30	120	150
10	97	15	126	141
0	100	0	130	130

For strategic purposes, market-risk managers typically set the VaR limits for the major desks and allow the heads of the desks to set limits for the subordinate desks. For subordinate desks, the limits may be translated from VaR into a measure that is more familiar to the trader, such as duration dollars or Greeks. To translate from VaR to duration dollars we reverse the process used to calculate VaR from duration:

$$VaR = 2.32 \ Duration\$ \times \sigma_r$$

Therefore:

$$Duration \ Limit = \frac{VaR \ Limit}{2.32\sigma_r}$$

After the limits have been set, each day the VaR limit for each desk and subdesk is compared with the calculated stand-alone VaR for that level. The calculated VaR includes the full correlation of all positions as they stand that day.

SUMMARY

In this chapter, we detailed how market-risk measurement is used to support market-risk-management decisions and control trading risks. This concludes our discussion of market risks in trading operations. Next, we will turn our attention to asset liability management (ALM), which comprises the market and liquidity risks associated with the rest of a bank's balance sheet.

CHAPTER 12

Introduction to Asset Liability Management

INTRODUCTION

In the previous chapters, we discussed the measurement and management of market risks for trading operations. Here, we discuss the market and liquidity risks associated with the rest of the bank's balance sheet, including commercial loans, mortgages, and customer deposits. The management of this part of the balance sheet is called *asset liability management* (ALM). There are two primary risks associated with ALM: interest-rate and liquidity risk. The interest-rate risk arises from the possibility that profits will change if interest rates change. The liquidity risk arises from the possibility of losses due to the bank having insufficient cash on hand to pay customers. Both risks are due to the difference between the bank's assets and liabilities.

Asset liability management deals with the management of the market risks that arise from a bank's structural position. The structural position is primarily created by the bank's intermediation between depositors and borrowers. The deposits are checking accounts, savings accounts, and fixed deposits. The loans to borrowers are commercial loans, personal loans, car loans, credit-card debt, home-improvement loans, and mortgages. Asset liability management is most important for universal or retail banks and less important for trading or investment banks.

Asset liability management is distinct from the management of market risk in trading operations because ALM positions are relatively illiquid. After origination, the assets and liabilities are typically held by the bank until they mature, although it is becoming increasingly common to bundle banking products such as loans into securities and sell or trade them with other banks. This is especially true of mortgage-backed securities (MBS). Mortgage-backed securities fall in the gray area between trading and ALM, and depending on the bank, they may be held either in the trading book or the ALM book. The rule of thumb is that positions that are commonly liquidated within a month are treated as traded instruments with the risk measured in the trading-VaR framework. Positions that cannot be quickly liquidated, and any associated hedge instruments, are treated in the ALM framework.

It is not crucially important whether an instrument is measured in the trading-VaR or ALM frameworks, so long as the risks are well monitored somewhere. Whereas trading VaR has a one-day horizon, ALM risks are typically managed on a monthly basis with a large amount of consideration being given to long-term trends and customer behavior.

The best illustration of ALM risks is given by the U.S. savings and loan (S&L) crisis. Savings and loan banks are local banks that are mandated to take in retail deposits and make retail loans. For many years, the Federal Reserve kept interest rates stable, and the S&Ls had a stable business. They took in deposits for which they paid around 4%, and they lent 30-year mortgages paying about 8% at fixed rates. This gave a 4% profit before noninterest expenses. Then in the 1980s, the Federal Reserve allowed interest rates to float. Short-term interest rates rose to 16%. Many deposit customers withdrew their funds or demanded the new higher rates. The S&Ls were then locked into receiving 8% from the long-term, fixed-rate mortgages and paying 16% to the short-term, floating-rate deposits. This caused many S&Ls to go bankrupt. The crisis could have been avoided if the S&Ls had practiced better asset liability management and not exposed themselves so badly to this risk.

In addition to interest-rate risks, asset liability management also includes the management of the funding liquidity risks. This is the challenge of ensuring that the bank has sufficient liquid assets available to meet all its required payments, including the possibility of a "run on the bank." A run on the bank occurs when deposit customers lose confidence in a bank's creditworthiness and rush to the bank to take out their savings before the bank collapses. This panic can be self-fulfilling, and if the bank does not have enough liquid assets available, it may not be able to meet the demand for cash, even though the total value of assets may be much higher than the value of liabilities. In most developed countries, this risk is greatly reduced by deposit insurance backed by the government. For example, in the United States the Federal Deposit Insurance Company (FDIC) guarantees that retail depositors will be compensated up to $100,000 if their bank fails. This reduces the incentive to panic.

A liquidity crunch can also occur if the bank has had a heavy reliance on short-term, interbank loans and the lending banks lose confidence in their creditworthiness. This was the situation faced by many of the Asian banks and companies in the crisis of 1997.

By modeling and understanding ALM risks, banks seek to minimize the risks and know how much to charge customers to cover the capital consumed by the risks. Another important aspect of ALM is determining the fair, risk-minimizing interest rates that should be charged internally between the bank's business units when they lend funds to each other. This helps the bank to minimize the risk within each unit and measure its profitability. This aspect of ALM is called funds transfer pricing.

With this basic understanding of interest-rate and liquidity risk, the ALM chapters are organized as follows:

- A discussion of the sources of interest-rate risks
- A discussion of the risk characteristics of ALM instruments, such as mortgages and checking accounts
- Measurement of ALM interest-rate risk at the bank level
- Measurement of ALM funding-liquidity risk at the bank level
- Allocation of ALM risks to business units through transfer pricing
- Organization of ALM risk management

The remainder of this chapter discusses the sources of interest-rate risk and the characteristics of ALM instruments.

SOURCES OF INTEREST-RATE RISK

Asset liability management oversees the management of the long-term, structural interest-rate position. All other market risks are typically managed by the trading room. However some banks also have large, structural foreign-exchange positions that cannot be quickly changed. For example, many banks in emerging-market countries have a large portion of their balance sheets in the form of loans denominated in U.S. dollars. In such cases, both the structural interest rate and the structural FX positions are managed in the ALM framework. The discussion below will focus on interest rates. FX positions can be treated using a combination of the techniques discussed in this chapter and the VaR chapter.

The primary cause of structural interest-rate risk is that customers want both long-term loans and quick access to any deposits that they have made. Furthermore customers like to have certainty in the interest payments that they will be required to make and therefore ask for fixed-rate loans. This leaves banks in a position in which they are receiving long-term, fixed-rate interest payments from borrowers and paying short-term, floating-rate interest to depositors. A simple model for this situation is that the bank is long a series of long-term, fixed-rate bonds and short a series of floating-rate bonds. Figure 12-1a illustrates a possible scenario. The upper arrows represent the fixed-rate payments into the bank, and the lower arrows represent the floating-rate payments made by the bank. Figure 12-1b shows the net interest income (NII), i.e., interest income minus interest costs. From this net income, we can also deduct non-interest expenses (NIE or NIX), such as staff costs. Noninterest expenses are partially floating (Figure 12-1c). The result is the net earnings for the bank (Figure 12-1d) and shows that risk arises from the mismatch between the interest-rate characteristics of the assets and liabilities.

The measurement of ALM risks is made more difficult than the management of a simple bond portfolio because of the indeterminate maturities of assets and liabilities. The *indeterminate maturity* describes the uncertainty as to when customers will make or ask for payments. Therefore, the risk of the structural interest-rate position is generally

FIGURE 12-1a

Illustration of Payment Volatility

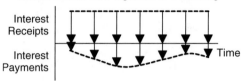

FIGURE 12-1b

Illustration of Volatility in Net Interest Income

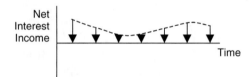

FIGURE 12-1c

Illustration of Volatility in Noninterest Expenses

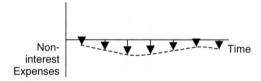

FIGURE 12-1d

Illustration of Volatility in Net Earnings

more difficult to measure than the market risk of the trading room. In the trading room, all transactions are clearly structured. With bonds, the maturity is known, and the term is fixed by the contract underlying the security. With options, the expectation is that every option will be exercised to maximize the advantage to the holder.

In contrast, ALM products such as mortgages and deposits have many implicit or embedded options that make the values dependent not only on market rates, but also on customer behavior. For example, customers have the option to withdraw their deposit accounts whenever they wish, or to prepay a mortgage early if they find a cheaper mortgage elsewhere.

Another feature of retail products is that customers pay rates that are not tightly linked to market rates. Retail customers typically have interest payments that are a fixed percentage above or below prime. *Prime* is the rate that the bank advertises for its retail customers, and is not directly determined by the market. Therefore, it is called an *administered rate*. Prime is typically held constant for several months and is only changed when there has been a significant change in the market rates. Optimally hedging a portfolio of prime-paying assets is one of the great challenges of ALM, as there will always be a difference between the yield from prime-based assets and the yield on market-based assets. This difference is called *basis risk*. It is the risk that arises from having assets and liabilities that reprice on a different basis.

MAIN PRODUCT CLASSES HELD IN ALM PORTFOLIOS

In this section, we review the characteristics of the main product classes that make up the portfolio to be managed by the asset liability manager. This facilitates the later discussion of risk measurement for these products. Retail transactions, such as deposits and mortgages, have many implicit or explicit options, such as the option for customers to prepay the principal before it is finally due, or the option for deposit customers to withdraw their money at any time. This introduces customer behavior into the modeling of the risks. The behavior depends on the structure and purpose of the product. The main classes of products for asset liability management are the following:

Assets

- Retail personal loans
- Retail mortgages
- Credit-card receivables
- Commercial loans
- Long-term investments
- Traded bonds
- Derivatives

Liabilities

- Retail checking accounts
- Retail savings accounts
- Retail fixed-deposits accounts
- Deposits from commercial customers
- Bonds issued by the bank

Below, each asset and liability will be examined in greater depth, beginning with the assets.

Retail Personal Loans

Retail personal loans may be either fixed or floating rate. If they are floating, they are priced off the prime rate. Fixed-rate loans are generally paid off in equal installments. The installments include both interest payments and a partial repayment of the outstanding principal. The amount of each installment (I) depends on the initial amount lent (L), the periodic interest rate (r), and the number of periods over which the payments will be made (T). The NPV of the installments must equal the initial amount lent:

$$L = \sum_{t=1}^{T} \frac{\text{Installment}}{(1+r)^t}$$

This equation can be rearranged to give the installment amount as a function of L, r, and T:

$$I = L \frac{r}{1 - \left(\frac{1}{1+r}\right)^T}$$

For example, if the annual rate is 8%, a \$100, 6-year loan would have annual installments of \$21.63.

Retail loan agreements generally allow the customer to pay the loan amount back to the bank earlier than originally required. Customers might do this if they had an unexpected windfall, or if rates had fallen and they were able to get a replacement loan elsewhere at a lower rate. This prepayment risk is not significant for loans of one or two years, but is significant for mortgages. Banks often discourage prepayment by requiring the customer to pay a fee called a prepayment penalty.

If the loan has a floating rate, there is less incentive to prepay because whenever rates fall, the required payment falls. However, floating-rate loans often have a cap on the maximum amount of interest that can be charged or the maximum increase per year. This effectively gives the customer a put option to force the bank to accept a liability paying the full rate in exchange for the capped rate.

Retail Mortgages

Most mortgages in the United States are fixed rate and have a maturity of many decades. In the emerging markets, mortgages tend to be for a shorter term and only fixed for the initial years. This reduces the interest-rate risk for the bank, but increases the probability of the customer being unable to pay if interest rates rise. From an ALM perspective, long-term, fixed-rate mortgages could be considered to be simple bonds if it was not for the prepayment option.

To see the importance of the prepayment option, consider a $100, 10-year bond paying 10% anually. If the current 10-year rate was 10%, the bond would be worth $100. If the rates dropped to 5% the bond would be worth $159, and the holder would have gained $59:

$$\text{Initial Value} = \frac{\$100(1 + 10\%)^{10}}{(1 + 10\%)^{10}} = \$100$$

$$\text{New Value} = \frac{\$100(1 + 10\%)^{10}}{(1 + 5\%)^{10}} = \$159$$

Now consider a similar bond, but structured as a mortgage with a prepayment option. If rates dropped to 5%, the borrower would be sensible to pay back the $100 and get a new mortgage at 5%. In this case, the bank issuing the mortgage simply receives $100 from the customer and does not gain the $59.

In the United States, there is a large market of traded mortgage-backed securities (MBS). In an MBS, the payments from many mortgages are pooled together. This pool of payments is then used to guarantee payments on several tranches of bonds. The most secure bonds are paid first, and once they have been paid the next tranche is entitled to payment, and so forth. The tranches can also be split as to whether they are entitled to the interest payments only (IO) or principal payments only (PO). The value of a tranche of principal payments increases when prepayments increase because the cash flows happen sooner. Tranches entitled to interest payments drop significantly in value when prepayments occur because the interest-payment stream stops. The valuation of the payment streams therefore depends heavily on customer behavior.

The Public Securities Association (PSA) has published a standard for the expected conditional prepayment rate (CPR). It says that 0% are expected to prepay in the first month, rising linearly to 6% per annum at month 30. Thereafter, each year 6% of the remaining borrowers are expected to prepay. An MBS with a prepayment rate matching this profile is said to be at 100% PSA. An MBS with twice the prepayment rate would be at 200% PSA.

A term related to the CPR is the SMM (single monthly mortality rate). This is the percentage of the remaining pool that prepays each month. The CPR and SMM are simply related:

$$(1 - CPR) = (1 - SMM)^{12}$$

Figure 12-2 shows the amount of principal outstanding on a 20-year, 8% mortgage, assuming that the installments are equal and there is no prepayment. Figure 12-3 shows the same mortgage but with prepayments at 100% PSA. With prepayments, the stream of interest payments is reduced, and the principal payments are early.

Table 12-1 shows the NPV of the principal and interest payments for different speeds of prepayment. Notice that as the PSA increases, the value of the principal payments increases, and the value of the interest payments decreases.

The PSA standard is a very simple model. The main simplification is that in reality, the prepayment rate is strongly affected by changes in interest rates. When market rates drop, new mortgages have lower interest payments, and homeowners are tempted to refinance their homes by taking out a new mortgage and prepaying the old one. Prepayments increase as the gap between the old and new mortgage rates widens. The value of the option to prepay is the difference in the NPV of the two alternative sets of interest payments, minus the strike price. The *strike price* includes any prepayment penalties and the plain hassle involved in refinancing. Prepayment also requires that customers be sufficiently financially sophisticated to realize that they can refinance more cheaply. Customers also exercise their prepayment option suboptimally whenever they sell their homes.

A typical prepayment function can be approximated as a *logistic function*. The form of the logistic function is as follows:

$$f(x) = \frac{1}{1 + e^x}$$

This function equals one when x equals negative infinity and equals zero when x equals positive infinity. The function has the shape of an S curve between one and zero. The prepayment rate as a percentage of the PSA can be modeled as follows:

FIGURE 12-2

Mortgage Amortization with No Prepayments

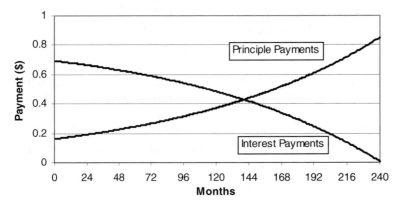

FIGURE 12-3

Mortgage Amortization with Prepayments at 100% PSA

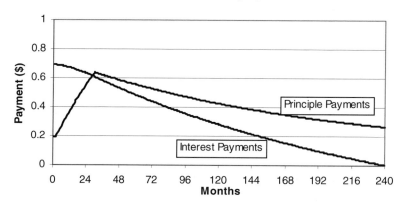

$$\%PSA = \frac{a}{1 + e^{b(r-c)}} + d$$

Here, r is the market-refinancing rate. a, b, c, and d are constants. a determines the maximum $\%PSA$, b determines the sharpness of the customer response, c determines the rate at which the refinancing is equal to 100% PSA. d is the residual amount of refinancing that will always take place, however adverse the market, because of people moving to new homes. Typical values for the parameters are given in the equation below:

$$\%PSA = \frac{1.8}{1 + e^{2(r-9\%)}} + 0.18$$

This function is shown in Figure 12-4.

TABLE 12-1

Effect of Prepayment Speed on NPV

% PSA	NPV of Principle Payments	NPV of Interest Payments
0	$39	$61
50	$47	$53
75	$50	$50
100	$53	$47
125	$56	$44
150	$58	$42
175	$60	$40
200	$62	$38

FIGURE 12-4

Rate of Prepayment as a Function of Prevailing Market Rates

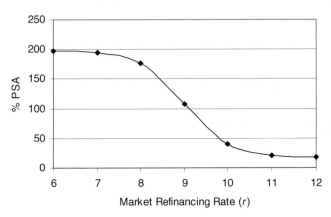

Knowing how changes in interest rates cause changes in the prepayment rate, we can estimate the effect of rate changes on the value of a mortgage-backed security.

Changes in market rates affect both the discount rate and the timing of the cash flows from the MBS. Figure 12-5 shows the effect of rate changes on the NPV of principal-only (PO) payments. The sudden drop in value occurs in the region where prepayment rates drop and the average time for the cash flows increases dramatically.

Figure 12-6 shows the effect of rate changes on the NPV of interest-only (IO) payments. This shape is very interesting. As the rate begins to increase from 6% to

FIGURE 12-5

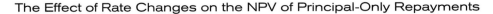

The Effect of Rate Changes on the NPV of Principal-Only Repayments

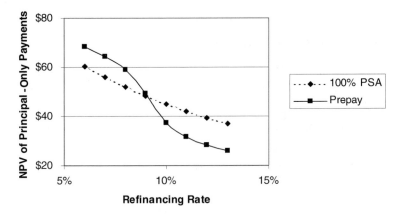

FIGURE 12-6

The Effect of Rate Changes on the NPV of Interest-Only Payments

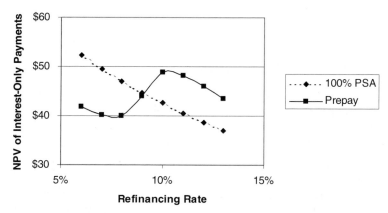

8%, the value drops because of the greater discounting. From 8% to 10% as rates increase, so does the value of the security. This is because there are significantly fewer prepayments of principal, and therefore more interest payments. Such regions in which value increases as rates increase are referred to as having *negative convexity*. Once the prepayment rate stabilizes at a new low level, the discounting effect again begins to dominate, and positive convexity returns above 10%. By slicing the payment streams, securities can be formed with many interest-rate characteristics.

The example above shows that the change in value of an MBS can be a complex function of interest rates. In reality, the value of an MBS is even more complex because customer payments are also path dependent. They are path dependent because the prepayment rates depend not only on the current market rate, but also on the previous rates. If rates have previously been low, most of the financially sophisticated borrowers will have already prepaid, and a renewed drop in rates will not cause a significant increase in prepayments.

In the example above, the security holders are entitled to all of the principle or interest cash flows. We could have sliced each of those cash flows into multiple tranches in which the most-secure tranches are always paid first, and the least-secure tranches get the residual payments. In this case, the most-secure tranches behave like normal bonds unless there is a very severe drop in rates, and the least-secure tranches have an even stronger response to changes in rates because they are effectively leveraged.

The accurate valuation of mortgage-backed securities is highly complex and the subject of many trading models, but the key points to be aware of are as follows:

- Mortgage-backed securities can be structured to have values that are very complex functions of interest rates.
- The value of an MBS is greatly dependent on the prepayment rate.

- The prepayment rate is a complex function of interest rates.
- The response to changes in interest rates can have significant negative convexity; i.e., the value can rise as rates rise.

Credit-Card Receivables

Many banks have a large portion of their assets in the form of credit-card receivables, either from credit cards that they have originated, or from asset-backed securities (ABS) that are backed by credit-card receivables. Interest payments are usually a fixed percentage above the prime rate, often with caps on the maximum that can be charged.

The value of credit-card receivables depends on two main factors: the default rate, and the difference between market rates and the rate charged on the cards. The most important factor is the default rate, which can be on the order of 10% to 20%. The default rate is generally measured as a credit risk, but it is also possible to model it as an ALM risk in a similar way to the modeling of prepayments for mortgages.

Commercial Loans

Large commercial loans are priced relative to the prevailing market rates, and can therefore be considered to have the characteristics of bonds, possibly with prepayment options that will be exercised as efficiently as if they were traded instruments.

Long-Term Investments

The ALM book often also includes such balance-sheet items as "strategic investments," which were bought by the senior management as a way of investing the bank's excess funds. The ALM book may also include real estate that is used by the bank or owned by the bank as an investment. Long-term investments such as these have values that are sensitive to interest-rate movements, and therefore should be included in the analysis of the bank's structural interest-rate position. It is difficult to model the interest-rate sensitivity of illiquid equities or real estate, but a reasonable proxy is to use the interest-rate sensitivity of market indices or to build cash-flow models for company income and real-estate rental rates.

Traded Bonds and Derivatives

The ALM book can also include liquidly traded instruments, such as bonds, swaps, and options. Identical instruments could also be held in the trading book, but the instruments in the ALM book are held either to modify the interest-rate position of the book, or as a temporary place to invest the bank's funds before they are used for customer transactions.

This concludes the discussion of assets, let us now turn to liabilities.

Retail Checking and Savings Accounts

Checking and savings accounts are also known as demand deposit accounts (DDA). Demand deposits such as checking and savings accounts have a contractual maturity of zero because they must be repaid to the customers as soon as they are demanded. Checking and savings accounts receive interest payments that are equal to or close to zero. Customers have DDAs for convenience and cash management. From a bank's point of view, the profitability of a checking account is the income the bank can make from investing the funds, plus any fees charged to the customer, minus all the administrative costs. Although checking accounts are demand deposits and can be withdrawn at any time, in practice the total balance for the sum of all checking accounts in a bank is typically relatively stable.[1] The net effect is that the banks can rely on having most of this money for many months or years. However, when interest rates rise, the total balance of checking accounts tends to fall as customers become more careful in sweeping their checking accounts into high-yielding savings accounts, money market accounts, or mutual funds.

In general, the value of a liability is the NPV of the cash flows from the liability. In the case of a noninterest-bearing checking account, the cash flows arise from changes in the net balance.

As an illustration, consider a simplified model for checking accounts. On the day the bank opens, a million customers come in, and they deposit $500 each. If the market remains stable, the net balance is expected to fluctuate between $400 million and $600 million. The bank can therefore consider $400 million to be "core" long-term deposits and the remaining as short-term funds. If the bank assumes that it will be in the checking-account business for at least 5 years, it can value the NPV of its liabilities as being $100 million owed immediately and $400 million to be paid in 4 years' time. Assuming an interest rate of 5%, this liability is worth $413 million (not including the administrative costs of servicing):

$$NPV = \$100\,M + \frac{\$400}{(1+5\%)^5} = \$413$$

If interest rates suddenly move to 10%, and the payments remain stable at $100 and $400, the value of the liability would fall to $348:

$$NPV = \$100\,M + \frac{\$400}{(1+10\%)^5} = \$348$$

However, if the customers withdraw half of the $400 million to invest elsewhere, the liability becomes worth $424:

$$\text{NPV} = \$300\,\text{M} + \frac{\$200}{(1 + 10\%)^5} = \$424$$

This demonstrates negative convexity. In this example, the change in value is strongly dependent on how the balance changes when rates change. A simple model for the changes in balance would be to say that there is an expected growth, a response to changes in rates, and a random element. This could be modeled by the equation below:

$$B_t = B_{t-1}(\gamma - \rho(r_t - r_{t-1}) + \varepsilon_t)$$

Here, B_t is the balance at time t, B_{t-1} is the balance at the previous time step, ρ determines the extent to which depositors withdraw their funds when rates increase, and ε_t is a random term. Such a model can be constructed by carrying out a regression between historical changes in balances and changes in rates. The model can then be used to estimate the value of the liability under different assumptions for rate changes.

Deposit accounts such as money market accounts may also pay a small amount of floating-rate interest. This makes their value more like the value of a floating rate bond paying the overnight rate. The NPV of a bond paying the overnight rate is always 100%. Therefore, the NPV of money market accounts is less sensitive to changes in market rates, as it is a less significant loss if customers withdraw early.

Retail Fixed Deposits

Fixed deposits (FDs) are offered in increments of months or years. Fixed deposits are also known as certificates of deposit (CDs). In FDs, customers guarantee not to withdraw the funds for a given period, and they are rewarded by receiving a relatively high fixed-interest payment. If the customers withdraw their funds early, they forfeit the interest income. If at the end of the deposit period, customers choose to redeposit (or "roll over") the funds, the new rate is based on the prevailing market rates. Fixed deposits therefore have interest-rate characteristics that are similar to short-term bonds or floating-rate bonds. The main difference between fixed deposits and bonds is that the interest rate is not tied directly to the market rate, but is more commonly tied to the prime rate minus a few percent. The prime rate is the rate posted by the bank to its retail customers. It is only changed when there is a significant change in market rates, and typically changes every one to six months. It is often modeled as a lagged response to changes in the three-month rate. The prime rate is changed by banks as a response to both the market rates and the competitive situation; the value of fixed deposits is therefore a complex function of the market behavior, customer behavior, and bank behavior.

Deposits from Commercial Customers

Large deposits from commercial customers are generally priced very close to the prevailing interbank rate, and are therefore well approximated as bonds.

Bonds Issued by the Bank

The ALM book also contains bonds issued by the bank. These bonds are occasionally issued by banks to adjust their interest-rate position, raise funds, or modify the capital structure. They are a useful benchmark in determining the bank's true cost of debt.

SUMMARY

In this chapter, we introduced the two risks associated with ALM, namely, interest-rate and liquidity risk. We also detailed the sources of these risks and the characteristics of ALM instruments. Next, we discuss the measurement of interest-rate risk for ALM.

NOTE

1 Although the total amount in retail checking accounts increases sharply on payday at the end of each month, the net balance from one month's end to the next is stable.

CHAPTER 13

Measurement of Interest-Rate Risk for ALM

INTRODUCTION

The previous chapter outlined the difference between the two primary ALM risks: liquidity and interest rates. This chapter will examine the measurement of interest-rate risk in greater detail.

The purposes of measuring ALM interest-rate risk are to establish the amount of economic capital to be held against such risks, and to show managers how the risks can be reduced. Risks can be reduced by buying or selling interest-rate-sensitive instruments, such as bonds and swaps, or by restructuring the products that the bank offers, e.g., promoting floating-rate mortgages over fixed-rate mortgages or encouraging more fixed deposits.

Although ALM risk is a form of market risk, it cannot be effectively measured using the trading-VaR framework. This VaR framework is inadequate for two reasons. First, the ALM cash flows are complex functions of customer behavior. Second, interest-rate movements over long time horizons are not well modeled by the simple assumptions used for VaR. Therefore, banks use three alternative approaches to measure ALM interest-rate risk, as listed below:

- Gap reports
- Rate-shift scenarios
- Simulation methods similar to Monte Carlo VaR

These approaches are now examined in greater detail.

GAP REPORTS

Gap reports have been in use for many years to monitor the interest-rate risk. They can also be used to measure liquidity risk. They characterize the balance sheet as a fixed series of cash flows. The "gap" is the difference between the cash flows from assets and liabilities.

Gap reports are useful because they are relatively easy to create, and they give a very intuitive appreciation of the overall position of the bank. Gap reports can also be used to estimate the duration of the cash flows, and therefore allow us to get an approximate measure of the risk. This measure is only approximate because gap reports do not include information on the way customers exercise their implicit options in different interest environments.

There are three types of gap reports: contractual maturity, repricing frequency, and effective maturity. Each is explained in greater detail below, then we explain how a crude estimate of required economic capital can be based on the gap report.

Contractual-Maturity Gap Reports

A *contractual-maturity gap report* indicates when cash flows are contracted to be paid. For liabilities, it is the time when payments would be due from the bank, assuming that customers did not roll over their accounts. For example, the contractual maturity for checking accounts is zero because customers have the right to withdraw their funds immediately. The contractual maturity for a portfolio of three-month certificates of deposit would (on average) be a ladder of equal payments from zero to three months. This ladder occurs because new deposits are continuously expiring and originating.

The contractual maturity for assets may or may not include assumptions about prepayments. In the most simple reports, all payments are assumed to occur on the last day of the contract. Such assumptions are made to ease the requirements for data gathering and analysis, but cause significant distortions in the risk measurement.

A contractual-maturity gap report is illustrated in Figure 13-1. Along the x-axis there is maturity. The height in the y-axis is the amount of assets and liabilities maturing in each time bucket. Assets appear above the line and liabilities below the line. In this figure, the bank has almost $30 billion of demand deposits, and assets whose maturity is more evenly spaced over the next 10 years.

The contractual-maturity gap report is useful in showing liquidity characteristics because it shows the mismatch of cash flows into the bank and the possible required cashflows out of the bank if customers exercised their rights to withdraw funds immediately. However, the contractual-maturity gap report gives little information on interest-rate risk.

Repricing Gap Reports

For interest-rate measurement, an improvement on the contractual gap report is a gap report based on repricing characteristics. *Repricing* refers to when and how the

FIGURE 13-1

Illustration of Contractual-Maturity Gap Report

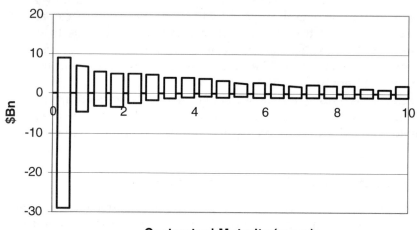

Contractual Maturity (years)

The *x*-axis in this maturity gap report reflects maturity. The *y*-axis shows the amount of assets and liabilities maturing in each time bucket.

interest payments will be reset. The repricing gap makes no assumptions about customer behavior but begins to capture the interest-rate characteristics of the balance sheet.

The report matches together all assets and liabilities that have the same interest-rate basis, e.g., prime, 3-month LIBOR, 5-year fixed rate, etc. Accounts based on prime are typically included in the 3-month bucket, but may also have a bucket of their own. Compared with the contractual gap report, the main difference is that medium-term, prime-based assets such as personal loans move from the 2-year and 4-year buckets down to the 3-month bucket. Similarly, any floating-rate mortgages will move down from 10 or 30 years to below the 1-year bucket.

Effective-Maturity Gap Reports

Although the repricing report includes the effect of interest-rate changes, it does not include the effects of customer behavior. This additional interest-rate risk is captured by showing the effective maturity. For example, the effective maturity for a mortgage includes the expected prepayments, and may include an adjustment to approximate the risk arising from the response of prepayments to changes in interest rates. The effective maturity for checking accounts typically includes the assumption that the total amount in the checking accounts will have a core component that will not be withdrawn in the near future. Checking accounts behave more like a ladder of bonds than an overnight loan.

The effective maturity for prime-based accounts is typically assumed to be two to four months, or a ladder of bonds from overnight to six months. The overall effect is as follows: assets have a shorter effective maturity than their contractual maturity, and liabilities have a longer effective maturity than their contractual maturity.

Gap reports give an intuitive view of the balance sheet, but they represent the instruments as fixed cash flows, and therefore do not allow any analysis of the nonlinearity of the value of the customers' options. To capture this nonlinear risk requires approaches that allow cash flows to change as a function of rates.

Estimating Economic Capital Based on Gap Reports

It is relatively easy to use gap reports to get a crude estimate of the economic capital required for ALM interest-rate risks. The gap reports give us a series of cash flows. We can treat these cash flows as if they are payments from a bond for which we can calculate duration dollars. Recall that duration dollars measure the sensitivity of the value of a bond to changes in interest rates:

$$Duration\$ = -\frac{dV}{dr} = \sum_t \frac{tC_t}{(1+r)^{t+1}}$$

Change in Value $= -Duration\$ \times$ Change in Rates

From historical data, we can estimate the standard deviation of rate changes. For economic-capital purposes, we need the annual standard deviation of rates. This can be calculated using annual data or from quarterly, monthly, or daily data, and then using the square-root-of-T approximation to convert to annual standard deviation:

$$\sigma_{Annual} \approx \sqrt{4}\sigma_{Quarterly} \approx \sqrt{12}\sigma_{Monthly} \approx \sqrt{250}\sigma_{Daily}$$

It is generally best to use quarterly data as the best compromise between using recent data and including long-term trends such as mean reversion.

We can now calculate the standard deviation of the change in the ALM portfolio over a year:

$$\sigma_{Value,Annual} = Duration\$ \times \sigma_{Rate,Annual}$$

Economic capital is several times the standard deviation of change in value. For example, if the bank's target creditworthiness is a 10-basis-point probability of default, and we assume the value is Normally distributed, the economic capital should cover 3 standard deviations of value:

$$Economic\ Capital \approx Duration\$ \times 3 \times \sigma_{Rate,Annual}$$

For this analysis, we made several significant assumptions. We assumed that value changes linearly with rate changes (i.e., there is no optionality, and bond convexity is negligible). We also assumed that the duration would be constant over the whole year; i.e., the portfolio composition would remain the same. Finally, we assumed that annual rate changes were Normally distributed. Combined, these assumptions could easily create a 20% to 50% error in the estimation of capital. We now discuss methods that do not require so many assumptions.

RATE-SHIFT SCENARIOS

Rate-shift scenarios attempt to capture the nonlinear behavior of customers. A common scenario test is to shift all rates up by 1%. After shifting the rates, the cash flows are changed according to the behavior expected in the new environment; for example, mortgage prepayments may increase, some of the checking and savings accounts may be withdrawn, and the prime rate may increase after a delay. The NPV of this new set of cash flows is then calculated using the new rates. The analysis is used to show the changes in earnings and value expected under different rate scenarios.

As an example, let us consider a bank with $90 million in savings accounts and $100 million in fixed-rate mortgages. Assume that the current interbank rate is 5%, the savings accounts pay 2%, and the mortgages pay 10%. The expected net income over the next year is $8.2 million:

$$Interest\ Income = 10\% \times \$100M - 2\% \times \$90M = \$8.2M$$

If interbank rates move up by 1%, assume that savings customers will expect to be paid an extra 25 basis points, and 10% of them will move from savings accounts to money-market accounts paying 5%. Nothing will happen to the mortgages. In this case the expected income falls slightly to $7.5 million:

$$Interest\ Income = 10\% \times \$100M - 2.25\% \times \$81M - 5\% \times \$9M = \$7.5M$$

Now assume that interbank rates fall by 1%. Savings customers are expected to be satisfied with 25 basis points less, but 10% of the mortgages are expected to prepay and refinance at 9%. The expected income in these circumstances is $8.3 million:

$$Interest\ Income = 10\% \times \$90M + 9\% \times \$10M - 1.75\% \times \$90M = \$8.3M$$

The example above shows the nonlinear change of income. We can extend this to show changes over several years. By discounting these changes, we can get a measure of the change in value.

An approximate estimate of the economic capital can be obtained by assuming that rates shift up or down equal to three times their annual standard deviation, and then calculating the cash flows and value changes in that scenario. The economic capital is then estimated as the worst loss from either the up or down shifts.

The rate-shift scenarios are useful in giving a measure of the changes in value and income caused by implicit options, but they can miss losses caused by complex changes in interest rates such as a shift up at one time followed by a fall. To capture such effects properly we need a simulation engine that assesses value changes in many scenarios.

SIMULATION METHODS

The purpose of using simulation methods is to test the nonlinear effects with many complex rate scenarios and obtain a probabilistic measure of the economic capital to be held against ALM interest-rate risks.

The primary simulation method is Monte Carlo evaluation. The process is similar to that used for calculating the Monte Carlo VaR for trading portfolios. However, there are two main differences: the simulation extends out over several years rather than just one day, and the models used are not simply pricing models for financial instruments, but also include models for customer behavior and the behavior of administered rates such as prime.

Monte Carlo simulation can use the same behavior models as the rate-shift scenarios. The difference is that in a simulation, the scenarios are complex, time-varying interest-rate paths rather than simple yield-curve shifts.

The Monte Carlo simulation is carried out as shown in Figure 13-2:

- Randomly create a scenario of future interest rates for the next month.
- Use models for each type of product to estimate the changes in the product's balance for that rate scenario, e.g., prepayments of loans and withdrawals of deposits.
- Model administered rates, such as prime, to get the interest to be paid on administered-rate products.

FIGURE 13-2

The Process for an ALM Monte Carlo Simulation

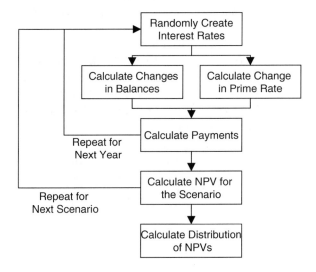

- Calculate payments of interest using the rate multiplied by the product's balance. Calculate payments of principal using the changes in balances. This produces the net income for the month.
- The simulation then randomly creates an interest-rate scenario for the next month and steadily moves forward to a horizon typically around three to five years. At this horizon, the value of each product is assumed to be equal to the remaining balance outstanding.
- The net value of the portfolio for the given scenario is the NPV of all the cash flows generated and the remaining balance.
- The process is then repeated for several hundred new scenarios. The result is a probability distribution for the earnings at each time step and a distribution for the portfolio's value.

Models to Create Interest-Rate Scenarios Randomly

An important component in the simulation approach is the stochastic (i.e., random) model used to generate interest-rate paths. Many models have been developed. The most basic model is the one commonly used in Monte Carlo VaR for trading portfolios. This basic interest-rate model assumes that the interest rate in the next period (r_{t+1}) will equal the current rate (r_t), plus a random number with a standard deviation of σ:

$$r_{t+1} = r_t + \sigma \times z_t$$
$$z_t \in N(0, 1)$$

This is inadequate for ALM purposes because over long periods, such as a year, the simulated interest rate can become negative. This model also lacks two features observed in historical interest rates: rates are mean reverting and heteroskedastic (their volatility varies over time).

Two classes of more sophisticated models have been developed for interest rates: general-equilibrium (GE) models and arbitrage-free (AF) models. The AF approach observes the current set of bond prices and deduces the stochastic model that would create those prices. This arbitrage-free approach provides prices that are tightly tied to the prices currently observed in the market, and therefore is generally good for trading.

The GE approach assumes a model for the random process that created the observed history of rates, and then estimates a yield curve that can be used to price bonds. The general equilibrium approach gives a better model of volatility. It therefore is better for risk management and is described here. A general model for the GE approach has a mean-reverting term and a factor that reduces the volatility as rates drop:

$$r_{t+1} = r_t + \kappa(\theta - r_t)\Delta t + \sigma\sqrt{\Delta t} \times r_t^{\gamma} \times z_t$$
$$z_t \in N(0, 1)$$

Here, θ is the level to which interest rates tend to revert over time. κ determines the speed of reversion. If κ is close to 1, the rates revert quickly; if it is close to 0, the model becomes like a random walk. σ gives the relative volatility of the disturbances to the rates. γ determines how significantly the volatility will be reduced as rates drop. If γ was 0, the volatility would not change if rates changed. The factor $\sqrt{\Delta t}$ scales the volatility according to the size of the timestep. If γ is fixed equal to 0.5, the GE equation is called the *Cox-Ingersoll-Ross* equation. If γ is fixed equal to 1, it is called the *Vasicek model*.

Values for the parameters θ, κ, σ, and γ can be determined from historical rate information using maximum likelihood estimation, as explained in Appendix A to this chapter. The equation below parameterizes the three-month U.S. T-bill rate from January 1990 to January 2001. (Δt is in units of years.)

$$r_{3m,t+1} = r_{3m,t} + 0.53(5.1\% - r_{3m,t})\Delta t + 0.03\sqrt{\Delta t} \times r_{3m,t}^{0.4} \times z_{3m,t}$$

The random driving term $z_{3m,t}$ is approximately Normal with a mean of zero and standard deviation of one. A common approach to finding the longer-term rates is to say that they are given by a complex equation depending on θ, κ, σ, γ, and the current value of the short rate $r_{3m,t}$. An alternative approach is suggested here.

The equations below parameterize the 3-month U.S. T-bill rate, the 1-year U.S. note rate, and the 10-year U.S. T-bond rate:

$$r_{3m,t+1} = r_{3m,t} + 0.53(5.1\% - r_{3m,t})\Delta t + 0.03\sqrt{\Delta t} \times r_{3m,t}^{0.4} \times z_{3m,t}$$

$$r_{1y,t+1} = r_{1y,t} + 0.55(5.4\% - r_{1y,t})\Delta t + 0.02\sqrt{\Delta t} \times r_{1y,t}^{0.3} \times z_{1y,t}$$

$$r_{10y,t+1} = r_{10y,t} + 0.56(6.6\% - r_{10y,t})\Delta t + 0.02\sqrt{\Delta t} \times r_{10y,t}^{0.3} \times z_{10y,t}$$

The correlation between the driving terms $z_{3m,t}$, $z_{1y,t}$, and $z_{10y,t}$ is as follows:

$$\rho_{3m,1y} = 0.061$$

$$\rho_{3m,10y} = 0.044$$

$$\rho_{1y,10y} = 0.741$$

This can also be expressed as a correlation matrix:

$$C = \begin{bmatrix} 1 & 0.061 & 0.044 \\ 0.061 & 1 & 0.741 \\ 0.044 & 0.741 & 1 \end{bmatrix}$$

We can carry out an Eigenvalue decomposition on this matrix, as described in the chapter on Monte Carlo VaR:

$$C = E\Lambda E^T$$

$$E = \begin{bmatrix} 0.099 & 0.995 & -0.016 \\ 0.704 & -0.059 & 0.708 \\ 0.703 & -0.081 & -0.706 \end{bmatrix}$$

$$\Lambda = \begin{bmatrix} 1.749 & 0 & 0 \\ 0 & 0.993 & 0 \\ 0 & 0 & 0.258 \end{bmatrix}$$

$$E\Lambda^{\frac{1}{2}} = \begin{bmatrix} 0.131 & 0.991 & -0.008 \\ 0.931 & -0.059 & 0.360 \\ 0.930 & -0.081 & -0.360 \end{bmatrix}$$

We can then use this to create properly correlated driving terms for the three rates:

$$Z = E\Lambda^{\frac{1}{2}}N$$

$$\begin{bmatrix} z_{3m,t} \\ z_{1y,t} \\ z_{10y,t} \end{bmatrix} = \begin{bmatrix} 0.131 & 0.991 & -0.008 \\ 0.931 & -0.059 & 0.360 \\ 0.930 & -0.081 & -0.360 \end{bmatrix} \begin{bmatrix} n_1 \\ n_2 \\ n_3 \end{bmatrix}$$

Here, N is a vector of n_1, n_2, and n_3, each of which is an uncorrelated, random number from a Standard Normal distribution. Z is the vector of $z_{3m,t}$, $z_{1y,t}$, and $z_{10y,t}$, which are random numbers each with a Standard Normal distribution and with the required correlation between them. The result of this is that all three rates are driven by correlated shocks, and therefore tend to move together.

Figure 13-3 shows an example in which a random scenario for the rates has been created using the above approach. In this example, the rates are simulated in monthly time steps out to 5 years. Notice that the 1-year and 10-year rates tend to move together, but the 3-month rate is more independent.

Stochastic Product Models

The rate scenarios created above are used to drive models of customer behavior. If we take the example of a checking account, a typical model for the balances would have a constant-growth term, changes in the balance according to the three-month rate, and changes due to uncorrelated random events:

$$B_{t+1} = B_t\left(1 + g + a \ r_{3m,t} + z_{b,t}\frac{\sigma_b}{\sqrt{\Delta t}}\right)\Delta t$$

$$z_{b,t} \in N(0,1)$$

FIGURE 13-3

Illustration of a Random Scenario for Interest Rates

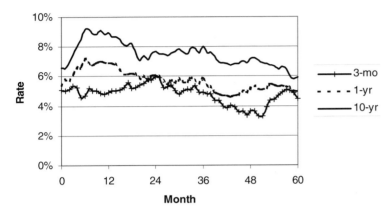

Here, g is the growth term, a is a constant giving the response of the balance to changes in rates, $z_{b,t}$ is from a Standard Normal distribution, and σ_b is the annual volatility caused by external events (i.e., the residual from the regression).

To give a numerical example, let us assume that the results of a regression between the rates and the balances finds that each factor has a 10% influence. (In this example, the coefficient on the rate has been scaled by the average rate.)

$$B_{t+1} = B_t + B_t \left(0.1 + \frac{0.1}{5.1\%} \, r_{3m,t} + z_{b,t} \, \frac{0.1}{\sqrt{\Delta t}} \right) \Delta t$$

Creation of Stochastic Cash Flows

Using this model for the balances, driven by the rate scenario, we produced the scenario result shown in Figure 13-4. By taking the difference in balance from one time step to the next, we get the cash flows to and from the checking account, including the final repayment of all balances assumed at the five-year horizon. The cash flows for the scenario are shown in Figure 13-5. The spike at the end is the assumed repayment of the remaining balances at the five-year horizon.

This example gives an indication of the process used to estimate earnings volatility for a single product. An evaluation for a full ALM portfolio follows the same procedure, but includes balance and payments models for all products. A more detailed model may also include costs of servicing, which become important when valuing products such as checking accounts. In the section below, we explore how to get from this to a measure of economic capital.

FIGURE 13-4

Illustration of a Random Scenario for Balances

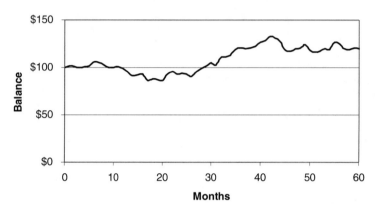

FIGURE 13-5

Illustration of a Random Scenario for Cash Flows

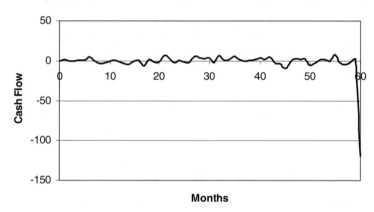

Value Volatility and Economic Capital Simulation

In measuring the economic capital, we want to know how much capital should be held at the beginning of the year, so there is a very high probability that the port-folio's value will still be positive at the end of the year. For example, an A-rated bank should have approximately a 99.9% chance of the value being positive at the end of the year.

Consider having a simulation that gives the NPV of the capital at the end of 10 years. If we held capital equal to the NPV of the 99.9%-confidence level of the value distribution, we would have enough capital to be sure that we could have a 99.9% chance of surviving 10 years. This is too much capital for a single A bank that only needs a 99.9% chance of surviving 1 year. One possibility is to say that if the bank plans to remain rated single A, it needs a 99% probability of surviving 10 years. This would lead us to use the NPV of the 99%-confidence level of the NPV of the 10-year distribution as the economic capital.

This is a slightly different definition of economic capital, but should give results that are close to the capital that would be calculated from the 99.9% confidence level over 1 year. Direct calculation of the 1-year capital involves a complex simulation in which we first simulate cash flows up to the 1-year point, and then do a second simulation from the 1-year point to assess the value of the remaining balances. Such a complex nested simulation takes a long time to run, and the extra accuracy rarely justifies the extra effort.

SUMMARY

In this chapter, we examined the measurement of interest-rate risk in great detail. Knowing how to measure this risk enables us to establish the amount of economic capital to be held against such risks, and shows managers how the risk can be reduced. Next, we discuss funding liquidity risk for ALM, along with how it can be measured and managed.

APPENDIX A: MAXIMUM LIKELIHOOD ESTIMATION

In building the interest-rate models, we applied maximum likelihood estimation to find the values for the parameters. In maximum likelihood estimation, we seek the model that maximizes the combined probability of the observed events. In the case of interest rates, we seek the model that best describes the observed changes in the time series of historical interest rates.

The process is as follows:

1. We pick a model for the process, e.g., the CIR model.
2. We guess values for the parameters in the model, i.e., θ, κ, σ, and γ.
3. From historical data, we calculate the expected value of the variable in the next time step. For the CIR model, the expected value is given by the following:

$$E[r_{t+1}] = r_t + \kappa(\theta - r_t)\Delta t$$

4. We also calculate the standard deviation of the error that is expected due to the random driving term:

$$Standard\ Deviation[r_{t+1}] = \sigma\sqrt{\Delta t} \times r_t^\gamma$$

5. We calculate the probability density of the observed result happening given the model that we have chosen. For the CIR model, the probability density is the value of the Normal probability-density function for the observed rate, given the expected value and standard deviation:

$$p[r_{t+1}] = \phi[r_{t+1}, E[r_{t+1}],\ Standard\ Deviation[r_{t+1}]]$$

6. We repeat this for all N time steps of historical data, then multiply all the probabilities together to get a single number, J, that measures the goodness of the model:

$$J[\theta, \kappa, \sigma, \gamma] = p(r_1) \times p(r_2) \times p(r_3) \times \cdots \times p(r_N)$$

7. We then slightly change the parameters in the model and repeat the process until we find the parameter values that maximize J.

In practice, there is a slight modification to the above algorithm because the product of the probabilities for hundreds of data points is a number that is too small for computers to handle. However, maximizing the product of a set of numbers is the same as maximizing the sum of the log of the numbers, so in step 6, the equation for J should be replaced by the following:

$$J[\theta, \kappa, \sigma, \gamma] = \ln[p(r_1)] + \ln[p(r_2)] + \ln[p(r_3)] + \cdots \ln[p(r_N)]$$

CHAPTER 14

Funding-Liquidity Risk in ALM

INTRODUCTION

In the previous chapter, we discussed the interest-rate risk that is caused by mismatches between the bank's assets and liabilities. One function of the ALM unit is to measure and manage this interest-rate risk. The ALM unit is also involved in the management of the funding-liquidity risk that arises from mismatches between the assets and liabilities.

This risk arises because banks generally fund themselves with liabilities that have very short contractual maturity (e.g., demand deposits such as checking accounts). Banks take the money they receive from these liabilities, set aside a small amount in cash, and invest the rest in assets that have long maturity, e.g., commercial loans. In general, customers leave most of their money in the demand deposits for a long time, and the small amount of cash that the bank sets aside is sufficient to meet customers' requests for withdrawals. However, if withdrawals are unusually high, there is a risk that the bank would not have enough cash to meet the demand. Such a situation could happen if there was a rumor that the bank could have a liquidity problem, which would lead customers to withdraw their funds, thereby creating a liquidity problem and increasing the rumors. This vicious cycle is called a "run on the bank."

In such a situation, the bank's choices can be simplified into three: borrow money from other banks, if they are willing and able to supply more cash; sell some of the loans, possibly at deeply discounted prices; or default to the customers, and go out of business. This risk of defaulting or being forced to sell at a loss is called *funding-liquidity risk* or *cash-crisis risk*.

Funding-liquidity risk is different from the liquidity risk discussed in the chapters on trading risk. The liquidity risk in trading arises from the possibility of the bank's losing money by being locked into a position that is losing value. But in ALM, we are concerned that the bank will be unable to raise enough cash to pay its customers, or that it will be forced to sell ("cash in") assets at an awkward moment, incurring a significant liquidation cost. There is also an important "reputation" element in funding risk because if a bank is seen scrambling for funds, other market participants will start charging the bank high interest rates on any funds it borrows. In this chapter, we discuss in more detail how funding-liquidity risk arises, how it can be measured, and how it can be managed.

MEASUREMENT OF LIQUIDITY RISK

Let us begin our analysis of liquidity risks by considering the bank's uses and sources of funds. The *uses* of funds are the outflows of payments from the bank to customers or other banks. The *sources* of funds are inflows from customers and other banks.

To structure our discussion, we classify payments as scheduled, unscheduled, semidiscretionary, and discretionary. *Scheduled payments* are those which have previously been agreed on by the counterparties. *Unscheduled payments* arise from customer behavior. *Semidiscretionary payments* occur as part of the bank's normal trading operations but can be quickly changed if necessary. The *discretionary transactions* are those carried out by the bank's funding unit to balance the net cash flow each day. Using this classification, the typical daily outflows are as follows:

- Scheduled loan disbursements to customers
- Scheduled repayments to customers, such as maturing fixed deposits (FDs)
- Scheduled loan repayments to other banks as well as corporations
- Unscheduled repayments to customers, such as withdrawals from checking-account deposits
- Unscheduled loan disbursements to customers, such as credit cards and lines of credit
- Unscheduled contracted payments to corporations, such as contingent standby lines of credit
- Semidiscretionary payments for the purchase of securities by the bank
- Semidiscretionary payments as cash collateral for borrowing securities or for reverse repos
- Discretionary lending to other banks in the short-term interbank market

The bank typically has the following inflows and sources of cash:

- Scheduled payments being made into the bank by customers, including loan repayments
- Unscheduled payments by customers, such as checking-account deposits, and rollover of expiring fixed deposits into new fixed deposits
- Semidiscretionary payments from the sale of normal trading securities

- Semidiscretionary payments as cash collateral for lending securities or for repos
- Discretionary payments from the sale of securities from a liquidity reserve
- Discretionary borrowing from other banks in the interbank market
- Discretionary calls on backup lines of credit prearranged with other banks
- Cash on hand, stored in the vault or deposited with the government
- In great emergency, calling on the government for expensive short-term funding

This classification allows us to construct a framework to measure funding-liquidity risk. The measurement of funding requirements can be considered for three situations: expected requirements, unusual requirements, and crisis conditions.

Expected Funding Requirements

The expected requirements are relatively easy to measure conceptually, although they require a large amount of daily data collection. The expected requirements are all the scheduled payments, plus the average levels of all the other payments. For example, if the total balance of the checking-account portfolio is expected to increase steadily over the next few months, this would create a net expected inflow. A more detailed, daily model would probably find that balances on personal checking accounts were expected to decline steadily towards the end of the month, then jump up as wages are paid. The mirror image of this is that corporate accounts would be expected to increase steadily, then drop as they pay wages. In this case, the net flow to the bank would be close to zero.

An important component of the scheduled funding requirements are new asset originations. For example, if the commercial lending unit is planning to give a $500 million loan to a corporation, this will cause an additional expected outflow of $500 million. For such a loan, the ALM and funding units should have advanced warning that they will need to source additional funds on the day that the loan is disbursed to the company.

Unusual Funding Requirements

The expected rarely happens. Instead, the unscheduled demand will usually be above or below the mean. As part of normal business, the bank should be ready to make payments easily on days when the net outflow of funds is 2 standard deviations above the daily mean. Two standard deviations for a Normal distribution corresponds to a 2% tail probability; therefore, such an event can be expected 5 times per year. This is not a crisis, just an unusual day. To meet this demand, the ALM desk will need to find funds from discretionary sources, such as interbank loans or selling liquid securities.

On any day, the net inflow of discretionary funds to be raised (I_D) equals the scheduled, unscheduled, and semidiscretionary outflows minus the scheduled, unscheduled, and semidiscretionary inflows:

$$I_D = (O_S + O_U + O_{SD}) - (I_S + I_U + I_{SD})$$

The scheduled flows are known, but the unscheduled and semidiscretionary flows evolve randomly according to the behavior of customers and the bank's normal operations. Let us group these random terms into a single variable, R:

$$R = (O_U + O_{SD}) - (I_U + I_{SD})$$

We can now say that the amount of discretionary funds to be raised (I_D) is equal to the scheduled flows plus the random term:

$$I_D = O_S - I_S + R$$

The funding requirement on unusual days is then the scheduled requirement, plus the average for R, plus an additional two standard deviations of R:

$$I_{D,2\sigma} = O_S - I_S + \overline{R} + 2\sigma_R$$

$\overline{R}$ and σ_R can be estimated by collecting historical data for O_U, O_{SD}, I_S, and I_U to calculate R for each past day.

The analysis above gives us the amount of funds that should be available to make payments on one unusual day. If we wish to be protected for an unusual period, we can make the bold assumption that cash flows from one day to the next are not correlated, and therefore can use the "square-root-of-T" approximation to scale up the standard deviation from one day to multiple days:

$$\sigma_{R,T} = \sqrt{T} \times \sigma_R$$

The results can be given as in Figure 14-1, which shows the cumulative scheduled funding and the scheduled funding plus two standard deviations of the uncertain requirements.

This analysis of the normal flows of funds gives a good measure for the amount of discretionary sources of funds that the ALM unit must keep available to continue conducting normal business on those unusual days that happen a few times each year.

It is tempting to use this analysis with a higher multiple of the standard deviation to get to a higher level of confidence. For example, if we had enough discretionary funding sources to cover 3 standard deviations of σ_R then, based on the shape of the Normal distribution, we might hope that the probability of meeting the payments would rise from 98% to 99.8%. However, this assumes that the underlying mechanisms causing an "unusual day" are the same as in a crisis. Unfortunately, this is not true, so we need to develop a different kind of model to cover crises.

FIGURE 14-1

Typical Results for the Required Payments

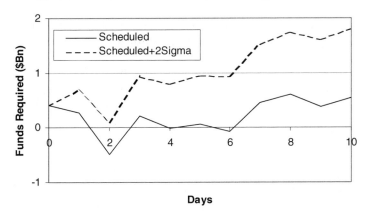

Crisis Funding Requirements and Economic Capital

By their nature, crises are rare, and there is little direct data to study. One possibility is to look at international crises and get a high-level indication of the behavior of customers and markets in such situations. However, such data is hard to find because banks naturally do not publish details about the occasions in which they almost defaulted.

An alternative approach to measuring the risk in a cash crisis is to use two steps. First, estimate the possible funding requirement by modifying the model that we used above. Then go on to estimate how much value would be lost in such a crisis. This gives us an indication of the economic capital required to be held against funding-liquidity risks.

The times of greatest liquidity risk are those in which there is a general market crisis. In such a crisis, customers lose confidence in the bank, and other banks are not able or willing to lend. In this situation, the bank may disrupt its normal business to minimize semidiscretionary outflows of cash, such as buying new securities. The bank will generally do everything it can to maximize its net cash available. It may also maximize the discretionary and semidiscretionary inflows, such as calling on standby lines of credit.

For a crisis, it would be reasonable to assume that the bank will make all its scheduled payments, and most of the scheduled inflows will be received, but there will be some defaults. We could also assume that customers made no unscheduled payments into the bank, and that the unscheduled payments to customers were a multiple of the usual standard deviation of unscheduled customer demands.

We can apply these assumptions to modify the requirement for funds on an "unusual" day, and thereby get an estimate of the amount of cash that would need to be generated in a crisis.

The next step is to estimate how much value the bank could lose in such a crisis. The loss would arise from selling assets that are usually illiquid but have been discounted to "fire-sale" prices to get cash.

The estimate of the loss can be achieved by making a list of the bank's assets in the order in which they would be sold to generate cash. Then, for each asset, estimate the amount of "fire-sale" discount that would be required to sell it immediately. Table 14-1 illustrates such a compilation. The columns list the amount of each asset class held by the bank, the discount that could be expected if they were sold in a crisis, and the consequent loss. If our analysis had shown that $13 billion of additional funds would be required in a crisis, then we would expect that we would need to sell all the cash, money-market instruments, and government bonds. This would give the bank the required $13 billion in cash to meet customers' demands.

However, in making these sales, the money-market instruments would be sold at $20 million below their value and the government bonds at $200 million below, making a total loss of $220 million. This would indicate that $220 million of economic capital should be maintained to absorb this potential loss.

LIQUIDITY-RISK MANAGEMENT

Once management has a picture of its current liquidity position and the associated probabilities of default, they can then begin to modify the position. This can be done in the following ways:

TABLE 14-1

Losses Due to Selling Assets in a Liquidity Crisis

Assets	Value ($Bn)	Cumulative Value ($Bn)	Fire-Sale Discount	Loss ($Bn)	Cumulative Loss ($Bn)
Cash	1	1	0%	0.00	0.00
Money Markets	2	3	1%	0.02	0.02
Treasuries	10	13	2%	0.20	0.22
Corp Bonds	10	23	3%	0.30	0.52
Equities	10	33	4%	0.40	0.92
Synd Loans	5	38	5%	0.25	1.17
Corporate Loans	25	63	15%	3.75	4.92
Retail Loans	40	103	30%	12.00	16.92

- Borrow long-term funds in the interbank market or issue bonds. Then use the proceeds to buy liquid assets, such as government bonds to be sold or pledged in times of crisis.
- Establish contingent standby lines of credit with other banks, whereby the bank providing the line of credit guarantees to give funds in a time of crisis. Establishing such a line can be expensive, especially if the bank providing the line sees that it is likely to be called when it is also in trouble.
- Limit the amount of funds that are lent for long maturities in the interbank market. The ultimate case would be to use only the overnight market for lending the proceeds from demand deposit accounts (DDAs) such as checking. This would perfectly match the contractual cash flows and eliminate liquidity risk, but it would give a relatively low yield.
- Reduce the liquidity of the bank's liabilities. For example, the bank could promote fixed deposits instead of savings accounts, and it could encourage customers with short-term FDs to move to longer-term FDs. This can be done by offering higher rates for more illiquid products. It can also reduce the value of the customer's option for early withdrawal by adding early-with-drawal penalties, and thereby increasing the exercise price.

It is also important that management should plan the optimal liquidation of the balance sheet for times of crisis. The funding desk should have a crisis-response plan prepared in advance so they know all the possible places in the bank that can either reduce their requirements for cash, get cash back if it has been lent or pledged, or increase cash inflow. The plan for generating cash inflow should list the order in which securities will be sold to minimize the amount of discount required.

SUMMARY

In this chapter, we discussed how ALM liquidity risk can be measured and managed. Next, we explain how to calculate funds-transfer pricing, which is the framework for establishing prices and moving interest-rate risk between business units.

CHAPTER 15

Funds-Transfer Pricing and the Management of ALM Risks

INTRODUCTION

In the preceding chapters, we examined the ALM interest-rate and liquidity risk to the bank. However, we did not specify which departments within the bank carry that risk. For example, we showed that if the bank has made long-term loans by using money from short-term savings accounts, the bank will suffer a loss if rates rise. However, we did not specify whether that loss should be counted as a loss on the loans, a loss on the savings accounts, or a loss to the fixed-income trading desk. The assignment of this profit and loss is important because it determines the risk and profitability of each business unit and product and therefore the price that the bank should charge its customers.

The way we determine where the risk is located is by using transfer pricing. Transfer pricing is a framework of internal transactions and payments between business units. For ALM purposes, the major units are the lending units, the deposit-taking units, the trading unit, and the ALM desk. The payments between the business units are fictitious in that they are recorded in the accounts for each unit, but no money actually leaves the bank as a whole.

The transfer payments significantly affect the measured accounting profitability of each unit. By affecting the measured profitability, we affect the prices that each unit must charge to its customers, and we affect the bonuses of the staff. If one unit is forced to pay a higher transfer price to another unit, the first unit's measured profitability will fall, their bonuses will be reduced, and senior management may decide to scale back the activities of the less-profitable unit. For these reasons, transfer pricing can be highly political. Transfer prices, along with capital charges and limits, set the rules within which bankers, traders, and business units must play.

Transfer payments between units are made for one of two reasons: services provided or funds provided. Transfer payments for services is not part of ALM. In this chapter, we are concerned only with *funds*-transfer pricing, which is also often called the *cost of funds* (COF). Funds-transfer pricing can be viewed as the interest payments charged when one unit lends funds to another. It is the structure of funds-transfer pricing which moves interest-rate and liquidity risks between units.

In this chapter, we first describe the traditional way of calculating funds-transfer prices and the associated problems of this traditional approach. The bulk of the chapter then discusses matched-funds-transfer pricing, which eliminates most of the problems. In discussing matched-funds-transfer pricing, we first show how it can be used to eliminate or move interest-rate risks, and we give the general rules for transfer pricing. We then discuss the difficulties of transfer pricing for indeterminate maturity products such as checking accounts. Most of the discussion deals with transfer pricing for debt costs, but towards the end we add the complication of transfer pricing for economic capital. Transfer pricing deals with the conceptual movement of funds between accounting entities to measure profit and risk. At the end of the chapter, we discuss how the real business groups within the bank access funds and manage risk.

TRADITIONAL TRANSFER PRICING AND ITS PROBLEMS

A typical situation in a universal bank is that the retail banking group takes in deposits and lends them out to retail customers. The amount of deposits generally exceeds retail loans, so the excess is given to the bank's ALM desk. The ALM desk is closely associated with the trading group. It is sometimes referred to as the "funding desk" or "treasury," although the term "treasury" may also be used to refer to the whole trading group. The ALM desk takes the excess funds from the retail unit and lends them out. It may lend them to another bank in the interbank market or to another group within the bank, such as commercial lending or the trading group. In return for providing these funds, the retail group receives some interest payments from the ALM desk. In the traditional framework, the transfer rate for these interest payments is typically either the overnight interbank rate or the retail deposit rate, plus a small spread to cover operating expenses. This traditional transfer-pricing framework has several negative consequences.

First, within the retail banking group, there is no clear line between the profitability of retail loans and deposits. If the retail group as a whole is profitable, it is not clear whether the profit is driven by raising cheap funds from deposits or giving well-priced loans. Consequently, it is not clear whether to expand either the deposit program, the loan program, or both.

Second, the interest rate given to the retail group for their excess funds tends to be lower than the rate they would have received if they had been able to lend the funds directly into the interbank capital market. This falsely reduces the measured profitability of the retail unit. The lower rate also falsely boosts the measured profit of the trading unit or commercial loan unit who would have paid more for their funds if they had been forced to borrow them from the interbank market.

Third, traditional transfer pricing makes it difficult to monitor and control interest-rate risk because a change in market rates may affect the profitability of all business units. Even if the commercial lending department had done a good job in making well-priced, well-structured loans to creditworthy customers, the department may still suffer a loss if their funding costs suddenly rise.

To avoid these problems, a transfer-pricing framework is needed that recognizes the true value of the funds and concentrates the interest-rate risk into one unit: the ALM desk. This can be achieved by matched-funds-transfer pricing.

INTRODUCTION TO MATCHED-FUNDS-TRANSFER PRICING

To introduce matched-funds-transfer pricing, let us start with an example using traditional transfer pricing, and then show how matched-funds-transfer pricing can be introduced to bring clarity to the risk and profitability.

Consider a traditional bank raising funds in the form of 3-month deposits (FDs) and lending 5-year, fixed-rate loans. If the bank pays 4% for the FDs and receives 11% for the loans, the nominal net interest margin (NIM) is 7%. This is illustrated in Figure 15-1.

The 7% spread between the loans and deposits should cover the administrative costs, the credit loss on the loan, and the interest-rate risks due to the mismatch between the 3-month funding and 5-year lending. There are two problems with this situation. One, it is not possible to attribute profitability separately to the loans and FDs. Two, there is interest-rate risk because if rates rise to 8% in 3 months, the bank will find itself with a net interest margin reduced to only 3%, which would not be enough to cover expenses.

As an alternative, consider taking in 3-month FDs, and lending the resulting funds for 3 months in the interbank market at the current available rate, e.g., 6%. Then to fund the loans, borrow money for 5 years in the capital markets fixed at the current available 5-year rate, e.g., 7%. This is illustrated in Figure 15-2.

FIGURE 15-1

Example of Traditional Transfer Pricing

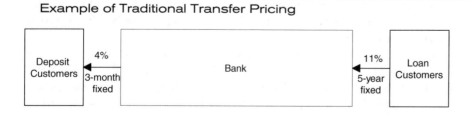

FIGURE 15-2

Transfer Pricing via the Interbank Market

In this arrangement, the bank has no interest-rate risk because the 3-month liabilities are matched with a 3-month asset, and the 5-year loans are matched with a 5-year liability. Furthermore, we can clearly see the profitability of each product. The net interest margin for the FDs is clearly 2% (6%–4%), and the NIM for the loans is 4% (11%–7%). The profitability for the FDs is therefore 2%, minus the FD administrative costs. The profitability for the loans is 4%, minus the loan administrative costs and the costs of credit risk.

Figure 15-3 illustrates how the rates are set relative to the current yield curve for interbank lending. This figure very clearly shows the spread that each unit receives. By funding the bank's assets and liabilities with matched interbank assets and liabilities, we have removed the interest-rate risk from both the business units and the bank as a whole, and we have brought clarity to the profitability of each product.

Notice that the bank has lost 1% of income to the capital markets, but in exchange, it has no interest-rate risk and therefore does not need to hold capital against ALM risks. You may also notice something strange about this bank. Its net

FIGURE 15-3

Pricing of Internal Transactions Relative to the Yield Curve

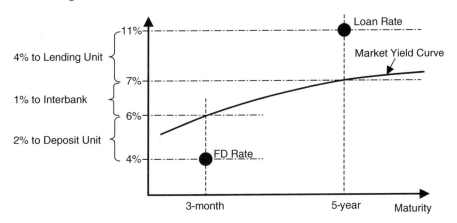

value is zero; i.e., it has no capital to cover other risks such as loan defaults. We return to the complications of capital later, but for now let us assume that the loans are risk free and concentrate on the transfer pricing required for the cost of raising debt.

In practice, it would be difficult and costly to implement a structure in which every individual deposit is lent separately into the market and every loan requires funds to be individually borrowed from the market. The practical alternative is to set up an internal market that aggregates all the individual transactions, and only to use the external market to borrow or lend the net amount. This is illustrated in Figure 15-4, in which the business units interact with the ALM desk as if it were the interbank market.

This concept of having an ALM desk that acts as internal reflection of the external market is the foundation of matched-funds-transfer pricing. In this framework, every business unit interacts with the ALM desk as if it were an external counterparty. The units give fictitious loans to each other, and the interest payments that they receive on the loans are the same as the rate they would have received by lending the funds in the external capital market.

The fictitious loans and trades are entered in the accounting system as if they were real trades with an external counterparty, except that both counterparties are different business units within the bank.

Consider the example of the commercial lending department making a five-year, fixed-rate loan to a customer. The department would borrow at a fixed rate for five years from the ALM desk. The rate quoted to the department for that internal loan would be the rate that it would cost the ALM desk to borrow the money in the interbank market for five years at a fixed rate. When the commercial lending department borrows from the ALM desk, a fictitious liability is created for the lending department. This is mirrored by a fictitious asset created for the ALM desk.

FIGURE 15-4

Transfer Pricing Using an Internal Reflection of the Market

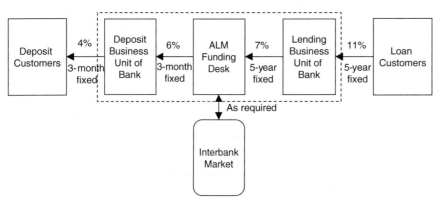

The department then lends the funds to the client, charging them the five-year interbank rate, plus a spread to cover operating expenses and the credit risk. This creates a real asset for the department. The resulting situation is that the lending unit has a real asset and a fictitious, matching liability. The ALM desk has a fictitious asset that has the interest-rate characteristics of the loan, but without credit risk.

On the day of making the loan, the commercial lending department knows that for the next five years it will receive fixed-interest payments from its client and make fixed-interest payments to the ALM desk. At the end of five years, the client will repay the loan, and the lending unit will use the proceeds to repay the ALM desk. The lending department therefore has locked-in its profit for this transaction and knows that the profit will not change if general market rates change.

By matching the real assets and liabilities with fictitious liabilities and assets of the same maturity, the business units are hedged, and changes in interest-rates will only affect the profitability of the ALM desk. The managers of the ALM desk chose how they wish to deal with this net interest-rate risk. They may choose to hedge it by doing real trades with the external capital market, or they may choose to keep it, thereby gaining a net expected profit but requiring the bank to hold additional economic capital to protect it from interest-rate risk.

GENERAL RULES FOR MATCHED-FUNDS-TRANSFER PRICING

Now that we have seen how matched-transfer pricing works for a specific example, let us lay out some general rules for setting up a matched-funds-transfer pricing framework.

1. For the purpose of transfer pricing, the funding requirements for all transactions are considered to go through the ALM desk. This process is illustrated in Figure 15-5. Notice that the business units do not just go to the ALM desk for their net requirements. Each business unit gives all of its deposits to the ALM desk to be invested at market rates, and goes to the ALM desk for all its funding requirements if it wishes to make loans.

2. For every transaction, there is an agreement between the business unit and the ALM desk about the terms of the fictitious asset or liability. These terms are the same as would be agreed between the bank and an external counterparty. The terms specify the amount, the repricing frequency, the time for final repayment of the principle, any amortization, any prepayment options, and the rate, which is the current market rate. These terms should mirror the interest-rate characteristics of the business unit's transaction with the customer.

3. For each transaction, the business unit receives a fictitious asset (liability) and the ALM desk receives the opposite fictitious liability (asset).

FIGURE 15-5

Conceptual Transfer of Funds between Units for Transfer Pricing

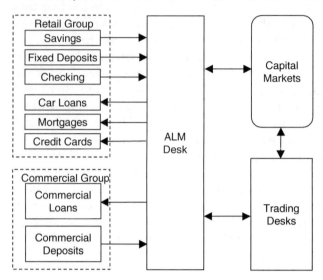

4. The trading unit is a special case. Like the other units, any transaction between the trading unit and the ALM desk has the price fixed according to the effective maturity of the loan. However, unlike the other business units, the trading unit has access directly to the interbank market and is not required go to the ALM desk to match every transaction. For risk-measurement purposes, any fictitious liability that the trading unit has goes into the trading VaR calculator, and the corresponding fictitious asset goes into the ALM simulation.

After all the internal transactions have been conducted, each business unit has a balance sheet showing its actual assets and liabilities and interest-rate matched fictitious liabilities and assets. The accounting unit charges and credits each business unit with the internal interest payments established by the matched-funds-transfer-pricing agreements and the consequent assets and liabilities on each unit's balance sheet. Figure 15-6 shows an example of a balance sheet. The real assets and liabilities are shown in bold. The fictitious liabilities and assets are denoted by an asterisk (*).

Let us examine this balance sheet in detail. Starting with the trading unit, we find that it has $30 billion in assets created by long positions, e.g., owning equities. It has real liabilities of $20 billion in short positions and $5 billion in money that it has borrowed from other banks in the interbank market. It also has a fictitious liability for

FIGURE 15-6

Balance Sheet for Transfer Pricing

Trading	Assets	Liabilities	$Bn	Assets ALM Desk	$Bn	Liabilities	$Bn
Trading Desks	Long Positions 30	Short Positions	20				
		Money-market loans	5				
		* 1-year loan	5	* 1-year loan	5		
Net Value		30	30				
Commercial							
Loans	Remaining Maturity						
	Within 6 months 10	* Overnight loan	10	* Overnight loan	10		
	6–18 months 20	* 1-year loan	20	* 1-year loan	20		
	18–30 months 25	* 2-year loan	26	* 2-year loan	26		
	30–42 months 20	* 3-year loan	21	* 3-year loan	21		
	42–54 months 10	* 4-year loan	12	* 4-year loan	12		
	54 months 5	* 5-year loan	7	* 5-year loan	7		
		* Option to prepay	-6	* Option to prepay	-6		
Deposits at Overnight	* Overnight loan 10	Deposits	10			* Overnight loan	10
Net Value		100	100				
Retail							
2-Year Prime Car Loans	Loans 40	* Overnight loan	10	* Overnight loan	10		
		* 3-month loan	20	* 3-month loan	20		
		* 6-month loan	10	* 6-month loan	10		
Checking Accounts	* Overnight loan 10	Deposits	100			* Overnight loan	10
	* 3-month notes 10					* 3-month notes	10
	* 1-year loan 40					* 1-year loan	40
	* 2-year loan 40					* 2-year loan	40
Net Value		140	140				
				Interbank Loans	8	Interbank Loans	5
				Pay-fixed swaps	1	5-year bond Issue	10
						* Equity	19
				Net Value	144		144

$5 billion that it has borrowed from the ALM desk for 1 year. This appears as an asset to the ALM desk.

The commercial lending group has made a series of loans to its customers. These are matched by a series of fictitious loans of similar maturities and almost the same value. The difference in value is because the true loans are prepayable, whereas the fictitious loans are not normally prepayable. However, the prepayment risk is captured by an option which allows the business units to put the fictitious notes to the ALM desk in case the customer prepays. The $10 billion of deposits from commercial customers are paid rates that are close to the interbank rate, and are therefore hedged with an overnight loan.

The retail unit has $40 billion of assets in the form of car loans. However, the interest-rate on these loans floats and is tied to prime. Because prime is an administered rate, it is not quite the same as any single market rate, and is therefore best hedged with a series of loans of different maturities, as we discuss later. The retail unit also has $100 billion of liabilities in the form of checking accounts. Although these accounts are demand deposits, it is unlikely that the whole amount will be withdrawn for at least 2 years, so the bank can be confident in lending out the deposit funds as a mixture of loans from overnight to 2 years.

Finally, let's look at the ALM desk. It has the reflection of all the fictitious assets and liabilities of the other business units, plus it also has some real assets and liabilities of its own. In this case is has lent $8 billion in the form of various interbank loans and has borrowed $5 billion at other times. It also has a swap that it is using to modify its interest-rate risk, and it has issued $10 billion of 5-year bonds in the name of the bank.

In this concept of transfer pricing, the net value of each business unit is zero, and all the available capital to support the business units is concentrated on the ALM desk. We discuss this and its alternatives in more depth later. But now, let us further investigate the strange mixture of loans that was used to hedge the checking accounts and prime-based loans.

TRANSFER PRICING FOR INDETERMINATE-MATURITY PRODUCTS

For products such as fixed-rate loans, it is relatively easy to find traded instruments in the interbank and capital markets that can be used to hedge the interest-rate risk. However, in the balance-sheet example, we introduced the problem of dealing with products such as checking accounts and prime-based loans that have indeterminate maturities and no fixed relationship to traded instruments. Products such as these are best hedged using a mixture of instruments.

The hedge can include not only bonds, but also options. For example, if customers are able to prepay when rates fall, the lending unit and the ALM desk should enter into an agreement in which the ALM desk agrees to take any prepaid funds. The ALM unit thereby commits to reinvesting the funds at the new market rates, without passing on any losses to the lending unit. Effectively in this arrangement, the lending unit has the right to prepay its loan from the ALM unit. In exchange, the ALM unit will charge an option premium to the lending unit when it first funds the prepayable loan. The ALM unit is left to manage or hedge the option as it sees fit.

Determining the best hedge for an indeterminate product is difficult. The best way is to model the payments from the product as described in the chapter on interest-rate risk. The product can then be put into the simulation model along with a series of traded instruments, such as loans and options. The best hedge is then the combination of traded instruments that best matches the product. In matching the product we have several choices. If the performance of all the business units is being measured according the value created each year, then the best hedge is the one whose change in value over one year is most similar to the change in value of the product. An alternative way of saying this is that the best hedge is the set of instruments that, when combined with the product, results in the minimum possible variation in value.

In the simulation, it is relatively easy to calculate the change in value of the traded instruments because we have pricing equations (e.g., the bond equation) that give their value as a function of the rates prevailing at the end of one year. However, for the indeterminate-maturity product, the value at the end of the year must be determined by a new set of nested simulations, as explained in the chapter on interest-rate risk.

ALLOCATION OF CAPITAL

After applying matched-funds-transfer pricing, the lending units should be left with only credit and operating risk, and the deposit-taking units are left with only operating risk. The ALM desk has the structural interest-rate risk, and the trading group has general market risk, counterparty-credit risk, and operating risk. This is illustrated in Figure 15-7, where the extent of shading reflects the amount of risk.

In our discussion so far, we have not specified how transfer pricing treats capital for credit and operating risk. For example, we implicitly assumed that the funding for a loan would be in the form of debt raised in the interbank market. However, if all loans were supported by 100% debt, the bank would not be able to repay the debt holders if any of the loans defaulted. Banks must therefore fund their customers' loans from a mixture of debt and equity.

The total funding requirement is the amount of the asset (A). The amount of equity (E) equals the economic capital required to support the credit risk of the loan. The remaining funding requirement is made up of debt (D):

$$A = E + D$$

FIGURE 15-7

Distribution of Risk after Transfer Pricing

	Interest-Rate Risk	Other Market Risk	Credit Risk	Operating Risk
Lending	○	○	●	◕
Deposits	○	○	○	◕
Trading	◑	●	◕	◑
ALM	●	○	○	◕

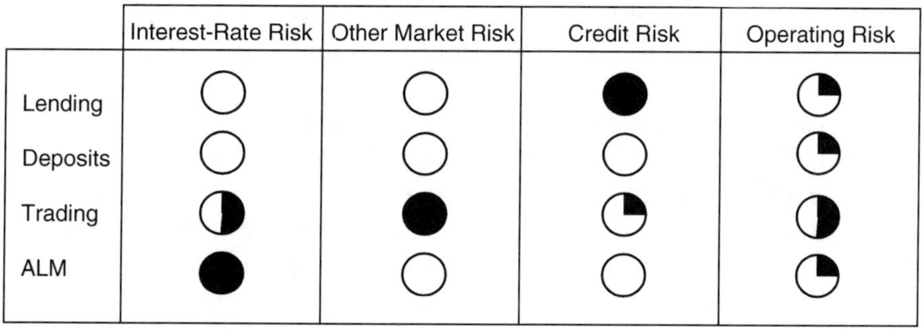

The extent of the shading reflects the amount of risk remaining in the business unit after transfer pricing.

This mixture of funding can be reflected in the transfer pricing in 1 of 2 almost equivalent ways. One way is that the business units can be charged their debt rate for 100% of their funding requirement. The required capital can be held by the ALM desk in the form of additional assets that can be sold to cover any losses in the business unit. These additional assets are safe assets (e.g., government bonds). Because there is the possibility that they will be sold to cover losses, these assets must be bought by raising equity from shareholders. As these are safe assets, they only give a return equal to the debt rate (e.g., 6%); however, the shareholders demand a high return equal to the hurdle rate for capital, e.g., 16%. The difference (e.g., 10%) is charged to the business units who create the risk requiring the capital to be held. The total charge to the business unit is then the full amount of the asset multiplied by the debt cost, plus the amount of equity times the required excess return:

$$Cost = A \times r_d + E \times (r_e - r_d)$$

This approach was illustrated in the balance sheet in Figure 15-6.

An alternative approach is to assume that the capital is held by each business unit rather than by the ALM desk. In this model, the business units are funded with a mixture of debt and equity. For example, a $100 loan requiring $8 of economic capital would be funded with $92 of debt and $8 of equity. The total charge to the unit would then be the amount of debt times the debt rate, plus the amount of equity times the equity rate:

$$Cost = D \times r_d + E \times r_e$$

This is equivalent to the previous formulation:

$$
\begin{aligned}
Cost &= D \times r_d + E \times r_e \\
&= D \times r_d + E \times r_d - E \times r_d + E \times r_e \\
&= A \times r_d + E \times (r_e - r_d)
\end{aligned}
$$

Figure 15-8 shows the balance sheet modified to have the equity held in the business units. Notice that the real assets and liabilities are the same. In this version, the ALM desk raises a mixture of debt and equity to fund each business unit. For assets such as loans, the amount of the fictitious debt is reduced and replaced by a transfer of equity.

For liabilities, the reasoning is less obvious because the amount of fictitious debt is increased. One way to think about this is that for a bank to take in deposits, it must first raise equity to cover the possibility of losses due to operating risks. It can then raise deposits. It then invests the deposits and the equity in the interbank market. When the deposits are to be repaid, the bank will be able to use the interbank investments to pay back the investors and pay any unusual costs due to operating risks. If there were no significant operating losses, the bank would be able to repay the equity holders, plus give them the profits from the deposit-taking business.

FIGURE 15-8

Balance Sheet Showing Alternative Treatment for Capital

	Assets	Liabilities	$Bn	ALM Desk Assets	$Bn	ALM Liabilities	$Bn
Trading ($Bn)							
Trading Desks	Long Positions 30	Short Positions	20				
		Money-market loans	5				
		* 1-year loan	2	* 1-year loan	2		
		* Equity	3	* Equity	3	* Equity	3
Net Value	30		30				
Commercial							
Loans	Remaining Maturity						
	within 6 months 10	* Overnight loan	10	* Overnight loan	10		
	6–18 months 20	* 1-year loan	19	* 1-year loan	19		
	18–30 months 25	* 2-year loan	24	* 2-year loan	24		
	30–42 months 20	* 3-year loan	19	* 3-year loan	19		
	42–54 months 10	* 4-year loan	10	* 4-year loan	10		
	54 months 5	* 5-year loan	6	* 5-year loan	6		
		* Option to prepay	-6	* Option to prepay	-6		
		* Equity	8	* Equity	8	* Equity	8
Deposits at Overnight	* Overnight loan 11	Deposits	10			* Overnight loan	11
		* Equity	1	* Equity	1	* Equity	1
Net Value	101		101				
Retail							
2-year Prime Car Loans **Loans**	40	* Overnight loan	9	* Overnight loan	9		
		* 3-month loan	19	* 3-month loan	19		
		* 6-month loan	9	* 6-month loan	9		
		* Equity	3	* Equity	3	* Equity	3
Checking Accounts	* Overnight loan 10	**Deposits**	100			* Overnight loan	10
	* 3-month notes 10					* 3-month notes	10
	* 1-year loan 41					* 1-year loan	41
	* 2-year loan 41					* 2-year loan	41
		* Equity	2	* Equity	2	* Equity	2
Net Value	142		142				
				Interbank Loans	8	Interbank Loans	5
				Pay-fixed swaps	1	5-year bond issue	10
						* ALM Equity	2
				Net Value	147		147

Notice that in the new balance sheet, the equity owed to the shareholders is tagged closely to each business unit, and the only equity "belonging" to the ALM desk is $2 to cover economic capital required for the ALM-mismatch risks.

The approach taken gives balancing accounts for each business unit. However, the balance sheet for the ALM unit is not an exact reflection of the balance sheet for the bank. The bank has $169 billion of real assets and liabilities, but the ALM balance sheet shows $147 billion.

This is because we used the net amount of the assets and liabilities in the trading group rather than the gross amounts. If we use the gross amounts, and enter economic capital for deposits as a negative asset, we can create the balance sheet in Figure 15-9, in which the total assets and liabilities of the ALM desk equal the total real assets and liabilities of the bank ($169).

FIGURE 15-9

Balance Sheet Reflecting All the Bank's Assets on the ALM Desk

Trading	Assets	$Bn	Liabilities	$Bn	ALM Desk Assets	$Bn	Liabilities	$Bn
Trading Desks	Long Positions	30	Short Positions	20	*Long positions 25		*Short Positions	20
			Money-market loans	5			*Money-market loans	5
			*1-year loan	2	*1-year loan 2			
			*Equity	3	*Equity 3		*Equity	3
Net Value		30		30				
Commercial								
Loans	Remaining Maturity							
	within 6 months	10	*Overnight loan	10	*Overnight loan 10			
	6–18 months	20	*1-year loan	19	*1-year loan 19			
	18–30 months	25	*2-year loan	24	*2-year loan 24			
	30–42 months	20	*3-year loan	19	*3-year loan 19			
	42–54 months	10	*4-year loan	10	*4-year loan 10			
	54 months	5	*5-year loan	6	*5-year loan 6			
			*Option to prepay	-6	*Option to prepay -6			
			*Equity	8	*Equity 8		*Equity	8
Deposits at Overnight	*Overnight loan	11	Deposits	10			*Overnight loan	11
	*Equity	-1					*Equity	-1
							*Equity	1
Net Value		100		100				
Retail								
2-year Prime Car Loans	Loans	40	*Overnight loan	9	*Overnight loan 9			
			*3-month loan	19	*3-month loan 19			
			*6-month loan	9	*6-month loan 9			
			*Equity	3	*Equity 3		*Equity	3
Checking Accounts	*Overnight loan	10	Deposits	100			*Overnight loan	10
	*3-month notes	10					*3-month notes	10
	*1-year loan	41					*1-year loan	41
	*2-year loan	41					*2-year loan	41
	*Equity	-2					*Equity	-2
							*Equity	2
Net Value		140		140				
					Interbank Loans	8	Interbank Loans	5
					Pay-fixed swaps	1	5-year bond issue	10
							*ALM Equity	2
					Net Value	169		169

THE ROLES OF ORGANIZATIONAL UNITS INVOLVED IN ALM

In dealing with transfer pricing, we have described the conceptual framework that is used to set transfer prices and measure risk. In the conceptual framework, all the funds flow through an ALM desk and the "invisible hand" of the transfer-pricing rules sets all the transactions to be at market rates. This works for measuring risk and profitability, but it is not how funds are handled in reality. Let us now look at the real organizational units within a bank that are responsible for operating the ALM system.

Although many groups throughout the bank are involved with asset liability management, the main ones are as follows:

- The Senior Risk Committee
- The Asset Liability Committee (ALCO)

- Asset Liability Manager
- The ALCO Support Group
- The Money-Market Funding Desk
- Financial Accounting Unit
- Business Units

We will look at their roles and responsibilities in detail.

The Senior Risk Committee and the Asset Liability Committee

The senior risk committee monitors all the risks of the bank. As a result, they are interested in the risk arising from the ALM book and the correlation of that risk with other risks, especially interest-rate positions on the fixed-income trading desk.

Many executives on the risk committee are also in the ALCO. The ALCO is typically chaired by the CFO, head trader, or in smaller banks by the CEO. The members of the ALCO typically include the heads of the business units. The ALCO typically meets monthly to review the structural interest-rate and liquidity positions of the bank. They also review transfer-pricing policy and decisions on administered rates, such as changes in the bank's prime rates or retail fixed-deposit rates. If the committee wishes to change the risk profile significantly, they will agree with the CFO to carry out large capital-markets transactions, such as issuing bonds or securitizing and selling parts of the balance sheet. Alternatively, the committee may agree that the business units should change the risk profile by modifying the mix of products that are offered to customers, e.g., by changing rates and marketing to encourage or discourage different types of products.

Smaller-scale tactical changes are delegated to the asset liability manager. In general, the structural interest-rate position should be mostly hedged, unless the ALCO decides that the expected return from "playing the gap" is sufficient to give a good return on the economic capital consumed by the risk.

Asset Liability Manager

The asset liability manager (AL manager) is a mid- or senior-level trader who has the daily responsibility of maintaining the interest-rate and liquidity profile targeted by the ALCO. This is done based on risk reports from the ALCO support group and is carried out by ordering trades such as swaps and interbank loans for the ALM book. The *ALM book* is an accounting entity holding all the fictitious assets and liabilities. The orders for the book may be placed directly with the market or, to increase efficiency, they are more commonly placed with the bank's own trading desks. The desks then execute the trades and transfer the security to the ALM book. In some institutions, the ALM book is managed as part of the bond desk, but more typically in large institutions, the ALM book is managed separately. The personnel staffing the ALM desk may be the same as those on some of the bond desks, but they are conceptually different.

If the ALM manager did nothing to hedge the ALM book, it would receive the spread between the long and short interbank rates, and it would run the risk of earnings compression if the rates moved. Because it is now the center of ALM interest-rate risk, it attracts the charge for the economic capital consumed by that risk, and should earn the hurdle rate on the capital. As the rates for the fictitious transactions are the rates at which the bank could borrow or lend in the interbank market, the ALM desk could theoretically hedge itself to be risk free with no cost. To hedge itself, the desk can use the usual fixed-income transactions such as buying or shorting bonds, or use derivatives such as futures, swaps, and options.

The ALCO Support Group

The ALCO support group is a team of analysts reporting to the AL manager. They provide weekly risk reports to enable the ALCO and AL manager to maintain the target profile. They also carry out analyses to estimate the effective maturity of the indeterminate-maturity products such as checking accounts. This information on duration is used to create the risk reports and is also supplied to the financial accounting group to determine the rates for funds-transfer pricing. In addition to identifying the sources of risk, the ALCO support group should suggest hedges to be approved by the AL manager and the executives on the ALCO. Hedges may include market transactions or changes in customer products.

The Money-Market Funding Desk

Conceptually, for transfer-pricing purposes, we said that all requests for funds from the business units are made to the ALM desk. In practice, daily requests for short-term funds are made directly from the business units to the money-market funding desk. For accounting purposes, they are later recorded as if they went to the ALM desk and then the ALM desk requested funds from the money-market desk.

The money-market desk is therefore responsible for sourcing and placing short-term funds to fulfil the cash requirements of the bank. This is a very reactive role, in which the desk receives funds or requests for funds from the rest of the bank, and goes to the overnight interbank market to place or borrow the funds at the best available rates. The money-market funding desk operates on a very quick time-scale of hours to ensure that the daily funding requirements are balanced, whereas the time scale for managing the structural interest-rate position of the ALM book is several weeks.

The Financial Accounting Group

The financial accounting group reports the profitability of each business unit, and therefore needs to be supplied with the rules for transfer pricing, the effective transfer rates to be applied, and the details of which transactions have happened.

Business Units

The individual business units, such as retail lending, are the ones creating the interest-rate mismatches. The business units have great personal interest in the transfer rates because they affect the units' profitability and the rates they can give to their customers. Changing the rates changes the profitability and the volume of business for each type of product. This change in volume affects the AL risk profile. For example, if the bank found that the basis risk for prime was consuming too much economic capital, it could ask the retail business to better balance the assets and liabilities based off of prime. This could be done as a decision in the ALCO, and by a capital charge made for the basis risk.

SUMMARY

In this chapter, we explained how matched-funds-transfer pricing can be use to bring clarity to risk and profitability measurement. This concludes the discussion of ALM. Next, we turn our attention to credit risk, starting with an explanation of what it is and why it needs to be measured.

CHAPTER 16

Introduction to Credit Risk

INTRODUCTION

The taking of credit risk has always been a core activity for banks. Over the last 10 years, quantitative measurement has been adopted by banks to improve their processes for selecting and pricing credit transactions. Quantitative measurement has become even more important since it was adopted by the Basel Committee on Banking as the basis for setting regulatory capital. In this chapter, we review the process for granting credit and the ways in which risk measurement supports credit decisions. In subsequent chapters, we review the different types of credit instruments, risk measurement for a single loan, risk measurement for a portfolio, and how the results are used for decision support. Most of the discussion focuses on estimating the economic capital, but we finish the credit-risk section with the Basel Committee's new framework for setting regulatory capital.

SOURCES OF CREDIT RISK

Credit risk arises from the possibility that borrowers or counterparties will fail to honor commitments that they have made to pay the bank. Credit-related losses can occur in the following ways:

- A customer fails to repay money that was lent by the bank.
- A customer enters into a derivative contract with the bank in which the payments are based on market prices, then the market moves so that the customer owes money, but the customer fails to pay.
- The bank holds a debt security (e.g., a bond or loan) and the credit quality of the security issuer falls, causing the value of the security to fall. Here, a default has not occurred, but the increased possibility of a default makes the security less valuable.

- The bank holds a debt security, and the market's price for risk changes. For example, the price for all BB-rated bonds may fall because the market is less willing to take risks. In this case, there is no credit event, just a change in market sentiment. This risk is therefore typically treated as market risk in the trading VaR calculator.

There is a gray area between market and credit risks. Generally, changes in value due to defaults and downgrades are considered to be credit risk because they depend on the behavior of the specific company. Changes in value due to changes in the risk-free interest-rate or changes in credit spread for a given grade are considered to be market risk because they depend on general market sentiment.

THE CREDIT LIFE CYCLE

To set the stage for examining credit-risk management, let us begin by considering the life cycle of a single loan. The process begins with business development, in which the lending group targets a potential customer. The customer then applies for credit and supplies some information about his or her creditworthiness. In the case of a retail customer, it is personal information such as income. In the case of a commercial customer, it is balance-sheet information such as total assets.

Based on this information, the bank's credit department determines the riskiness of the customer and assigns a credit grade, which is a form of risk score. Often, banks will supplement their grading processes with information from external rating agencies. For retail customers, data is provided by credit bureaus who collect information from many banks and collate it for resale to any bank considering lending to an individual. In the United States the main credit bureaus are Equifax, TRW, and Experian. The information includes personal details, such as income, and financial information, such as the total number of credit cards and whether the customer has defaulted.

For lending to corporations, the main credit-rating agencies for large corporations in the United States are Standard & Poor's, Moody's, and Fitch IBCA. For the middle market, Dunn and Bradstreet is the primary rating agency. These rating agencies carry out a process that is very similar to that of a credit analyst in a bank. They take information on a company and an associated facility (a particular bond, for example), and they rate the facility based on subjective judgments and objective models. The models use information on the company's balance sheet and profitability. The result is a letter grade that indicates the "riskiness" of the facility. There are also companies (principally, KMV, now owned by Moody's) who rate corporations based on the volatility of their equity prices, which we will later discuss in depth.

Based on the grade, the bank decides whether to offer credit to the customer, in what amount, at what interest rate, and with what terms. The difference between the risk-free rate and the rate charged to the customer is called the spread. The terms can include the requirement for collateral and the right of the bank to change the price or loan amount if the customer's credit quality changes. The customer decides whether to accept the given price, and then there may be a final round of bank approval before the deal is closed. The process up to closing the actual deal is called *origination*.

After the deal is closed, a series of disbursements are made to the borrower, and the loan becomes part of the bank's portfolio of assets. The portfolio is managed to minimize the risk/return ratio of the portfolio. This may require selling the loan to another bank, either stand-alone, or packaged with other loans into an asset-backed security. The portfolio management process may also influence the decision to originate new loans that create diversification or concentration in the portfolio.

Eventually, most of the loans are paid back by the customers, but some default and go to the collections department, who takes time to recover as much of the outstanding amount as possible. The collections department may also be called the *workout group* or the *special assets group*.

CREDIT APPROVALS FOR TRADING COUNTERPARTIES

The process described above is generally applicable when the granting of credit is the main purpose of the transaction. However, in transactions such as derivatives trading, credit risk is an unwelcome by-product of the transaction. In this case, the emphasis is much more about setting limits on exposure and mitigating the exposure through collateral. The decision is couched in terms of the expected profit to be made by trading with the counterparty and the limit on the maximum exposure (or "line") that the bank can risk having with any one counterparty.

Two types of limits are set: the total exposure and the daily settlement limit. The *total exposure* is the net present value of all the transactions that the bank has with a counterparty. If all trades were completed and then the counterparty defaulted, the amount lost would be the total exposure minus any later recoveries.

The *daily settlement limit* is the amount that the bank is prepared to exchange with the counterparty on any given day. This limits the Herstatt risk, i.e., the loss if the bank makes one side of a payment, but the counterparty defaults midway through settlement and fails to make the payment for the other side of the transaction.

WHY MEASURE CREDIT RISK?

Before launching into the analysis and calculation of credit risk, let us first consider what risk measurements would be useful to support the decisions in the process we discussed above. There are three main sets of decisions: origination, portfolio optimization, and capitalization.

Supporting Origination Decisions

The most basic decision is whether to accept a new asset into the portfolio. The origination decision can be framed in two possible ways:

- Given the risk and a fixed price, is the asset worth taking?
- Given the risk, what price is required to make the asset worth buying?

The first is more often asked in a rigid system where there is little opportunity to modify the price, and therefore the decision becomes "yes/no." This is the type of decision made when dealing with a large volume of retail customers. The question can be recast as, "Is the expected return on capital for this transaction greater than the bank's minimum return on capital?" To support this decision, we need to know the expected return, adjusted for expected losses and expenses, and the amount of capital that this transaction will consume.

The second approach is typically used in a flexible, liquid trading environment, or in negotiating rates and fees for a corporate loan. Here, we start with the capital consumed and the known hurdle rate for the return on capital to calculate the minimum acceptable return for the overall loan.

Supporting Portfolio Optimization

In optimizing a portfolio, the manager seeks to minimize the ratio of risk to return. To reduce the portfolio's risk, the manager must know where there are concentrations of risk and how the risk can be diversified. This requires a credit-portfolio model that includes all the correlations between assets to show where there are concentrations of assets that are highly correlated. The high correlation may arise from being in the same industry or geography, or because they are driven by the same economic factors, such as oil prices. The portfolio model must show the current risk concentrations and allow the manager to try "what-if" analyses to test strategies for diversifying the portfolio.

Supporting Capital Management

Given the risk in the portfolio, the CFO needs to set the provisions for expected losses over the next year, and the reserves, in case losses are unusually bad. The CFO also needs to ensure that the total economic capital available is sufficient to maintain the bank's target credit rating given the risks. If it is insufficient, the bank must raise more capital, reduce the risk, or expect to be downgraded. To set the provisions, the CFO needs to know the average losses that are to be expected. To set reserves, it is necessary to know the loss that could be experienced in an unusually bad year, e.g., losses that have a 1-in-20 chance of happening. To set capital, we need the loss level that could be experienced in an extraordinarily bad year, e.g., losses that have a 1-in-

1000 chance of happening. These statistics can be obtained if we can calculate the probability-density function for the portfolio-loss rate, which is the focus of the next few chapters.

SUMMARY

In this chapter, we introduced readers to the concept of credit risk. Next, we detail the most common credit structures as a foundation for quantifying the risk.

Types of Credit Structure

INTRODUCTION

Credit risk can arise in many ways, from granting loans to trading derivatives. The amount of credit risk depends largely on the structure of the agreement between the bank and its customers; for example, in a loan, the amount that the customer owes is fixed, whereas in a line of credit, the customer chooses how much to borrow each month. An agreement between a bank and a customer that creates credit exposure is often called a *credit structure* or a *credit facility*.

This chapter describes the most common credit structures. It is useful to know these structures for two reasons: to be able to have a meaningful conversation with bank credit staff, and to model the potential credit losses for each structure.

For a single facility, there are three parameters that are important in quantifying the credit risk: the exposure at default (EAD), the loss in the event of default (LIED), and the probability of default (PD). The probability of default is also known as the *default rate* or the *expected default frequency* (EDF). It is most strongly associated with the characteristics of the counterparty or customer.

The exposure at default (EAD) is also known as the *loan equivalence* (LEQ) and is the outstanding amount at the time of default. The loss in the event of default (LIED) is the loss as a percentage of the EAD. It is also known as *loss given default* (LGD) or *severity* (S). The amount of loss is the full EAD, plus all administrative costs associated with the default, minus the net present value of any amount that is later recovered from the defaulted company:

$$LIED = \frac{EAD + Admin - Recoveries}{EAD}$$

The EAD and LIED are strongly influenced by the type of credit structure. In discussing the alternative types of credit, we focus on how the structure affects these two loss parameters.

The credit structures discussed in this chapter are as follows:

Credit exposures to large corporations
- Commercial loans
- Commercial lines
- Letters of credit and guarantees
- Leases
- Credit derivatives

Credit exposures to retail customers
- Personal loans
- Credit cards
- Car loans
- Leases and hire-purchase agreements
- Mortgages
- Home-equity lines of credit

Credit exposures in trading operations
- Bonds
- Asset-backed securities
- Securities lending and repos
- Margin accounts
- Credit exposure for derivatives

CREDIT EXPOSURES TO LARGE CORPORATIONS
Commercial Loans

Typically, commercial loans have a fixed structure for disbursements from the bank to the company and have a fixed schedule of repayments, including interest payments. There may also be a fee paid by the company at the initiation of the loan. The fee acts to reduce required interest payments later. The loan may be secured (collateralized) or unsecured. If it is secured, then in the event of default, the bank will take legal possession of some specified asset and be able to sell this to reduce the loss. The collateral may be in the form of traded securities, the rights to a physical inventory or building, or the rights to a stream of cash flows, such as accounts payable from customers to the corporation. An unsecured loan is a general obligation of the company, and in the case of default, the bank will just get its share of the residual value of the company. The loan may also be classified as senior or subordinated (also called junior). When a company liquidates, it pays off the senior loans first; then if there are any remaining assets, it pays off the subordinated loans. As senior loans always get paid before subordinated loans, they have a lower loss in the event of default.

For credit-risk measurement, the most important loan features are the collateral type, the level of seniority, the term (or maturity), and the scheduled amounts that are expected to be outstanding (i.e., the amount that the company owes the bank at any given time).

Very large corporate loans may be syndicated to spread the risk among several banks and reduce the concentration risk for any one bank. In the syndication process there will be one or possibly two lead banks that arrange the deal, and then get agreement from other banks to take portions of the loan. Typically, all banks share equally in the risks, in that they have equal seniority and an equal claim on collateral. Once the deal has been closed, there may be secondary trading in which banks sell the loan between each other. This is almost like bond trading except that the number of investors is limited, and much more legal paperwork needs to be completed to transfer the rights of the loan from one party to another.

The syndicated-loan market is a prime example of the way in which the loan and bond markets are converging, with loans becoming more liquid, and the business model becoming one in which bankers originate and structure the deal then sell it to external portfolio managers who are looking for investments.

Commercial Lines

In a standard loan, the pattern of disbursements and repayments is set on the day of closing the deal. For a line of credit (also known as a *revolver* or a *commitment*), only a maximum amount is set in advance. The company then draws on the line according to its needs and repays it when it wishes. This means that the bank cannot be certain about the exposure at default (EAD). Historical studies have found that companies going into default tend to draw down more than healthy companies. There are three models used for the EAD of a line of credit. The choice depends on the data available in any given situation.

$$EAD = A \times Drawn\ Amount \qquad\qquad\qquad\qquad A \geq 1$$
$$EAD = B \times Line \qquad\qquad\qquad\qquad\qquad\qquad 0 \geq B \geq 1$$
$$EAD = Drawn\ Amount + C \times (Line - Drawn\ Amount) \quad 0 \geq C \geq 1$$

In this formulation, the *Drawn Amount* is the amount that the customer has currently borrowed, and the *Line* is the maximum amount that the customer can borrow. *A*, *B*, and *C* are constants that are found by looking at historical data to compare the actual exposure at default for companies that have defaulted with the *Drawn Amount* or the *Line* several months before the default happened. This is discussed later in the chapter on estimating parameter values for single facilities.

With a line of credit, the bank faces the possibility of loss on both the drawn and undrawn amounts, and should therefore set aside capital for each. However, it need only provide debt funding for the drawn amount. This is reflected in the pricing schedule, which charges the company one rate of interest for the drawn portion and another, lower, rate of interest for the additional amount that the bank has committed to lend. The charge on the drawn portion is the cost of debt plus the cost of capital. The charge on the undrawn portion is just the cost of capital.

To minimize the risk, the line agreement may also include covenants that allow the bank to limit further drawdowns if the company is downgraded. There may also be covenants so that under certain conditions, the bank can convert the line into a loan with a fixed term for repayments.

Letters of Credit

There are two primary types of letters of credit (LC): trade LCs and backup LCs. *Trade LCs* are tied to specific export transactions. A trade LC guarantees payment from a local importer to an overseas exporter; if the importer fails to pay, the bank will pay, and then try to reclaim the amount from the importer. For the bank, this creates a short-term exposure to the local importer.

A *back-up letter of credit* is a general form of guarantee or credit enhancement in which the bank agrees to make payments to a third party if the bank's customer fails. This is used to lower the cost of the customer's getting credit from the third party, because the third party now only faces the risk of a bank default. The bank faces the full default risk from its customer and has the same risk as if it had given the customer a direct loan. In the treatment of credit risk, such a letter of credit is considered to be a full loan, and the customer is charged by the bank for the economic capital it must set aside in case the customer defaults.

Leases

Leases are a form of collateralized loan, but with different tax treatment in certain situations. In an equipment lease, the equipment is given to the customer, and in return, the customer makes rental payments. After sufficient payments, the customer may keep the equipment. In terms of credit risk, this is equivalent to giving the customer a loan, having them buy the equipment, and pledging the equipment as collateral to secure the loan. In both cases, if the customer stops making payments, the bank ends up owning the equipment. Depending on the terms of the lease, the bank may or may not have a further claim on the company if the value of the equipment is less than the amount of the loan. The risk of leases can be treated in a very similar way to the risk of collateralized loans.

Credit Derivatives

The derivatives that we discussed in the market-risk chapters have their value determined according to a market variable such as the price of an equity or the prevailing interbank lending rate. Credit derivatives are different in that they are designed so their value is primarily determined by credit events, such as a default or a downgrade. Credit derivatives have been commonly used for several years, but are still highly tailored, over-the-counter instruments. Credit derivatives are useful for several reasons:

- They allow the relatively easy transfer of credit risk without the complex legal agreements that are required to transfer the ownership of a loan.
- They allow just a part of the loan's risk to be transferred.
- They can be tailored in many ways to transfer just one portion of the risk if desired; e.g., they could transfer the risk of default but not the risk of downgrades.

In almost all cases, the calculation of the risk for credit derivatives can be based on the analysis that would be used for the underlying loan.

As a simple example, consider a derivative in which one bank agrees to pay an initial amount, and in return, a second bank agrees to make payments equal to all the payments they receive from a particular corporate loan. For the first bank, if the corporation defaults, the bank will receive less money and will therefore make a loss. For the second bank, if the corporation defaults, the bank will receive less money from the corporation, but it will also need to pay less to the first bank. The changes in payments therefore cancel each other out, and they make no loss. Through this agreement, the economic risk of the loan has been transferred from the second bank to the first. In measuring the risk for the first bank, we would treat this credit derivative as if it were just a loan to the corporation. The example above is very similar to a total return swap except that in a total return swap, a series of fixed payments is made by the first bank rather than an initial lump sum.

In a total return swap, all the credit risk is transferred. However, it is also perfectly possible to write credit-derivatives contracts that have many different structures. For example, if a loan is traded, the payments each month could be equal to the face value of the loan minus the trading price. This would be equivalent to one side paying a fixed amount and in return owning the loan.

Another structure might be that if the corporation defaults, one side pays a fixed amount and the contract terminates. If the fixed amount was set to be equal to the expected loss in the event of a default (LIED), then a bank owning both the loan and the credit derivative would expect to make no loss if the corporation defaulted. However, there is the possibility of the bank making a loss or profit if the actual LIED is different from the derivative payment. Such a derivative would be treated as a loan with a variable LIED minus a loan with a fixed LIED.

CREDIT EXPOSURES TO RETAIL CUSTOMERS

Credit exposures to retail customers take generally the same form as exposures to corporations in that they can be structured as loans or lines, and they can be secured or unsecured. Let us briefly review the main characteristics of each type of structure.

Personal Loans

Personal loans are typically unsecured and may be used by the customer for any purpose. They are generally structured to have a fixed time for repayment. The interest charges may be fixed at the time of origination, or may float according to the bank's published prime rate, which the bank may change at its discretion.

Credit Cards

Credit cards are again generally unsecured by collateral, but they have no fixed time for repayment. The interest-rate is typically 10% to 15% above the floating prime rate, to compensate for the very heavy default rates experienced on credit cards.

Car Loans

Car loans are the same as personal loans except that they are for a specific purpose and have the car as collateral. They tend to have a lower loss given default than personal loans because of the collateral, and they have a lower probability of default because the customer is unwilling to lose the car.

Leases and Hire-Purchase Agreements

In a lease, the customer is allowed to use a physical asset (such as a car) that is owned by the bank. Leases are typically structured so that at the end of a finite period, the asset will be returned to the bank. The customer makes regular payments to cover the interest that would have been required to purchase the asset and to cover depreciation. The customer typically has the option to buy the asset outright at the end of the lease for a prespecified lump sum.

Hire-purchase agreements are similar to leases except that the payments include the full value of the asset, and the customer is certain to own the asset at the end of the agreement.

Leases and hire-purchase agreements are similar to car loans in that they are secured by the physical asset that has been purchased. Leases are structured such that the bank continues to own the physical asset legally until all lease payments have been made. This makes repossession easier and reduces the loss given default.

Mortgages

Mortgages use the customer's home as collateral. This minimizes the probability of default. Furthermore, banks generally ensure that the loan-to-value (LTV) ratio is less than 90%, so even if the property value drops by 10%, the bank will still have a loss given default of 0.

Home-Equity Lines of Credit

A home-equity line of credit (HELOC) is like a credit card but secured by the customer's house. This ensures a low probability of default. However, HELOCs are generally subordinated to the customer's primary mortgage, meaning that in the event of default, the house will be sold and the mortgage will be fully paid off before any payments are made towards the HELOC. This means that the loss given default for a HELOC is much higher than the LGD on the corresponding mortgage.

General Approach for Credit Risk from Retail Customers

Loans to corporations are generally large, and correspondingly large amounts of data and analysis are available on each corporation. In contrast, loans to retail customers are relatively small, and only a small amount is known about each customer. However, there are many more retail customers than there are corporations, so the total size of a bank's retail portfolio is often larger than its corporate-loan portfolio.

Another significant difference between corporate loans and retail loans is that the terms of the agreements between a bank and its customer are much more standardized because of the relatively massive volume of retail customers compared with the number of corporations. This allows retail exposures to be analyzed as a homogeneous mass.

Although there is a relatively small amount of information known about each customer, the average behavior of a large number of customers can be predicted reasonably well. Risk for retail customers is usually estimated by grouping them according to automated credit scores, such as the FICO score, and then gathering historical default and loss data on each group. The FICO score is the score from one of the models created by Fair, Isaac & Company. The model takes credit-bureau information on a retail customer, such as age, income, total number of credit cards, and number of delinquencies in the last three years, and produces a single number, the score. The score generally corresponds to the customer's probability of default, but models can also be used to predict other aspects of customer behavior, such as the probability of delinquency or the probability of the customer's actually using a credit card.

CREDIT EXPOSURES IN TRADING OPERATIONS

Bonds

Bonds were discussed at length in the market-risk section. The value of a bond depends on the risk-free interest-rate, the credit rating, the spread for that credit rating, and whether or not the corporation issuing the bond has defaulted. Changes in value due to interest-rates and the spread for a given rating are generally treated in the market-risk framework. Changes in the credit grade and actual default are either neglected or treated in the credit-risk framework. One rationale for this is that since bonds are liquidly traded, it is assumed that they can be sold with only a small loss whenever a downgrade occurs, and long before a default.

If the bonds are not sufficiently liquid to be easily sold before a default, they can be treated along with the loans. As with loans, a bond's credit risk depends on the level of seniority and whether it is secured with collateral.

From this discussion, you may wonder what happens to the interest-rate risk of loans. The interest-rate risk from loans is removed in the ALM transfer-pricing process and is relocated onto the ALM desk, as discussed earlier.

Asset-Backed Securities

Asset-backed securitization is used with retail assets, such as credit cards and mortgages. In an asset-backed security, the payments from many uniform assets are bundled together to form a pool. This pool is then used to make payments to several sets (or tranches) of bonds. Typically, there will be one set of bonds that is highly rated (e.g., AAA) and one set that is rated lower (e.g., BB). Any residual between the pool payments and the bond payments is typically retained by the institution originating the security. This residual amount is very volatile and is often called "toxic waste." This is illustrated in Figure 17-1.

If the payments into the pool are insufficient to pay the bondholders, it is possible that some of the bond payments will be less than scheduled. The probability of such underpayment depends on the degree of overcollateralization, i.e., the extent to which the value of the assets is expected to exceed the value of the bonds. The probability of underpayment also depends on the volatility of the value of the assets.

Asset-backed securities have often been used by banks to sell assets nominally to other investors, thereby removing the assets from the official balance sheet of the bank. If the assets are removed from the official balance sheet, the bank no longer needs to hold regulatory capital for the assets. However, if all the tranches of the security are highly rated, and the bank retains all of the toxic waste, then very little of the economic risk has been transferred from the bank. In effect, the regulatory-capital requirement has been reduced, but the economic-capital requirement is unchanged. This is useful to a bank if the market is inefficient, and investors in the bank can only

FIGURE 17-1

Illustration of an Asset-Backed Security

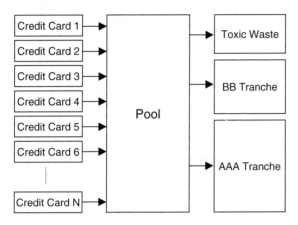

judge the risk by the regulatory capital and cannot observe the required economic capital. In this case, the bank can seem to remain safe, and obtain low-cost funding, while taking large risks and (hopefully) getting large returns.

The analysis of the credit risk of an asset-backed security is the same as the analysis of a portfolio of loans. In this case, we calculate the probability distribution of the payments from the pool of underlying assets and use this to estimate the probability that the pool will be sufficient to pay the bonds. The calculation of the probability distribution depends on the risk of the individual assets and the correlation between them. Estimation of this correlation is difficult and is discussed in the later chapter on risk measurement for a credit portfolio.

Securities Lending and Repurchase Agreements

Securities lending (*sec lending*) and repurchase agreements (*repos*) are common functions in trading. From a credit-risk perspective, both sec lending and repos are short-term collateralized loans. In securities lending, a counterparty asks to borrow a security from the bank for a limited period of time. The security is typically a share or bond. To minimize the credit risk, the counterparty gives collateral to the bank that is worth slightly more than the borrowed security. The collateral is typically in the form of cash. At the end of the trade, the counterparty returns the security and the bank returns the cash, less a small amount as a fee.

Repos are very similar to securities lending except that they are used to gain funding. In a repo, a security is sold by the bank with a guarantee from the bank to repurchase it at a fixed price and date. At the time of sale, the bank receives cash. At the time of repurchase, the bank sends the cash back to the counterparty, plus a small additional amount, which is effectively an interest payment for the loan.

In both sec lending and repos, the bank could make a credit loss if the counterparty defaults and the value of the security has risen to be higher than the amount of cash that the bank was expecting to pay to get the security back. The expected exposure at default will be the average amount by which the value of the security can be expected to exceed the cash. This can be calculated from the probability distribution of the security's value over the life of the deal. For example, Figure 17-2 shows the probability distribution for a security and the value of the cash held by the bank.

The average exposure at default is calculated from the possible exposure, times the probability of that exposure's happening. The exposure amount is the maximum of zero, or the difference between the security's value and the cash. Mathematically, the average exposure is the probability-weighted integral of the extent to which the security's value (V) exceeds the cash value (C):

$$Average\ Exposure = \int_0^\infty \max[0, (V - C)]pr(V)dV$$
$$= \int_C^\infty (V - C)pr(V)dV$$

In the above analysis, we did not specify how to estimate the probability distribution for the security, $pr(V)$. The simplest choice would be to assume that it was a Normal distribution with a mean equal to the current value of the security, and a standard deviation equal to the standard deviation of daily price changes times the square root of the number of days for the transaction. This analysis assumes that the

FIGURE 17-2

Illustration of Average Credit Exposure for a Repo

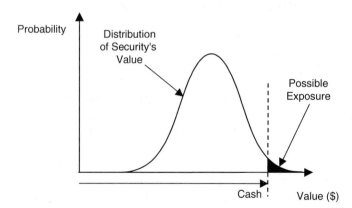

behavior of the security is unaffected by whether the counterparty defaults. This would not be the case if the security was a bond issued by the counterparty. In that case, default and change in value would be highly correlated. Standard good practice is to accept only collateral that is not related to the counterparty, in which case our analysis above is valid.

Margin Accounts

A margin account is another form of collateralized loan. In a margin account, a customer takes a loan from the bank, and then with the loan and his own funds, purchases a security. The security is then held by the bank as collateral against the loan. The pledging of the security as collateral by the customer to the bank is called *hypothecation*. It is also possible for the bank to pledge the security to another bank to get a loan. This is called *rehypothecation*.

Margin accounts are used by customers who want to leverage their position and increase their potential returns. As an example, consider a customer who has $10,000 and takes a loan for $10,000. This is used to buy $20,000 worth of securities. If the price rises by 10% to $22,000 and the customer sells, then after paying back the loan with interest, the customer has a little less than $12,000, a 20% gain. Conversely, if the price falls by 10%, the customer makes a 20% loss.

Typically, retail customers are allowed to borrow only up to half the value of the securities they own. If the value of the securities falls, the bank will ask the customer for more cash to maintain the 50% ratio; this is called a *margin call*. If the customer does not respond, the bank will sell all or part of the shares. After paying off the loan, any residual value is given back to the customer. If the securities lost more than 50% of their value before they were liquidated, and the customer failed to make up the difference, the bank would suffer a credit loss.

The potential exposure at default is quantified by the probability distribution of the security's value over the days from the security's first being worth over 200% of the loan, through the time it takes for the bank to make a margin call, plus the time it takes for the bank to liquidate the position if the customer does not respond. The simplest approach is to assume that the security value has a Normal or log-Normal distribution with a mean equal to the current value (V_0) and standard deviation equal to the daily standard deviation of the value multiplied by square root of the time to liquidation. The potential exposure is illustrated in Figure 17-3. The average exposure at default for a 50% margin account is given by the equation below:

$$Average\ Exposure = \int_0^{\frac{V_0}{2}} \left(\frac{V_0}{2} - V\right) pr(V)dV$$

If the value is greater than $V_0/2$, the exposure is zero.

FIGURE 17-3

Possible Exposure for a Margin Account

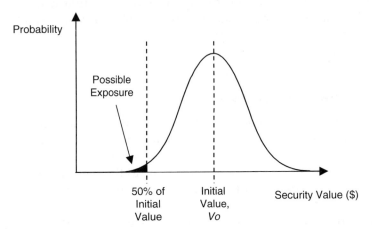

Credit Exposure for Derivatives

For normal derivatives, credit risk is a by-product of an essentially market-risk transaction. The estimation of credit exposures for derivatives is quite complex and discussed here in three sections: how credit risks arise, how they can be quantified, and how they can be reduced.

How Credit Risks Arise in Derivatives Trading

The derivatives that we discussed in the earlier market-risk chapters have their values determined according to a market variable, such as the price of an equity or the prevailing interbank lending rate. When trading derivatives, such as swaps and options, there is the possibility, indeed the hope, that over the life of the derivative contract, the market rates will change and the counterparty will owe money to the bank. When this is the case, the derivative is said to be "in the money" to the bank.

As an example, consider the bank being long a call option on an equity. If the value of the equity increases, the bank can exercise the option and receive the highly valued equity in return for the strike price. The bank's profit would be the difference between the equity price and the strike price. If the counterparty went bankrupt before the option was exercised, the bank would lose this potential profit. If the idea of losing potential profit seems a little obscure, consider what would happen if the bank had also entered into an agreement with another customer to deliver the equity. If the counterparty defaults on the option, the bank will need to use its own reserves to buy the equity for delivery to the customer.

Notice that if the option had been out of the money, the counterparty's bankruptcy would have had no effect on the bank. In general, there can only be a credit loss if the derivatives contract is in the money to the bank. If it is out of the money, then when the counterparty goes bankrupt, there is no credit loss because the counterparty does not owe the bank anything. In this case, the bank simply pays any remaining amount it owes to the counterparty and closes the contract.

Because the exposure can vary greatly depending on changes in the market, when managing credit exposures to derivatives-trading counterparties, the bank needs to consider not just the current market-to-market exposure, but also the potential future exposure. Returning to the example of the call option, on the day of initiating the option, the mark-to-market value will be close to zero, which would seem to indicate no credit risk, but if equity prices move, there is the potential that the exposure could become very great.

Let us now discuss how credit risk can be quantified for the three most common types of derivatives: vanilla options, FX swaps, and interest-rate swaps.

Quantifying Credit Exposure for Vanilla Options

For a vanilla call option, there is no exposure if the bank has sold the option (gone short). In this case, the bank has received the option premium and now simply has to face the possibility of paying the counterparty if market rates change. If the bank is long the option, there will always be a credit exposure until the contract expires because the option will always have time value. Theoretically, the credit exposure from a call option could become infinite if the value of the underlying went to infinity.

Saying that the credit exposure could be infinity is not terribly useful for managing the credit risk of a derivatives portfolio. Instead, the potential future exposure over the remaining life of the instrument can be better described using statistical measures. The potential credit exposure is usually described in terms of the expected exposure (EE) and the maximum likely exposure (MLE). The *expected exposure* is the average exposure across all possible market movements, weighted by the probability of the movement. The *maximum likely exposure* is a measure of how bad the exposure could be, given a certain level of confidence. Typically, the 95% confidence interval is used. This means that we can be 95% sure that the exposure will be less than the MLE.

Both the EE and MLE have a term structure; i.e., the amount changes as we look into the future. As an example, consider a vanilla call option with a strike price close to the current equity price. Over the next day, the price is likely to be only a little higher than the strike price, but over several months, it could become much higher. There is the potential that in a few months' time, the counterparty could owe the bank a large amount.

For simple instruments with single payments, such as vanilla options, it is relatively easy to calculate the EE and MLE analytically in a closed-form equation. The 95% MLE is the option price if the stock price is equal to the 95% worst case. If we assume that the stock price has a Normal probability distribution, then the 95% worst case is 1.64 standard deviations from the current stock price. The standard deviation over T days is the standard deviation over one day multiplied by the square root of T. For a call option, the MLE T days in the future is given by the following equation:

$$MLE_T = C[S_{95\%}, (T_e - T)]$$
$$= C\left[\left(S_0 + 1.64\sqrt{T}\sigma_S\right), (T_e - T)\right]$$

Here, $C[s, t]$ is the value of the call option with the stock price equal to s, and t days left to expiration. $S_{95\%}$ is the 95% worst case stock price, T_e is the time from now to expiration, T is the number of days into the future that we want to evaluate the MLE, and σ_S is the daily standard deviation of the stock price.

The expected exposure (EE) is a little more difficult to evaluate because we need to calculate the value of the call, weighted by the probability density of the stock price:

$$EE_T = \int_{S=0}^{\infty} C[S, (T_e - T)]pr(S)dS$$

Figure 17-4 shows a random walk for the price of an equity, and Figure 17-5 shows the corresponding credit exposure for a call option on that equity. Notice that because there is only a single payment, and uncertainty increases as we look further into the future, EE and MLE for a vanilla option keep increasing up to the final settlement date.

FIGURE 17-4

Change in the Price of an Equity Underlying an Option

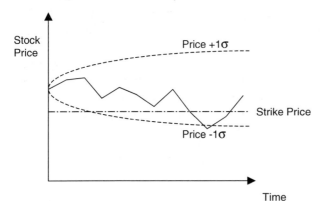

FIGURE 17-5

Change in the Credit Exposure in an Option Contract

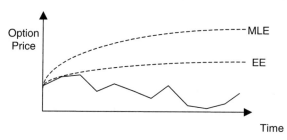

Quantifying Credit Exposure for FX Swaps

In an FX swap, the parties agree to exchange fixed amounts of each currency on the last day of the contract. If we are based in dollars, and paying D dollars and receiving P pounds, then the value of the swap is the difference in the NPV of each cash flow converted back into dollars:

$$V = \left[FX_{P,D}\,\frac{P}{\left(1+r_{P,T}\right)^{T}}\right] - \left[\frac{D}{\left(1+r_{D,T}\right)^{T}}\right]$$

Here, $FX_{P,D}$ is the spot exchange rate, $r_{P,T}$ is the sterling discount rate for maturity T, and $r_{D,T}$ is the corresponding dollar discount rate. The credit exposure on the swap is the maximum of zero or the value of the swap. For there to be an exposure, the value of the currency to be received should be greater than the value of the currency to be paid. The maximum exposure would occur if the currency to be paid had a massive devaluation. In this case, the value of the currency to be paid would be close to zero, and the credit exposure would be equal to the value of the currency to be received.

A reasonable estimate of the EE and MLE for an FX swap can be obtained by using the parametric-VaR framework to calculate the volatility of the value of the contract, σ_V. The 95% maximum likely exposure of the swap is then the maximum of 0 or the current price plus 1.64 standard deviations:

$$MLE = \max\left[0,\,\left(V_0 + 1.64\sigma_V\sqrt{T}\right)\right]$$

The expected exposure is the integral of the positive value, weighted by the probability density of V:

$$EE_T = \int_{V=-\infty}^{\infty} \max[0,V]pr(V)dV$$
$$= \int_{V=0}^{\infty} Vpr(V)dV$$

If we assume that the value is Normally distributed with a mean equal to the current value and a daily standard deviation of σ_V, then the expected exposure is obtained by integrating the Normal probability-density function:

$$EE_T = \int_{V=0}^{\infty} VN(V_0, \sqrt{T}\sigma_v, V)\, dV$$

We were able to obtain these neat analytical expressions for EE and MLE because the payment structure was simple and because we made simplifying assumptions about the valuation model and the probability-density function for the random variables. For more complex products or models, we need to resort again to using a simulation tool, such as Monte Carlo.

Quantifying Credit Exposure for Interest-Rate Swaps

The measurement of exposure for interest-rate swaps is made complex by the multiple payments and by the complex form of interest-rate movements over long periods. In an interest-rate swap, the parties regularly exchange the difference between a notional amount times a fixed rate, and the same notional amount times a floating rate:

$$Payment = Nr_{fix} - Nr_{float}$$

For a swap making payment every six months, the floating rate is typically equal to six-month LIBOR plus a spread.

An interest-rate swap is equivalent to one side making payments on a fixed-rate bond and the other side making payments on a floating-rate bond. The value of a swap is therefore equal to the value of a fixed-rate bond minus the value of a floating-rate bond.

The value of a fixed-rate bond is the NPV of the fixed-interest payments, plus the NPV of the final principal payment:

$$V_{Fixed} = \left[\sum_{t=t_{next}}^{T_{final}} \frac{Nr_{fix}}{(1+r_t)^t}\right] + \left[\frac{N}{\left(1 + r_{T_{final}}\right)^{T_{final}}}\right]$$

Here, N is the notional amount, r_{fix} is the fixed rate, and t_{next} is the time to the next coupon payment.

To value a floating-rate bond, we assume that at the next payment date, the required coupon will be paid and the new coupon will be set such that the value of the bond on that day will equal the face value (i.e., the bond will be at par). The total value of the floating-rate bond on the next payment date is therefore equal to the following:

$$V_{Floating,t_{next}} = Nr_{float} + N$$

Here, r_{float} is the rate that was fixed for the next coupon payment on the floating side. The value of the bond today is the value of the bond on the next payment date, discounted to today:

$$V_{Floating} = \frac{V_{Floating,t_{next}}}{\left(1 + r_{t_{next}}\right)^{t_{next}}}$$

$$= \frac{Nr_{float}}{\left(1 + r_{t_{next}}\right)^{t_{next}}} + \frac{N}{\left(1 + r_{t_{next}}\right)^{t_{next}}}$$

The value of the swap can then be calculated as follows:

$$V_{Swap} = NPV_{Fixed} - NPV_{Floating}$$

$$= \left[\sum_{t=t_{next}}^{T_{final}} \frac{Nr_{fix}}{\left(1 + r_t\right)^t} + \frac{N}{\left(1 + r_{T_{final}}\right)^{T_{final}}}\right] - \left[\frac{Nr_{float}}{\left(1 + r_{t_{next}}\right)^{t_{next}}} + \frac{N}{\left(1 + r_{t_{next}}\right)^{t_{next}}}\right]$$

The equation above gives us the value of a swap in terms of the rates of today's yield curve. This equation can be used in a simulation to estimate the distribution of possible future values for the swap, and therefore the distribution of the possible future credit exposure. The simulation creates a random interest-rate path and then uses the above equation to value the option at each point along the path.

Figure 17-6 shows a scenario for the value of an interest-rate swap, and Figure 17-7 shows the corresponding credit exposure.

By repeating this analysis for multiple scenarios (in this case, 1000) we can obtain an ensemble of exposures from which we can calculate the expected exposure and maximum likely exposure. These are shown in Figure 17-8 for an interest-rate swap that at the initial time (i.e., today) has a mark-to-market value of zero. Notice that interest-rate swaps have the maximum likely exposure approximately one-third of the time from the date that the swap is started to the time when the last payment is made. The sawtooth appearance occurs when interest payments are made and the outstanding exposure drops.

Monte Carlo evaluation takes a long time, so some banks carry out a set of simulations for generic instruments, then store the results in a table. The exposure is then approximated as "mark-to-market plus add-on," where the add-on comes from the table. The add-on is typically a percentage of the notional amount, and depends on the time left to maturity and the extent to which the derivative is in the money. This "add-on" technique works for single instruments, but does not work well for netting agreements, as discussed in the next section.

FIGURE 17-6

One Scenario of Interest-Rate-Swap Value

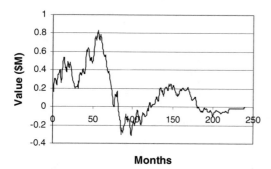

Months

FIGURE 17-7

Scenario for Interest-Rate-Swap Credit Exposure

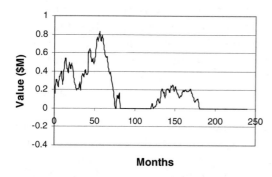

Months

FIGURE 17-8

Expected and Maximum Likely Exposure for an Interest-Rate Swap

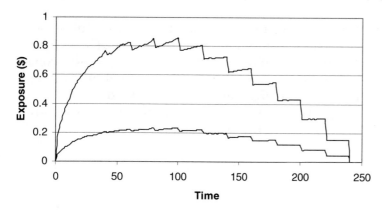

Mitigating Credit Risk when Trading Derivatives

In this section, we discuss seven common ways for managing counterparty credit risk:

1. Requiring collateral
2. Settling according to the mark-to-market
3. Early settlement in the event of a downgrade
4. Using a special-purpose vehicle (SPV)
5. A netting master agreement
6. Counterparty exposure limits
7. Pricing for credit risk

Requiring Collateral

If the bank considers that its counterparty has a significantly high probability of default, it can reduce the potential loss by requiring collateral. For example, if the current mark-to-market value of a derivatives contract with a counterparty is $100, the bank may ask the counterparty for $100 in cash to be held as collateral. If the counterparty later defaults on the derivatives contract, the bank will keep the cash, thereby making no net loss. If changes in the market reduce the value of the derivative to $90, the bank would release $10 of collateral back to the counterparty. If the market changes so the value of the contract is negative (i.e., the bank owes money to the counterparty) then the amount of collateral would drop to 0.

Typically, the amount of collateral that the bank requires is equal to or slightly higher than the current mark-to-market value of the contract. The bank will require the collateral to be more than the current value of the contract if the contract value is highly volatile or if the value of the collateral is volatile, e.g., if the collateral is in the form of bonds or equities rather than cash.

Settling According to Mark-to-Market

Settling according to mark-to-market is very similar to using cash collateral, except that if the value of the contract becomes negative, the bank has to give cash to the counterparty. Settling according to mark-to-market is rare and is only used when the credit risk is very high, for example for a large swap in a project finance deal. (Project finance deals are generally risky because payments depend on the profits from a single project.)

Settling according to mark-to-market reduces the credit exposure, but it increases the cash-flow volatility for the counterparty and may increase the counterparty's probability of default. The probability of default is affected because the company is forced to pay the full change in value as soon as the market moves, rather than having a series of slightly increased swap payments. This sudden need for a large payment can cause the company to have a cashflow crisis.

Early Settlement in the Event of a Downgrade

A bank can protect itself from the default of a counterparty by adding a clause in the derivatives contract that states that if the counterparty's credit rating falls at all from its current level, the contract will be terminated and immediately settled at the existing mark-to-market value. To be effective, this requires the rating agencies to identify the need for a downgrade well in advance of any default. Such an agreement is also onerous to the counterparty because in a time of trouble (the downgrade), the counterparty could suddenly be forced to make a large payment to the bank to close the contract.

Using a Special-Purpose Vehicle

Derivatives traders want to concentrate on market risks and generally do not want to be distracted by the credit risks of their counterparties. Ideally, they would deal with a AAA-rated counterparty so that default is extremely unlikely. There are relatively few AAA-rated banks, but this problem has been solved by setting up AAA-rated *special-purpose vehicles* (SPVs) to trade derivatives. An SPV is a separate legal entity. It is set up by a parent bank, and is given a large amount of capital. It is effectively a minibank that only trades derivatives and is fully owned by the parent bank. Although the bank is legally separate, it shares the staff and facilities of the parent bank.

The legal structure is such that in the event of the parent bank's defaulting, the creditors will not be able make any claims on the SPV. This makes the SPV "bank-ruptcy remote" from the parent bank and will allow it to continue operating to honor its current derivatives contracts.

Using a Netting Master Agreement

A *netting master agreement* is a legal agreement that covers all the derivatives trans-actions between two institutions. The agreement states that in the event of default, the bank is only liable for the net amount that it owes the counterparty under all con-tracts, and not the gross sum. As an example, consider a bank that has bought an option from a counterparty and sold a very similar option to the same counterparty. Assume that the counterparty defaults, and at that time the bank owes $100 for one option, and the counterparty owes $90 for the other option. If there was no netting agreement, the bank would have to pay $100 and then get in line with all the other creditors to try to recover what it could of the $90. However, if the bank has a netting agreement, then the bank only owes the net amount of $10. Under the netting agree-ment, the bank pays the $10, and then there are no further claims on either side.

Although simple in concept, netting agreements can be legally difficult to enforce. It is also difficult to measure the exposure properly under a netting agree-ment. The measurement problem arises because the net exposure is highly dependent on the correlation between the value of all the instruments traded between the bank and the counterparty. The normal solution to estimating the net exposure is to net the current mark-to-market exposure with the counterparty, and then add on the gross amount of the individual future exposures as if there were no netting agreement.

A more refined but computationally expensive approach is to use simulation. In using simulation, a scenario is created for market conditions, the value of every transaction is calculated under those conditions, and then the net exposure for that scenario is calculated. By carrying out many simulations, we can calculate the expected net exposure and the maximum likely net exposure.

Counterparty Exposure Limits

Another approach to managing credit risk is to accept its existence, but limit the total exposure to any one counterparty. The limits have a term structure to limit the exposure at each point in the future. Typically, the allowed exposure reduces as the bank looks further into the future. The limits are in terms of the maximum-allowed EE or MLE. The allowed limits are compared with the measured EE and MLE of the bank's current transactions.

As an example, consider Figure 17-9, which shows the exposure profile for three transactions with one counterparty: a loan, an interest-rate swap, and an FX swap. Figure 17-9 also shows the net MLE for the combination of all three transactions. Figure 17-10 shows the allowed limit for the MLE to this counterparty. In this example, assume the loan and interest-rate swap transactions have taken place previously, and now the risk management group is being asked by a trader to approve the new FX-swap transaction. Before allowing the new transaction, the risk management group compares the limits with the net MLE that would occur with all three trades. Figure 17-11 shows the limit imposed on the expected MLE. In this case, the MLE would exceed the limit. Given that the limit will be exceeded, the risk management group could refuse to approve the new trade in its current form, or could increase the limit slightly if they thought that the counterparty was reasonably creditworthy.

Pricing for Credit Risk

For every risk the bank assumes, it should ensure that the shareholders are compensated. This includes the credit risk in the derivatives-trading operation. Using the exposure profiles we discussed above and the credit-portfolio analytics we discuss in later chapters, it is possible to calculate the amount of economic capital to be held for each derivatives transaction. The required return on this capital can then be added to the price of the derivatives contract, for example, by modifying the swap interest rate.

A simplified approach is to decompose the derivative transaction into a pure market-risk component, and a loan of an amount equal to the exposure, then charge the counterparty a credit spread on that loan. The amount of the credit spread would be equal to the spread on a loan to a company of the same creditworthiness.

CHAPTER 17

FIGURE 17-9

Stand-Alone Credit Exposures for a Loan, Interest-Rate Swap, and FX Swap

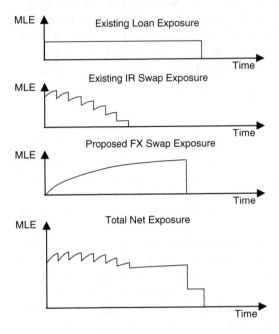

FIGURE 17-10

Limit of Maximum-Allowed Exposure

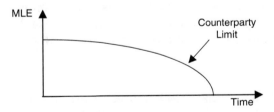

FIGURE 17-11

Comparison of Net Exposure with the Allowed Limit

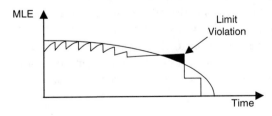

SUMMARY

In this chapter, we described the common ways in which credit risk is structured, taking particular note of the factors that affect the probability and amount of loss. In the next chapter, we build the framework for calculating credit risk for a single transaction.

Risk Measurement for a Single Facility

INTRODUCTION

To quantify credit risk, we wish to obtain the probability distribution of the losses from a credit portfolio and also to have a measure of the contribution of each loan to the portfolio loss. In this chapter, we lay the foundation for quantifying the credit risk of a portfolio by quantifying the risk for individual facilities.

We start by considering the simple case of modeling the losses that could occur over one year due to a default. We then add the complication of additional losses due to the possibility of downgrades. Finally, we look at how the risk can be calculated for a credit exposure that lasts for multiple years (e.g., a five-year loan).

DETERMINING LOSSES DUE TO DEFAULT

For a single facility, we describe the credit-loss distribution by the mean and standard deviation of the loss over a year. The mean is commonly called the expected loss (EL). The expected loss can be interpreted as being the amount that a lender could expect to lose on average over a number of years, from transactions with similar levels of creditworthiness, exposure, and security. The EL can be viewed as a cost of doing business because over the long run, the bank should expect to lose an amount equal to EL each year. The standard deviation of the loss is typically called the unexpected loss (UL).

In this section, we consider the potential losses due to default. The actual loss (L) can be described as the exposure at default (E), multiplied by the loss in the event of default or severity (S), multiplied by an indicator of default (I). The indicator is a discrete variable that equals one if a default occurs, and zero otherwise:

[handwritten annotations: "Loss in event of default", "severity", "exposure", "EXPOSURE AT DEFAULT"]

$$L = I \times S \times E$$
$$L = 0 \qquad \text{if } I = 0$$
$$L = S \times E \quad \text{if } I = 1$$

In deriving expressions for EL and UL, we first get results quickly, using the simplifying assumptions that S and E are fixed. We then repeat their derivation in more detail without the simplifying assumptions.

If we assume that LIED and EAD are fixed, the only remaining uncertainty is whether a default occurs. The two possible conditions at the end of the year are: there is a default or there is no default, with probabilities of P and $(1 - P)$ respectively. The expected loss is then the amount that is lost in each condition, multiplied by the probability of being in each condition:

$$EL = P[1 \times E \times S] + (1 - P)[0 \times E \times S]$$
$$= P \times E \times S$$

This is a fairly intuitive result, as it says that the average is the probability of default times the amount that is lost if default occurs. If we loaned \$100 to a BBB-rated company, then P would be around 22 basis points. Assuming that S is 30%, the EL is 0.066 :

$$EL = 0.0022 \times \$100 \times 0.3 = \$0.066$$

The next step is to calculate the standard deviation of losses (UL). Let us again assume that LIED and EAD are fixed. For a discrete variable, such as our indicator function, the variance is the probability of each state times the difference between the result and the mean squared. For clarity, we use $\overline{L}$ instead of EL to denote the mean loss:

$$UL^2 = P[1 \times E \times S - \overline{L}]^2 + (1 - P)[0 \times E \times S - \overline{L}]^2$$
$$= P\left[E^2 S^2 - 2ES\overline{L} + \overline{L}^2\right] + (1 - P)\left[\overline{L}\right]^2$$
$$= P\left[E^2 S^2 - 2ES\overline{L} + \overline{L}^2\right] + [\overline{L}]^2 - P[\overline{L}]^2$$
$$= P\left[E^2 S^2 - 2ES\overline{L}\right] + [\overline{L}]^2$$
$$= P\left[E^2 S^2 - 2ESPES\right] + [P^2 E^2 S^2]$$
$$= PE^2 S^2 - P^2 E^2 S^2$$
$$= [P - P^2][ES]^2$$

By taking the square root, we obtain the simple expression for the unexpected loss:

$$UL = \sqrt{P - P^2} \times E \times S$$

For the loan of $100 to a BBB company, the UL would be $1.41:

$$UL = \sqrt{0.0022 - 0.0022^2} \times \$100 \times 0.3 = \$1.41$$

This result can also be obtained by realizing that the indicator, I, is a Bernoulli variable. A *Bernoulli variable* can only equal one or zero and the variance of a Bernoulli variable is $P(1 - P)$.

These simple expressions for the EL and UL are the ones most commonly used. However, if we also want to include the possibility of uncertainty in LIED and EAD, we must use more a complex derivation. The math gets quite detailed, so you may want to review the derivations quickly, focus on the results, then come back to the math if you need it later.

Now we repeat the derivations of EL and UL but without assuming fixed values for the exposure at default (E) and the loss in the event of default (S). In this general case, the expected loss is the mean loss in each state, multiplied by the probability of being in that state:

$$EL = \sum_{I=0,1} p(I) \int_S \int_E ISE\, pr(S, E|I)dSdE$$

$$= (1 - P) \times 0 + P \times \int_S \int_E SE\, pr(S, E|I = 1)dSdE$$

Here, $p(I)$ is the probability of event I taking a particular value (0 or 1). $pr(S, E|I)$ is the joint probability-density function for S and E given that I equals a particular value. In practice, we only care about $pr(S, E|I = 1)$, which is the probability-density function for S and E in the case when there is a default. Notice that the term inside the double integral is similar to the definition of the covariance of S and E:

$$\int_S \int_E SE\, pr(S, E)dSdE = \sigma_{S,E}^2 + \overline{S}\,\overline{E}$$

Using this definition, the equation for EL can be simplified to the following result:

$$EL = P \times \left(\overline{S}\,\overline{E} + \sigma_{S,E}^2\right)$$

This result is the same as the equation we had before for EL, but with an additional term for the covariance between S and E. If the S and E are uncertain, but the correlation between them is zero, then the expected loss is simply the product of the expected value of each component:

$$EL = P \times \overline{S} \times \overline{E}$$

Let us now turn our attention to UL. In the general case where E and S are uncertain, the variance of the loss (UL^2) is the square of the deviation of the loss in each state, multiplied by the probability of being in that state. Again, we use $\overline{L}$ to denote the expected loss:

$$UL^2 = \sum_{I=0,1} p(I) \int_S \int_E (ISE - \bar{L})^2 \, pr(S,E|I)dSdE$$

$\bar{L}$ has already been found and is constant over the summation and integration, so it can be pulled out and evaluated separately, as in the equations below:

$$UL^2 = \left(\sum_{I=0,1} p(I) \int_S \int_E (ISE)^2 \, pr(S,E|I)dSdE \right)$$

$$- \left(2\bar{L} \sum_{I=0,1} p(I) \int_S \int_E (ISE)pr(S,E|I)dSdE \right)$$

$$+ \left(\bar{L}^2 \sum_{I=0,1} p(I) \int_S \int_E pr(S,E|I)dSdE \right)$$

$$= \left(\sum_{I=0,1} p(I) \int_S \int_E (ISE)^2 \, pr(S,E|I)dSdE \right) - \left(\bar{L}^2 \right)$$

We can now carry out the summation over the two possible values for I. When I equals zero, the term inside the integrals equals zero:

$$UL^2 = \left((1-P) \times 0 + P \times \int_S \int_E (SE)^2 \, pr(S,E|I=1)dSdE \right) - \left(\bar{L}^2 \right)$$

$$= \left(P \times \int_S \int_E (SE)^2 \, pr(S,E|I=1)dSdE \right) - \left(\bar{L}^2 \right)$$

This double integral is difficult to evaluate unless we assume that the values of S and E are independent, meaning that the severity of the loss is independent of the exposure at the time of default. In that case, the probability distribution can be separated into the product of two distributions, each of which can be integrated separately:

$$UL^2 = \left(P \times \int_S \int_E (SE)^2 \, pr(S)pr(E)dSdE \right) - \left(\bar{L}^2 \right)$$

$$= \left(P \times \int_S S^2 \, pr(S)dS \times \int_E E^2 pr(E)dE \right) - \left(\bar{L}^2 \right)$$

Now we can recognize that the integrals are almost the same as the equations for variance, and use this to produce the following result:

$$UL^2 = P \times \left(\sigma_S^2 + \bar{S}^2 \right) \left(\sigma_E^2 + \bar{E}^2 \right) - \left(\bar{L}^2 \right)$$

$$= P \times \left(\sigma_S^2 + \bar{S}^2 \right) \left(\sigma_E^2 + \bar{E}^2 \right) - \left(P^2 \bar{S}^2 \bar{E}^2 \right)$$

$$= (P - P^2)\bar{S}^2\bar{E}^2 + P \times \left(\sigma_S^2 \bar{E}^2 + \sigma_E^2 \bar{S}^2 + \sigma_S^2 \sigma_E^2 \right)$$

This result is the same equation as before for UL, but with additional terms for the variances of S and E. For a loan, the variance of the exposure, E, is close to zero.[1] As we see in the next chapter, the standard deviation of the loss in the event of default (LIED or S) is typically around 25%. For our example of the BBB loan, this gives a UL of $1.83, which is a 30% increase from the UL that was calculated assuming that the LIED was fixed:

$$UL = \sqrt{((0.0022 - 0.0022^2)(0.3^2 100^2) + 0.0022 \times (0.25^2 100^2))}$$

$$= \$1.83$$

In summary, if the loss given default and exposure amount are fixed, the EL and UL for the losses due to default are given by the following:

$$EL = P \times E \times S$$

$$UL = \sqrt{P - P^2} \times E \times S$$

If E and S can vary, EL is given as follows:

$$EL = P \times \left(\overline{S}\,\overline{E} + \sigma_{S,E}^2 \right)$$

If S and E are uncorrelated, UL is given as follows:

$$UL = \sqrt{(P - P^2)\overline{S}^2\overline{E}^2 + P \times \left(\sigma_S^2\overline{E}^2 + \sigma_E^2\overline{S}^2 + \sigma_S^2\sigma_E^2 \right)}$$

DETERMINING LOSSES DUE TO BOTH DEFAULT AND DOWNGRADES

In the section above, we calculated the statistics of loss due to the possibility of default. It is also possible for bonds and loans to lose value because the issuing company is downgraded. When a company is downgraded, it means that the rating agency believes that the probability of default has risen. A promise by this downgraded company to make a future payment is no longer as valuable as it was because there is an increased probability that the company will not be able to fulfill its promise. Consequently, there is a fall in the value of the bond or loan.

As an example, consider a case in which the one-year (risk-free) government note is trading at a price of 95 cents per dollar of the nominal final payment (implying a risk-free discount rate of 5.25%). A promise by a single-A company to make a payment in one year would have a price around 94 cents per dollar, and a BBB company would trade around 93 cents on the dollar. This implies discount rates of 6.35% and 7.5%, or credit spreads of 1.1% and 2.25% relative to the risk-free rate. If you had bought the bond of the single-A company for 94 cents, and then it was downgraded to BBB, you would lose 1 cent.

To obtain the EL and UL for this risk, we require the probability of a grade change and the loss if such a change occurs. The probability of a grade change has been researched and published by the credit-rating agencies. Table 18-1 shows the probability of a company of one grade migrating to another grade over one year. (Appendix A describes how this table is derived.) To understand how to read this table, let us use it to find the grade migration probabilities for a company that is rated single-A at the start of the year. Looking down the third column, we see that the company has a 7-basis-point chance of becoming AAA rated by the end of the year. It has a 2.25% chance of being rated AA, a 91.76% chance of remaining single-A, and a 5.19% chance of being downgraded to BBB. Looking down to the bottom of the column, we see that it has a 4-basis-points chance of falling into default. Notice that the last row gives the probability of a company's defaulting over the year; for example, a company rated CCC at the beginning of the year has a 21.94% chance of having defaulted by the end of the year.

From Table 18-1, we can get any company's probability of moving to a different grade by the end of the year. Associated with each grade is a discount rate relative to the risk-free rate. This varies with the market's appetite for risk, but Table 18-2 shows the spread between U.S. corporate bonds and U.S. Treasuries in October, 2001. These spreads are calculated for zero-coupon bonds.

With these spreads, we can calculate the value of a bond or loan, and thereby estimate the change in value if the grade changes. As an example, let us calculate the EL and UL for a BBB-rated bond with a single payment of $100 that is currently due in 3 years. At the end of the year the bond will have 2 years to maturity. If we assume

TABLE 18-1

Probability of Grade Migration (bps)

Rating at Start of Year

		AAA	AA	A	BBB	BB	B	CCC	Default
	AAA	9366	66	7	3	3	0	16	0
	AA	583	9172	225	25	7	10	0	0
Rating	A	40	694	9176	483	44	33	31	0
at	BBB	8	49	519	8926	667	46	93	0
End	BB	3	6	49	444	8331	576	200	0
of Year	B	0	9	20	81	747	8418	1074	0
	CCC	0	2	1	16	105	387	6395	0
	Default	0	1	4	22	98	530	2194	10000

Table showing the probability of a company of one grade migrating to another grade before the end of the year.

Adapted from "Corporate Defaults: Will things get worse before they get better?" Leo Brand, Reza Bahar, Standard & Poor's *Credit Week*, January 31, 2001. See Appendix A to this chapter for notes on the creation of this table.

TABLE 18-2

Corporate Bond Spreads Above the Risk-Free Rate (basis points)

Rating	1 yr	2 yr	3 yr	5 yr	7 yr	10 yr	30 yr
AAA	38	43	48	62	72	81	92
AA	48	58	63	77	92	101	112
A	73	83	103	117	137	156	165
BBB	118	133	148	162	182	201	220
BB	275	300	325	350	375	450	575
B	500	550	600	675	725	775	950
CCC	700	750	900	1000	1100	1250	1500

From www.bondsonline.com/asp/corp/spreadfin.html

a risk-free discount rate of 5%, and the bond is still rated BBB, the value will be $88.45:

$$Value_{BBB} = \frac{\$100}{(1 + 5\% + 1.33\%)^2} = \$88.45$$

However, if the bond rating falls to single B, the value of the bond will fall to $81.90 :

$$Value_{BB} = \frac{\$100}{(1 + 5\% + 5.50\%)^2} = \$81.90$$

This is a loss of $6.55.

We can repeat this calculation for all possible grades to give the values shown in Table 18-3. The value in default corresponds to our assumption of a 30% LIED. Table 18-3 also shows the loss in value compared with the value if the bond retained its BBB-rating.

From Table 18-1, we have the probability of a change in credit grade, and from Table 18-3, we have the loss amount if the bond changes grades. We can now bring these together to calculate EL and UL. The expected loss is calculated from the probability of being in a given grade (P_G), multiplied by the loss for that grade (L_G):

$$EL = \sum_G P_G L_G$$

The unexpected loss is given by the square root of the probability-weighted sum of the differences squared:

$$UL = \sqrt{\sum_G (L_G - EL)^2 P_G}$$

TABLE 18-3

Change in Values for a BBB Bond due to Credit Events

Rating	Value	Loss
Aaa/AAA	$89.96	$-1.52
Aa2/AA	$89.71	$-1.26
A2/A	$89.29	$-0.84
Baa2/BBB	$88.45	$0.00
Ba2/BB	$85.73	$2.71
B2/B	$81.90	$6.55
Caa/CCC	$79.01	$9.44
Default	$61.91	$26.53

Table 18-4 shows the elements of the EL and UL calculation for the example BBB bond. The result is that EL is $0.18 and UL is $1.25.

It is also interesting to compare this with the result of considering only the default. If we only consider default, EL is the probability of default times the loss, given default:

$$EL = P_D L_D$$
$$= 0.0022 \times \$26.5 = \$0.058$$

This is much less than the EL calculated including downgrades. To calculate UL for default only, we only consider the default and zero-loss cases:

$$UL = \sqrt{(L_D - EL)^2 P_D + (0 - EL)^2(1 - P_D)}$$
$$= \sqrt{(26.5 - 0.058)^2\, 0.0022 + (0 - 0.058)^2(1 - 0.0022)} = \$1.24$$

UL for just default is a little less than UL including downgrades. The downgrades are relatively insignificant to UL because UL is largely determined by the extreme losses, and the extreme losses depend mostly on defaults and not on downgrades.

The next logical step would be to add complication to the analysis by considering the uncertainty to the loss in the event of default (LIED). This is normally done by simulation, in which we first randomly choose the grade at the end of the year. If the grade is CCC or higher, we value the bond as above. If the grade is a default, we then randomly choose the LIED. We discuss simulation for credit risk in great depth in the later chapter on portfolio analysis.

TABLE 18-4

Calculation of Expected and Unexpected Loss, Including Downgrades

Year-End Rating	Probability (P_G, bps)	Loss (L_G)	Expected Loss $(P_G L_G)$	Unexpected Loss $(L_G - EL)^2 P_G$
AAA	3	$(1.52)	$(0.000)	$0.001
AA	25	$(1.26)	$(0.003)	$0.005
A	483	$(0.84)	$(0.040)	$0.051
BBB	8926	$—	$—	$0.031
BB	444	$2.71	$0.121	$0.284
B	81	$6.55	$0.053	$0.328
CCC	16	$9.44	$0.015	$0.137
Default	22	$26.53	$0.058	$1.525
Total (sqrt of total for UL)			$0.203	$1.537

DETERMINING DEFAULT PROBABILITIES OVER MULTIPLE YEARS

In the discussion above, we dealt with the probability of the company's defaulting or being downgraded at some point over the next year. We are now going to tackle the problem of quantifying the risk over multiple years.

One approach is to look at historical data. The approach groups the companies according to their ratings at one snapshot of time. Then calculates how many defaulted in the first year, how many in the second year, and so forth. If we want to look out over many years, this requires a large amount of data. An alternative is to derive the default rate over several years from the one-year grade-migration matrix in Table 18-1.

From our discussion on grade migrations, we know the probability of a company's transitioning from one grade to another by the end of a year. And we know the probability of each grade's defaulting. From these two pieces of information, we can estimate the probability of the company's defaulting in the second year. The probability of default in the second year $(P_{D,2})$ is given by the probability of transitioning to each grade (P_G), multiplied by the probability of default for a company of that grade $(P_{D|G})$:

$$P_{D,2} = \sum_G P_G P_{D|G}$$

For a single-A rated bond, the probability of default in the first year is 4 basis points. The probability of defaulting by the end of the second year is given by the following sum:

$$P_{D,2} = \sum_G P_G P_{D|G}$$

$$= P_{AAA}P_{D|AAA} + P_{AA}P_{D|AA} + P_A P_{D|A}$$

$$+ P_{BBB}P_{D|BBB} + P_{BB}P_{D|BB} + P_B P_{D|B}$$

$$+ P_{CCC}P_{D|CCC} + P_D P_{D|D}$$

$$= 0.07\% \times 0\% + 2.25\% \times 0.01\% + 91.76\% \times 0.04\%$$

$$+ 5.19\% \times 0.22\% + 0.49\% \times 0.98\% + 0.2\% \times 5.3\%$$

$$+ 0.01\% \times 21.94\% + 0.04\% \times 100\%$$

$$= 0.11\%$$

Here, P_{AAA} is the probability of becoming AAA rated, and $P_{D|AAA}$ is the one-year probability of default for a company that is rated AAA at the start of a year. Notice that this calculation multiplies the elements of the third column (the single-A row) of the migration matrix in Table 18-1 by the bottom row of the matrix.

If we want to know the probability of default by the end of the third year, we need to calculate the probability of migrating to each grade over the first year, followed by the probability of migrating to another grade over the second year, followed by the probability of default over the third year. This is quite painful to do with normal algebra, but is easy to do with matrix multiplication if we treat the migration matrix as a *state transition matrix*.

Let us use the symbol M for the migration matrix in Table 18-1, and define G to be a vector giving the probability of being in each grade:

$$G = \begin{bmatrix} P_{AAA} \\ P_{AA} \\ P_A \\ P_{BBB} \\ P_{BB} \\ P_B \\ P_{CCC} \\ P_D \end{bmatrix}$$

At the beginning of the first year, a single-A-rated bond has a 100% chance of being rated single A:

$$G_{T=0} = \begin{bmatrix} 0 \\ 0 \\ 1 \\ 0 \\ 0 \\ 0 \\ 0 \\ 0 \end{bmatrix}$$

The probability distribution of ratings at the end of the year is given by M times G:

$$G_{T=1} = M\ G_{T=0}$$

This equation can be used recursively to get the probability distribution of grades after N years:

$$G_{T=1} = M\ G_{T=0}$$
$$G_{T=2} = M\ G_{T=1}$$
$$= MM\ G_{T=0}$$

$$\vdots$$

$$G_{T=N} = M^N G_{T=0}$$

For a company that is initially rated single A, we get the following results:

$$G_0 = \begin{bmatrix} 0 \\ 0 \\ 1 \\ 0 \\ 0 \\ 0 \\ 0 \\ 0 \end{bmatrix}, \quad G_1 = \begin{bmatrix} 0.0007 \\ 0.0225 \\ 0.9176 \\ 0.0519 \\ 0.0049 \\ 0.0020 \\ 0.0001 \\ 0.0004 \end{bmatrix}, \quad G_2 = \begin{bmatrix} 0.0015 \\ 0.0415 \\ 0.8461 \\ 0.0943 \\ 0.0110 \\ 0.0043 \\ 0.0004 \\ 0.0011 \end{bmatrix}, \quad G_3 = \begin{bmatrix} 0.0024 \\ 0.0575 \\ 0.7838 \\ 0.1290 \\ 0.0178 \\ 0.0070 \\ 0.0008 \\ 0.0020 \end{bmatrix}, \quad G_4 = \begin{bmatrix} 0.0032 \\ 0.0709 \\ 0.7296 \\ 0.1573 \\ 0.0248 \\ 0.0099 \\ 0.0012 \\ 0.0033 \end{bmatrix}$$

The most interesting element of this result is the bottom row, which gives the probability of having fallen into the default grade. From these results, the probability of default after 2 years is 0.11%, after 3 years it is 0.20%, and after 4 years it is 0.33%.

Figure 18-1 shows the probability of default over 10 years for companies with different initial grades. The results are also shown numerically in Table 18-5 for reference.

Notice that these are cumulative probabilities of default. Two other measures of default probability are also of interest to us: the marginal probability of default, and the conditional probability of default. The *marginal probability* is the probability that the company will default in any given year. It is calculated by taking the difference in the cumulative probability:

$$P_{D,Marginal,T} = P_{D,Cumulative,T} - P_{D,Cumulative,T-1}$$

FIGURE 18-1

Probability of Default over 10 Years Depending on Initial Rating

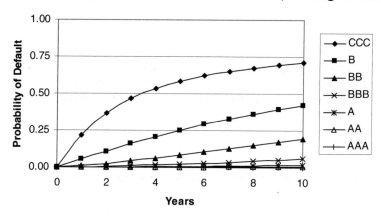

TABLE 18-5

Cumulative Probability of Default over 10 Years Depending on Initial Rating
(basis points)

				Initial Rating			
Year	AAA	AA	A	BBB	BB	B	CCC
1	0	1	4	22	98	530	2194
2	0	3	11	54	244	1067	3656
3	0	7	20	96	423	1584	4652
4	1	12	33	147	624	2068	5349
5	2	18	50	208	838	2515	5851
6	4	26	71	277	1060	2923	6224
7	6	36	96	353	1283	3294	6512
8	9	48	125	436	1506	3631	6742
9	12	61	157	524	1724	3937	6930
10	17	77	194	617	1937	4215	7088

The *conditional probability* is the probability that it will default in the given year, given that it did not default in any of the previous years. The conditional probability is the marginal probability divided by the probability that it has survived so far:

$$P_{D,Conditional,T} = \frac{P_{D,Cumulative,T} - P_{D,Cumulative,T-1}}{1 - P_{D,Cumulative,T-1}}$$

Figure 18-2 shows the conditional probability of default over 10 years. Notice that as time increases, the probabilities converge. One way of thinking about this is to say that if a company is still surviving many years from now, we cannot predict what will be its rating.

FIGURE 18-2

Conditional Probability of Default over 10 Years Depending on Initial Rating

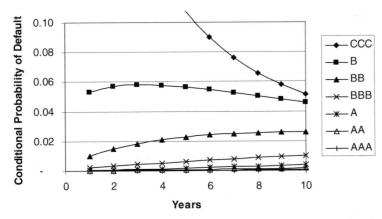

SUMMARY

In this chapter, we explored quantitative frameworks for calculating the credit losses that can occur due to defaults and downgrades. In the next chapter, we explain the process for calculating the values of the parameters used in these equations.

APPENDIX A: DERIVATION OF THE MIGRATION MATRIX

The migration matrix in Table 18-1 is based on the observation of historical data. Such studies are published by the rating agencies. The agencies take several years of historical data on bond ratings and observe the ratings at the beginning and end of each year. From this, they calculate the probability of a grade change. The results of such a study are shown in Table 18-A1.

TABLE 18-A1

Historical Grade-Migration Probabilities (basis points)

		Rating at Start of Year						
		AAA	AA	A	BBB	BB	B	CCC
	AAA	9034	64	7	3	3	0	13
	AA	562	8878	216	24	6	9	0
Rating	A	39	672	8794	456	40	29	26
at	BBB	8	47	497	8426	609	41	77
End	BB	3	6	47	419	7609	511	166
of Year	B	0	9	19	76	682	7462	893
	CCC	0	2	1	15	96	343	5319
	Default	0	1	4	22	98	530	2194
	NR	354	321	416	559	858	1076	1314

From Table 6 in "Corporate Defaults: Will things get worse before they get better?" Leo Brand, Reza Bahar, Standard & Poor's *Credit Week*, January 31, 2001.

The category "NR" means that at the end of the year, the companies had not defaulted but were not rated. The rating may be withdrawn for a variety of reasons, including that the company had no outstanding rated debt at the end of the year, or the company was in sufficient financial trouble that it was no longer cooperating with the rating agencies. For simplicity, we can assume that the unrated companies have the same probability distribution as the other companies that did not default. By doing this, we can remove the NR row and rescale the other migration probabilities.

We also make one other change to the data to obtain the migration matrix. We assume that once a company goes into default, it stays in default. So, if its initial rating is D, there is a 100% chance that the final rating will be D. With these modifications, we produce the migration matrix in Table 18-1.

Notice that the probability of default for AAA companies is shown to be 0. In reality, AAA companies do not have a 1-year probability of default that is exactly 0. Other studies have found that AAA companies can default within a year, but because the true default rate is around 1 basis point, we would only expect to observe a default every 10,000 company-years, which means that there is typically insufficient data to estimate reliably the default rate for AAA companies. A common alternative assumption is that AAA companies have a default rate of 1 basis point, but for the purpose of the migration examples, we will leave the 1-year default rate for AAA companies equal to 0.

NOTE

1 There may be some variance if the loan is amortizing and the time of default is unknown.

CHAPTER 19

Estimating Parameter Values for Single Facilities

INTRODUCTION

In the previous chapter, we discussed the framework and equations to calculate the expected loss and unexpected loss for a single facility. These equations depended critically on three parameters: the probability of default (PD), the loss in the event of default (LIED), and the exposure at default (EAD). As we will find later, these three parameters are also important for calculating regulatory capital under the new guidelines from the Basel Committee.

In this chapter, we discuss the methods that banks use to find values for these three parameters, and we show example calculations of EL and UL. Most of the methods rely on the analysis of historical information; therefore, at the end of the chapter there will be a short discussion on the types of data that should be recorded by banks.

ESTIMATING THE PROBABILITY OF DEFAULT

Traditionally, the likelihood of a customer's repaying a loan was determined in a conversation between the bank staff and the customer, possibly supplemented by discreet inquiries at the country club to ensure that the customer was trustworthy. This situation still persists in some regional banks and less-developed countries, but leading banks are now maximizing the amount of objectivity used to assess borrowers. The approaches to estimating the credit quality of a borrower can be grouped into four categories: expert credit grading, quantitative scores based on customer data, equity-based credit scoring, and cash-flow simulation. Each will be explored in more detail below.

Expert Credit Grading

There are 3 steps to estimating the probability of default through expert grading. The first step is to define a series of buckets or grades into which customers of differing credit quality can be assigned. The second step is to assign each customer to one of the grades. The final step is to look at historical data for all the customers in each grade and calculate their average probability of default. The most difficult of these 3 steps is assigning each customer into a grade.

The highest grade may be defined to contain customers who are "exceptionally strong companies or individuals who are very unlikely to default;" the lower grades may contain customers who "have a significant chance of default." Credit-rating agencies use around 20 grades, as shown in Table 19-1. The default rating may be

TABLE 19-1

Ratings used by Standard & Poor's, Fitch, and Moody's

S&P and Fitch Scale	Moody's Scale
AAA	Aaa
AA+	Aa1
AA	Aa2
AA−	Aa3
A+	A1
A	A2
A−	A3
BBB+	Baa1
BBB	Baa2
BBB−	Baa3
BB+	Ba1
BB	Ba2
BB−	Ba3
B+	B1
B	B2
B−	B3
CCC+	Caa1
CCC	Caa2
CCC−	Caa3
CC	Ca
C	C
D (Default)	D (Default)

further broken down according to the amount that is expected to be recovered from the defaulted company.

Typically, banks have around eight grades. They often think of the highest grade as corresponding to a credit-rating-agency grade of AAA, and the lowest as corresponding to a default. Traditionally, banks assigned a grade that reflected the expected loss, i.e., the combined probability of the counterparty's defaulting (PD) and the loss in the event of default (LIED). Now banks are moving to rating the counterparty according to the PD, and using a separate rating to reflect the LIED.

Customers are assigned to each grade using expert opinion. The experts are the credit-rating staff of the bank or the rating agency. They base their opinions on all the information that they can gather about the customers. They gather quantitative balance-sheet information, such as the total assets and historical profitability; they also gather qualitative information such as the customers' planned use of the funds and their business strategies relative to their competitors.

From many years of experience, and by studying previous defaults, the experts have an intuitive sense of the quantitative and qualitative indicators of trouble. For example, they know that any company whose annual sales are less than their assets is likely to default.

For large, single transactions, such as loans to large corporations, banks will rely heavily on the opinion of experts. However, experts are expensive because it takes many years of experience to train them. An alternative is to use an expert system. An expert system is a database of rules and questions that tries to mirror the credit expert's decision process. Based on the answers, there are a series of decisions and further questions that finally produce a credit grade. Although an expert system is systematic, it is still qualitative. Expert systems have been used successfully for credit analysis, but are not widespread.

For large-volume, small exposures, such as retail loans, the bank reduces costs by relying mostly on quantitative data, and only using expert opinion if the results of the quantitative analysis put the customer in the gray area between being accepted and rejected.

Quantitative Scores Based on Customer Data

Quantitative scoring seeks to assign grades based on the measurable characteristics of borrowers that, at times, may include some subjective variables such as the quality of the management team of a company. The quantitative rating models are often called scorecards because they produce a score based on the given information. Table 19-2 shows the types of information typically used in a model to rate corporations, and Table 19-3 shows information used to rate individuals.

To link customer characteristics to later default behavior, data is also required to show when a customer misses any payments, defaults, or becomes bankrupt. At such

TABLE 19-2

Information Used to Rate Corporations

Company Type	**Profitability**
Customer segment or industry group	Historical profitability
Geography	Annual growth rate of profitability
Age of company	Sales growth rate
Total assets	Profit divided by assets
Total sales	Profit divided by costs
Total equity	
	Market Data
Financial Ratios	Credit-agency rating on any outstanding debt
Equity divided by assets	Current stock price
Debt divided by equity	Volatility of stock price
Working capital divided by debt	
Accounts payable divided by debt	**Facility Information**
Long-term debt divided by debt	Facility type
Sales divided by assets	Length of facility
	Size of facility
	Collateral type

a time of default, the outstanding balance should be recorded, and then every future recovery from the customer should be recorded with its timing and, if possible, the administrative expense associated with the collection. For traded credits, such as bonds and syndicated loans, a record should be kept of their trading prices. As we

TABLE 19-3

Information Used to Rate Retail Customers

Personal Information	**Financial Information**
Income	Number of loans outstanding
Age	Number of credit cards
Occupation	Balance on each card or loan
Home value	Maximum line on each card or loan
Mortgage amount	Any defaults in last 3 years
	Any payment overdue by 30/60/90 days

see later, this is useful in calculating the loss given default. By linking customer characteristics with default behavior, we can create models that predict default.

So far as possible, the variables used in the default model should be chosen so that they stay within a reasonable range. For example, it is better to use equity over assets rather than assets over equity, because as equity drops to zero, the latter ratio goes to infinity.

The variables used should also be relatively independent from one another. An advanced technique to ensure this is to transform the variables according to their principal components (Eigenvalues).

The number of variables in the model should be limited to those that are strongly predictive. Also, there should be an intuitive explanation as to why each variable in the model is meaningful in predicting default; for example, low profitability would intuitively signal a higher probability of default. If the variables used in the model are not intuitive, the model will probably not be accepted by the credit officers who are the ultimate users.

There are two common approaches: discriminant analysis and logistic regression. These are discussed below.

Discriminant Analysis

Discriminant analysis attempts to classify customers into two groups: those that will default and those that will not. It does this by assigning a score to each customer. The score is the weighted sum of the customer data:

$$Discriminant\ Score_c = \sum_i w_i X_{i,c}$$

Here, w_i is the weight on data type i, and X_i is one piece of customer data. The values for the weights are chosen to maximize the difference between the average score of the customers that later defaulted and the average score of the customers who did not default. The actual optimization process to find the weights is quite complex. The most famous discriminant scorecard is Altman's Z Score.[1] For publicly owned manufacturing firms, the Z Score was found to be as follows:

$$Z = 1.2X_1 + 1.4X_2 + 3.3X_3 + 0.6X_4 + 1.0X_5$$

where:

X_1 = Working Capital/Total Assets
X_2 = Retained Earnings/Total Assets
X_3 = Earnings Before Interest and Taxes/Total Assets
X_4 = Market Value of Equity/Total Assets
X_5 = Sales/Total Assets

Typical ratios for the bankrupt and nonbankrupt companies in the study were as follows:

	Bankrupt	Not Bankrupt
X_1	−6.1%	41.4%
X_2	−62.6%	35.5%
X_3	−31.8%	15.4%
X_4	40%	248%
X_5	1.5%	1.9%

A company scoring less than 1.81 was "very likely" to go bankrupt later. A company scoring more than 2.99 was "unlikely" to go bankrupt. The scores in between were considered inconclusive.

This approach has been adopted by many banks. Some banks use the equation exactly as it was created by Altman, but most use Altman's approach on their own customer data to get scoring models that are tailored to the bank.

To obtain the probability of default from the scores, we group companies according their scores at the beginning of a year, and then calculate the percentage of companies within each group who defaulted by the end of the year.

Logistic Regression

Logistic regression is very similar to discriminant analysis except that it goes one step further by relating the score directly to the probability of default. Logistic regression uses a logit function as follows:

$$P_C = \frac{1}{1 + e^{Y_C}}$$

Here, P_C is the customer's probability of default, and Y_C is a single number describing the credit quality of the customer. Y_C is a constant, plus a weighted sum of the observable customer data:

$$Y_C = w_0 + \sum_i w_i X_{i,C}$$

When Y_C is negative, the probability of default is close to 100%. When Y_C is a positive number, the probability drops towards 0. The probability transitions from 1 to 0 with an "S-curve," as in Figure 19-1.

To create the best model, we want to find the set of weights that produces the best fit between P_C and the observed defaults. We would like P_C to be close to 100% for a customer that later defaults and close to 0 if the customer does not default. This can be accomplished using maximum likelihood estimation (MLE).

FIGURE 19-1

Illustration of the Logit Curve

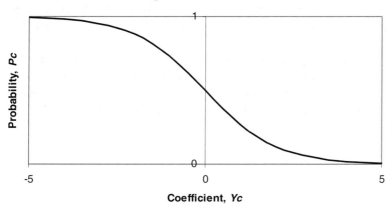

In MLE, we define the likelihood function L_C for the customer, to be equal to P_C if the customer did default, and $1 - P_C$ if the customer did not default:

$$L_C = P_C \qquad \text{if default}$$
$$L_C = 1 - P_C \quad \text{if no default}$$

We then create a single number, J, that is the product of the likelihood function for all customers:

$$J = L_{Company1} \times L_{Company2} \times \cdots \times L_{CompanyN}$$

J will be maximized if we choose the weights[2] in Y_C such that for every company, whenever there is a default, P_C is close to 1, and when there is no default, P_C is close to 0. If we can choose the weights such that J equals 1, we have a perfect model that predicts with 100% accuracy whether or not a customer will default. In reality, it is very unlikely that we will achieve a perfect model, and we settle for the set of weights that makes J as close as possible to 1.

The final result is a model of the form:

$$P_C = \frac{1}{1 + e^{\left(w_0 + \sum w_i X_i\right)}}$$

Where the values for all the weights are fixed. Now, given the data (X_i) for any new company, we can estimate its probability of default.

Testing Quantitative Scorecards

An important final step in building quantitative models is testing. The models should be tested to see if they work reliably. One way to do this is to use them in practice and see if they are useful in predicting default. Although this is the ultimate test, it can be an expensive way to find mistakes.

The usual testing procedure is to use hold-out samples. Before building the models, the historical customer data is separated randomly into two sets: the model set and the test set. The model set is used to calculate the weights. The final model is then run on the data in the test set to see whether it can predict defaults.

The results of the test can be presented as a *power curve*. The power curve is constructed by sorting the customers according to their scores, and then constructing a graph with the percentage of all the customers on the x-axis and the percentage of all the defaults on the y-axis. For this graph, x and y are given by the following equations:

$$x_k = \frac{k}{N}$$

$$y_k = \frac{1}{N_D} \sum_{c=1}^{k} I_c$$

Here, k is the cumulative number of customers, N is the total number of customers, and N_D is the total number of defaulted customers in the sample. I_c is an indicator that equals 1 if company c failed, and equals 0 otherwise. A perfect model is one in which the scores are perfectly correlated with default, and the power curve rises quickly to 100%, as in Figure 19-2. A completely random model will not predict default, giving a 45-degree line, as in Figure 19-3.

Most models will have a performance curve somewhere between Figure 19-2 and Figure 19-3.

FIGURE 19-2

Illustration of Power Curve for a Perfect Model

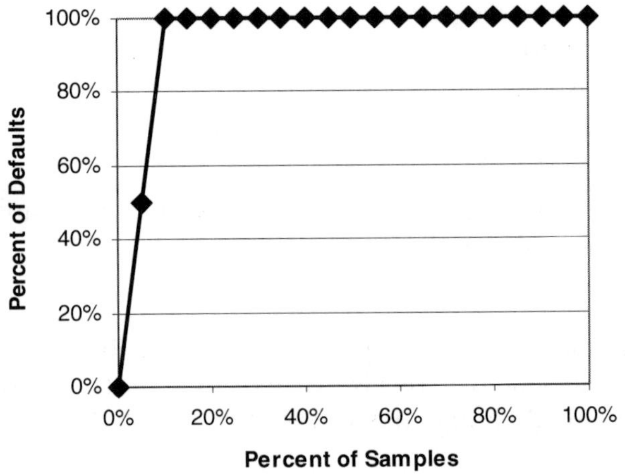

FIGURE 19-3

Illustration of Power Curve for a Random Model

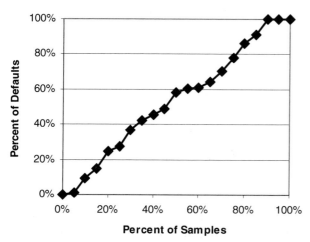

Equity-Based Credit Scoring

The scoring methods described above relied mostly on examination of the inner workings of the company and its balance sheet. A completely different approach is based on work by Merton[3] and has been enhanced by the company KMV.[4] Merton observed that holding the debt of a risky company was equivalent to holding the debt of a risk-free company plus being short a put option on the assets of the company. The put option arises because if the value of the assets falls below the value of the debt, the shareholders can put the assets to debt holders, and in return, receive the right not to repay the full amount of the debt. In this analogy, the underlying for the put option is the company assets, and the strike price is the amount of debt.

This observation led Merton to develop a pricing model for risky debt and allowed the calculation of the probability of default. This calculation is illustrated in Figure 19-4.

It is relatively difficult to observe directly the total value of a company's assets, but it is reasonable to assume that the value of the assets equals the value of the debt plus equity, and the value of the debt is approximately stable. This assumption allows us to say that changes in asset value equal changes in the equity price. This approach is attractive because equity information is readily available for publicly traded companies, and it reflects the market's collective opinion on the strength of the company.

We can then use the volatility of the equity price to predict the probability that the asset value will fall below the debt value, causing the company to default. If we

FIGURE 19-4

Relationship between Asset Volatility and Probability of Default

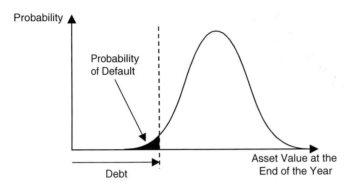

assume that the equity value (E) has a Normal probability distribution, the probability that the equity value will be less than zero is given by the following:

$$P = \int_{-\infty}^{0} p(E, \overline{E}, \sigma_E)\, dE$$

Here, $p(E, \overline{E}, \sigma_E)$ is the Normal probability-density function with a mean equal to the current equity price $(\overline{E})$ and a standard deviation equal to the standard deviation of the equity (σ_E). This integral is equivalent to the integral of the Standard Normal distribution (ϕ) from negative infinity up to $-E/\sigma_E$ (for proof, see Appendix A):

$$P = \int_{-\infty}^{-\overline{E}/\sigma_E} \phi(z)\, dz = \Phi\left(-\overline{E}/\sigma_E\right)$$

Here, ϕ is the Normal probability-density function with a mean of zero and a standard deviation of one. Φ is the cumulative Normal probability function.

Most spreadsheets and statistical packages have commands to calculate these functions. For example, in Microsoft's Excel spreadsheet, $\phi(x)$ is calculated from the command "=normdist(x,0,1,0)". $\Phi(x)$ is calculated from the command "=normdist(x,0,1,1)".

The value $\overline{E}/\sigma_E$ is called the *critical value* or the *distance to default*. It is the number of standard deviations between the current price and zero. With these simplifying assumptions, for any given distance to default we can calculate the probability of default, as in Table 19-4. This table also shows the ratings that correspond to each distance to default.

Unfortunately, there are a few practical problems that require modifications of the above approach to create accurate estimates for the probability of default. One problem is that equity prices have a distribution that is closer to log-Normal than

TABLE 19-4

Idealized Relationship Between Distance to Default and Probability of Default

Critical Distance to Default: $\overline{E}/\sigma_E$	Probability of Default: $\Phi(-\overline{E}/\sigma_E)$	Corresponding Rating
3.72	0.01%	AA
3.35	0.04%	A
2.85	0.22%	BBB
2.33	0.98%	BB
1.62	5.30%	B
0.77	21.94%	CCC

Normal. A related problem is that in reality, the value of the debt is not stable, and changes in the equity price do not capture all of the changes in the asset value. This is especially the case as a company moves towards default because the equity value has a floor of zero.

A practical alternative is to treat the distance to default and the predicted probabilities as just another type of score. As with the other types of credit score, the score is calibrated to the probability of default as follows:

- Find historical data on companies.
- Estimate what their scores would have been based on the equity volatility at the time.
- Group the companies according to their scores.
- Calculate what proportion of the group defaulted over the next year.

The greatest advantage of credit ratings based on equity prices is that they automatically incorporate the latest market data, and therefore, they very quickly respond when a company starts to get into problems.

Cash-Flow Simulation

The methods described above rely on having historical data on company financial ratios or stock prices. For new ventures, there is no historical data. However, if the deal is tightly structured, as in project finance, we can evaluate the risk using a cash-flow simulation.

Project finance is used for large projects, such as the building of a power station, toll roads, or a telecoms infrastructure. In project finance, a stand-alone project company is established by one or more parent companies. This project company raises funds in the form of debt and equity, and builds the infrastructure needed for the project. The debt and equity holders are then paid from the profits of the project. If the profits are insufficient, the debt holders have no recourse to the parent companies who were involved in setting up the project company.

Such deals are carefully planned and tightly structured so it is clear who will be paid in each circumstance. Because the operations of the project company are so well defined, it is possible to build a cash-flow model that predicts what the company's profits will be under different economic circumstances.

With this cash-flow model, we can apply Monte Carlo evaluation to obtain cash-flow statistics, including occasions in which the cumulative cash flows are so negative that default occurs. This approach is discussed in "Risk Measurement for Project Finance Guarantees," Marrison, C.I., *The Journal of Project Finance*, Volume 7, Number 2, pp. 43–53, 2001.

As a simplified example, consider a project-finance deal to build an oil refinery. The refinery is built using money from shareholders and debt holders. The shareholders and debt holders are repaid from the operating profit. In year T, the operating profit is the income from selling refined oil, minus the cost of crude oil and the operating cost:

$$Operating\ Profit_T = R_T \times V_{R,T} - C_T \times V_{C,T} - O_T$$

Here, R_T and C_T are the costs per barrel of refined and crude oil. $V_{R,T}$ is the volume of refined oil produced, which depends on the plant's efficiency and the volume of crude oil, $V_{C,T}$. O_T represents the operating expenses.

The volumes and costs per barrel will depend on the structure of the project-finance deal. For example, the costs could float according to the market price of oil, or there could be a purchase contract in which another company guarantees to buy the oil at a fixed price. For this example, let us assume that the costs vary with the market prices for refined and crude oil. There is then a risk if the difference between the prices becomes too small for the operating profit to repay the debt holders.

This risk can be quantified by building a random model to simulate oil prices and then calculating the operating profit each year for each random scenario. A simple stochastic model for random oil prices would be as follows:

$$C_{T+1} = a + bC_T + c\varepsilon_{1,T}$$
$$S_{T+1} = d + eS_T + f\varepsilon_{2,T}$$
$$R_{T+1} = C_{T+1} + S_{T+1}$$

S is the "crack-spread" between the prices of crude and refined oil. a, b, c, d, e, and f are constants. The constants a, b, c, d, e, and f are found from regressions on historical oil prices. ε_1 and ε_2 are random numbers. The initial values for the prices would be today's prices.

The model works as follows. We use the random models to create a scenario for prices. With these prices, we calculate the operating profit and test to see if it is sufficient to pay the outstanding debt. Any remaining profit after paying the debt is given to the shareholders or retained into the next year, according to the project contract. We then step forward in time and create another random set of prices and repeat the calculations. This is repeated for the life of the planned project. Then, we go back to year 0 and repeat the whole process again, typically 1000 times. At the end, we can calculate the probability of default as the number of scenarios in which debt payments were missed, divided by the total number of scenarios tested.

The model described above was very simple and only had two uncertain parameters: the oil prices. Other random factors in the project could be the efficiency of the plant, the operating expenses, and foreign exchange rates if, as is common, some the debt is denominated in a different currency. A full model, including all random factors, taxes, and management options, can become very complex.

The simulation can be used to not only give the probability of default, but also the exposure at default, the loss given default, and the net present value of the losses. The structure of the cash-flow model is illustrated in Figure 19-5.

Notice that in Figure 19-5, there is a module called the *event model*. This is an optional addition that can be added if there are significant discrete events that could affect the project but are not part of the project. For an international project, the event model can include the event of the country's defaulting. This can be driven by currency devaluations or collapses in GDP generated by the macroeconomic simulation. If a country default occurs, we record the appropriate losses, and that becomes part of the payment probability distribution.

Now let's move from the probability of default to discuss the exposure of default.

FIGURE 19-5

Illustration of the Structure of a Cash-Flow Simulation

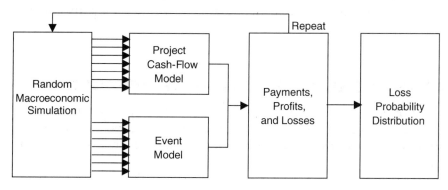

ESTIMATING THE EXPOSURE AT DEFAULT

The exposure at default (EAD) is the outstanding amount at the time of default. For a loan, the exposure amount is set by the amortization rate. The EAD then only depends on how much the customer has paid back by the time of default. Typically, the exposure for a loan is assumed to be fixed for each year and equal to the average outstanding for the year. This methodology neglects some of the uncertainty, but greatly simplifies the analysis.

For derivatives contracts, the EAD is calculated by simulation as described in the previous chapter.

For a line of credit, the EAD depends on how much the customer draws on the line before defaulting. This customer behavior is estimated based on historical information. The procedure entails collecting information on defaulted companies, noting how much they had drawn on the line by the time they defaulted; and noting how much they had drawn on the line, the limit on the line, and their credit rating before default, one year before default.

Many banks have carried out internal analyses of EAD for lines of credit, but few of the results have been published. The article by Elliot Asarnow and James Marker, "Historical Performance of the US Corporate Loan Market: 1988–1993," *The Journal of Commercial Lending*, Vol. 10, No. 2, Spring 1995, pp. 13–32, calculated the EAD as the average use of the line plus the additional use at the time of default:

$$EAD = L(\bar{E} + (1 - \bar{E})e_d)$$

Here, L is the dollar amount of the total line of credit, $\bar{E}$ is the average percentage of use, and e_d is the additional use of the normally unused line at the time of default. Asarnow and Marker found that the EAD depended on the initial credit grade as shown in Table 19-5.

In applying these results to the assessment of a line of credit, a typical assumption would be to replace the average exposure for the grade with the actual current exposure for the line of credit being assessed. As an example, consider a BBB company that has currently drawn 42% of its line. The additional use at default would be expected to be 38% (58% times 65%), making the total EAD for this company equal to 80% (42% plus 38%).

ESTIMATING THE LOSS IN THE EVENT OF DEFAULT

The loss in the event of default (LIED) is the percentage of the exposure amount that the bank loses if the customer defaults. It is proportional to the exposure at default, plus all administrative costs associated with the default, minus the net present value of any recoveries:

TABLE 19-5

Exposure at Default for Lines of Credit

Grade	Average Use of Line	Additional Use of Normally Unused Line	Average Exposure at Default
AAA	0.1%	69%	69%
AA	1.6%	73%	73%
A	4.6%	71%	72%
BBB	20.0%	65%	72%
BB	46.8%	52%	74%
B	63.7%	48%	81%
CCC	75.0%	44%	86%

From Asarnow, Elliot, and Marker, James "Historical Performance of the US Corporate Loan Market: 1988–1993," *The Journal of Commercial Lending*, Vol. 10, No. 2, Spring, 1995, pp. 13–32.

$$LIED = \frac{EAD - Recovery\$ + Admin\$}{EAD}$$
$$= 1 - Recovery\% + Admin$$

The definition above is most useful for illiquid securities, such as bank loans, where the bank takes many months to recover whatever it can from the defaulted company. An alternative definition for liquid securities, such as bonds, is to say that the LIED is the percentage drop in the market value of the bond after default:

$$LIED = \frac{Value\ Before - Value\ After}{Value\ Before}$$

Theoretically, for any one security, the LIED calculated with each of the above definitions should be the same because the value of the bond after default should equal the NPV of the recoveries, minus the administration costs.

In this section, we review three empirical studies that estimated LIED as a function of the security's collateral, structure, and industry. As we review the studies, we also use a simple technique for estimating the standard deviation of LIED.

We require the standard deviation of LIED to estimate accurately the unexpected loss. We often face the situation in which we have an estimate for the average LIED but no information on the standard deviation. In this case, we can estimate the standard deviation from the following equation:

$$\sigma_{LIED} \approx A \times \sqrt{\overline{LIED} - \overline{LIED}^2}$$

Here, $\overline{LIED}$ is the average LIED and A is a constant. The term $\sqrt{\overline{LIED} - \overline{LIED}^2}$ is the largest possible standard deviation for LIED, given that the average is $\overline{LIED}$. This largest standard deviation happens if the LIED after each default equals either 0 or 100%. Note that the standard deviation of LIED is the same as the standard deviation of recoveries. Also, the worst case for LIED is the same as the worst case for recoveries:

$$\sigma_{LIED,Worst} = \sqrt{\overline{LIED} - \overline{LIED}^2}$$
$$= \sqrt{1 - \overline{R} - (1 - \overline{R})^2}$$
$$= \sqrt{1 - \overline{R} - (1 - 2\overline{R} + \overline{R}^2)}$$
$$= \sqrt{\overline{R} - \overline{R}^2}$$

The three studies discussed below show both the average LIED and the standard deviation of LIED for different types of collateral, structure, and industry. This allows us to estimate A by comparing the actual standard deviation with the worst case:

$$A = \frac{\sigma_{LIED,Actual}}{\sqrt{\overline{LIED} - \overline{LIED}^2}}$$

Let us now look at the empirical studies.

Lee V. Carty, David Hamilton, et al. (*Bankrupt Bank Loan Recoveries*, Moody's Investors Services, Special Comment, June 1998), looked at how much had been recovered from hundreds of defaulted bank loans. One of their results was an estimate of the probability-density function for the recovery rates.

The distribution was estimated in 2 ways: first, using the NPV of recoveries, and then by using the change in the price of traded loans. The results are shown in Figure 19-6 and Figure 19-7. They show that recovery rates are highly variable, and the distribution is strongly skewed. The mean and standard deviation for Figure 19-6 is 87% and 23%, and for Figure 19-7 is 70% and 23%. The difference in the mean is most likely because the discount rate used in calculating the NPV of the recoveries was lower than the discount rates used by the market.

Carty, Hamilton, et al. also examined the effect that collateral has on loss rates, and found the results shown in Table 19-6. The results indicate that the highest recovery was 90% for loans secured by cash. Unsecured loans only recovered 79%. Surprisingly, unsecured loans have a higher recovery rate than loans secured by stock in subsidiaries; there could be a fundamental reason for this, or it may be due to the small sample size. (There were only 19 unsecured loans in the study.) Table 19-6 also shows that the factor A was on average equal to 0.66; i.e., if we only knew the average recovery rate, a reasonable estimate for the standard deviation would be 0.66 times the worst case of $\sqrt{\overline{LIED} - \overline{LIED}^2}$.

FIGURE 19-6

Distribution of Loss-Recovery Rates Estimated from Recovery Experience

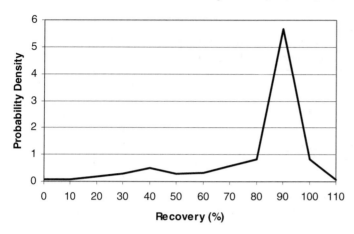

FIGURE 19-7

Distribution of Recovery Rates Estimated from Prices

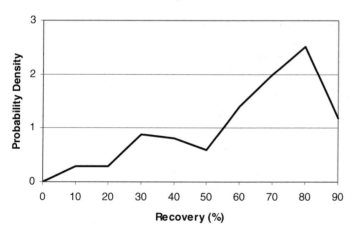

A study by Standard & Poor's Karen Van de Castle and David Keismann ("Recovering Your Money: Insights Into Losses from Defaults," *Standard & Poor's Credit Week*, June 16, 1999, pp. 29–34) gives the recovery rates of bank loans and different classes of bonds. The results, in Table 19-7, show that recoveries on bank loans are higher than for bonds. Of the bonds, senior secured bonds have the highest recovery rate (84%) and junior subordinated bonds have the lowest recovery rate (14%). This clearly shows us that the structure has a great effect on the risk.

TABLE 19-6

The Effect of Collateral on Recovery Rate

Collateral Type	Average Recovery	Standard Deviation of Recovery	Factor *A*
Unsecured	79%	27%	0.66
Stock of Subsidiaries	74%	31%	0.71
Property, Plant, & Equipment	85%	23%	0.64
Substantially All Assets	89%	18%	0.58
Accounts Receivable/Cash/Inventory	90%	21%	0.70
Average	83%	24%	0.66

From Lee V. Carty, David Hamilton, et al. in *Bankrupt Bank Loan Recoveries*, Moody's Investors Services, Special Comment, June 1998.

TABLE 19-7

The Effect of Structure on Recovery Rate

Collateral Type	Average Recovery	Standard Deviation of Recovery	Factor *A*
Bank Loans	84%	25%	0.68
Senior Secured Bonds	66%	28%	0.59
Senior Unsecured Bonds	49%	36%	0.72
Senior Subordinated Bonds	37%	31%	0.64
Subordinated Bonds	26%	30%	0.68
Junior Subordinated Bonds	14%	24%	0.69
Average	46%	29%	0.67

From Karen Van de Castle, David Keismann, "Recovering Your Money: Insights Into Losses From Defaults," *Standard & Poor's Credit Week*, June 16, 1999, pp. 29–34.

The industry of the borrower also affects the recovery rate. This may be due to the quality of the collateral that is available in each industry. Table 19-8 shows the recovery rates reported by Edward I. Altman and Vellore M. Kishore ("Almost Everything You Wanted to Know about Recoveries on Defaulted Bonds," *Financial Analysts Journal*, November/December 1996, pp. 57–64). The table also shows that the actual standard deviation that is experienced for LIED is on average 0.48 times the theoretically worst case.

TABLE 19-8

The Effect of Industry on Recovery Rate

Industry	Average Recovery	Standard Deviation of Recovery	Factor *A*
Public Utilities	70%	19%	0.41
Chemicals & Petroleum	63%	27%	0.56
Machinery & Instruments	49%	20%	0.40
Services	46%	25%	0.50
Food	45%	21%	0.42
Wholesale & Retail Trade	44%	22%	0.44
Diversified Manufacturing	42%	24%	0.49
Casinos, Hotels, & Recreation	40%	26%	0.53
Building Materials	39%	23%	0.47
Transportation	38%	28%	0.58
Media	37%	21%	0.43
Financial Institutions	36%	26%	0.54
Construction & Real Estate	35%	29%	0.61
General Stores	33%	21%	0.45
Mining & Petroleum Drilling	33%	18%	0.38
Textiles	32%	15%	0.32
Wood Paper & Leather	30%	24%	0.52
Lodging & Hospitals	26%	23%	0.52
Average	41%	23%	0.48

From Edward I. Altman and Vellore M. Kishore, "Almost Everything You Wanted to Know about Recoveries on Defaulted Bonds," *Financial Analysts Journal*, November/December, 1996, pp. 57–64.

EXAMPLE CALCULATION OF EL & UL FOR A LOAN

To demonstrate the use of these results, let us work through an example. Consider a 1-year line of credit of $100 million to a BBB-rated public utility, with a 40% utilization. From the tables above, the probability of default is 0.22%, the average additional exposure at default for a BBB corporation is expected to be 65% of the unused portion of the line. The average recovery for a utility is 70% with a standard deviation of 19%.

As derived earlier, the expected loss is given by:

$$EL = P \times \overline{S} \times \overline{E}$$
$$= 0.22\% \times (1 - 70\%) \times \$100M \times (40\% + 60\% \times 65\%)$$
$$= \$0.052M = \$52,000$$

$\overline{S}$ is the average loss in the event of default (severity), and $\overline{E}$ is the average exposure at default.

Assuming that changes in exposure and severity are uncorrelated, the unexpected loss is given by:

$$UL = \sqrt{(P - P^2)\overline{S}^2\overline{E}^2 + P \times \left(\sigma_S^2\overline{E}^2 + \sigma_E^2\overline{S}^2 + \sigma_S^2\sigma_E^2 \right)}$$

σ_S is the standard deviation of severity (equal to the standard deviation of LIED). σ_E is the standard deviation of exposure for the line of credit. Here, the only thing we do not have a value for is the standard deviation of exposure. There are no published results for the standard deviation of additional exposure of default for a line of credit. In a practical application, this would be obtained by studying the bank's historical data. Here, let us assume that the standard deviation of exposure follows the same pattern as LIED, i.e., that the standard deviation of the additional exposure is approximately half the worst case that could occur given the average additional exposure $\overline{A}$:

$$\sigma_A = \frac{\sqrt{\overline{A} - \overline{A}^2}}{2}$$
$$= \frac{\sqrt{0.65 - 0.65^2}}{2}$$
$$= 0.24$$

The volatility of the overall exposure is the volatility of the additional exposure, multiplied by the amount of the unused line:

$$\sigma_E = \sigma_A(1 - D)L_{Max}$$
$$= 0.24 \times (1 - 40\%) \times \$100M$$
$$= \$14M$$

Here, D is the percentage of the line that has already been drawn down (40% in our example), and L_{Max} is the total line ($100 million in our example). We now have all the elements required to calculate UL:

$$UL = \sqrt{(P - P^2)\overline{S}^2\overline{E}^2 + P \times \left(\sigma_S^2\overline{E}^2 + \sigma_E^2\overline{S}^2 + \sigma_S^2\sigma_E^2\right)}$$

$$P = 0.22\%$$

$$\overline{S} = 1 - 70\%$$

$$\overline{E} = \$100M \times (40\% + 60\% \times 65\%)$$

$$\sigma_S = 19\%$$

$$\sigma_E = \$14$$

$$UL = \$1.335M$$

For the BBB company, we have the results shown in Table 19-9.

We can repeat this calculation for the same line of credit but to companies of different grades. The results are shown in Table 19-10 and plotted in Figure 19-8 (assuming AAA companies have a one-basis-point default rate). Figure 19-8 shows that EL and UL tend to converge as the credit quality decreases.

TABLE 19-9

Example of Calculation of Expected and Unexpected Loss for a BBB Company

	BBB
Probability of Default (P)	0.22%
Limit On Line Size (L_{max})	$100
Drawn-Down Percentage (D)	40%
Average Additional Use of Normally Unused Line ($\overline{A}$)	65%
Average Exposure at Default ($\overline{E}$)	$79
Standard Deviation of Exposure at Default (σ_E)	$14
Average Loss in the Event of Default ($\overline{S}$)	30%
Standard Deviation of Loss in the Event of Default (σ_S)	19%
Expected Loss	$52
Unexpected Loss	$1335

INFORMATION REQUIREMENTS

All of the methods described above require large amounts of historical data on company characteristics and later default behavior. The first step in model building is the collection of this data. This data should be easily accessible to model builders and the collection should be established as soon as possible to start accumulating

TABLE 19-10

Example of Calculation of Expected and Unexpected Loss for Several Different Company Credit Grades

	AAA	AA	A	BBB	BB	B	CCC
Line Size (millions)	$100	$100	$100	$100	$100	$100	$100
Drawn-Down Percentage	40%	40%	40%	40%	40%	40%	40%
Probability of Default	0.01%	0.01%	0.04%	0.22%	0.98%	5.30%	21.94%
Average Additional EAD	69%	73%	71%	65%	52%	48%	44%
Average EAD	$81	$84	$83	$79	$71	$69	$66
Standard Deviation of EAD	$14	$13	$14	$14	$15	$15	$15
Average LIED	30%	30%	30%	30%	30%	30%	30%
Standard Deviation of LIED	19%	19%	19%	19%	19%	19%	19%
Expected Loss (thousands)	$2	$3	$10	$52	$209	$1097	$4344
Unexpected Loss (thousands)	$292	$302	$598	$1335	$2542	$5667	$10,386

Example of Calculation of Expected and Unexpected Loss for Several Different Company Credit Grades

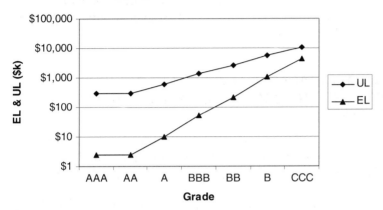

Note that EL and UL tend to converge when credit quality decreases

history. Three types of information must be collected: information on the customer and facility at the time the loan was granted (as in Table 19-2 and Table 19-3), information on the results of the models used to approve the facility, and information on later default behavior.

The information on the models should be collected to back test the models. It should include information such as the credit rating, predicted exposure at default, and predicted loss in the event of default.

The information on later default behavior is compared with the predicted behavior, and is used to build models relating the customer information to the default behavior. Table 19-11 shows the minimum data requirements for recording default behavior.

Requirements for Collecting Historical Data

Probability of Default	Loss in the Event of Default
Date of any changes in credit grade	Dates of recovered amounts
Date of first delinquency or default	Recovered amounts
Default or termination date	Legal fees
	Administrative costs or time
EAD	Trading price one year before default
Exposure at default	Trading price one month before default
Line size at default	Trading price one month after default

SUMMARY

In this chapter, we discussed the methods banks employ to find values for the probability of default, the loss in the event of default, and the exposure at default. In the next few chapters, we move from measuring the risk of isolated credit facilities to measuring the credit risk of an entire portfolio.

APPENDIX A: TRANSFORMATION OF A NORMAL PROBABILITY DISTRIBUTION INTO A STANDARD NORMAL DISTRIBUTION

The Standard Normal distribution is a Normal distribution with a mean of zero and a standard deviation of one. It is often easier to use than a general Normal distribution. This appendix addresses the problem of transforming from a general distribution to a Standard distribution.

The probability-density function for a Normal distribution with mean $\overline{E}$ and standard deviation σ_E is as follows:

$$p(E, \overline{E}, \sigma_E) = \frac{1}{(2\pi)^{1/2}\sigma_E} e\left[-\frac{1}{2}\frac{(E - \overline{E})^2}{\sigma_E^2}\right]$$

The probability of E being less than zero is given by integrating the probability-density function:

$$P = \int_{-\infty}^{0} p(E, \overline{E}, \sigma_E)\, dE$$

To transform to a Standard distribution, let us define a variable z:

$$z = \frac{E - \overline{E}}{\sigma_E}$$

Given this definition, note the following:

1) $E = z\sigma_E + \overline{E}$

2) when $E = 0$, $z = \dfrac{-\overline{E}}{\sigma_E}$

3) $dE = dz\sigma_E$

We can now write the probability as follows:

$$P = \int_{-\infty}^{\frac{-\overline{E}}{\sigma_E}} p(z\sigma_E - \overline{E},\ \overline{E},\ \sigma_E)\, \sigma_E dz$$

By substituting z into the probability-density equation, we can write it in terms of the Standard Normal distribution:

$$p(E, \overline{E}, \sigma_E)\sigma_E = \sigma_E \frac{1}{(2\pi)^{1/2}\sigma_E} \, e\left[-\frac{1}{2}\frac{\left(z\sigma_E + \overline{E} - \overline{E}\right)^2}{\sigma_E^2}\right]$$

$$= \frac{1}{(2\pi)^{1/2}} \, e\left[-\frac{1}{2}z^2\right] = \phi(z)$$

$\phi(z)$ is the symbol for the Standard Normal probability-density function. The probability can now be written as follows:

$$P = \int_{-\infty}^{\frac{-\overline{E}}{\sigma_E}} \phi(z)dz = \Phi\left(\frac{-\overline{E}}{\sigma_E}\right)$$

Φ is the symbol for the cumulative Standard Normal probability function.

NOTES

1. Altman E.I., 1968, "Financial Ratios, Discriminant Analysis and the Prediction of Corporate Bankruptcy," *Journal of Finance* 23 pp. 189–209.
2. The weights are chosen using an optimization method such as the "solver" function in Microsoft's Excel.
3. Merton, Robert, "On the Pricing of Corporate Debt: The Risk Structure of Interest Rates," *Journal of Finance*, vol. 29, 1974.
4. Kealhoffer, Stephen, "Managing Default Risk in Derivative Portfolios," in *Derivative Credit Risk: Advances in Measurement and Management*, Renaissance Risk Publications, London 1995.

Risk Measurement for a Credit Portfolio: Part One

INTRODUCTION

In the preceding chapters, we created a framework for measuring and quantifying the risk of isolated credit facilities such as loans. We now need to do the same for a portfolio of credit risks. However, this effort requires a different set of tools because we need to include the effects of correlation. Correlation describes the extent to which loans tend to default at the same time. Intuitively, we would expect that companies would have some tendency to default together. This could happen because the whole economy is in recession, forcing many companies into bankruptcy at the same time, or it could be that the default of one company triggers the default of another company. For example, the collapse of a car factory would tend to push suppliers and businesses in the local town closer to default. These correlation effects produce loss distributions that are highly skewed: there are many years of low losses, then a few years of "surprisingly" high loss. The description of this correlation and skew is one of the most difficult problems in credit-risk measurement. In this chapter and the next, we describe the five most common approaches used to measure the credit risk of a portfolio.

Each approach estimates the probability distribution for the credit losses and specifically estimates the portfolio's expected loss, unexpected loss, and economic capital. This allows us to determine how much capital the bank should hold to maintain its credit rating. Also, in Chapter 22, we use the economic capital to calculate the risk-adjusted profitability of each loan in the portfolio.

MODELING TECHNIQUES TO MEASURE AND QUANTIFY A PORTFOLIO OF CREDIT RISKS

Correlation effects for credit defaults are difficult to observe because defaults are relatively infrequent. For example, in any given year we would only expect 1 in 1000 single-A-rated companies to default. This contrasts with market-risk analysis in which we collect new price data on all traded securities every day. Given the scarcity of data, credit-risk models use assumptions and financial theories to estimate loss statistics based on the small amounts of observable data. There are five common approaches:

- The covariance model
- The actuarial model
- The Merton-based simulation model
- The macroeconomic default model
- The macroeconomic cash-flow model

The fundamental difference between each model is the approach taken to characterize the correlation. We discuss each model in detail, but for reference, the main features of each model are shown in Table 20-1. In this table, the correlation mechanism is the approach used to model the tendency for defaults to occur at the same time. The parameterization column shows the most important variables that must be quantified to capture the portfolio effects. The capital column shows the method used to evaluate the portfolio's economic capital.

Each of these model approaches has been integrated into software packages created by different companies. In this discussion, we do not describe the specific details of each package, but describe the fundamental concepts behind each model and possible ways in which each model can be developed.

In this chapter, we describe the covariance approach to modeling credit risk. We spend a lot of time on this approach for two reasons: it lays the foundation for the other approaches, and it is the easiest to use if you need to build a credit-portfolio model from scratch. In the next chapter, we discuss the underlying mechanisms for the other types of models.

THE COVARIANCE CREDIT-PORTFOLIO MODEL

The covariance portfolio model is also sometimes referred to as the *Markowitz model*. It is largely the same as the parametric approach for VaR except that the correlations used are default correlations and the probability distribution is assumed to be a Beta distribution rather than a Normal distribution. Another difference is that for credit risk, one of the results we are concerned about is the mean of the distribution (the expected loss), whereas for market risks, we assume the mean is zero. In this discussion, we use the term "loan" to refer to any general credit exposure. This discussion

TABLE 20-1

Summary of Credit-Portfolio Models

	Correlation Mechanism	Parameterization	Capital
Covariance model	• Observation of historical defaults	• Default correlations	• Assumption of Beta distribution
Actuarial model	• Gamma-distributed mean default rates	• Parameters of Gamma distribution	• Analytic integration of Gamma distribution with Poisson distribution
Merton simulation model	• Correlated asset values	• Asset correlations • Critical asset levels	• Simulation
Macroeconomic default model	• Changes in macro-variables driving changes in mean default rates	• Random macromodel • Default rate as a function of macro-variables	• Simulation
Macroeconomic cash-flow model	• Changes in macro-variables driving changes in cash flows	• Random macromodel • Structural model of companies' balance sheets	• Simulation

applies equally to other types of credit exposures, such as bonds, lines, and derivatives exposures.

There are four steps required in the covariance model:

1. Defining the expected loss (EL) and unexpected loss (UL) of the portfolio in terms of the EL and UL of the individual loans.
2. Estimating the default correlation, which is the longest step.
3. Estimating the portfolio's overall probability distribution based on its EL and UL.
4. Allocating the capital of the whole portfolio to the individual loans using the concept of unexpected loss contribution.

Defining the Expected Loss and Unexpected Loss

The expected loss for the portfolio (EL_p) is simply the sum of the expected losses for the individual loans (EL_i) within the portfolio:

$$EL_P = \sum_{i=1}^{N} EL_i$$

As with parametric VaR, the standard deviation for the portfolio (UL_P) is obtained from the sum of the variances for the individual loans. If there are only two loans, UL_P would be as follows:

$$UL_P^2 = UL_1^2 + 2\rho_{1,2}UL_1UL_2 + UL_2^2$$

Where $\rho_{1,2}$ is the loss correlation between loan 1 and loan 2. For N loans, we can use summation notation:

$$UL_P^2 = \sum_{i=1}^{N} \sum_{j=1}^{N} \rho_{i,j} UL_i UL_j$$

This can also be expressed in matrix notation:

$$UL_P^2 = U^T R U$$
$$U^T = [\,UL_1 \quad UL_2 \quad \ldots \quad UL_N\,]$$
$$R = \begin{bmatrix} 1 & \rho_{1,2} & \rho_{1,N} \\ \rho_{2,1} & 1 & \rho_{2,N} \\ \rho_{N,1} & \rho_{N,2} & 1 \end{bmatrix}$$

The next step is to estimate values for the correlations.

Estimation of Loss Correlation

Loss correlations can be estimated based on the historical data of losses or on asset correlations. The approach taken in any given situation depends mostly on the data available. Ideally, correlations should be calculated using both methods, and then compared.

Using Historical Observations to Estimate Loss Correlation

Let us begin by considering the simple case of a portfolio of two loans. The UL for this portfolio is given by the variance equation:

$$UL_P^2 = UL_1^2 + 2\rho_{1,2}UL_1UL_2 + UL_2^2$$

If we knew the values for UL_P, UL_1, and UL_2 we could solve the equation to get $\rho_{1,2}$:

$$\rho_{1,2} = \frac{UL_P^2 - UL_1^2 - UL_2^2}{UL_1 UL_2}$$

If we have a large number of loans, we said that UL_P is given by the following:

$$UL_P^2 = \sum_{i=1}^{N} \sum_{j=1}^{N} \rho_{i,j} UL_i UL_j$$

We can get an estimate for the correlation if we assume that the correlation between each loan is identical:

$$\rho_{i,j} = \overline{\rho} \qquad \text{for all } i \text{ and } j$$

By doing this, we have neglected the fact that the correlation between a loan and itself must equal one. This becomes unimportant if there is a large number of loans, but the proof is quite tedious, and is therefore relegated to Appendix A. Given the assumption of a fixed correlation, we can separate the two summations because they no longer depend on each other:

$$UL_P^2 = \sum_{i=1}^{N} \sum_{j=1}^{N} \overline{\rho}\, UL_i UL_j$$

$$= \overline{\rho} \sum_{i=1}^{N} \sum_{j=1}^{N} UL_i UL_j$$

$$= \overline{\rho} \sum_{i=1}^{N} UL_i \sum_{j=1}^{N} UL_j$$

$$= \overline{\rho} \left(\sum_{i=1}^{N} UL_i \right)^2$$

If we now assume that each loan has the same UL, we can estimate the correlation as follows:

$$\overline{\rho} = \frac{UL_P^2}{\left(\sum_{i=1}^{N} UL_i \right)^2}$$

$$= \frac{UL_P^2}{(N \times UL_i)^2}$$

Here, N is the total number of loans in the portfolio. You would use this approach (giving UL_P) if the only information available was a time series of losses from the portfolio and (giving P_D and therefore UL_i) an estimate of the average percentage loss given default. As an example, consider the loss information in Table 20-2. This is the type of information that you could get from the bank's annual reports. The loss is written in percentage terms to reduce the effect of the changing size of the portfolio. The historical expected loss of the portfolio ($EL_{P,H}$) is simply the

TABLE 20-2

Example of Historical Losses Used to Estimate
the Unexpected Loss of the Portfolio

Year	Assets $Bn	Write-offs $Bn	% Loss
1990	231	1.2	0.5%
1991	236	2.6	1.1%
1992	243	0.7	0.3%
1993	245	5.6	2.3%
1994	250	5.9	2.4%
1995	269	9.4	3.5%
1996	284	2.1	0.7%
1997	309	1.8	0.6%
1998	333	0.2	0.1%
1999	352	11.7	3.3%
2000	386	2.5	0.7%
EL% $_{P,H}$			1.4%
UL% $_{P,H}$			1.2%

average of the losses and the historical percentage UL ($UL_{P,H}$) is the standard deviation.

In dollar terms, the UL for the portfolio is the UL as a percentage, multiplied by the total size of the portfolio:

$$UL_{P,H} = N \overline{E} \, UL\%_{P,H}$$

Here, $\overline{E}$ is the average loan size, and N is the number of loans.

We now wish to estimate UL for the individual loans. If we assume that the loss given default (LGD) is 75%, then the average probability of default for loans in this portfolio is 1.9%:

$$P = \frac{EL\%}{LGD} = \frac{1.4\%}{75\%} = 1.9\%$$

The UL for an individual loan is estimated as follows:

$$UL_i = \overline{E} \, LGD \sqrt{P - P^2} = 10\% \, \overline{E}$$

We can now calculate the correlation as follows:

$$\bar{\rho} = \frac{UL_P^2}{(N \times UL_i)^2}$$

$$= \frac{\left(N \, \bar{E} \, UL\%_{P,H}\right)^2}{\left(N \, \bar{E} \, LGD \, \sqrt{P - P^2}\right)^2}$$

$$= \left(\frac{N \, \bar{E} \, 1.4\%}{N \, \bar{E} \, 10\%}\right)^2 = 1.9\%$$

The calculation of $\bar{\rho}$ using this method is useful for getting estimates of $\bar{\rho}$ to use in the calculation of the unexpected loss contribution, as discussed later. It is also a useful cross-check on results obtained using other methods.

A better estimate of $\bar{\rho}$ can be made if we have an idea of the distribution of the creditworthiness of the loans. This extension to the methodology is demonstrated in Appendix B.

The calculation of loss correlations directly from historical data can produce a quick estimate for the correlation, but it has a couple of problems. First, it only gives us one correlation for the whole portfolio so it is not possible to differentiate between loans that have different correlations. The second problem is that the reported historical loss data is often corrupted because the amount of losses reported each year is manipulated by the bank's managers.

The manipulation of reported losses is done to maintain the appearance of stable earnings. Banks tend to underreport the losses in bad times and overreport them in good times. Banks can postpone the declaration of losses by restructuring loans that are about to default. For example, if a company is unable to pay back a loan, the bank has two choices: it can force the company into bankruptcy and take over its remaining assets, or the bank could give it a new loan that it can use to repay the old loan and thereby delay the official default. The bank will probably never recover its money, but by making such deals, banks have had some leeway in manipulating the reported losses, thereby reducing UL_P and the accuracy of this approach.

This corruption of the data exacerbates the problems of only having a few data points, and can produce results that significantly undercount the risk.

Using Asset Correlations to Estimate Default Correlations

The analysis above used portfolio-level data. We now discuss the asset-correlation approach, which calculates the loss correlation between two individual companies. The loss correlation is estimated based on the correlation between their net asset values or equity prices.

The approach calculates the loss correlation from the joint default probability. The *joint default probability* between two loans, 1 and 2 ($JDP_{1,2}$), is the probability that both loans will default at the same time. The relationship between the joint default probability and the loss correlation is detailed in Appendix C to this chapter. The result is that the loss correlation between loans 1 and 2 ($\rho_{1,2}$) can be expressed in terms of the joint default probability and the individual probabilities of default for the loans (P_1, P_2) as follows:

$$\rho_{1,2} = \frac{JDP_{1,2} - P_1 P_2}{\sqrt{(P_1 - P_1^2)(P_2 - P_2^2)}}$$

We can estimate P_1 and P_2 from the calculation of default probabilities as in Chapter 19. The problem now is to calculate $JDP_{1,2}$.

The calculation of the joint default probability can be based on the Merton approach that was discussed in Chapter 19. In Chapter 19, we estimated the probability of default for a single company as the probability that its asset value would fall below its debt value. For this calculation, we assumed that the equity (E) was a good measure of the difference between the assets and debts. The probability of default was then calculated as the probability that the equity price would fall below zero:

$$P = \int_{-\infty}^{0} p(E, \overline{E}, \sigma_E) \, dE$$

We transformed this equation to say that the default probability was equal to the probability that a Standard Normal variable would fall below a critical value (C), which depends on the equity price and its volatility:

$$P = \int_{-\infty}^{0} p(E, \overline{E}, \sigma_E) \, dE$$
$$= \int_{-\infty}^{-\overline{E}/\sigma_E} \phi(z) \, dz$$
$$= \int_{-\infty}^{-C} \phi(z) \, dz$$

$\overline{E}/\sigma_E$ is the distance to default or the critical value, and ϕ is the Standard Normal probability-density function. This gave us the probability that one company will default. We now want to know the probability of two companies' defaulting at the same time.

Let us define z_1 and z_2 as follows:

$$z_1 = \frac{E_1 - \overline{E}_1}{\sigma_{E_1}}$$

$$z_2 = \frac{E_2 - \overline{E}_2}{\sigma_{E_2}}$$

Here, E_1 is the equity value for company 1, and E_2 is the value for company 2. If we assume that the equity values are Normally distributed, then z_1 and z_2 will be

Normally distributed, each with a mean of 0 and standard deviation of 1. The probability of each company's defaulting is as follows:

$$P_1 = \int_{-\infty}^{-C_1} \phi(z_1)\, dz_1$$

$$P_2 = \int_{-\infty}^{-C_2} \phi(z_2)\, dz_2$$

The correlation between z_1 and z_2 equals the correlation between the equity prices, ρ_E. Figure 20-1 shows a scatter plot for 1000 possible changes in z_1 and z_2 for 2 companies with an equity correlation equal to 0.7. Notice that when one company has a low value, the other also tends to have a low value. The probability of both companies' having a particular value is described by the joint-probability density function. The formula for the joint probability density for 2 correlated Standard Normal variables is given below:

$$\phi(z_1, z_2, \rho_E) = \frac{1}{2\pi\sqrt{1 - \rho_E^2}}\, e\left[-\frac{1}{2}\frac{(z_1^2 - 2\rho z_1 z_2 + z_2^2)}{\sqrt{1 - \rho_E^2}}\right]$$

This function is plotted in Figure 20-2 for a correlation of 0.7. Notice that the plot is flattened and twisted along a 45-degree line. If the correlation was lower, the twist

FIGURE 20-1

Illustration of the Correlation Between the Standard Asset Values of Two Companies

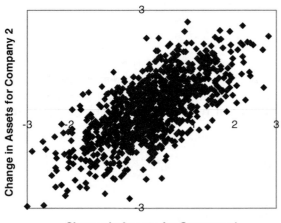

Change in Assets for Company 1

This figure depicts a scatter plot for 1000 possible changes in asset values *z1* and *z2* for two companies with an equity correlation equal to 0.7.

FIGURE 20-2

Illustration of the Joint Normal Probability-Density Function with a Correlation of 0.7

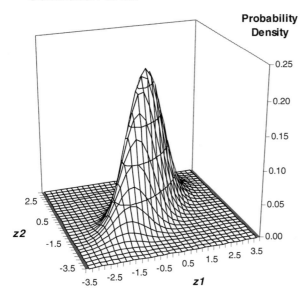

This figure plots the joint probability density for two Standard Normal variables with a correlation of 0.7. The height of the plot corresponds to the probability of z1 and z2 both falling in the given cell.

along the 45-degree line would be less pronounced. Figure 20-3 shows the probability-density function for a correlation of 0.1. Notice that the height of the function is now much less in the area where both companies have low values.

The probability of z_1 and z_2 falling in a small area is given by the probability-density function, multiplied by the size of the area:

$$P[\alpha_1 < z_1 < (\alpha_1 + \Delta_1), \alpha_2 < z_2 < (\alpha_2 + \Delta_2)] = \phi(\alpha_1, \alpha_2, \rho_E)\Delta_1\Delta_2$$

The joint probability that both companies will default is equal to the probability that z_1 falls in the range below $-C_1$, and z_2 falls in the range below $-C_2$. This probability is evaluated by integrating the probability-density function over the area in which both companies default:

$$JDP = P[z_1 < -C_1, z_2 < -C_2] = \int_{-\infty}^{-C_1} \int_{-\infty}^{-C_2} \phi(z_1, z_2, \rho)\, dz_1 dz_2$$

Let us summarize the results so far. We calculated the critical distance to default from the equity-price information:

$$C_1 = \overline{E}_1/\sigma_{E_1}$$

FIGURE 20-3

Illustration of the Joint Normal Probability-Density Function with a Correlation of 0.1

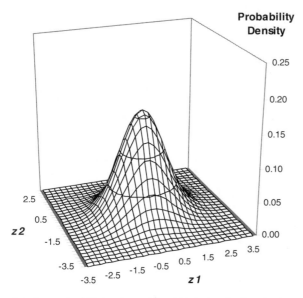

This figure plots the joint probability density for two Standard Normal variables with a correlation of 0.1.

We calculated the probability of default for a single company using the Merton model and the cumulative Standard Normal probability-density function, Φ:

$$P_1 = \int_{-\infty}^{-C_1} \phi(z_1)\, dz_1 \equiv \Phi(-C_1)$$

We calculated the joint probability of default from the critical values, the two-dimensional Standard Normal probability-density function, and the correlation between the equity prices:

$$JDP = \int_{-\infty}^{-C_1} \int_{-\infty}^{-C_2} \phi(z_1, z_2, \rho_E)\, dz_1 dz_2$$

Finally, the loss correlation was calculated from the probabilities and the JDP:

$$\rho_{1,2} = \frac{JDP_{1,2} - P_1 P_2}{\sqrt{\left(P_1 - P_1^2\right)\left(P_2 - P_2^2\right)}}$$

The process just described is a reasonable way of estimating the default correlation; however, it requires that we know all the equity information. Alternatively, if we already know the individual probabilities of default (e.g., if we know the credit grades) we can take a short-cut and calculate the critical values from Table 19-4 or by using the inverse of the cumulative probability function:

$$-C_1 = \Phi^{-1}(P_1)$$

Φ^{-1} is available in most spreadsheet programs (e.g., "norminv(P,0,1)" in Excel). Knowing the critical values and the correlation between equity prices, we can step directly to evaluating the JDP.

The evaluation of the integral cannot be done analytically, and instead, numerical integration is required. Numerical integration takes the sum of the probability over many small areas:

$$JDP = \int_{-\infty}^{-C_1} \int_{-\infty}^{-C_2} \phi(z_1, z_2, \rho_E)\, dz_1 dz_2$$

$$\approx \sum_{k=0}^{N} \sum_{m=0}^{N} \phi((-C_1 - k\Delta_1), (-C_2 - m\Delta_2), \rho_E)\Delta_1\Delta_2$$

In this scheme, we evaluate ϕ at a total of N^2 points. Δ_1 is the distance between each point in the z_1 direction, and Δ_2 in the z_2 direction. The size of the steps is chosen so that the difference between evaluation points is not too large. N is chosen so that $\phi((-C_1 - N\Delta_1), (-C_2 - N\Delta_2), \rho)$ is very small.

Table 20-3 and Table 20-4 show the results for companies of differing credit quality and asset correlation. In each table, the credit quality of the companies is increased from a default rate of 0.01% per year (1 basis point) to 10% per year (1000 basis points). As the default rate increases, the default correlation also increases. Comparison of Table 20-3 and Table 20-4 also shows that an increase in the equity correlation causes an increase in the default correlation.

TABLE 20-3

Default Correlation for Companies with Equity Correlation of 20%

Probability of Default for Company 2	Probability of Default for Company 1			
	1 bp	10 bps	100 bps	1000 bps
1 bp	0.1%	0.3%	0.5%	0.7%
10 bps	0.3%	0.6%	1.1%	1.8%
100 bps	0.5%	1.1%	2.4%	4.1%
1000 bps	0.7%	1.8%	4.1%	8.0%

TABLE 20-4

Default Correlation for Companies with Equity Correlation of 40%

Probability of Default for Company 2	Probability of Default for Company 1			
	1 bp	10 bps	100 bps	1000 bps
1 bp	1.0%	1.6%	2.0%	1.7%
10 bps	1.6%	2.8%	4.3%	4.5%
100 bps	2.0%	4.3%	7.7%	10.3%
1000 bps	1.7%	4.5%	10.3%	18.5%

Estimation of the Economic Capital for Credit Losses Using the Covariance Portfolio Model

From the discussions above, we can calculate the portfolio's EL and UL. We now wish to use those results to estimate the portfolio's economic capital. To do this, we need to estimate the probability distribution of the portfolio's losses.

In the covariance model, the losses are typically assumed to have a Beta distribution. The Beta distribution is used for three reasons:

1. It can have highly skewed shapes similar to the distributions that have been observed for historical credit losses.
2. It only requires two parameters to determine the shape (EL_P and UL_P).
3. The possible losses are limited to being between 0 and 100%.

The formula for the Beta probability-density function for % losses (L) is as follows:

$$\beta(L) = \frac{L^{a-1}(1-L)^{b-1}}{\int_0^1 L^{a-1}(1-L)^{b-1}dL}$$

The Beta function can be integrated numerically and is available in most spreadsheet programs. To use it, the variables a and b can be expressed in terms of the required mean (EL_P) and standard deviation (UL_P):

$$a = (1 - EL_P)\left(\frac{EL_P}{UL_P}\right)^2 - EL_P$$

$$b = \frac{a(1 - EL_P)}{EL_P}$$

Figure 20-4 shows three Beta distributions for which (UL_P) is held constant at 1%, and EL_P equals 1%, 2%, and 3%. Notice that as EL becomes larger relative to UL,

FIGURE 20-4

Illustration of Beta Distribution for Credit Losses

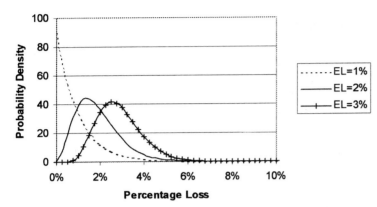

the distribution becomes more like a Normal distribution. Portfolios of lower-quality loans (e.g., credit cards) have a higher ratio of EL to UL, and therefore, have Beta distributions that tend to look like Normal distributions.

From the tail of the Beta distributions, we can obtain estimates of the economic capital required for the portfolio. In Chapter 2, we discussed risk measurement at the corporate level and said that the common definition of economic capital for credit losses is the maximum probable loss minus the expected loss:

$$EC_P = MPL_P - EL_P$$

The maximum probable loss is the point in the tail where there is a "very low" probability that losses will exceed that point. The "very low" probability is chosen to match the bank's desired credit rating. For example, a single-A-rated bank would require that there should be only 10 basis points of probability in the tail, whereas AAA banks require around 1 basis point. For the 3 distributions shown in Figure 20-4, the 10-basis-point confidence level is close to 7%, and the 1-basis-point confidence level is between 8% and 9%.

Figure 20-5 shows the process for calculating the economic capital using the covariance model with default correlations estimated from asset correlations.

Calculation of the Unexpected Loss Contribution

We have now calculated the UL and economic capital of the portfolio as a whole. Using the unexpected loss contribution, we can allocate the capital to the individual loans in the portfolio. The unexpected loss contribution (ULC) allocates the total UL of the portfolio to the individual loans in the portfolio in such as way that the ULCs

F I G U R E 20-5

Illustration of the Process for the Covariance Approach

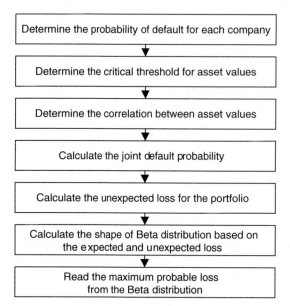

sum back up to the UL_P of the portfolio. In Chapter 22, we use this capital allocation to calculate the risk-adjusted profitability for each loan.

The unexpected loss contribution takes the same approach as the Value at Risk contribution (VaRC). One approach is to differentiate UL_P with respect to UL_i, as shown in Appendix D. An alternative derivation is simply to rearrange the terms in the summation notation:

$$UL_P^2 = \sum_{i=1}^{N}\sum_{j=1}^{N} \rho_{i,j} UL_i UL_j$$

$$= \sum_{i=1}^{N}\left(UL_i \sum_{j=1}^{N} \rho_{i,j} UL_j \right)$$

We now divide both sides by UL_P:

$$UL_P = \sum_{i=1}^{N} UL_i \frac{\sum_{j=1}^{N} \rho_{i,j} UL_j}{UL_P}$$

By analogy, with the case in which all the correlations were assumed to be equal, the second term is called the square root of the average correlation between loan i and the rest of the portfolio:

$$\sqrt{\bar{\rho}_i} \equiv \frac{\sum\limits_{j=1}^{N} \rho_{i,j} UL_j}{UL_P}$$

With this notation, the portfolio UL can now be written as a sum of the individual ULs weighted by their average correlations:

$$UL_P = \sum_{i=1}^{N} \sqrt{\bar{\rho}_i} UL_i$$

The term inside the summation is called the *unexpected loss contribution* (ULC). By construction, the sum of the ULCs equals the portfolio UL:

$$ULC_i \equiv \sqrt{\bar{\rho}_i} UL_i$$

$$UL_P = \sum_{i=1}^{N} ULC_i$$

Let us summarize the ULC approach. By using the variance formula, we can calculate the UL_P for the portfolio, based on the UL of the individual loans:

$$UL_P^2 = \sum_{i=1}^{N} \sum_{j=1}^{N} \rho_{i,j} UL_i UL_j$$

Knowing the UL_P, we can calculate the unexpected loss contribution in such a way as to ensure that the sum gives us the UL_P:

$$ULC_i \equiv \sqrt{\bar{\rho}_i} UL_i$$

$$UL_P = \sum_{i=1}^{N} ULC_i$$

ULC is useful because we can use it to allocate the economic capital of the whole portfolio (EC_P) the individual loans. The economic capital contribution for loan i (ECC_i) can be allocated according to its unexpected loss contribution:

$$ECC_i = EC_P \frac{ULC_i}{UL_P}$$

This has the property that the sum of the individual ECCs equals the total portfolio capital. The ratio of the economic capital to the unexpected loss is sometimes called the *capital multiplier*, M:

$$M = \frac{EC_P}{UL_P}$$

This allows the economic capital contribution to be written simply as follows:

$$ECC_i = M \times ULC_i$$

Knowing the economic capital contribution for an individual loan, we can calculate the risk-adjusted return on capital (RAROC) for that loan and set the required price if it is a new loan. Pricing is discussed in Chapter 22 once we have explored the other approaches for quantifying the risk of credit portfolios.

SUMMARY

In this chapter, we described the covariance approach to measuring the credit risk of a portfolio. In the next chapter, we discuss four alternatives to the covariance approach.

APPENDIX A: THE DOMINANCE OF CORRELATION

For a large portfolio (large N), the correlation (or systematic risk) becomes the dominant term in determining UL_P, and the correlation of each loan with itself becomes unimportant. To see this, consider a portfolio of N identical loans. Assume that all the off-diagonal correlations are equal, and the UL for each loan is equal:

$$\rho_{i,j} = 1 \quad \text{if } i = j$$
$$\rho_{i,j} = \widehat{\rho} \quad \text{if } i \neq j$$
$$UL_i = \widehat{UL} \ \forall i$$

The summation can now be written as:

$$UL_P^2 = \sum_{i=1}^{N} \sum_{j=1}^{N} \rho_{i,j} \widehat{UL}^2$$

$$= \sum_{i=1}^{N} \left[\widehat{UL}^2 + \sum_{j=1, j\neq i}^{N} \widehat{\rho} \, \widehat{UL}^2 \right]$$

$$= N \left[\widehat{UL}^2 + (N-1) \widehat{\rho} \, \widehat{UL}^2 \right]$$

$$= N \, \widehat{UL}^2 + N(N-1) \widehat{\rho} \, \widehat{UL}^2$$

If N is much larger than $1/\widehat{\rho}$ (e.g., if N is greater than 100), the second term dominates, and we can approximate UL_P as follows:

$$UL_P^2 \approx N(N) \widehat{\rho} \, \widehat{UL}^2$$

$$UL_P \approx N \sqrt{\widehat{\rho}} \, \widehat{UL}$$

This equation shows that for a large portfolio, the systematic risk dominates the idiosyncratic risk of the individual loans.

APPENDIX B: DERIVATION OF DEFAULT CORRELATION GIVEN INFORMATION ON THE PORTFOLIO'S CREDITWORTHINESS

In the section on estimating the loss correlation from historical data, we assumed that all the loans were identical. As a next step of complication, assume that we know the historical loss on the portfolio as before in Table 20-2, and in addition, we have an idea of the distribution of the creditworthiness of the loans in the portfolio as in the first two columns of Table 20B-1.

With the information in Table 20B-1, we no longer need to assume that all the loans are the same, and we can go back to the correlation equation and develop it more carefully. Assuming that the correlation is the same for all loans, the correlation equation was as follows:

$$\overline{\rho} = \frac{UL_P^2}{\left(\sum_{i=1}^{N} UL_i\right)^2}$$

Now we can sum up the ULs of the individual loans according to the loan's credit grade:

$$\sum_{i=1}^{N} UL_i = \sum_{i=1}^{G1} UL_i + \sum_{i=G1+1}^{G2} UL_i + \sum_{i=G2+1}^{G3} UL_i + \cdots + \sum_{i=Gx+1}^{N} UL_i$$

TABLE 20-B1

Example of a Portfolio's Credit-Grade Allocation Used to Estimate the Unexpected Loss of the Individual Grades

Grade	Allocation of Exposure (R_G)	Probability of Default (P_G)	UL%
AAA	5%	0.01%	0.04%
AA	10%	0.01%	0.07%
A	25%	0.04%	0.37%
BBB	30%	0.22%	1.05%
BB	15%	0.98%	1.11%
B	10%	5.30%	1.68%
CCC	5%	21.94%	1.55%
$\sum_{i=1}^{N} UL\%_i$			5.88%

In this equation, UL_i can be estimated as follows:

$$UL_i = E_i \, LGD \, \sqrt{P_i - P_i^2}$$

Here, E_i is the exposure at default for the loan, and P_i is the probability of default for the given credit grade. If we assume that LGD is fixed for the whole portfolio, we can calculate the sum of UL for each grade from the sum of the total exposure to the credit grade:

$$\sum_{i=1}^{G1} UL_i = \sum_{i=1}^{G1} E_i \, LGD \, \sqrt{P_G - P_G^2} = LGD \, \sqrt{P_G - P_G^2} \sum_{i=1}^{G1} E_i$$

This can be expressed as a percentage by dividing by the total exposure of the portfolio:

$$\sum_{i=1}^{G1} UL\%_i = LGD \, \sqrt{P_G - P_G^2} \, \frac{\sum_{i=1}^{G1} E_i}{E_{Total}} = LGD \, \sqrt{P_G - P_G^2} \, R_G$$

Here, R_G is just the proportion of the portfolio's exposure that is in each grade:

$$R_G = \frac{\sum_{i=1}^{G1} E_i}{E_{Total}}$$

The result is shown in the fifth column of Table 20B-1.

From Table 20-2, we know that $UL\%_P$ is 1.2%, and from Table 20B-1, we know that the sum of UL for the individual loans is 5.88%. From this we can calculate $\bar{\rho}$:

$$\bar{\rho} = \frac{UL\%_P^2}{\left(\sum_{i=1}^{N} UL\%_i\right)^2} = \left(\frac{1.2\%}{5.88\%}\right)^2 = 4.2\%$$

APPENDIX C: THE RELATIONSHIP BETWEEN LOSS CORRELATION AND THE JOINT PROBABILITY OF DEFAULT

Recall that correlation between two variables, x and y, can be defined from the variances and covariance of the two variables:

$$\rho_{x,y} = \frac{\sigma_{x,y}^2}{\sigma_x \sigma_y}$$

Where the covariance is calculated as follows:

$$\sigma_{x,y}^2 = \int_x \int_y (x - \bar{x})(y - \bar{y})\, p(x,y)\, dx\, dy$$

$$= \int_x \int_y xy\, p(x,y)\, dx\, dy - \bar{x}\bar{y}$$

The covariance between two losses L_1 and L_2 is therefore:

$$\sigma_{1,2}^2 = \int_1 \int_2 L_1 L_2\, p(L_1, L_2)\, dL_1\, dL_2 - \overline{L_1}\,\overline{L_2}$$

In Chapter 18, our formula for loss was made up of an indicator function (I), the severity of loss in the event of default (S), and the exposure at default (E).

$$L = I \times S \times E$$

Substituting this into the covariance equation gives a fairly complex expression:

$$\sigma_{1,2}^2 = \sum_{I_1} \int_{S_1} \int_{E_1} \sum_{I_2} \int_{S_2} \int_{E_2} I_1 S_1 E_1 I_2 S_2 E_2 P(I_1, I_2) p(S_1, E_1, S_2, E_2 | I_1, I_2)\, dS_1 dE_1 dS_2 dE_2$$
$$- \bar{I}_1 \bar{S}_1 \bar{E}_1 \bar{I}_2 \bar{S}_2 \bar{E}_2$$

The usual approach for estimating the correlation is to bypass the complexity and assume that the severities and exposures are constants. This allows us to simplify the equation to the following:

$$\sigma_{Lx,Ly}^2 = S_1 E_1 S_2 E_2 \left(\left[\sum_1 \sum_2 I_1 I_2 P(I_1, I_2) \right] - \bar{I}_1 \bar{I}_2 \right)$$

We can now simplify the summation term. If I_1 or I_2 equals 0, the term inside the summation equals 0. Therefore, we are only concerned with the case where both I_1 and I_2 equal 1, i.e., that both companies default. $P(I_1 = 1, I_2 = 1)$ is called the *joint default probability* of I_1 and I_2. The JDP is the probability that both companies default at the same time. We can now write the loss covariance in terms of the joint default probability:

$$\sigma_{1,2}^2 = S_1 E_1 S_2 E_2 (JDP_{1,2} - P_1 P_2)$$

We can find similar equations for the variances:

$$\sigma_{1,1}^2 = S_1 E_1 S_1 E_1 \left(\left[\sum_1 \sum_1 I_1 I_1 P(I_1, I_1) \right] - \bar{I}_1 \bar{I}_1 \right)$$
$$= S_1^2 E_1^2 (P_1 - P_1^2)$$
$$\sigma_{1,1} = S_1 E_1 \sqrt{P_1 - P_1^2}$$
$$\sigma_{2,2} = S_2 E_2 \sqrt{P_2 - P_2^2}$$

Note that this is the familiar expression for UL for an individual facility. If we put these expressions into the equation for the correlation, the severities and exposures cancel out, allowing us to write the correlation in terms of the independent probabilities and the joint probability:

$$\rho_{1,2} = \frac{JDP_{1,2} - P_1 P_2}{\sqrt{(P_1 - P_1^2)(P_2 - P_2^2)}}$$

Notice that if the defaults were independent, then the joint probability would simply be the product of their independent probabilities $(P_1 P_2)$ and therefore the correlation would equal zero.

Strictly speaking, $\rho_{1,2}$ is the default correlation; if we assume that the severity and exposure amounts are constant, it is also equal to the loss correlation. Be aware that in many credit-risk discussions "default correlation" and "loss correlation" are used interchangeably.

APPENDIX D: DERIVATION OF THE UNEXPECTED LOSS CONTRIBUTION BY DIFFERENTIATION

The unexpected loss contribution can be thought of as the sensitivity of the portfolio UL to a change in the UL of an individual transaction. We can obtain ULC by differentiating UL_P with respect to UL_i:

$$UL_P = \sum_i ULC_i$$

$$ULC_i = UL_i \frac{\partial UL_P}{\partial UL_i}$$

Where:

$$\frac{\partial UL_P}{\partial UL_i} = \frac{\partial \sqrt{(UL_P^2)}}{\partial (UL_P^2)} \frac{\partial (UL_P^2)}{\partial UL_i}$$

$$= \frac{\frac{1}{2}}{UL_P} \frac{\partial \left(\sum_{i=1}^{N} \sum_{j=1}^{N} \rho_{i,j} UL_i UL_j \right)}{\partial UL_i}$$

$$= \frac{\sum_{j=1}^{N} \rho_{i,j} UL_j}{UL_P}$$

CHAPTER 21

Risk Measurement for a Credit Portfolio: Part Two

INTRODUCTION

In the previous chapter, we discussed the covariance approach to calculating portfolio credit losses. The main limitations of the covariance approach are that we need to have faith that the Beta distribution is a good description of the loss distribution, and it is difficult to include details such as correlated changes in credit grades and changes in exposure amount. This chapter discusses four popular alternative credit-portfolio models:

- The actuarial model
- The Merton-based simulation model
- The macroeconomic default model
- The macroeconomic cash-flow model

At the end, we show that most of the models can be combined into a unified model.

THE ACTUARIAL CREDIT-PORTFOLIO MODEL

The actuarial credit model is an approach for estimating the loss distribution for a portfolio of loans. It is called an *actuarial* approach because it directly uses the statistics of historical losses rather than trying to define an underlying mechanism for the cause of losses. The actuarial credit model has been implemented by Credit Suisse Financial Products in their CreditRisk+[TM] software.[1] The approach is quite complex, and you would probably not want to build such a model from scratch; however, as a risk professional, you should be aware of the principles underlying this approach.

The approach begins by grouping the loans in the portfolio according to their sector and size. The sectors can be by industry or geography. The size is measured according to the dollar amount of the loss given default. The dollar amount is the usual percentage LGD multiplied by the exposure at default:

$$LGD\$ = LGD \times EAD$$

For a given "condition of the world," the losses within a group are assumed to be conditionally independent from each other. This means that the default correlation is zero within the group for that "condition of the world." Such a group of loans, with independent default events of equal size, will have a binomial loss distribution.

With N loans in the group, and an average probability of default equal to p, the binomial distribution gives the following probability of having k defaults:

$$P(k) = \binom{N}{k} p^k (1-p)^{N-k}$$

Here, the term in parentheses is the factorial expression:

$$\binom{N}{k} \equiv \frac{N!}{k!(N-k)!}$$

As N becomes large and p becomes small, the binomial distribution converges towards the Poisson distribution. The Poisson distribution is given by:

$$P(k) = \frac{e^{-p} p^k}{k!}$$

This distribution has a mean of p and a standard deviation equal to the square root of p. The Poisson distribution is useful because it requires only one parameter (p), and it is relatively easy to derive analytical expressions for combinations of Poisson distributions. The actuarial approach therefore approximates the loss distribution of the group of loans in the given "condition of the world" as a Poisson distribution.

Having established the loss distribution for one condition of the world, the next step is to include variations in the world's condition. This is reflected in variations in the mean probability, p. We can think of this as saying that in a recession, for all loans, the probability of default will increase.

The mean probability is assumed to have a Gamma distribution. This distribution has long tails similar to those observed for credit losses, and again, it is possible to manipulate the Gamma distribution to derive analytic results. If we assume that the average default rate p in the Poisson distribution has a Gamma distribution, it can be shown that the overall losses in all conditions of the world will have the form of a negative binomial distribution. The probability of having k losses is calculated from negative binomial distribution as follows:

$$P(k) = (1-p)^\alpha \binom{k+\alpha-1}{k} p^k$$

Here, α is determined by the mean and standard deviation of the Gamma function:

$$\alpha = \frac{\mu^2}{\sigma^2}$$

The mean of the Gamma function is chosen to be the mean probability of default for the group for all conditions of the world. There are several approaches for selecting the standard deviation of the Gamma distribution. One approach is to select the standard deviation to ensure that the final result has the same kurtosis as historically observed defaults. Another approach is to look at the historical default volatility within a sector and try to determine how much of the volatility was caused by systematic changes in the underlying mean probability of default (the Gamma distribution), and how much was caused by sampling from a population with a constant probability of default (the Poisson distribution).

Up to this point, we have discussed the method for calculating the probability distribution for a single group of loans. The groups are combined back into a portfolio by assuming that the losses from each group are independent from losses in the other groups.

The amount of loss from group g equals the number of defaults (k) and the dollar amount of loss given default for that group:

$$L_g = k \times LDG\$$$

The probability of having such a loss amount is given by the group's negative binomial distribution for k:

$$P_{L_g} = P(k)$$

To estimate the portfolio's loss distribution, we now need to step through every possible combination of k for each group.

For a given combination, the loss amount for the portfolio as a whole is the sum of the losses from each group:

$$L_c = \sum_g L_g$$

The probability of having this combination is the product of the probabilities of each group's having its given level of loss:

$$P_c = \prod_g P_{L_g}$$

For example, consider two groups, A and B, each with two possible loss levels and the following probabilities:

$$P_A(k=1) = 70\%, \quad P_A(k=2) = 30\%$$
$$P_B(k=1) = 80\%, \quad P_B(k=2) = 20\%$$

If the LDG for A is \$25 and for B is \$16. The corresponding losses are as follows:
$$L_A(k=1) = \$25, \quad L_A(k=2) = \$50$$
$$L_B(k=1) = \$16, \quad L_B(k=2) = \$32$$
The four possible losses for the portfolio are as follows:
$$P_1 = 70\% \times 80\%, \quad L_1 = \$25 + \$16$$
$$P_2 = 70\% \times 20\%, \quad L_2 = \$25 + \$32$$
$$P_3 = 30\% \times 80\%, \quad L_3 = \$50 + \$16$$
$$P_4 = 30\% \times 20\%, \quad L_4 = \$50 + \$32$$
Finally, we sort the combinations according to the size of the loss, and calculate the cumulative probability to give us the cumulative-probability function for the losses.

If we had x possible loss levels for each group and y groups, the total number of combinations that we would have to calculate is x^y. If there were many groups or many levels of loss to be considered, the number of combinations quickly becomes too large for efficient computation. As a practical alternative, the CSFP software uses a recurrence relationship for the probabilities. The relationship is mathematically complex but computationally efficient.

The overall process for the actuarial approach is summarized in Figure 21-1.

The main difficulty in using the actuarial approach is defining the standard deviations of the Gamma functions that effectively drive the correlations. A second

FIGURE 21-1

The Calculation Process for the Actuarial Approach

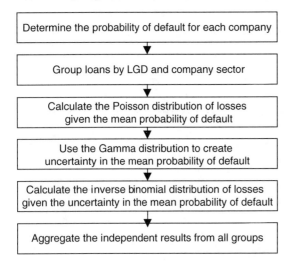

difficulty is that there is no easy way to link credit and market risks in the actuarial model. Both of these difficulties are overcome in the Merton simulation approach.

THE MERTON-BASED SIMULATION MODELS

In Chapter 19, we used the Merton approach to estimate a company's probability of default based on changes in the value of its assets. In Chapter 20, we described the covariance credit-portfolio model, in which we used the Merton approach to calculate the probability that two companies would default at the same time. Here we describe another use of the Merton model: simulating correlated defaults for a portfolio of loans.

The Merton-based simulation models create random values for each company's assets, and if the value is too low, the model simulates a default. For all the companies in the loan portfolio, the changes in the asset values are correlated, and as we will show, this produces correlated defaults.

There are three main advantages to this approach:

- There is no need to assume a probability distribution for the losses because a distribution is produced by the simulation.
- It is relatively easy to include uncertainties in not only the number of defaults but also in the exposure at default, loss given default, and changes in value due to changes in credit grade.
- It allows the simulation of market variables, such as interest-rates, in parallel with the simulation of asset values. This allows us to calculate the credit exposure for derivatives and correctly correlate the exposure with counter-party defaults. It also opens the way to calculating credit risk and market risk in the same framework, thereby allowing them to be properly correlated.

The approach has been adopted in several forms by different banks and software companies. Models are commercially available from KMV Corporation in their PortfolioManager[TM] software[2] and from Risk Metrics in their CreditMetrics[TM] software.[3]

Calculating Losses Due to Default Using the Merton-Based Approach

Let us start by looking at how the approach works if we just want to consider uncertainty in the default rate. Later, we will add uncertainty in the loss given default and the final credit grade. If we are just interested in uncertainty in the default rate, the process is as follows.

For each company in the portfolio, we need to find the probability of default, the exposure at default (EAD) and the loss given default (LGD). For now, we assume EAD and LGD are fixed. From the probability of default for each company, we calculate the critical distance to default using the inverse cumulative-probability function:

$$-C = \Phi^{-1}(P)$$

This calculation was described in Chapter 20 when we used the Merton model to calculate the joint default probability.

Next, we calculate the correlation between the asset values of each company. The most obvious way to do this is to use the correlation between the equity values, but there is a more commonly used alternative, which we discuss later.

Once we know all the parameter values, we can begin the simulation. The first step is to create a set of random numbers that have the same correlation as the company asset values. If we had just two companies, we could use the following approach:

$$z_1 = n_1 \qquad\qquad n_1 \sim N(0,1)$$

$$z_2 = \rho z_1 + \sqrt{1 - \rho^2} n_2 \qquad n_2 \sim N(0,1)$$

Here, z_1 represents the change in the asset value for company 1, n_1 is a random number from a Standard Normal distribution, and ρ is the correlation between the asset values of the two companies. For more than two companies, correlated random values for the assets are created using Cholesky decomposition or Eigenvalue decomposition, as we discussed in the chapter on Monte Carlo VaR.

After creating the random number for each company, we test to see if it is less than the critical value. If it is, we say that the company has defaulted and record the loss given default. The losses from all companies are then summed to give the portfolio's loss.

The process is repeated several thousand times with different sets of random asset values until we have enough results to create the loss distribution. The maximum probable loss and the economic capital can then be read from the distribution. For example, if we carried out 10,000 trials, the 10-basis-point maximum probable loss would be estimated from the tenth-worst result. Figure 21-2 summarizes the process for calculating the economic capital using the Merton-based simulation approach.

In the description above, we noted that there were alternative ways of creating the correlation between asset values. One approach is to set the correlation equal to the correlation between the equity values. The main problem with this is that if we have N companies in the portfolio, and we calculate the correlation between each company, we need to create an N-by-N correlation matrix with N times $(N-1)/2$ unique correlations. If N is large, the method would be slow.

A practical alternative is that instead of using equity prices directly to calculate asset correlations, equity indices are used. This greatly reduces the amount of correlated random numbers that must be created by the Eigenvalue decomposition. In the most simple case, the asset value for each individual company (z_i) could be modeled

FIGURE 21-2

The Calculation Process for the Merton Simulation Approach for Defaults

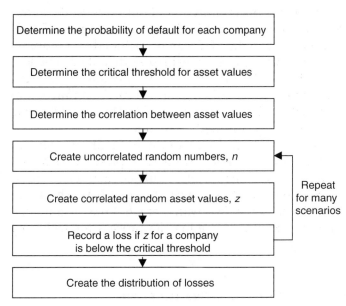

according to its Beta with a single market index (m) and a company-specific idiosyncratic term, ε_i:

$$z_i = \beta_i m + \varepsilon_i$$
$$\beta_i = \frac{\rho_{i,m} \sigma_i}{\sigma_m}$$

With this model, it would only be necessary to produce a single random value for the market index, and then N uncorrelated idiosyncratic terms. The model used in practice is slightly more complex than this.

In practice, the value of each company is set to depend on a series of indices. One index, for example, could represent energy prices, and another could represent the performance of high-tech companies. A high-tech company in the energy field would then be modeled as having its assets depend on both indices:

$$z_i = \beta_{i,energy} m_{energy} + \beta_{i,tech} m_{tech} + \varepsilon_i$$

These weights can be found by regressing the equity price against the indices.

Including Uncertainty in the Exposure at Default and Loss in the Event of Default

Until this point, we have only modeled the uncertainty in default rates. In the simulation model, it is relatively easy to add uncertainties in the loss given default (LGD) and exposure at default (EAD). Uncertainty in the LGD can be included by randomly picking an amount of loss after a company has been classified as defaulted. The loss can be purely random, with a suitable standard deviation and probability distribution (as discussed in the section on parameterizing LGD), or it could be a function of the extent to which the assets fall below the critical threshold. This would create correlation between the LGD experienced by different companies.

Uncertainty in the exposure at default can be modeled by a simple random number for a product such as a line of credit. For a derivative product such as a swap, the exposure may be modeled as a function of simulated market rates, as discussed in the section on measuring the credit exposure of derivatives. The simulated market rates would be created in the same Eigenvalue or Cholesky decomposition that creates the correlated indices. Figure 21-3 adds the process for including uncertainty in LGD and EAD.

Including Losses Due to Downgrades

It is also relatively easy to extend the Merton simulation model to include the effect of credit losses due not only to defaults but also due to downgrades. A downgrade occurs if the credit-rating agencies believe that a company's probability of default has increased. If a downgrade occurs, investors are less willing to hold the loan because of the risk of nonpayment. Therefore, the value of the loan falls, even though there has not yet been a default. For a single loan, this phenomenon was discussed in Chapter 18, in which we described losses due to both default and downgrades. Now, we wish to calculate these losses for a whole portfolio and ensure that changes in grades are correctly correlated with each other and with defaults.

From the migration matrix in Table 18-1, we know the probability of a grade change. This is reproduced in Table 21-1 for a company that is rated BBB at the start of the year. We can see that there is an 89% probability that the company will still be BBB at the end of the year. There is also a 4.8% chance of being upgraded to single-A, and a 4.4% chance of being downgraded to single-B.

Given these probabilities, we can define bands for a variable with a Standard Normal distribution, such that the probability of falling in a band equals the probability of migrating to a specific grade. These bands are illustrated in Figure 21-4.

The position of the critical threshold between each band corresponds to the probability of falling below the threshold. The threshold is calculated from the inverse for the cumulative Normal distribution:

$$\textit{Threshold} = \Phi^{-1}(\text{Probability of Falling Below})$$

FIGURE 21-3

The Calculation Process Used to Include Uncertainty in Exposure and Loss in the Event of Default

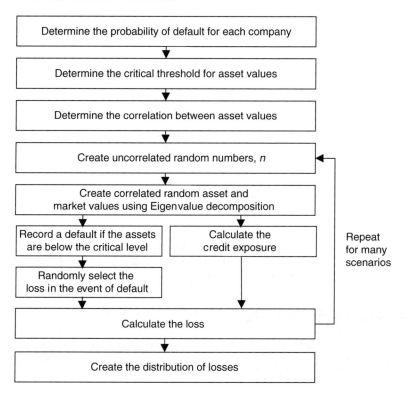

TABLE 21-1

Probability of Grade Migration for a Company Initially Rated BBB

		Probability (basis points)
	AAA	3
	AA	25
Rating	A	483
at the	BBB	8926
end of	BB	444
the year	B	81
	CCC	16
	Default	22

FIGURE 21-4

Illustration of Probability of Grade Migration for a Company Initially Rated BBB

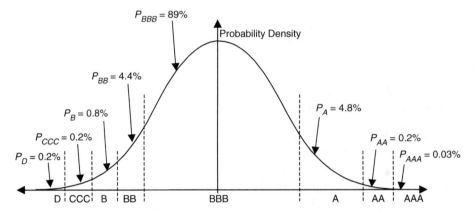

For a BBB company, the thresholds are given in Table 21-2.

If we now randomly select a value from a Standard Normal probability function, the probability of falling in a specified band will equal the probability of migration to the band.

So far, this is not very useful; we have simply created a way of simulating probabilities that we already know. The useful part of this analysis is that if we have two companies, we can correlate the random values that we use to predict rating changes. Each company will have the correct probability of a grade change,

TABLE 21-2

Critical Thresholds for Grade Migration for a BBB Company

	Probability of Falling Below (bps)	Threshold Value $\Phi^{-1}(P)$
AAA to AA	9997	3.4
AA to A	9972	2.8
A to BBB	9489	1.6
BBB to BB	563	−1.6
BB to B	119	−2.3
B to CCC	38	−2.7
CCC to Default	22	−2.8

and because the random numbers are correlated, they will tend to change grades at the same time.

The obvious way to do this is to use the same approach as the Merton default model and assume that rating changes correspond to changes in the asset value, and that the random values represent the net asset values. With this assumption, we can bring the probability of grade changes into the same model as the probability of default. For each company, we create a Standard Normal variable, z, representing the asset value with the variables for different companies correlated according to the equity correlations. We then test z to see if it passed any of the critical thresholds. If it did, we record a loss equal to the difference in value between a loan of the initial grade and a loan of the final grade.

THE MACROECONOMIC DEFAULT MODEL

In the actuarial model, we assumed that for the given condition of the world, all defaults were independent, and we calculated the loss distribution for that condition of the world. We then said that the condition of the world can change, and that the probability of default for each loan changes as the world changes. The macro-economic default model is very similar in that in any given economic condition, defaults are considered to be independent, but the probability of default for all loans is expected to change when the economy changes.

One form of the macroeconomic default model was developed by McKinsey and Company, and is implemented in their CreditPortfolioView™ software.[4] Here, we describe not only the McKinsey model, but also other ways in which these concepts can be used.

In general, the macroeconomic default model works as follows. For each company, the probability of default is found using one of the methods discussed in Chapter 19. The probability used should be the "cycle-neutral" probability of default. The cycle-neutral probability of default is the average probability of default for that type of company across all phases of the business cycle, from boom to recession.

The next step is to create a model for the overall economy that links economic conditions to the overall probability of default for all loans. The simplest such model would be to say that the number of defaults was equal to a constant, plus a proportion of GDP Growth:

$$P_{Overall} = a + b \times G$$

Here, a and b are constants, and G is the GDP growth rate. A slightly more complex model would be to use a logit function:

$$P_{Overall} = \frac{1}{1 + e^Y}$$
$$Y = a + b \times G$$

Here, a and b are again constants, but will have different values than in the previous equation. The values for a and b can be found by carrying out a regression between historical GDP growth and loss information. The loss information may be the bank's own aggregate losses each year, or may be national data, such as the number of bond defaults in each past year.

The next step is to create a model that can randomly create different scenarios for economic conditions such as GDP. A simple model is to say that future GDP growth will equal current GDP growth plus a Normally-distributed random number:

$$G_k = G_0 + \sigma_G \varepsilon_k, \quad \varepsilon_k N(0,1)$$

Here, G_k is the growth for random scenario number k, and σ_G is the standard deviation of the growth rate from one year to the next.

Now we have the probability of each company's defaulting, a model for how the probability changes in different economic conditions, and a model to create different conditions. These can be combined into a simulation model as follows.

In the simulation model, we randomly create a macroscenario, we calculate the default rate for the whole economy in that scenario, and then modify the default rate of individual companies according to the overall change in defaults:

$$G_k = G_0 + \sigma_G \varepsilon_k$$

$$P_{Overall,k} = \frac{1}{1 + e^{a + b \times G_k}}$$

$$P_{Company,k} = \frac{P_{Overall,k}}{\overline{P_{Overall}}} \times \overline{P_{Company}}$$

Here, $P_{Company,k}$ is the probability of default for the company in scenario k, and $\overline{P_{Company}}$ is the cycle-neutral probability of default. In this process, correlation between defaults is created by the common change in the whole portfolio's probability of default.

Once we know the probability of default for each company in this scenario, we "flip a coin" to decide whether or not the company will actually default. The flipping of the coin has to work in such a way that the probability of default equals $P_{Company,k}$. The usual way to do this is to create a random number from a uniform distribution between zero and one. If the random number is less than $P_{Company,k}$, we say that the company has defaulted and we record the loss.[5] We do this for all companies in this scenario and calculate the total loss for the portfolio. We then repeat the whole process for several thousand different scenarios, giving a distribution of possible losses. The process is illustrated in Figure 21-5.

The description above outlines a basic macroeconomic default model. Many enhancements can be added. One enhancement would be to describe the economy with several variables, such as GDP and inflation. These variables would then be correlated using the usual Eigenvalue decomposition. Another enhancement would be to add the possibility of grade migration. The cycle-neutral grade-migration prob-

FIGURE 21-5

Calculation for the Macroeconomic Default Model

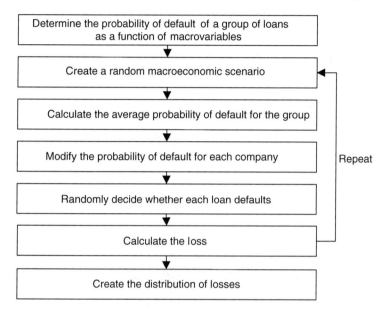

abilities are taken from the migration matrix, and the probabilities are then modified to cause more downgrades when the economy is doing badly. The final enhancement that we discuss here is a modification to the assumption that the probability of default for all companies must move in the same way.

In the basic model, we said that a company's probability of default would be given by the following equation:

$$P_{Overall,k} = \frac{1}{1 + e^{a + b \times G_k}}$$

$$P_{Company,k} = \frac{P_{Overall,k}}{\overline{P}_{Overall}} \times \overline{P}_{Company}$$

This forces us to assume that the probability of default for all companies changes by the same degree. As an alternative, recall that in Chapter 19, one of the models for predicting a company's probability of default was the logistic regression:

$$P = \frac{1}{1 + e^Y}$$

$$Y = w_0 + \sum_i w_i X_i$$

Here, X_i represents data on the customers, such as their financial ratios. When carrying out this regression, we can add a term to describe the economy:

$$Y = w_0 + \sum_i w_i X_i + w_G G$$

By adding the extra term, the model should be able to predict more accurately a company's probability of default. We can also use this model directly in the simulation as follows:

$$G_k = G_0 + \sigma_G \varepsilon_k$$

$$Y_{C,k} = w_{C,0} + \sum_i w_{C,i} X_{C,i} + w_{C,G} G_k$$

$$P_{Company,k} = \frac{1}{1 + e^{Y_{C,k}}}$$

This allows us to model individually each company's response to changes in the economy.

THE MACROECONOMIC CASH-FLOW MODEL

In Chapter 19, we described one technique for calculating the probability of default, which was to use a cash-flow model in which the cash flows for a project company changed according to different macroeconomic conditions. This approach can also be used to calculate the loss from a portfolio of projects. The key is to feed the same scenario into each model in parallel, then calculate the loss for each project and sum the losses to get the portfolio's loss in that scenario. This is discussed in "Risk Measurement for Project Finance Guarantees," Marrison, C.I., *The Journal of Project Finance*, Volume 7, Number 2, pp. 43–53, 2001, and illustrated in Figure 21-6.

UNIFIED SIMULATION MODEL

From the discussions of the different types of models, you probably got the sense that there were several recurring themes and that, at some level, the models must be similar. A nice discussion of the differences and similarities between the analytic versions of the covariance, actuarial, and Merton models is given in Koyluoglu, Ugur and Hickman, Andrew, "Reconcilable Differences," *Risk*, October 1998, pp. 56–62.

For the simulation models, the underlying principles are so similar that they can all be combined into one model. It is relatively easy to build a model that simultaneously creates correlated scenarios for equity indices, macroeconomic variables (e.g., GDP, FX, inflation), and other market variables (e.g., oil prices, implied volatility).

FIGURE 21-6

Calculation of Portfolio Losses Using a Macroeconomic Model and Cash-Flow Models

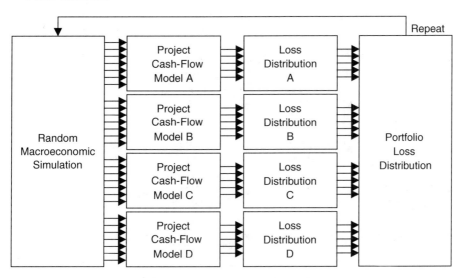

The equity indices can be fed into the Merton model, the macrovariables can be fed into the macrodefault model, and the macrovariables and market variables can be fed into the cash-flow model. The changes in the market variables can also be used to estimate the exposure amount for derivatives, and can even be used to drive changes in the value of the traded instruments and ALM portfolio. This combines credit risk with market risk.

You can use this unified approach to bring together results for risks that have been modeled in different ways. For example, it is usually easiest to model the defaults of retail customers and small businesses using the logistic regression of the macrodefault model. For large, publicly traded companies, it is more accurate to use the Merton approach, and for project finance deals, it is best to use the cash-flow approach.

Obviously, for market risks, the approach is completely different than for credit risk because we use Value-at-Risk (VaR). However, even VaR can be driven by the Monte Carlo simulation of macroeconomic factors and market rates.

The key is to create a single scenario in which the changes in all the variables are correlated (typically using Eigenvalue decomposition). That single scenario is fed separately into each portfolio model. Each model holds a different part of the portfolio and gives the loss for that part of the portfolio. The overall loss in that scenario is the sum of the losses in each model. The structure of the unified model is illustrated in Figure 21-7.

FIGURE 21-7

Structure of a Unified Simulation Model

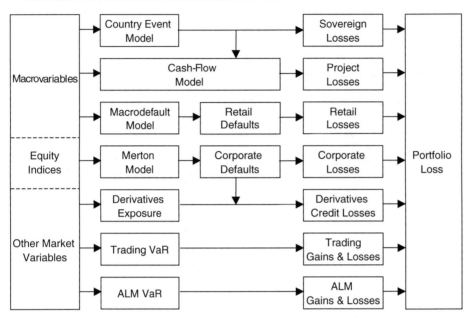

SUMMARY

In this chapter, we completed our discussion of the common approaches used to quantify the risk in credit portfolios. Having established the amount of capital consumed by credit risk, we now use that result in calculating the risk-adjusted return on capital for loans.

NOTES

1. Credit Suisse Financial Products, "CreditRisk+: A Credit Risk Management Framework," 1997.

2. Kealhoffer, Stephen, "Managing Default Risk in Derivative Portfolios," in *Derivative Credit Risk: Advances in Measurement and Management*, Renaissance Risk Publications, London, 1995.

3. Gupton, Greg, Christopher Finger, and Mickey Bhatia, "CreditMetrics Technical Document," Morgan Guaranty Trust Co., 1997.

4. Wilson, Tom, "Portfolio Credit Risk," September 1997 (Part I) and October 1997 (Part II).

5. In Excel this can be done using the command "IF (RAND()<P,1,0)".

CHAPTER 22

Risk-Adjusted Performance and Pricing for Loans

INTRODUCTION

We have spent the last few chapters discussing methods for calculating the expected loss and economic capital required for credit risks. Economic capital is useful for identifying large risks and setting the total amount of capital to be held by the bank, but when deciding whether to carry out a transaction, the bank is not only concerned about the risk, it is also interested in profitability relative to that risk. In Chapter 2, we discussed the concepts of risk-adjusted return on capital (RAROC) and shareholder valued added (SVA). In this chapter, we briefly review those concepts for loans. In Chapter 2, we implicitly only discussed RAROC for a transaction that happens over a single time period, e.g., a year. However, banks often grant multiyear loans, so the second half of this chapter discusses the application of RAROC over multiple years.

RISK-ADJUSTED PERFORMANCE OVER ONE YEAR

In Chapter 2, we defined RAROC to be the expected net risk-adjusted profit divided by the economic capital required to support the transaction:

$$RAROC = \frac{ENP}{EC}$$

The return on the transaction is the net increase in value. For a loan, the expected net profit is the interest income on the loan, plus any fees (F), minus interest to be paid on debt, minus operating costs (OC), and minus the expected loss (EL).

The interest income on the loan asset is the initial loan amount (A_0), multiplied by the interest rate on the loan (r_A). The interest to be paid on the debt is the amount of debt (D_0), multiplied by the interest rate on the debt (r_D). The amount of debt required is the loan amount minus the economic capital. The RAROC equation for a loan is therefore as follows:

$$RAROC = \frac{A_0 r_A + F - D_0 r_D - OC - EL}{EC}$$

$$= \frac{A_0 r_A + F - (A_0 - EC)r_D - OC - EL}{EC}$$

The term $EC\, r_D$ is sometimes called the "capital benefit" because it is a reduction in the debt interest charge because part of the loan is funded by capital.

The equation above determines the RAROC based on the risk and the expected income. Alternatively, for a new loan, we can fix the RAROC equal to the hurdle rate (H), and calculate the required fees and spread:

$$A_0 r_A + F = (A_0 - EC)r_D + OC + EL + H \times EC$$

Another twist to the RAROC equation is to calculate the SVA, which is defined as the expected net profit, minus the required return on capital:

$$SVA = ENP - H \times EC$$

$$= [A_0 r_A + F - (A_0 - EC)r_D - OC - EL] - H \times EC$$

To clarify these concepts, let us consider an example. Consider our previous example of a loan of $100 for 1 year to a company rated BBB with the following assumptions:

- The collateral is such that the loss in the event of default (LIED) is 30% with no uncertainty.
- The average default correlation with the rest of the portfolio is 3%.
- The capital multiplier for the portfolio is 6.

Using the covariance-portfolio approach, we calculate the EL for this loan to be $0.066:

$$EL = \$100 \times 30\% \times 0.22\% = \$0.066$$

The UL is $1.41, and the UL contribution is $0.24.

$$UL = \$100 \times 30\% \times \sqrt{0.22\% - 0.22\%^2} = \$1.41$$

$$ULC = \sqrt{3\%} \times \$1.41 = \$0.24$$

With a capital multiplier of 6, the economic capital for this loan is $1.46:

$$EC = 6 \times \$0.24 = \$1.46$$

We now know the risk characteristics of the loan, but to calculate RAROC, we also need the income and costs. Let us assume the following:

- The interbank rate for one-year debt is 5% (r_D).
- The customer is being charged 6.5% interest (r_A).
- The operating costs are $1 ($OC$).

We can now calculate that the RAROC is 35%:

$$RAROC = \frac{\$100 \times 6.5\% - (\$100 - \$1.46) \times 5\% - \$1 - \$0.066}{\$1.46} = 35\%$$

If we assume a pretax hurdle rate of 25%, the SVA is $0.13:

$$SVA = [\$100 \times 6.5\% - (\$100 - \$1.46) \times 5\% - \$1 - \$0.066] - 25\% \times \$1.46$$

RISK-ADJUSTED PERFORMANCE OVER MULTIPLE YEARS

In the analyses above, we defined RAROC to be simply the expected net profit divided by the economic capital:

$$RAROC = \frac{ENP}{EC}$$

For a one-year loan, this is quite adequate, and as we saw, it is relatively easy to calculate. The multiyear case is more complicated for several reasons:

- Over time, the probability of the company defaulting changes, as predicted by the migration matrices in Chapter 18. This affects the required economic capital, and therefore the required debt.
- After one or more years, there is the possibility that the loan will have defaulted, thus slightly reducing the expected value of the costs and interest income.
- The outstanding amount may vary over time, for example, if the loan is amortizing.
- Over time, the collateral value may change as a percentage of the exposure amount, thereby changing the LIED.

To deal with these effects, we need a more subtle definition of RAROC.

Redefinition of RAROC

We can define RAROC to be the internal rate of return on the set of expected cash flows. The internal rate of return (*irr*) is the discount rate that sets the net present value of a series of cash flows (C_t) to equal zero:

$$0 = \sum_t \frac{C_t}{(1 + irr)^t}$$

To see the connection with the earlier definition of RAROC, consider that at the beginning of the period we invest the economic capital. Thus, the cash flow at the $t = 0$ equals the economic capital. At the end of the period ($t = 1$), we expect to receive the capital back, plus the additional net expected profit. The *irr* equation is then as follows:

$$0 = -EC + \frac{EC + ENP}{1 + irr}$$

We can rearrange this expression to take us back to the original definition of RAROC for a one-year loan:

$$EC(1 + irr) = EC + ENP$$

$$irr = \frac{ENP}{EC}$$

As a further step toward calculating multiyear RAROC, let us again look at the one-year case but more carefully decomposing the cash flows. This is a complex way to get to the same result we already have, but it gives a good introduction into the process we use to calculate RAROC over multiple years.

At the beginning of the year, the bank pays the customer the amount of the loan (A). To fund this loan, the bank will invest some of its economic capital, and will raise some debt (D). The net cash flow to the bank at the beginning of the year is $D - A$. This is a negative amount equal to the economic capital that has effectively been paid to the customer.

At the end of the year, the bank will pay back the debt (D) with interest (Dr_D), and it will have paid some operating costs (OC). If the customer does not default, the bank will receive the principle amount (A) with interest (Ar_A). If the customer does default, the bank can sell the defaulted loan and receive the recovery amount, R. The expected cash flow from the customer is calculated from these two possibilities weighted by the probability of default (p):

$$\text{Expected Payment} = A(1 + r_A)(1 - p) + Rp$$

These cash flows are summarized in Table 22-1 and illustrated in Figure 22-1. In this figure, the central line represents the bank, and the arrows indicate flows into or out of the bank. The flows to the customer are above the line, and the flows to the capital markets and internal expenses are below the line. The cash flows from the customer at the end of the year are dashed because they are alternatives depending on default.

We put these expected cash flows into the equation for the internal rate of return:

$$0 = (D - A) + \frac{[A(1 + r_A)(1 - p) + Rp] - [D(1 + r_D) + OC]}{(1 + irr)}$$

We can replace D with $A - EC$:

$$0 = (A - EC - A) + \frac{[A(1 + r_A)(1 - p) + Rp] - [(A - EC)(1 + r_D) + OC]}{(1 + irr)}$$

TABLE 22-1

Expected Cash Flows for a One-Year Loan

Year	Cash Flows Received	Cash Flows Paid Out
0	D	A
1	$A(1 + r_A)(1 - p) + R(p)$	$D(1 + r_D) + OC$

FIGURE 22-1

Illustration of Cash-Flows for a One-Year Loan

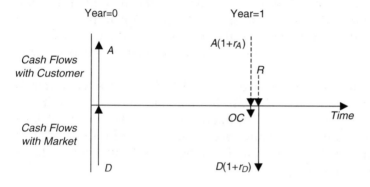

And rearrange as follows to get the original one-year equation for RAROC:

$$EC = \frac{[A(1 + r_A)(1 - p) + Rp] - [(A - EC)(1 + r_D) + OC]}{(1 + irr)}$$

$$1 + irr = \frac{[A(1 + r_A)(1 - p) + Rp] - [(A - EC)(1 + r_D) + OC]}{EC}$$

$$1 + irr = \frac{A + Ar_A - (A - R)p - Ar_Ap - A + EC - (A - EC)r_D - OC}{EC}$$

$$irr = \frac{Ar_A - EL - Ar_Ap - (A - EC)r_D - OC}{EC}$$

The final step in this arrangement recognizes that $(A - R)p$ is the probability of default multiplied by the loss given default (in dollars), which is the definition of EL.

Compared with the original definition of RAROC, we have a small extra term: $-Ar_Ap$. This is the amount of interest income that is expected to be lost due to default and was neglected in the original calculation of EL.

RAROC for a Two-Year Loan

Using this framework, we are now ready to get into the algebra for the case of a two-year loan. For a two-year loan, two effects are important: the changing amount of economic capital, and survivorship.

For a two-year loan, the percentage of capital that we expect to hold will change in the second year due to the changing marginal probability of default from p_1 in the first year to p_2 in the second, as predicted by the migration matrices in Chapter 18. The change in capital has the effect of changing the amount of debt required from one year to the next. For clarity, we assume that all the first-year debt (D_1) is paid back at the end of the first year, and then a new amount of debt (D_2) is raised at the same interest rate, but with an amount depending on the new capital.

We also need to include the survivorship effects. The survivorship effects arise because if the loan defaults in the first year, there will be no need to raise debt or pay operating costs in the second year. We therefore multiply the second year's debt and operating costs by one minus the probability of a default in the first year. Similarly, if the loan defaults in the first year, it cannot default in the second year.

Let us use X to denote cash received by the bank, and Y for cash paid out as in Table 22-2 and Figure 22-2. The cash flows at the start of the first year are the same as before.

The cash flows at the end of the first year do not have a repayment of the principal A, but do have the possible payment of the amount that would be recovered if the loan defaulted in the first year, R_1. At the end of the first year, there is also an amount $D_2(1 - p_1)$ that is the debt to be raised to cover the loan in the second year, multiplied by the probability of surviving through the first year. The cash flows at the end of the second year are almost the same as the cash flows at the end of the one-year example in Table 22-1, except that all the terms are multiplied by $(1 - p_1)$. If the loan was amortizing, we would include the expected repayments of principal and the consequent changes in capital and debt.

Once we have established the set of expected cash flows, the RAROC is simply found by solving for the internal rate of return.

TABLE 22-2

Expected Cash Flows for a Two-Year Loan

Year	Cash Flows Received	Cash Flows Paid Out
0	$X_0 = D_1$	$Y_0 = A$
1	$X_1 = A(r_A)(1 - p_1) + R_1(p_1) + D_2(1 - p_1)$	$Y_1 = D_1(1 + r_D) + OC_1$
2	$X_2 = A(1 + r_A)(1 - p_1)(1 - p_2) + R_2(1 - p_1)(p_2)$	$Y_2 = D_2(1 - p_1)(1 + r_D) + OC_2(1 - p_1)$

FIGURE 22-2

Illustration of Cash Flows for a Two-Year Loan

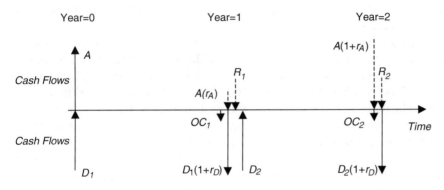

(In Microsoft's Excel spreadsheet you can use the command "irr()").

$$0 = \frac{X_0 - Y_0}{(1 + irr)^0} + \frac{X_1 - Y_1}{(1 + irr)^1} + \frac{X_2 - Y_2}{(1 + irr)^2}$$

The internal rate of return found from this equation is the RAROC for the loan. If we are dealing with a new loan and want to find the spread to be charged, the internal rate of return is fixed equal to the hurdle rate, and we solve the equation for r_A, which is lengthy but not difficult.

As an example, let us reconsider the loan to a BBB company. Let us keep all other factors the same in the second year as in the first except for the probability of default and the LIED. Assume that the probability of default increases from 0.22% in the first year to 0.32% in the second year (as predicted by the migration matrix in Table 18-5), and the LIED increases from 30% to 40% because of some deterioration in the collateral value. The calculation of the cash flows are shown in Table 22-3 and Table 22-4. In this case, a loan with a 6.5% interest-rate will have a RAROC of 26%. We would need to charge 6.65% to bring the RAROC back up to 34%.

SUMMARY

In this chapter, we reviewed the concepts of risk-adjusted return on capital (RAROC) and shareholder value added (SVA), and applied them to measuring the profitability of loans. Now, we shift focus slightly and move from a discussion of economic capital to a discussion of regulatory capital.

TABLE 22-3

Calculation of Parameters for a Two-Year Loan

Parameter	Year1	Year2
Exposure (A)	$100	$100
Interest Charge (r_A)	6.5%	6.5%
Probability of Default (p)	0.0022	0.0032
LIED	30%	40%
Recovery ($R = A(1 - \text{LIED})$)	$70.00	$60.00
EL	$0.066	$0.13
UL	$1.41	$2.26
Rho	3%	3%
ULC	$0.24	$0.39
Capital Multiplier	6	6
Economic Capital	$1.46	$2.35
Debt	$8.54	$97.65
Cost of Debt (r_D)	5%	5%
Operating Cost	$1.00	$1.00

TABLE 22-4

Calculation of Cash Flows for a Two-Year Loan

Year	X	Y	Difference
0	$98.54	$100.00	$(1.46)
1	$104.08	$104.47	$(0.39)
2	$106.12	$103.31	$2.81
Internal Rate of Return			26.0%

Regulatory Capital for Credit Risk

INTRODUCTION

In the previous chapters, we have discussed methodologies that a bank can use to get the best possible estimate of its required economic capital. Here, we discuss regulatory capital and specifically the recommendations of the Basel Committee on Banking Supervision.

In our previous discussion, the required economic capital was interpreted as the minimum amount of capital that a bank should hold to maintain its desired debt rating. In the economic-capital framework, the amount of capital available is the net present value or market value of the assets minus the liabilities.

As in the economic-capital framework, regulators are concerned with the difference between required capital and available capital. The required regulatory capital depends on the regulator's assessment of the bank's risks. The available capital is the regulator's assessment of the current net value of the bank. It is calculated from the value of the assets minus the liabilities, according to accounting principles. As we will see, the concepts of economic capital and regulatory capital are slowly converging, and by 2006 they should be almost, but not completely, identical.

In this chapter, we focus on credit risk and discuss the history of the capital accords, define the regulatory capital more closely, and discuss the implications of the New Capital Accord proposed in January 2001. We will conclude with a discussion of managing the differences between regulatory and economic capital.

THE BASEL COMMITTEE

The Basel Committee on Banking Supervision was established in the mid-1980s. It is a committee of national banking regulators, such as the Bank of England and the Federal Reserve Board. It has representatives from 12 industrial countries:

Belgium, Canada, France, Germany, Italy, Japan, Luxembourg, the Netherlands, Sweden, Switzerland, the United Kingdom, and the United States. The committee meets in the offices of the Bank for International Settlements in Basel, Switzerland, and is therefore often referred to as the "BIS Committee," although strictly speaking, the BIS and the Basel Committee are separate entities.

The purpose of the committee is to set common standards for banking regulations and to improve the stability of the international banking system. Its publications can be classified into 3 categories: research papers, consultative documents, and accords. They are available at www.bis.org. The consultative documents suggest new guidelines for accords and allow industry feedback before the publication of a formal accord. The accords lay out the rules to be followed by the national regulators in such matters as setting the minimum capital requirements. The accords are binding, but they give national regulators significant leeway in how they interpret and implement certain parts of the accords.

Although the committee only has 12 formal members, the guidelines have been adopted by regulators in many other countries. These countries adopt the accords because they want to ensure that they are recognized as having a banking system that meets international standards.

THE HISTORY OF THE CAPITAL ACCORDS

The most important publications by the Basel Committee have been the 1988 capital accord,[1] the 1996 amendment to the accord,[2] and the consultative document issued in 2001 proposing the New Capital Accord.[3]

The 1988 accord defined Tier I and Tier II capital and set minimum standards for the amount of capital to be held against credit risks. The 1996 accord required additional capital to be held against market risks, and for the first time, allowed banks to measure their own riskiness using internal models, namely Value-at-Risk calculators. The 2001 document suggests a much more refined measurement of credit risks based on methodologies similar to economic capital. It also proposes holding capital specifically for operating risks. The 2001 proposals do not change the definition of Tier I and Tier II available capital; the measurement of market risks is unchanged, and the measurement of credit risk for derivatives is unchanged from the 1988 Accord. No attempt is made to set capital specifically for "interest-rate risk in the banking book," i.e., asset/liability (ALM) risks.

THE 1988 ACCORD ON CREDIT-RISK CAPITAL

The 1988 accord was motivated largely by the low amount of available capital kept by Japanese banks in relation to the risks in their lending portfolios. This low ratio was believed to allow the Japanese banks to make loans at "unfairly" low rates. This was because Japanese depositors and shareholders were not demanding high returns to compensate for the increased risk.

The 1988 accord required that all banks should hold available capital equal to at least 8% of their risk-weighted assets (RWA). Let us first discuss the accord's concept of available capital, and then the calculation of RWA.

Definition of Available Regulatory Capital

If all banks were able to reliably measure the market value of their assets and liabilities, then the definition of capital would be simply the difference between the value of assets and liabilities. However, it is very difficult to get an accurate measure of the true value of illiquid assets such as loans. As a practical alternative, available capital is defined according to accounting measures that are commonly available in all countries.

To explain the calculation of available capital, we must first define some accounting terms. Accounting frameworks start from the face value of liabilities and assets. They then make several deductions and additions to estimate the true value.

The value of the assets is initially estimated as the sum of the face value of the assets (A), minus specific provisions (SP) for assets that have defaulted or are considered to be close to default:

$$Balance\ Sheet\ Assets = A - SP$$

In addition to the assets formally declared on the balance sheet, there may also be revaluations (RV) and undisclosed profits (UP). Revaluations mostly apply to long-term investments such as equities and real estate. The *revaluation* is a recognition that the market value of an asset has increased above its initial face value. The revaluation may appear as an item in the formal balance sheet statement, or it may be in a footnote "off balance sheet." *Undisclosed profits* are allowed in some countries. They are retained earnings that the bank's management prefers to treat as a hidden reserve, rather than publish as additional available assets. The estimate of the total assets can therefore be defined as follows:

$$Total\ Assets = A - SP + RV + UP$$

The liabilities have two parts: the actual liabilities, and accounting partitions that divide up the difference between the balance-sheet asset value and the liability value. The difference is divided into three major components: general provisions, equity, and reserves. *General provisions* (GP) are partitions to account for future possible loan losses, and correspond roughly to the expected loss that we calculate in the economic-capital framework. *Equity* (E) is the face value of the bank's shares at the time they were sold. The remaining difference is called *reserves* (R):

$$Balance\ Sheet\ Assets - Liabilities = GP + E + R$$

The liabilities can be divided into hard debt (*HD*) and soft debt (*SD*):

$$Liabilities - SD = HD$$

Hard debt is the most common form. If the bank does not pay its hard debt, it is considered to have defaulted. The *soft debt* comes in the form of special quasidebt instruments that are halfway between debt and equity; for example, they may be allowed to pay no interest for many years if the bank is unprofitable, but pay very high interest-rates whenever shareholders receive dividends.

From these concepts, we can estimate the net book value of assets in excess of the hard debt:

$$Net\ Value = Total\ Assets - HD$$
$$= (Balance\ Sheet\ Assets + RV + UP) - (Liabilities - SD)$$
$$= RV + UP + SD + (Balance\ Sheet\ Assets - Liabilities)$$
$$= RV + UP + SD + GP + E + R$$

From these concepts, the Basel Committee derived their requirements for the minimum amount of capital to be held. The net value was divided into two parts, or *Tiers*. *Tier I capital* consists of equity and reserves. *Tier II capital* consists of revaluations, undeclared profits, soft debt, and general provisions:

$$Tier\ I\ Capital = E + R$$
$$Tier\ II\ Capital = RV + UP + SD + GP$$

The 1988 accord required that the sum of Tier I and Tier II capital should be equal to 8% of the risk-weighted assets (*RWA*), and that the Tier I capital alone must be at least 4% of RWA. A common way of expressing the strength of a bank is its capital adequacy ratio, defined as the available capital divided by the required capital:

$$Capital\ Adequacy\ Ratio = \frac{Tier\ I\ Capital + Tier\ II\ Capital}{8\% \times RWA}$$

Now let us turn our attention to the calculation of RWA.

The Calculation of Required Capital in the 1988 Accord

The risk-weighted assets is the sum of the face value of all assets, weighted according to the asset's credit risk:

$$\$RWA = \sum w_i\ \$A_i$$

In the 1988 accord, a loan to a private company or individual was considered to have a risk weighting of 100%. Other assets were given reduced weights according to their approximate credit risks as shown in Table 23-1.

The 1988 accord also specified weights for the credit risk of traded and off-balance-sheet assets. For assets such as lines of credit and forward agreements, the risk weighting corresponded to the risk of the underlying company or asset, typically

TABLE 23-1

Credit-Risk Weights Under the 1988 Accord

Instrument	Risk Weight
Cash	0%
Loans to governments in their own currencies	0%
Loans to any OECD government	0%
Loans to OECD banks	20%
Short-term loans to non-OECD banks	20%
Housing mortgages	50%
Loans to private companies and individuals	100%
Long-term loans to non-OECD banks	100%
Loans to non-OECD governments, foreign currency	100%
All other assets	100%

100%. For derivatives such as interest-rate swaps, the accord gave the option of counting the risk either as a fixed percentage of the notional amount, or as 100% of the current mark-to-market value plus an "add-on," which was calculated as a percentage of the notional amount. The mark-to-market plus add-on is now the most common approach for major banks. The "add-ons" are shown in Table 23-2.

This simplified counting of risk in the 1988 accord was required so that it could be implemented easily and clearly by all banks. It had the great advantage of improving the capital adequacy of banks and is often used by less-sophisticated banks to calculate a form of risk-adjusted profitability, namely the return on RWA.

As the economic-capital methodology has developed over the last decade, banks have asked their regulators to use more-accurate methods in assessing the capital to be held. This has led to the introduction of the New Basel Capital Accord.

TABLE 23-2

Add-On Values to Calculate the Risk Weight for Derivatives

Residual Maturity	Interest-Rate Contracts	Exchange-Rate Contracts
Less than one year	0%	1.0%
One year and over	0.5%	5.0%

THE NEW BASEL CAPITAL ACCORD

The suggested form of the new accord was published in January 2001 to obtain comments from the banking industry. The final accord will be implemented around 2006. The new accord retains the same concepts of RWA and Tier I and Tier II available capital, but it changes the method for calculating RWA.

The new accord has three "Pillars:" measurement of the minimum capital requirements, supervisory review, and market discipline. The measurement of capital gives many formulas to replace the simple calculations of the 1988 accord. The *supervisory review* pillar requires regulators to ensure that the bank has effective risk management, and requires the regulators to increase the required capital if they think that the risks are not being adequately measured. The *market discipline pillar* requires banks to disclose large amounts of information so that depositors and investors can decide for themselves the riskiness of the bank and require commensurately high interest-rates and return on capital. We will discuss each pillar in turn, but we concentrate on the measurement and data requirements.

Measurement of the Minimum Capital Requirements

The accord allows banks to calculate their required regulatory capital using one of two approaches: the standardized approach or the internal ratings-based approach.

The Standardized Approach

The standardized approach is more complex than the 1988 accord and has sections dealing with many specific cases, but the broad intention is that risk weights should be set according to the credit rating of the customer. In the standardized approach, the credit rating must be made by an organization outside the bank such as a credit rating agency, e.g., Standard & Poor's. One set of suggested risk weights for governments and banks is shown in Table 23-3. Table 23-4 shows the risk weights for exposures to corporations.

There are two significant implications of setting capital according to credit ratings. It puts great pressure on the rating agencies, and it requires the bank to have a system that can track and retrieve the rating for every loan. Despite these difficulties, it is a great advance over the simplicity of the 1988 weightings.

The approach also allows an additional reduction in RWA for assets that are collateralized by financial instruments, e.g., bonds and equities.

In its most basic form, the risk weight with collateral is calculated from the initial risk weight, the exposure (E), and the adjusted value of the collateral (C_A):

$$RWA_C = RWA \frac{E - C_A}{E}$$

The adjusted value of the collateral is calculated by taking its current value (C) and dividing it by "haircut" factors that trim off a little of the value according to the

TABLE 23-3

Risk Weights for Governments and Banks Under the New Standardized Approach

Grade	AAA to AA−	A+ to A−	BBB+ to BBB−	BB+ to B−	Below B−	Unrated
Governments	0%	20%	50%	100%	150%	100%
Banks	20%	50%	100%	100%	150%	100%

TABLE 23-4

Risk Weights for Corporate Exposures Under the New Standardized Approach

Grade	AAA to AA−	A+ to A−	BBB+ to BB−	Below BB−	Unrated
Corporations	20%	50%	100%	150%	100%

volatility of the exposure (H_E), the volatility in the collateral value (H_C), and any exchange-rate volatility (H_{FX}):

$$C_A = \frac{C}{1 + H_E + H_C + H_{FX}}$$

For cash, the haircut is zero. For bonds, the typical haircut is between 1% and 12% depending on the remaining maturity and credit grade of the bond. For equities, the haircut is between 20% and 30%. The haircut for exchange-rate volatility (H_{FX}) is 8%.

As an example, if we were lending a "main index" equity, the exposure haircut (H_E) would be 20%. If as collateral we took a BBB-rated, 4-year government bond, the collateral haircut (H_C) would be 3%. If the bond was in a different currency than the equity, we would add an additional haircut (H_{FX}) of 8%. The adjusted collateral value would therefore be 76% of the current value:

$$\frac{1}{1 + H_E + H_C + H_{FX}} = \frac{1}{1 + 20\% + 3\% + 8\%} = 76\%$$

The standardized approach is relatively easy to implement, but gives inaccurate assessments of risk when compared with the economic-capital measures that we discussed in previous chapters.

The Internal Ratings-Based Approach

For those banks with the tools in place to measure risk more finely, the new Basel accord will allow banks the option of going beyond the standardized approach to measure credit risk using their own internal models. To encourage more sophisticated risk measurement, the Basel Committee intends that the regulatory capital for the internal ratings-based (IRB) approach should in general be less conservative than the standardized approach. This means that if banks choose to go to the trouble of using the IRB approach, they should expect to reduce the amount of required regulatory capital.

At its core, the IRB approach is very similar to economic capital. For loans to banks, governments, and corporations, the starting point is an equation that gives the benchmark risk weight (*BRW*). The BRW is the risk weight for a $100 loan of 3 years' maturity and a loss given default of 50%. The BRW is specified to be a function of the probability of default (*P*):

$$BRW = 976.5 \times \Phi\left[1.118 \times \Phi^{-1}(P) + 1.288\right] \times \left[1 + \frac{0.047(1 - P)}{P^{0.44}}\right]$$

Here, Φ is the cumulative Normal distribution, and Φ^{-1} is its inverse. In Excel, these are given by Normdist(x,0,1,1) and Norminv(x,0,1). For a standard loan, the regulatory capital will be 8% of BRW, multiplied by the dollar amount of the loan, divided by 100.

Table 23-5 compares the capital required by the IRB approach with the capital required by the standardized approach. This table is constructed by approximately mapping the probability of default to the implied rating, and then calculating the standardized capital from 8% multiplied by Table 23-4. The results show that for highly rated companies, the IRB approach will tend to give a lower capital. However, for lowly rated companies, the standardized approach gives lower capital. This table is for the benchmark loan and does not take into account the possibility of a loss given default other than 50%.

We can also compare the regulatory capital with economic capital. Notice that the calculation of BRW is very similar to our earlier calculation of the economic capital using the covariance credit-portfolio approach. In Chapter 20, we calculated the unexpected loss contribution of a loan to the portfolio based on its stand-alone UL and its average correlation with the rest of the portfolio:

$$ULC \equiv \sqrt{\bar{\rho}}\,UL$$

$$UL = LGD\sqrt{P - P^2}$$

The required economic capital attributed to a loan was shown to be a simple multiple of ULC. Let us conservatively estimate that the capital multiplier is 8:

$$EC = 8 \times \sqrt{\bar{\rho}} \times LGD\sqrt{P - P^2}$$

TABLE 23-5

Approximate Comparison of Regulatory Capital Required by the Standardized and Internal Ratings-Based Approaches

Probability of Default	Capital Required by the IRB Approach (Benchmark Loan)	Rating Implied by the Probability of Default	Capital Required by the Standardized Approach
0.03%	1.1	AAA/AA	1.6
0.05%	1.5	A	4.0
0.10%	2.3	A	4.0
0.20%	3.6	BBB	8.0
0.40%	5.6	BBB	8.0
0.50%	6.4	BBB	8.0
0.70%	8.0	BB	8.0
1.00%	10.0	BB	8.0
2.00%	15.4	BB	8.0
3.00%	19.7	BB	8.0
5.00%	26.5	B	12.0
10.00%	38.6	B	12.0
15.00%	47.0	B	12.0
20.00%	50.0	CCC	12.0

Furthermore, assume that the customer has an asset correlation of 40% with the rest of the portfolio, then from Table 20-4 we can read off the default correlations. If we assume that the average loan in the portfolio has a probability of default of 100 basis points, we can see from Table 20-4 that a loan with a 10-basis-point probability of default will have an average default correlation of 4.3%. Using this information, we can compare the regulatory capital and the estimate of the economic capital as in Table 23-6. With the mildly conservative assumptions of a high capital multiplier and a high asset correlation, the economic capital comes out to be virtually the same as the regulatory capital.

In this table, the dollar amounts are with reference to a $100 loan. Notice that the formula for BRW implicitly contains the information about the correlation of the assets with the rest of the portfolio. This was a deliberate decision by the Basel Committee because they did not feel that the credit-risk portfolio methodologies were sufficiently reliable to use them for setting regulatory capital. The major problem is the difficulty of back-testing credit-portfolio models. For a further discussion, see the

TABLE 23-6

Comparison of Regulatory and Economic Capital Results

Probability of Default	Benchmark Risk Weight	IRB Capital ($)	Stand-Alone UL ($)	Default Correlation	Economic Capital ($)
0.03%	14	1.1	0.9	2.0%	1.0
0.05%	19	1.5	1.1	3.2%	1.6
0.1%	29	2.3	1.6	4.3%	2.6
0.2%	45	3.6	2.2	4.7%	3.9
0.4%	70	5.6	3.2	5.6%	6.0
0.5%	81	6.4	3.5	6.0%	6.9
0.7%	100	8.0	4.2	6.9%	8.7
1.0%	125	10.0	5.0	7.7%	11.0
2.0%	192	15.4	7.0	8.0%	15.8
3.0%	246	19.7	8.5	8.3%	19.6
5.0%	331	26.5	10.9	8.9%	25.9
10.0%	482	38.6	15.0	10.3%	38.5
15.0%	588	47.0	17.9	10.3%	45.8
20.0%	625	50.0	20.0	10.3%	51.3

committee's survey paper: "Credit Risk Modelling: Current Practices and Applications," Basel Committee on Banking Supervision, April 1999.

Once the BRW has been calculated for the standard loan, the accord allows it to be modified depending on the maturity of the loan and its estimated loss given default. This gives the risk weight for the particular loan:

$$RW = BRW \times \frac{LGD}{50} \times [1 + b(P)(M - 3)]$$

Here, $b(P)$ is a function of the probability, and M is the effective maturity in years. The final step in calculating the risk weight for the asset is to multiply it by the dollar amount of the exposure at default (divided by 100):

$$RWA = RW \times EAD$$

Once the RWA has been calculated for each asset, they are summed to get the RWA for the portfolio as a whole. Finally, the portfolio's total RWA is adjusted to account for any concentrations and large loans. This "granularity" adjustment requires summation involving the probability of default, LGD, and EAD of every loan in the portfolio. Importantly, to carry out this adjustment, the bank needs to know the total exposure to each borrower. This is difficult to accomplish because one company may have slightly different names in different geographies or be recorded differently in different branches of the bank.

To use the IRB approach, we need to know values for the probability of default, LGD, the EAD, and the effective maturity (*M*) for each loan. In estimating these parameters the accord allows for two levels of sophistication: the foundation IRB approach, and the advanced IRB approach.

In the *foundation approach*, the bank needs to specify only the probability of default. The values for all the other variables are specified in the accord or by the national regulator, depending on the type of collateral, whether there are associated guarantees or credit derivatives, and the type of credit exposure. For example, the exposure of a line of credit is set at the current disbursed amount, plus 75% of the remaining line. In the *advanced approach*, the bank may specify the LGD and EAD for each product.

The discussion above applies to exposures to governments, banks, and corporations. The procedure for retail exposures is similar, whereby customers are grouped into segments, and then a BRW equation is used to set the capital for each segment. However, the exact form of the BRW equation is still under discussion.

To be allowed to use the IRB approach, the bank must show that it has a reliable process for measuring and managing risk. Specifically, the bank must establish a credit-grading system with at least 6 buckets arranged such that no more than 30% of the portfolio falls in any one bucket. There must be separate grading systems to measure the probability of default and the loss given default. There must also be strong formal control and documentation over the use of models and data. Specifically, the models must be controlled by a group that is independent from the group who profits by making loans, and any changes to the models must be documented and justified.

To ensure that the models are performing well, their predictions must be regularly compared to the actual results. For example, the bank should collect information on all defaults and compare each loss given default with that predicted by the models at the time of granting the loan.

As proof that the bank fundamentally believes in the models that it is using to calculate the regulatory capital, the numbers must pass the "use test." The use test requires that any numbers (such as LGD) used in the calculation of the regulatory capital must also be used in the models that the bank uses to run its business, namely the pricing models and economic capital calculator.

Although economic capital is not directly used for the calculation of RWA, we will see that if the bank adopts the advanced IRB approach, it is required to disclose its economic capital as part of the market discipline pillar. This effectively means that any bank using the advanced IRB must also calculate economic capital.

Supervisory Review

The supervisory review pillar is a set of qualitative recommendations meant to fill any unforeseen gaps in the capital measurement pillar. It also seeks to ensure that the bank has a strong risk-management process and culture. It requires that the bank's board and senior management should be aware and approve of the risk-management process, and that the process should be comprehensive and reliable. Most of the details of the supervisory review are left to the national regulators.

Market Discipline

An important and potentially difficult part of the accord is the requirement to disclose information so that other capital-markets players can judge the bank's creditworthiness. This provides incentive for the bank's management to have sound risk management so they will not be charged high interest-rates when borrowing from other banks. The disclosures are expected to be semiannual or quarterly. The list below gives a sample of the information that a bank should disclose if it wants to use the advanced IRB approach.

- For each risk grade, the nominal exposure amount, the effect of collateral, and the weighted average maturity
- For each risk grade, the actual experience of losses compared with the predicted experience, and for LGD the standard deviation of losses
- A comparison of economic capital, actual capital, and minimum regulatory capital
- The risk-weighted assets per risk grade, including and excluding the effects of collateral, netting, guarantees, and credit derivatives

This disclosure is difficult for two main reasons: it requires large amounts of data collection, and it requires the bank to disclose information that it could consider proprietary or the source of competitive advantage. For example, a bank that has invested in sufficient information technology to predict default probabilities and losses accurately will have a competitive advantage when pricing and selecting new loans. Giving away such information will help other banks become equally selective.

IMPLEMENTING THE NEW ACCORD

There are five major steps that a bank must take to implement the new accord: save historical data, decide the best approach, understand the full data requirements, build models, and build a system to report the results.

Saving Historical Customer Data

The first step in implementing the new accord is to start building a set of historical data. The accord requires that probabilities of default should be based on five years of data, although when a bank first adopts the IRB, it may be allowed to use only two years of data. Without data, a bank limits its future options for adopting one of the IRB options and for building economic-capital models. The data does not initially need to be in a grand centralized database; it can even be on paper, so long as it exists somewhere and can be extracted later.

The types of data to be collected were discussed in Chapter 19. Data needs to be collected on the characteristics of the borrower at the initial time of application, the characteristics of the product (loan or line, type of collateral, seniority, etc.), and the ratings given at that time. Data should also be collected on any significant changes in the customer over time, such as a change in rating. For products with variable balances, such as lines of credit, the exposure should be tracked over time. Ideally, a snapshot should be taken of all customer data at the end of each year.

The data on the customer at the time of application can be used to make loan-application models and pricing models. The snapshot data can be used to make portfolio models to answer the question: given this portfolio at the beginning of the year, how much capital do I need to survive until the end of the year?

To create the models for probability of default, loss given default, and exposure at default, information must be captured on any customer that defaults. This information should include the date of default, the exposure at default, the timing and amount of any repayments, and if available, the trading price of the bond or loan before and after default. There must also be a mechanism for keying the default information back to the original customer information.

Deciding the Best Approach to Adopt

The bank must decide which approach it will aim to adopt: standardized, foundation IRB, or advanced IRB. Part of that decision can include a migration plan first to adopt one approach, then to evolve to another. The main factors in the decision should be as follows:

- How much cost and management effort will be required to implement the plan, given the bank's current systems?
- How much of the work overlaps with the work that will be required for the bank's current plans to calculate economic capital?
- What will be the saving in required regulatory capital under each approach, given the bank's portfolio?
- What is the significance of reducing required regulatory capital? Is the bank's current required economic capital far in excess of the regulatory capital?

- If the bank adopts a more advanced approach, it will be seen by the regulators and the rest of the banking industry as a sophisticated player. How important is this? Will it reduce the burden of regulatory oversight, or increase the bank's influence in setting regulatory policy? Will its reputation as a sophisticated bank help it attract more customers or increase its share price?
- If the required regulatory capital was reduced, would the bank be able to improve its credit rating?
- If the bank is seen as sophisticated, and has a high regulatory-capital ratio, will this significantly reduce the bank's cost of raising debt? If the bank raises most of its debt from financially unsophisticated retail depositors, the change in the debt-funding cost will be minimal. If most of the debt is from the interbank market, the change could be significant.
- How much sensitive information would the bank have to disclose? Would the use of that information aid competitors; e.g., could they use high-quality loss data in their models to compete more effectively against the bank?

Table 23-7 gives a comparison of some of the costs and benefits for the three approaches.

TABLE 23-7

Comparison of the Costs and Benefits from Adopting Each of the New Regulatory-Capital Approaches

	Costs	Benefits
Standardized Approach	• Need to collect external credit-rating information and link it to the exposure to each customer • Gives the bank the reputation of being unsophisticated • The effort used to build the reporting system may be wasted if the bank later adopts a more sophisticated approach • There will be regulatory pressure on major banks to go beyond the standardized approach	• Minimal effort required for implementation
Foundation Internal Ratings-Based Approach	• Systems required to gather historical customer and default data • Need to set up a well-documented credit-grading system • Need to know the total exposure to each company to calculate the granularity adjustment	• Possible reduction in required regulatory capital • For the proper running of a bank, most of these systems should be in place anyway • It is relatively easy to upgrade to the advanced IRB approach if desired

	• Possible increase in required capital if the portfolio contains many lowly rated companies • Need to collect and disclose detailed information on the composition of the portfolio and loss experience	• The bank will have a reasonable level of respect from regulators, customers, and other capital-market players
Advanced Internal Ratings-Based Approach	• Need to collect additional historical information on loss given default and exposure at default • Need to have well-documented data collection, model building, and reporting systems for these many additional models • Need to calculate the weighted average maturity of each loan in the current portfolio • Need to disclose large amounts of very detailed information that may impose a date-collection burden and be useful to competitors.	• There will be a good set of information for calculating economic capital and determining risk-adjusted profitability • The bank will have a high level of respect from regulators, customers, and other capital-market players

Understanding the Full Data Requirements

The data requirements fall into three categories: historical data needed to build the models, live data needed to calculate the required capital, and data needed for disclosure. The data needed for disclosure is very extensive, especially for the IRB approaches, and will only be summarized here.

For the standardized approach, to calculate the capital, the bank needs only to collect exposure and rating information for each of its customers. The rating information must be from standardized sources and be well documented.

In addition to calculating the capital, the bank is required, under pillar three, to disclose the composition of its portfolio in terms of its total exposure to each geography, industry, and type of product (e.g., loans or lines). The bank also needs to be able to disclose the maturity distribution, e.g., what percentage of the loans is for more than one year.

For the foundation IRB approach, the capital is calculated based on the probability of default, which requires the bank to have a system or model to link customer characteristics to default probabilities. If models are used, they will be constructed based on historical default data, which the bank must collect or obtain from an external source. To calculate the granularity adjustment, the bank must know the total exposure to each customer, which means having unified customer codes across the bank. If the bank chooses to reduce its capital by counting collateral, it must also collect collateral information for each loan.

In addition to calculating the capital, the bank must disclose the exposure amount in each probability grade and the effects of any collateral adjustments. It must also disclose information on the performance of its models by publishing the number of loans in each probability grade that later went on to default.

In the advanced approach, the bank must collect and disclose the same information on LDG and EDA. It must also publish statistics on the LGD and EAD that it experienced. Significantly, it must also publish its estimate of economic capital, which implies that the bank must also have a portfolio model such as the ones discussed in Chapter 20 and Chapter 21.

Building Models

The historical data is used to create models that link borrower and product characteristics to expected probabilities of default, LGD, and EAD. Building the models proceeds in the same way as discussed in Chapter 19. The main difference is that the risk-management organization needs to document all the processes used to create the models. The documentation should ensure that the models are repeatable, independent of individuals, and not open to manipulation. Also, there will be little room to make ad hoc adjustments that are based on the model builder's intuition.

Reporting

The reporting process must pull together all the elements described above. This will typically require that a person in each business unit should be designated to be in charge of the data-collection effort to aggregate results for that unit. In consultation with the local regulators, a schedule for reporting will need to be established. For the pillar-three disclosures, this will be semiannual or quarterly. For the calculation of required and available capital, this will be quarterly or monthly. The whole reporting process should be documented with guidelines to ensure that the reporting can be repeated even if individuals change.

MANAGING THE DIFFERENCES BETWEEN REGULATORY AND ECONOMIC CAPITAL

In this section, we discuss what the bank should and can do if the required regulatory capital is significantly different from the required economic capital. In this discussion, we use four concepts: the available capital, the required economic capital, the minimum required regulatory capital, and the target required regulatory capital.

In the rest of the chapter we have concentrated on calculating the minimum required regulatory capital. However, if the bank's available capital falls below this amount, it is in trouble. Therefore, the bank normally has a target of ensuring that the available capital is some margin (e.g., 2%) above the minimum required capital. We call this the bank's *target required regulatory capital*.

The bank should keep two sets of accounts: economic capital based and regulatory capital based. In general, the bank should be managed so the required economic capital, the target required regulatory capital, and the available capital are approximately equal. This applies at the highest level of the total bank, but does not need to apply at lower levels, such as individual business units or transactions.

Bear in mind that economic capital is the bank's best assessment of the amount of capital that it actually needs, given its portfolio, operations, and desired credit rating, whereas regulatory capital, especially under the 1988 accord, is a crude measure of risk that is relatively easy for an external regulating body to calculate and check.

If the required economic capital is more than the required regulatory capital, it means either that the bank has risks that are not captured by the regulatory capital, or the bank has a higher target debt rating than the one implied by regulatory capital. In either case, both the regulatory-capital requirement and the economic-capital requirement will be satisfied if the bank holds capital equal to the required economic capital.

If the target regulatory capital is greater than the economic capital, this means either that the bank is actually safer than the regulators believe, or that it has a low target debt rating. In this case, the bank should reduce the difference between the required regulatory capital and the economic capital.

The bank can reduce the difference by shifting into assets with greater risk but the same regulatory capital requirement. Under the 1988 accord, this can be done simply by giving loans to lowly rated companies and refusing loans to highly rated companies. This can be accomplished by an ad hoc modification of the hurdle rate used in the profitability and pricing calculations to include a penalty if the asset attracts regulatory capital. Such a modification is illustrated in the equation below:

$$Usual\ Charge = H \times EC_i$$

$$Modified\ Charge = H \times \left(EC_i + RC_i \left(\frac{RC_T - EC_T}{EC_T} \right) \right)$$

Here, EC_i and RC_i are the economic and regulatory capitals for the individual transaction, and RC_T and EC_T are the capitals for the total bank. A refinement to this equation would be to add a scaling factor (s) and only add a charge if the total regulatory capital was greater than the economic capital. If the scaling factor was made larger, the business units would have a stronger incentive to move to assets with a high ratio of EC_i to RC_i:

$$Modified\ Charge = H \times \left(EC_i + s \times RC_i \times \min\left[0, \left(\frac{RC_T - EC_T}{EC_T} \right) \right] \right)$$

Banks can also reduce their regulatory capital by manipulating the accounting. This entails entering into trades that remove assets from the formal balance sheet. Such trades include issuing heavily collateralized asset-backed securities. In this case, the assets are counted as if they have been transferred away from the bank and into a legally independent company that is a "special-purpose vehicle" (SPV). The SPV then issues bonds backed by the assets. Most of these bonds are bought by other banks and investors. The SPV gives the proceeds of the bond issuance to the bank in payment for the assets. On the balance sheet, the assets are now replaced with cash, which attracts a risk weighting of zero.

However, part of the structure of the SPV will be an agreement by the bank to buy the most risky of the bonds issued by the SPV (i.e., the "toxic waste"). These bonds appear on the balance sheet with a small face value and small risk weight, but with great underlying economic risk. By such complex accounting games, the bank can reduce its required regulatory capital without significantly reducing the risk or economic capital. However, regulators tend to view such transactions dimly if they are too blatant.

A third alternative for balancing the capital is to keep the risk the same but increase the required economic capital up to the level of required regulatory capital, by increasing the target debt rating. The reasoning behind this is that if the available capital is greater than the required economic capital, the bank is actually safer than the current rating implies. If this is the case, the bank should be able to convince the rating agencies to improve its rating, thereby reducing the bank's cost of borrowing and its required rate of equity return.

To increase its rating, the bank would have to make the case to the credit-rating agencies that it is safer than the agencies currently believe. It could make this case by presenting the economic-capital calculations, showing that with the bank's risks, and the capital that it is holding, it has a very low probability of default, and therefore should be rated more highly.

As the calculation of regulatory capital becomes more similar to the calculation of economic capital, there should be less need to manage the differences.

SUMMARY

In this chapter, we discussed required regulatory capital for credit risks with a focus on the choices available to management and the steps required to use the new accord. Next, we explore the capital needed to cover operational risk.

NOTES

1. International Convergence of Capital Measurement and Capital Standards, Basel Committee on Banking Supervision, July 1988.
2. Amendment to the Capital Accord to Incorporate Market Risks, Basel Committee on Banking Supervision, January 1996.
3. Consultative Document, The New Basel Capital Accord, Basel Committee on Banking Supervision, January 2001.

CHAPTER 24

Operating Risk

INTRODUCTION

In the preceding chapters, we calculated the capital that the bank should hold to cover the credit and market risks caused by trading or holding securities. However, the bank should also hold capital to cover other risks. To understand the nature of these risks, consider nonfinancial institutions, such as industrial companies and software companies. Although such companies are not primarily focused on trading or holding securities, they do hold a large amount of capital. For such a nonfinancial institution, the capital is the sum of all the assets minus the liabilities, where the assets are typically not securities, but production equipment.

Industrial companies hold such capital so they can continue to operate if there are fluctuations in sales, accidents, mistakes, or legal action against the company. The companies are expected to compensate their shareholders with a return on capital that is commensurate with the risks. Banks have similar risks from being in business, and should hold appropriate capital and plan to compensate their shareholders. In practical terms, this requires the bank to estimate the amount that could be lost due to operating risks. This estimate is used to ensure that it has an excess of assets over liabilities to absorb such losses, and ensure that the business units charge their customers a sufficient amount to make each business profitable for the shareholders.

Operational-risk capital accounts for between 10% to 25% of the overall capital held by a bank; but for individual business lines, such as retail brokerage and advisory work, all of the required capital may be for operating risks. The banking industry is just beginning to understand how to measure and manage operating risks. In this chapter, we discuss the definitions of risk that are currently being used, the leading approaches for measuring operating risk, and the New Basel Accord for operational-risk capital.

DEFINITION OF OPERATING, OPERATIONAL, AND OPERATIONS RISK

Until recently, operating risk was defined simply as risks other than credit and market risks. Now, as the industry has begun to focus on operating risk, several often confusing and contradictory definitions have arisen. One problem is that practitioners use the terms operating, operational, and operations risk to mean slightly different things. As illustrated in Figure 24-1, operations risk is a subset of operational risk, which in turn is a subset of operating risk.

To minimize the confusion in this discussion, we will use different names for each set of risks. We shall use the term *processing risk* to be synonymous with operations risk, *failure risk* to be synonymous with operational risk, and *company risk* to be synonymous with operating risk.

Operations or *processing risk* covers losses from the back-office operations of processing trades and information. It includes losses from the following sources:

- Incorrectly entering trades
- Losing information on trades
- The failure of a computer system, such as a quotes system or an order-routing system
- The accidental destruction of a database
- Losses due to the failure of a vendor to correctly perform outsourced processing functions

The term may also be used to cover losses due to internal or external fraud that were possible because of poor processing procedures.

FIGURE 24-1

The Relationship Between Operating, Operational, and Operations Risk

Operational or *failure risk* is defined by the New Basel accord as follows: "The risk of direct or indirect loss resulting from inadequate or failed internal processes, people, and systems, or from external events." Failure risk includes losses from the following:

- Processing risks
- Human mistakes by traders, such as buying 100,000 shares instead of 10,000 shares, or using the wrong parameters in a pricing model
- Fraud by employees, such as employees covering up losses, placing unauthorized trades, or transferring money into their own bank accounts
- Fraud by external criminals, such as illegal withdrawals from automatic teller machines
- Mistakes in applying laws, such as mistakenly thinking that the bank holds rights to collateral that turns out not to be legally enforceable, or misunderstanding terms of a securitization agreement
- Mistakes or misconduct by staff, such as unfairly exploiting customers leading to legal action against the bank

Operating or *company risk* encompasses all the risks faced by a nonfinancial company, including the following:

- Processing risks
- Failure risks
- Business risks due to changes in the competitive environment, such as the introduction of a new product by a competitor
- Business risks due to miscalculation in the amount of costs or revenue associated with a new product
- Business risks due to falls in income caused by customers' responses to changes in the market.

Clearly, operating risk is not just one type of risk; it is a general term used to cover many different sources of risk.

APPROACHES FOR MEASURING OPERATING RISK

Given the very diverse nature of the risks, it is not surprising that there is no single effective methodology for estimating the required capital. A good risk-measurement framework should do two things:

1. It should measure the absolute level of risk to allow pricing and capital assignment from an estimate of the expected loss and the economic capital.
2. It should show managers what they must do if they want to reduce the risks and therefore reduce the corresponding capital charge. This requires a granular bottom-up model showing the specific sources of risk. The model must

create the right incentives. An example of a measurement approach with a poor incentive structure is to base the operational-risk charge on noninterest expenses. If the bank's operational-risk capital is allocated on the basis of noninterest expenses, a manager could reduce the capital charge by reducing the number of staff. This is a poor incentive structure because reducing staff would typically increase the actual operating risk.

We use these two principles to assess the different approaches that are being developed. The risk-estimation approaches can be categorized as either qualitative, structural, actuarial, or a blend of all three. We discuss examples of each.

Qualitative Approaches

Qualitative approaches use management's judgment to detect sources of risk. They are typically based on surveys or questionnaires to be filled out by management and operations staff within each department. The questionnaires include questions on historical events, the current state of the system, and the manager's main concerns.

Historical events of interest are any financial losses, charge-offs, or write-downs, and any events that were close misses and could have led to losses. The questionnaire should also get an indication of the amount of low-level mistakes that occur without leading to losses, such as the number of trades that fail to be settled on the first attempt.

Questions on the current state seek to show the reliability of the system and the amount of stress that it is under. The reliability of the system depends on the level of automation and the quality of the staff. Danger signs include high levels of manual entry, records kept on paper or spreadsheets, multiple systems, inexperienced staff, high turnover rates for staff, and large amounts of overtime being worked. The risk also depends on the complexity of the operation. If the operation has many different, tailored products traded across many geographies, it will tend to have more failures and mistakes. The questionnaires also typically cover each department's monitoring and control policies, including its disaster-recovery plan.

Some banks use the results of the questionnaire to assign judgmental scores to each department, and to assign operating-risk capital based on those scores. However, when such qualitative decisions affect measured profitability and bonuses, the approach is quickly called into question.

Qualitative approaches are useful because they focus management's attention on the risks in question and allow the incorporation of the bank management's best understanding of the bank's processes, the weak links, and the consequent risks. The major disadvantage is that the process is time-consuming and open to misuse if a manager wants to reduce the perceived risks and the capital charge in his or her department. Also, if the question is not on the list, the risk may be missed.

Structural Approaches

Structural approaches require a model of causality that defines a set of linkages between observable information and the probability of loss events. The structural approach is very good for showing managers where they should concentrate their efforts to reduce the risks. Although this is not possible for all operational risks, some well-defined risks lend themselves to this approach. As an illustration of the structural approach, we discuss the structural assessment of processing risk and business risk.

The Structural Assessment of Processing Risk

One approach to estimating processing risk is to build a map of the process, then examine which links in the process could fail, and the consequent losses. The effort required to build the process map will often show management where they should concentrate their attention. This is especially useful for complex legacy systems whose origins predate the IT staff who maintain and operate them.

The map can be used to estimate the loss given an event (LGE) by manually tracing through the map and asking what would happen if each link failed. To quantify the expected loss, it is necessary to have an estimate of the probability of each link's failing. For failures that happen more frequently than once per year, it is relatively easy to collect probability information. The probability of less-frequent events must be based on management's judgment or the experience of other banks. Systems with backup plans should be assessed using the probability of an initial failure and the probability that the backup will work, given the initial failure.

Manual examination of the process map can work for relatively simple processes to calculate the expected loss. However, to estimate the probability distribution for a complex process, it is necessary to build the process map into a simulation model.

The Structural Assessment of Business Risk

Business risk arises because changes in the market can affect the volume of business that the bank has, and the level of fees that it can charge. For example, when the market falls, retail customs make fewer trades, and a broker's income from commissions will fall.

This risk can be assessed by a relatively simple model that relates the level of the market, the response of the customers, and the consequent amount of fees. For example, if the fees were fixed, and the volume of retail customer trades fell by 2% every time the market fell by 1%, the annual volatility of the earnings would depend on the volatility of the market:

$$\sigma_{Fee\ Income} = F \times 2 \times \sigma_{Market,annual} \times 0.6$$

The factor of 0.6 converts from year-end volatility to an average yearly volatility. This is used because fee income depends on the average market over the year, not just the value on the last day. With our usual simplified assumptions about VaR, $\sigma_{Market,\ annual}$ can be calculated as daily VaR, divided by 2.32, and multiplied by the square root of the number of trading days:

$$\sigma_{Market,annual} = \sqrt{250}\,\frac{VaR}{2.32}$$

This approach to estimating the volatility of earnings is explained further in "Institution-Level Risk Measurement for Asset Managers," Marrison, C.I., *Risk*, September 2001.

In the model above, the customer behavior is very simple. In reality, the behavior will be nonlinear and time dependent; e.g., customer trades will drop off if the market falls and then stays low for several months. If the behavior of the customers is known, the risk can be easily calculated using a simulation. In the simulation, random values for the market are generated and the customer's response is calculated for each case.

Business volumes and profitability can also be affected by competitive pressures. These are much more difficult to quantify, and if a structural model is used, it must be based on a model of the trends in the external market or rely more on management's intuition as to what could happen. In this case, the model simply provides a structured way of guessing.

Actuarial Approaches

Actuarial approaches make minimal assumptions about the underlying causes and mechanism of losses. They simply note that losses tend to occur, and try to estimate some of the parameters of the loss distribution. Actuarial approaches have the disadvantage of not identifying the sources of risk, but have the advantage of including all the risks, not just the ones that management can identify. We discuss actuarial estimation using the residual and analog approaches.

The Actuarial Approach Using Residuals

If we return to the definition of operating risk as losses arising from risks other than market risk and credit risk, the residual approach automatically suggests itself. If we can get a history of losses and subtract the losses due to market and credit risks, then by definition, what remains is a history of losses due to operating risks. The history can be used to estimate the probability distribution of operating-risk losses. This approach is useful as a cross-check on the other approaches, but the residual method is not very accurate. One problem is that because market and credit risks are often much larger than operating risks, any mistake in calculating the credit- and market-risk losses will have a large effect on the calculated values for operating risk.

A different residual approach is to look at a series of banks, calculate their required economic credit and market-risk capital given their ratings, and then subtract these amounts from the actual capital that they hold. The remaining capital theoretically should be the overall operating-risk capital required by the bank to maintain its rating. This approach has multiple problems. One is that it is even more difficult to calculate capital accurately than to get clean historical-loss data, so the errors in the residual will tend to be larger. Another problem is that it is difficult to calculate economic capital reasonably without all the detailed internal information held by each bank, although this may be less of a problem if banks start to publish their economic-capital numbers, as suggested by the Basel accord.

The Actuarial Approach Using Analogs

The analog method avoids the problem of needing to assess market and credit risk accurately by looking at the capital held by companies whose main risk is operating risk, namely nonfinancial companies. The ideal is to find companies that have the same sort of processes as the bank but do not take credit and market risks; e.g., companies that process data such as payroll and tax information can be used to characterize the risk in the bank's processing activities. Similarly, the capital held by pure asset-management companies can be used to estimate the operating-risk capital for the bank's fee-based businesses, such as private banking.

Once such analogous companies have been identified, their capital is calculated as a ratio of some indicator of scale, such as gross revenue, net income, or number of employees. The operating-risk capital for the bank is then calculated according to the same measure of scale for the bank. For example, if the measure of scale was gross revenue, the operating risk capital would be estimated as follows:

$$Capital_{Ops,Bank} = \frac{Gross\ Revenue_{Bank}}{Gross\ Revenue_{NonBank}} Capital_{NonBank}$$

It is difficult to find nonfinancial companies whose operations are the same as those of a bank, so the calculated capital should be averaged across the results from several similar companies. If there is a difference in credit rating between the company and the bank, the capital should be adjusted. This adjustment may be based on the relative distance to default (D) for each grade. The final estimate for the bank's operating-risk capital would be as follows:

$$Capital_{Ops,Bank} = Average\left\{ \frac{D_{Bank}}{D_{NonBank}} \frac{Gross\ Revenue_{Bank}}{Gross\ Revenue_{NonBank}} Capital_{NonBank} \right\}$$

The main difficulties with this method are finding suitable companies and the fact that it misses those risks that are unique to financial companies, such as fraud by traders. Although the approach can give an estimate of the total operating-risk capital for a business unit, unlike the structural approaches, it does not give the manager a reasonable way of reducing the amount of operating-risk capital. For example, the manager is unlikely to want to reduce gross revenue to reduce the capital charge.

Approaches Blending Qualitative, Structural, and Actuarial Methods

The approaches most favored by the Basel Committee combine judgment, structure, and loss experience. The two main approaches can be described as historical loss mapping and key risk indicators. As banks start to collect data for both of these metrics, the hope is that they can be combined.

Historical Loss Mapping

Historical loss mapping estimates the probability distribution of losses based on historical data. The process is as follows:

1. Historical data is collected on operating loss events within the institution and at other institutions. The information from other institutions may be either public information on losses they have suffered or anonymous information from many banks, pooled together by a consortium. Several consortiums of banks have agreed to pool their loss data anonymously in return for getting a better overall picture of the types of losses that banks face.

2. The loss data is classified according to the type of event that caused the loss, and the type of process and business unit in which the loss occurred. A measure of the size of the unit in which the loss occurred is also recorded, e.g., the total number of trades processed by the unit.

3. The bank's own processes and business units are classified in the same way, and the losses in the database are applied to each business unit to estimate the expected loss and unexpected loss.

The main problem with this approach is that it is difficult to map external experience to the bank's internal processes. A second problem is that the information does not include the fact that the bank's processes may be better than the average of the industry. Despite these drawbacks, it is probably one of the best ways available for quantifying operating-risk.

Key Risk Indicators

Key risk indicators (KRIs) are quantifiable measures of the performance of the bank's processes. If chosen well, changes in a KRI should correspond closely to a change in the probability of a loss. Key risk indicators for operational risk include the following:

- The volume of trades processed
- The number of trades that failed to settle when expected
- The volatility in the P&L compared with normal
- The size of differences between different accounting methods, e.g., the profitability reported by the trader and the profitability reported by the VaR calculator

- The rate of staff turnover
- The average hours of overtime per person
- The number of systems outages

One of the advantages in KRIs is that they are quantitative and objective, and can therefore be gathered automatically, or at least they can be more quickly produced than answers to qualitative questionnaires. They also have the advantage of being tailored to the bank and quickly showing management when there are changes in the bank's operations.

KRIs are very useful as a management tool, but they will be less useful for quantifying economic capital until historical data has been gathered to show how KRIs are related to the losses that later occur. With such a linkage, KRIs are potentially one of the most useful metrics for measuring operating-risk capital. An intermediate step is to use KRIs as the scale factor to relate the experienced losses in a pool of banks to the anticipated losses in an individual bank. This would use an equation such as the following:

$$Expected\ Loss = \frac{Bank's\ KRI}{Average\ Industry\ KRI} Average\ Industry\ Loss$$

This is similar to the internal measurement approach being suggested by the Basel Committee for operational-risk capital.

REGULATORY CAPITAL FOR OPERATIONAL RISKS

A regulatory requirement for holding capital against operational (failure) risks is proposed by the Basel Committee for the New Capital Accord.[1] The proposal is available at www.bis.org. The committee found it necessary to include an explicit calculation of capital for operational risks because as they more closely defined the capital for market and credit risks, they realized that there was no longer an implicit cushion for other risks. The operational-risk capital is controversial, but necessary if regulatory capital is to be measured in a similar way to economic capital.

The committee proposed that banks should adopt one, or a combination, of three alternative approaches for calculating operating-risk capital. The approaches differ in their levels of sophistication:

- The basic indicator approach
- The standardized approach
- The internal measurement approach

The basic indicator approach is very easy to implement, whereas the internal measurement approach is beyond the current capabilities of most or all banks. The committee intends that the more sophisticated approaches should be less conservative, and will on average require banks to hold less capital for operating-risks. This provides an additional incentive for banks to monitor and control their risks. We now discuss each of the approaches, concentrating on how the capital is calculated, and what the bank must do to be able to make the calculation.

The Basic Indicator Approach

The basic indicator approach takes an easily calculated indicator of the bank's scale of activity and applies a multiplier to give the required regulatory capital. In January, 2001, the Basel Committee proposed that the indicator of activity should be the bank's gross income, and that the multiplier should be 30%, giving the capital as follows:

$$Regulatory\ Capital_{Operational} = 0.3 \times Gross\ Income$$

The value of 30% was proposed after the committee studied a small number of international banks. Many banks objected that this was too high, and it may be reduced in the final accord. To implement this approach, the bank simply needs to know its gross income.

The Standardized Approach

The standardized approach allows for different indicators and multipliers for each of seven different lines of business. The lines of business and suggested indicators of scale are shown in Table 24-1.

TABLE 24-1

Scale Indicators for the Standardized Approach to Operating-Risk Capital

Business Units	Business Lines	Scale Indicator
Investment Banking	Corporate Finance	Gross Income
	Trading and Sales	Gross Income
Banking	Retail Banking	Annual Average Assets
	Commercial Banking	Annual Average Assets
	Payment and Settlement	Annual Throughput
Others	Retail Brokerage	Gross Income
	Asset Management	Assets Under Management

From Operational Risk, Consultative Document, Basel Committee on Banking Supervision, January, 2001.

The total operational-risk capital for the bank is the sum of the indicators multiplied by a factor, β, for each line of business:

$$Regulatory\,Capital_{Operational} = \sum_{i=1}^{7} \beta_i \times Indicator_i$$

Here, i denotes an individual line of business. The values of β_i for each business will be set by the regulators. To implement this approach, the bank needs to categorize each of its activities into one of the standard lines of business, and then calculate the scale indicator for that business. In most cases, this information is readily available, but there will be controversy about the indicators to be used and the values fixed for β_i.

The Internal Measurement Approach

The internal measurement (IRM) approach keeps the definition of standard business lines, but takes two further steps. The first step is that it allows the risks within each business to be measured separately, with a separate indicator. It proposes six different types of risk, as follows:

- Write-downs
- Loss of recourse
- Restitution
- Legal liability
- Regulatory and compliance
- Loss or damage to assets

For each of the six risk types and each of the seven businesses, it proposes a different indicator and a different multiplying factor, m. The minimum regulatory capital would be the weighted sum of the indicators:

$$Regulatory\,Capital_{Operational} = \sum_{i=1}^{7} \sum_{j=1}^{6} \left(m_{i,j} \times Indicator_{i,j} \right)$$

The second step of complication is that the multiplier, $m_{i,j}$, would be made up of three components:

- The probability of an event (PE) given an indicator equal to one
- The loss given an event (LGE)
- A multiplying factor, gamma (γ)

The final formula for capital is therefore as follows:

$$Regulatory\,Capital_{Operational} = \sum_{i=1}^{7} \sum_{j=1}^{6} \left(\gamma_{i,j} \times PE_{i,j} \times LGE_{i,j} \times Indicator_{i,j} \right)$$

The idea is that the term $PE_{i,j} \times LGE_{i,j} \times Indicator_{i,j}$ should be an estimate of the expected loss due to risk type j in business unit i. The factor $\gamma_{i,j}$ would effectively convert from expected loss to capital.

In this framework, the regulators would set standard values for each of the 42 factors of $\gamma_{i,j}$, and the bank would estimate the other terms. This makes the measurement highly tailored to the bank, but gives it a difficult task in calculating PE and LGE.

To implement this approach, a bank would need to categorize its businesses into the 7 standard lines and then categorize its losses in each of the lines into 6 different types. In each of the 42 cells, it would then need to collect data on the indicator, all loss events, and the loss given each event. This is a significant amount of effort, and is probably not justified if it is simply to reduce the required capital. However, the process of collecting the data should give management better tools for managing and minimizing the losses that it actually suffers.

A NOTE ON CORRELATION

In the discussion above, we did not mention correlation. Data on operational loss experiences is currently so fragmented that it has not been possible to estimate correlations between different sources of operating-risks or between operating-risk and market and credit risks. As data-collection efforts proceed, this will become possible, and it is highly important because the amount of capital to be held depends strongly on the correlation.

Let us consider a simple calculation that will show the relative importance of operating risk compared with the other risks. Consider a bank that has losses from credit and market risks with a mean of $100 and a standard deviation of $80. On a stand-alone basis, let us assume that the losses from operating risks have a mean of $30 and a standard deviation of $20. The mean loss for the bank as a whole will be $130. The standard deviation of losses, for the bank as a whole will depend on the correlation (ρ) between the losses, as follows:

$$\sigma^2_{Bank} = 80^2 + 20^2 + 2 \times 80 \times 20 \times \rho$$

Table 24-2 shows the total standard deviation of the bank's losses, assuming correlations of +0.5, 0, and −0.5. A negative correlation would mean that the operating risks peak when the bank has minimal losses on its portfolio. This may be the case if operating risks increase with the volume of trades, and the volume of trades increases in a rising market. The table also shows the amount of the bank's total standard deviation that would be attributed to each risk according to the unexpected loss contribution.

If the correlation is +0.5, the amount of capital attributed to operating risks would still be high. If there is 0 correlation, the operating risks are swamped by

TABLE 24-2

Operating-Risk Capital as a Function of its Correlation with Other Risks

Standard Deviation for Market and Credit Risks	Standard Deviation for Operating Risk	Correlation	Standard Deviation for Bank as a Whole	Market and Credit Risk Contribution	Operating Risk Contribution
$80	$20	+0.5	$91.7	$78.6	$13.1
$80	$20	0	$82.5	$77.6	$4.8
$80	$20	−0.5	$72.1	$77.7	$−5.6

the much larger credit and market risks. With negative correlation, the total amount of capital would be reduced, although the expected loss would remain at $130.

As banks focus their efforts on collecting data on operating-risk losses, it will become possible to make these adjustments for correlation and combine credit risk, market risk, and operating-risk, as we discuss in the next chapter.

SUMMARY

In this chapter, we explored the concept of operational risk and the capital needed to cover it. In the final chapter, we discuss how to view all types of bank risk in an integrated fashion.

NOTE

1. Operational Risk, Consultative Document, Basel Committee on Banking Supervision, January 2001.

Inter-Risk Diversification and Bank-Level RAROC

INTRODUCTION

In Chapter 2, we discussed risk measurement at the highest level of the bank. In the following chapters, we looked in depth at the techniques used to individually measure market, ALM, credit risk, and operating risk. With this detailed knowledge, we can now return to the bank level and discuss how all the disparate risk models fit together to give a picture of the bank's overall risk.

The first section discusses how the risk is calculated for the bank as a whole, including diversification between different types of risks. The second section discusses how the different models fit together. Finally, we discuss a high-level implementation plan for calculating bankwide economic capital and RAROC.

INTER-RISK DIVERSIFICATION AND BANK-LEVEL CAPITAL

In this section, we first discuss ways in which the capital can be calculated for the bank as a whole, including the correlation between risks. Then, we show ways in which the total capital for the bank is allocated to individual business units and transactions. This is similar to finding the unexpected loss for a whole credit portfolio, and then calculating the unexpected loss contribution for each loan. The difference here is that we are not only dealing with credit risk, but also market, ALM, and operating risks.

Conceptually, the most straightforward way to calculate the risk for the bank is to have a single "grand machine" that concurrently simulates all the risks for the bank, similar to Figure 21-7, but with the addition of operating risks. With such a machine, the total capital for the bank comes automatically by summing the losses in each scenario to get the loss distribution for the bank as a whole. However, such a large calculation is difficult to construct because it requires many sources of data, and requires a coordinated team that can apply all the techniques needed for market, credit, and operating risks.

It is much more common that a bank will have separate calculators for each risk: a VaR calculator for trading risks, a simulator for ALM risks, a portfolio model for credit risks, and specialized models for operating-risk. In this case, it is necessary to construct a framework and a model that can tie all these risks together.

Broadly, there are two approaches: analytical estimation of the capital, and simulation. The analytical approach is more straightforward, but the simulation is a little more accurate.

Analytical Estimation of Bank-Level Capital

To estimate the capital, we first calculate the variance of the losses, and then estimate the capital multiplier.

Estimating Inter-Risk Correlations

We use the usual variance equation to get the variance for the whole bank based on the variance of the individual risk-types:

$$\sigma^2_{Bank} = \sigma^2_{Credit} + \sigma^2_{Mkt} + \sigma^2_{ALM} + \sigma^2_{Ops}$$
$$+ 2\left(\rho_{Credit,Mkt}\sigma_{Credit}\sigma_{Mkt} + \rho_{Credit,ALM}\sigma_{Credit}\sigma_{ALM} + \rho_{Credit,Ops}\sigma_{Credit}\sigma_{Ops}\right)$$
$$+ 2\left(\rho_{Mkt,ALM}\sigma_{Mkt}\sigma_{ALM} + \rho_{Mkt,Ops}\sigma_{Mkt}\sigma_{Ops} + \rho_{ALM,Ops}\sigma_{ALM}\sigma_{Ops}\right)$$

From the individual credit, market, ALM, and operating-risk models, we will already know the stand-alone variances: σ^2_{Credit}, σ^2_{Mkt}, σ^2_{ALM} and σ^2_{Ops}. The difficulty is in estimating the six correlations. There are three common ways of estimating correlations: historical loss data, equity prices of monoline companies, and simulation.

The analysis of historical data simply takes the time series of losses from each of the types of risk and calculates the correlation. Ideally, the time series would be losses from each of the bank's operations over several years. If such data are not available over a long period (e.g., due to mergers), national data can be used. For example, Table 25-1 shows bond-default rates and changes in the S&P 500 equity index over the last 20 years. The correlation between these 2 series is −40%. (When the market goes up, default rates fall.) Forty percent would therefore be a reasonable correlation to expect between losses in a portfolio of corporate loans and a trading operation that was highly correlated with the market.

An estimate of correlation can also be observed from historical equity prices of monoline companies. A *monoline company* is a company that only has one line of business, e.g., trading or lending. The correlation between the equity price of a monoline trading company and a monoline lending bank will give an indication of the

TABLE 25-1

Historical Correlation Between Bond Defaults and Equity Returns

Year	Bond-Default Rate	Change in the S&P 500 Index
1982	1.3%	17.3%
1983	0.7%	1.4%
1984	0.8%	26.3%
1985	1.0%	14.6%
1986	1.8%	2.0%
1987	0.9%	12.4%
1988	1.5%	27.3%
1989	1.7%	−6.6%
1990	2.8%	26.3%
1991	3.9%	4.5%
1992	1.3%	7.1%
1993	0.5%	−1.5%
1994	0.5%	34.1%
1995	0.9%	20.3%
1996	0.4%	31.0%
1997	0.5%	26.7%
1998	1.2%	19.5%
1999	2.0%	−10.1%
2000	2.1%	−13.9%

Bond-default rates from "Corporate Defaults: Will Things Get Worse Before They Get Better?" Leo Brand & Reza Bahar, Standard & Poor's *Credit Week*, January 31, 2001.

correlation between the capital needed for a trading business and a loan business. This approach is quite crude because the credit quality of the loans and the style of trading in the monoline companies are likely to be different from the bank of interest.

Estimation of correlation from simulation is done by using a small version of the grand machine. In this approach, a few representative loans and trades are simulated to get an example of the correlation between losses.

Allocating Capital to Individual Risks

Once we know the variance for the bank as a whole, we can calculate the contribution for each of the risks using the usual VaRC or ULC approach:

$$\sigma_{Bank} = \sigma c_{Credit} + \sigma c_{Mkt} + \sigma c_{ALM} + \sigma c_{Ops}$$

$$\sigma c_{Credit} = \frac{\sigma_{Credit}\left(\sigma_{Credit} + \rho_{Credit,Mkt}\sigma_{Mkt} + \rho_{Credit,ALM}\sigma_{ALM} + \rho_{Credit,Ops}\sigma_{Ops}\right)}{\sigma_{Bank}}$$

$$\sigma c_{Mkt} = \text{etc.}$$

Here, σc_{Credit} represents the contribution of credit risk to the bank's total standard deviation.

The ratio between the contribution and the stand-alone standard deviation is often called the inter-risk diversification factor, F:

$$F_{Credit} = \frac{\sigma c_{Credit}}{\sigma_{Credit}}$$

$$F_{Mkt} = \frac{\sigma c_{Mkt}}{\sigma_{Mkt}}$$

$$F_{ALM} = \frac{\sigma c_{ALM}}{\sigma_{ALM}}$$

$$F_{Ops} = \frac{\sigma c_{Ops}}{\sigma_{Ops}}$$

Notice that the factor depends not only on the correlation between risks, but also on the absolute size of one risk compared with the others. For example, consider a bank with only credit and market risks with a correlation of 40%. If the variance of both market and credit risks were equal to 100, the diversification factors would both be 84%:

$$\sigma_{Bank}^2 = \sigma_{Credit}^2 + \sigma_{Mkt}^2 + 2\rho_{Credit,\ Mkt}\sigma_{Credit}\sigma_{Mkt}$$

$$\sigma_{Bank}^2 = 100 + 100 + 2 \times 0.4 \times 10 \times 10 = 280$$

$$\sigma c_{Credit} = \frac{100 + 0.4 \times 10 \times 10}{\sqrt{280}} = 8.4$$

$$F_{Credit} = \frac{8.4}{10} = 84\%$$

$$\sigma c_{Mkt} = \frac{100 + 0.4 \times 10 \times 10}{\sqrt{280}} = 8.4$$

$$F_{Mkt} = \frac{8.4}{10} = 84\%$$

If the variance of credit risks was 4 times that of market risks, the diversification factor for credit risks would be 93%, and for market risks, 70%:

$$\sigma^2_{Bank} = \sigma^2_{Credit} + \sigma^2_{Mkt} + 2\rho_{Credit, Mkt}\sigma_{Credit}\sigma_{Mkt}$$

$$\sigma^2_{Bank} = 400 + 100 + 2 \times 0.4 \times 20 \times 10 = 660$$

$$\sigma c_{Credit} = \frac{400 + 0.4 \times 20 \times 10}{\sqrt{660}} = 18.7$$

$$F_{Credit} = \frac{18.7}{20} = 93\%$$

$$\sigma c_{Mkt} = \frac{100 + 0.4 \times 10 \times 20}{\sqrt{660}} = 7.0$$

$$F_{Mkt} = \frac{7.0}{10} = 70\%$$

For an individual transaction, the capital can be allocated according to the contribution of the transaction to the stand-alone portfolio, multiplied by the portfolio's inter-risk-diversification factor. For example, the capital allocated to a loan would be based on its ULC relative to the loan portfolio, multiplied by the inter-risk-diversification factor of the loan portfolio within the bank:

$$ULC_{Loan} = F_{Credit}\sqrt{\rho_{Loan,Portfolio}}\, UL_{Loan}$$

This ensures that the sum of the capital for the individual transactions equals the total capital for the bank; however, it gives a slightly different answer than if the ULC of the loan to the bank had been calculated in one step. This is because by using a single inter-risk-diversification factor for the whole credit portfolio, we are assuming that the correlation between every loan and the rest of the portfolio is the same. This point is explored further in Appendix A.

Calculating the Capital Multiplier for the Bank

Having established the variance for the bank as a whole, it is necessary to calculate a capital multiplier for the bank. Recall from Chapter 20 that the capital multiplier (M) is the required economic capital divided by the standard deviation:

$$M_{Bank} = \frac{EC_{Bank}}{\sigma_{Bank}}$$

In our current discussion, we know σ_{Bank}, and we want to determine M_{Bank} so we can estimate the capital.

The multiplier is determined by the shape of the probability distribution. It is difficult to calculate the shape of the probability distribution for the whole bank because it is the combination of several different distributions, such as a Normal distribution for market-risk losses and a Beta distribution for credit losses.

If we do not know the shape of the distribution for the bank as a whole, it is a reasonable approximation to use the weighted sum of the multipliers for the individual risks:

$$M_{Bank} = \frac{M_{Credit}\sigma c_{Credit} + M_{Mkt}\sigma c_{Mkt} + M_{ALM}\sigma c_{ALM} + M_{Ops}\sigma c_{Ops}}{\sigma_{Bank}}$$

This is equivalent to the following expression for the bank's capital:

$$EC_{Bank} = M_{Credit}\sigma c_{Credit} + M_{Mkt}\sigma c_{Mkt} + M_{ALM}\sigma c_{ALM} + M_{Ops}\sigma c_{Ops}$$

If this approach is used for estimating the total capital, the capital allocated to an individual transaction is calculated simply using the multiplier for the transaction's portfolio; for example, the capital allocated to a loan is as follows:

$$EC_{Loan} = F_{Credit}M_{Credit}\sqrt{\rho_{Loan,Portfolio}}\,UL_{Loan}$$

This approximation is sufficiently accurate for most purposes, but if a more refined estimation of the multiplier is required, it can be found through a simulation that properly combines the losses from different distributions. This simulation method is detailed in Appendix B.

CONNECTING MODELS TO CALCULATE BANKWIDE RISK

In the section above, we described a model to calculate the overall risk of the bank based on the risk produced from many individual models. Let us now step back and look at how all these models fit together.

In the last few chapters, we discussed the following models:

Trading Risk
- Value at risk (Chapter 6)
- Economic capital for trading based on VaR (Chapter 9)
- Simulation to estimate the likely exposure for derivatives (Chapter 17)

ALM
- Rules for transfer pricing (Chapter 15)
- Customer and interest-rate behavior models (Chapter 13)
- Simulation to estimate ALM economic capital (Chapter 13)

Credit Risk
- Models for probability of default (PD), loss given default (LGD), exposure at default (EAD), and correlation (Chapter 19)
- Portfolio models (Chapters 20 and 21)
- Loan-pricing models (Chapter 22)

Operating Risk
- Models for overall operating-risk capital (Chapter 24)
- Structural models for individual risks (Chapter 24)

Bank Level
- Models to estimate inter-risk diversification (Chapter 25)

These models fit together to calculate bank-level capital, as illustrated in Figure 25-1. We will step through each component in detail describing its function, the data that it requires, and the results that it provides.

We start with transfer pricing (shown with dashed lines). Transfer pricing in itself is not a model but a set of rules for internal trades. The internal trades move interest-rate risks from one group to another; most importantly, they remove the interest-rate risk from the lending business, leaving only credit and operating-risks. This means that the credit risk of the loan can be measured in a credit-portfolio model, and the interest-rate risk can be measured separately in the ALM model.

FIGURE 25-1

Connections Between Models to Calculate Bankwide Economic Capital

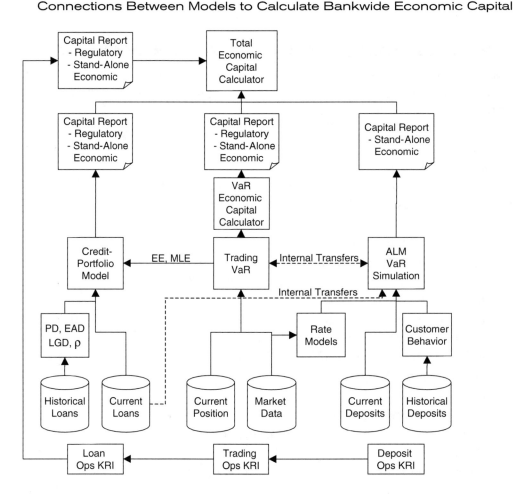

For transfers between the ALM desk and the trading desk, opposite fictitious assets and liabilities should appear in the ALM and VaR calculators to reflect each side of the internal trade.

Now let us look at the calculation of credit risk. The credit-portfolio calculator is supplied with current information on the loan portfolio and current information on the exposure to derivatives from the VaR calculator. The credit-portfolio calculator is also supplied with models that can estimate PD, LGD, EAD, and correlation, given the characteristics of the current loans. These models are typically based on regressions with historical loan data.

The credit-portfolio calculator is used to estimate the economic capital required for the portfolio as a whole, and for each transaction. The economic capital for the portfolio as a whole is fed into the bank-level capital calculator. The capital for each transaction is used to assess risk-adjusted performance, such as RAROC, and is used to create reports identifying concentrations of risk.

Importantly, the credit-portfolio calculator also provides the average correlation between each transaction and the rest of the credit-portfolio. This average correlation is used in loan-pricing models so the loan officers and traders know how much they will be charged for capital when taking on a new risk.

The information in the credit-portfolio model can be used to calculate both the economic capital and the regulatory capital for credit risk.

The calculation of trading market risks is made in the VaR calculator based on market and position information. The regulatory capital is a direct multiplication of VaR by $3\sqrt{10}$. The economic capital is based on VaR and a separate simulation that models trading behavior and potential losses over a year.

The ALM calculator is similar to VaR, except that the position information is largely from internal transfers from the loan and deposit groups. An important part of the ALM calculator is the customer behavior models, based on historical rate and balance data.

The operating-risk models collect information, such as key risk indicators, and try to estimate both the total capital to be set aside for operating-risks and the allocation of the capital to each business group.

Once the total economic capital for the bank is calculated, it can be allocated to the individual business units and the transactions that caused the risk. A separate exercise can be conducted to allocate all the income, interest expenses, and operating expenses to each business unit and transaction. This allows the calculation of risk-adjusted performance. The allocation of interest expenses should be made according to the rules of matched-funds-transfer pricing. The allocation of income and costs may use an approach such as activity-based costing (ABC).

As illustrated in Figure 25-2, the results of the credit-portfolio calculation are also fed to the loan-pricing model as a set of average correlations for each type of counterparty (e.g., by credit grade and industry). The loan-pricing model also has copies of the models for PD, EAD, and LGD, so it can evaluate any new customer. It

FIGURE 25-2

Data Feeds from Portfolio-Level Calculators to Desk-Level Calculators

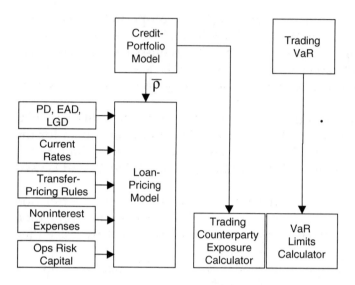

contains a set of matched-funds-transfer-pricing rules and is fed with current rates to estimate the interest expense. It also has the rules for the noninterest expenses that will be allocated to the loan.

The credit-portfolio calculator can also feed results to the trading group, so they can limit their credit exposure according to the economic capital consumed by exposure to each counterparty. Separately, at the start of the day, the VaR calculator supplies results to each portfolio that has a VaR limit, so the total VaR caused by any new intraday trade can be calculated.

IMPLEMENTATION OF RAROC

We have now discussed almost all the models required to calculate RAROC. In this section, we simply pull them together to present them as a list of things to be done to calculate the bank's profitability in terms of RAROC. In the detailed chapters, we discussed the many options available at each step. Here, we do not include every option, but just give a sense of the types of steps that need to be taken.

Implementation of RAROC needs three broad streams: capital calculation, funds-transfer pricing, and allocation of noninterest expenses.

Stream 1: Calculate the Total Economic Capital for the Bank

Trading Market Risk

- Decide which instruments are liquidly traded, and which should be treated as ALM instruments.
- Build pricing models for each type of security if using historical or Monte Carlo VaR. Build derivative models if using parametric VaR.
- Decide the set of market data that is required by the pricing models and collect it.
- Build a VaR calculator (Chapter 6).
- Build a model to convert from daily VaR to annual capital (Chapter 9).

ALM Market and Liquidity Risk

- Collect historical data on the behavior of customers.
- Build models showing how balances and implicit options respond to changes in rates (Chapter 13).
- Collect data on current deposit accounts.
- Transfer-price loan accounts to bring the risk into the ALM portfolio (Chapter 15).
- Build a simulation model to estimate economic capital for interest-rate risk (Chapter 13).
- Collect data on daily flows of funds.
- Build a simulation model to estimate economic capital for liquidity risk (Chapter 14).

Credit Risk

- Collect historical data on all companies that defaulted and at least an equal amount that did not default. (See Chapter 19 for types of data to collect.)
- Carry out regressions to relate company and loan characteristics to probability of default, loss given default, and exposure at default (Chapter 19).
- Collect information on the current portfolio.
- Calculate the expected loss.
- Estimate the asset or default correlation (Chapter 20).
- Build a portfolio model to calculate the economic capital (Chapters 20 and 21).

Operating Risk

- Collect historical loss data both inside the bank and externally.

- Collect scale and key risk indicators.
- Calculate capital (Chapter 24).

Calculate Inter-Risk diversification

- Collect historical data on losses.
- Estimate correlations and calculate the standard deviation of losses for the whole bank.
- Use the Merton approach (Chapter 21) or transformation simulation (Chapter 25, Appendix B) to estimate the shape of the bank's probability distribution.

Allocate the Capital to Individual Business Lines and Transactions

- Use the VaR contribution (Chapter 7) or unexpected loss contribution (Chapter 20), multiplied by the inter-risk-diversification factor (Chapter 25).

Stream 2: Calculate Income and Interest Costs

- Reverse any internal charges or credits for interest costs.
- Apply matched-funds-transfer pricing (Chapter 15) to charge and credit business units according to the interest-rate characteristics of their assets and liabilities.

Stream 3: Calculate Noninterest Expenses

- Either accept the bank's current transfer pricing for noninterest expenses, or reverse all charges and apply charges according to the preferred methodology, e.g., activity-based costing.

Final Step: Calculate RAROC

- Use the standard RAROC equations. (Use the definition in Chapter 2 for most occasions, but use Chapter 22 for the rare occasions when you need to calculate RAROC over multiple years.)

If, in addition to calculating RAROC, we wish to calculate the shareholder value added, or price a new transaction, we need to set a hurdle rate for using economic capital. This is discussed in Appendix C.

SUMMARY

In this chapter, we showed how the overall risk for a bank can be calculated based on the results from all the models that we discussed in the earlier chapters. You should now have a good idea of all the tools that are currently used by banks to measure their risk.

APPENDIX A: DISCREPANCIES IN CAPITAL ALLOCATION CAUSED BY USING AN INTER-RISK DIVERSIFICATION FACTOR

One approach to allocating capital to an individual loan is first to calculate the contribution of the loan to the risk in the credit-portfolio, and then calculate the contribution of the credit-portfolio to the risk of the whole bank. This gives a slightly different answer than directly calculating the contribution of the loan to the risk of the whole bank. This appendix explores the source of the discrepancy.

Consider a portfolio made up of two subportfolios, A and B. As usual, the variance of the total portfolio depends on the two subportfolios and their correlation:

$$\sigma_P^2 = \sigma_A^2 + \sigma_B^2 + 2\rho_{A,B}\sigma_A\sigma_B$$

We calculate the contributions of A and B as follows:

$$\sigma_P = \sigma_A\left(\frac{\sigma_A + \rho_{A,B}\sigma_B}{\sigma_P}\right) + \sigma_B\left(\frac{\sigma_B + \rho_{A,B}\sigma_A}{\sigma_P}\right)$$
$$= \sigma_A\sqrt{\overline{\rho_{A,P}}} + \sigma_B\sqrt{\overline{\rho_{B,P}}}$$

Here, $\sqrt{\overline{\rho_{B,P}}}$ is defined as the average correlation between B and the total portfolio. Now consider portfolio B to have 2 components, 1 and 2:

$$\sigma_B^2 = \sigma_1^2 + \sigma_2^2 + 2\rho_{1,2}\sigma_{1,2}\sigma_1\sigma_2$$
$$\sigma_B = \sigma_1\left(\frac{\sigma_1 + \rho_{1,2}\sigma_2}{\sigma_B}\right) + \sigma_2\left(\frac{\sigma_2 + \rho_{1,2}\sigma_1}{\sigma_B}\right)$$
$$= \sigma_1\sqrt{\overline{\rho_{1,B}}} + \sigma_2\sqrt{\overline{\rho_{2,B}}}$$

We could now calculate the portfolio's standard deviation as follows:

$$\sigma_P = \sigma_A\sqrt{\overline{\rho_{A,P}}} + \sigma_B\sqrt{\overline{\rho_{B,P}}}$$
$$= \sigma_A\sqrt{\overline{\rho_{A,P}}} + \sqrt{\overline{\rho_{B,P}}}\left(\sigma_1\sqrt{\overline{\rho_{1,B}}} + \sigma_2\sqrt{\overline{\rho_{2,B}}}\right)$$

The contribution of item 1 to the total portfolio could therefore be defined as follows:

$$\sigma_1 c = \sqrt{\overline{\rho_{B,P}}}\sqrt{\overline{\rho_{1,B}}}\,\sigma_1$$

Slightly different results for the unexpected loss contribution are obtained if the whole portfolio is considered:

$$\sigma_P^2 = \sigma_A^2 + \sigma_1^2 + \sigma_2^2 + 2\rho_{A,1}\sigma_A\sigma_1 + 2\rho_{A,2}\sigma_A\sigma_2 + 2\rho_{1,2}\sigma_1\sigma_2$$

$$\sigma_P = \sigma_A \left(\frac{\sigma_A + \rho_{A,1}\sigma_1 + \rho_{A,2}\sigma_2}{\sigma_P} \right) + \sigma_1 \left(\frac{\sigma_1 + \rho_{A,1}\sigma_A + \rho_{1,2}\sigma_2}{\sigma_P} \right)$$

$$+ \sigma_2 \left(\frac{\sigma_2 + \rho_{A,2}\sigma_A + \rho_{1,2}\sigma_1}{\sigma_P} \right)$$

$$= \sigma_A \sqrt{\rho_{A,P}} + \sigma_1 \sqrt{\rho_{1,P}} + \sigma_2 \sqrt{\rho_{2,P}}$$

In general, the unexpected loss contribution calculated in this way will not be the same as the contribution calculated in two stages, i.e.:

$$\sqrt{\rho_{1,P}} \neq \sqrt{\rho_{B,P}} \sqrt{\rho_{1,B}}$$

In matrix notation, the true correlation matrix is as follows:

$$C = \begin{bmatrix} 1 & \rho_{A,1} & \rho_{A,2} \\ \rho_{A,1} & 1 & \rho_{1,2} \\ \rho_{A,2} & \rho_{1,2} & 1 \end{bmatrix}$$

But by making the calculation of ULC in two steps, we effectively use the following correlations:

$$C = \begin{bmatrix} 1 & \rho_{A,B} & \rho_{A,B} \\ \rho_{A,B} & 1 & \rho_{1,2} \\ \rho_{A,B} & \rho_{1,2} & 1 \end{bmatrix}$$

APPENDIX B: ESTIMATION OF BANK-LEVEL CAPITAL MULTIPLIER BY SIMULATION

This appendix discusses a method for determining the shape of the probability distribution for a bank's combined losses, and thereby estimating the bank's overall capital multiplier. In this approach, simulation is used to create losses from each risk source, and to ensure that the distribution of losses for each source is correct and that the losses are properly correlated.

Over the one-year horizon used for capital calculations, trading and ALM risks have probability distributions that are close to Normal. As we discussed in the chapter on Monte Carlo VaR, it is relatively easy to create correlated scenarios with Joint-Normal distributions by using Eigen-value decomposition. However, credit losses have distributions that are close to a Beta distribution.

These distributions can be combined by simulating credit events along with market-risk losses to get the loss distribution for the portfolio. We can make the credit data amenable to simulation by transforming the credit-loss data from a Beta distribution to a Normal distribution. We then carry out the simulation using a Joint-Normal distribution and transform the credit losses back to having a Beta distribution.

This process can be considered to be a stretching of the credit-loss distribution into the shape of a Normal distribution. This is done by converting the loss data from loss-amounts to probabilities, then from probabilities into a Normally distributed loss. The first step is to calculate the mean and standard deviation of the historical loss data (L). We can then calculate the a and b parameters of the Beta distribution, as in Chapter 20. We then use the Beta function (e.g., x=Betadist(L,a,b,1) in Excel) to calculate the cumulative probability of each event's occurring. At this point the data should have a uniform distribution between 0 and 1. We then take the inverse Normal function to create a transformed series of losses $(\widehat{L})$ $(\widehat{L}=\text{Norminv}(x,0,1))$. This transformed series has a Normal distribution. The transformation equation is given below and illustrated in Figure 25-B1.

$$\widehat{L}_t = \Phi^{-1}\,\beta(L_t, a, b)$$

At this stage, we have a time series of trading losses, ALM losses, and transformed credit-risk losses, all with Normal distributions. We can then calculate the covariance of these losses and use Eigenvalue or Cholesky decomposition to create random scenarios with the same correlation structure. The result is a number of scenarios each containing actual trading risk and ALM losses, and Normally distributed credit losses.

To calculate the actual credit-risk losses, we run the transformation in the opposite direction to produce credit losses with a Beta distribution, as illustrated in Figure 25-B2.

FIGURE 25-B1

Illustration of the Transformation of Historical Data from a Beta Distribution to a Normal Distribution

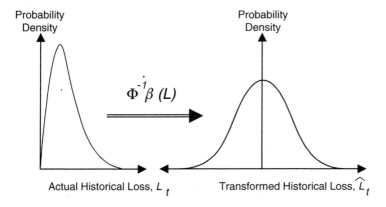

FIGURE 25-B2

Illustration of the Transformation of Simulated Losses from a Normal
Distribution to a Beta Distribution

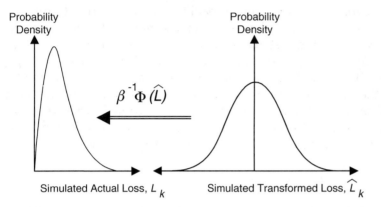

$$L_k = \beta^{-1}\Phi(\widehat{L}_k)$$

The next step is simply to add the credit losses to the trading and ALM losses to calculate the portfolio's total loss. After running thousands of simulations, we sort the results according to the size of the loss and read off the loss for the required confidence level. For example, if we wanted to know the 10-basis-point confidence level for capital, we could run 10,000 simulations and estimate the required capital to be the tenth-worst loss.

We calculate the capital multiplier by dividing the tenth-worst loss by the standard deviation of losses. The inter-risk-diversification factors can then be defined according to the multiplier, m, required to balance the following equation:

$$M_{Bank}\sigma_{Bank} = m(M_{Credit}\sigma c_{Credit} + M_{Mkt}\sigma c_{Mkt} + M_{ALM}\sigma c_{ALM} + M_{Ops}\sigma c_{Ops})$$

$$F_{Credit} = m\frac{\sigma c_{Credit}}{\sigma_{Credit}}$$

$$F_{Mkt} = m\frac{\sigma c_{Mkt}}{\sigma_{Mkt}}$$

$$F_{ALM} = m\frac{\sigma c_{ALM}}{\sigma_{ALM}}$$

$$F_{Ops} = m\frac{\sigma c_{Ops}}{\sigma_{Ops}}$$

The capital allocated to a loan is then as follows:

$$EC_{Loan} = m\, M_{Credit}F_{Credit}\sqrt{\rho_{Loan,Portfolio}}\, UL_{Loan}$$

m should be expected to have a value close to one. The use of m forces the equations to balance and forces the sum of the economic capital allocated to individual transactions to equal the total capital of the bank. However, this is not the only way that capital can be allocated.

An alternative scheme for allocating capital is to use the results of the simulation. We can define the capital contribution of a portfolio from the total loss from that portfolio in all scenarios when the capital is exceeded, divided by the total loss for the whole bank when the capital is exceeded. For a credit-portfolio, this would be as follows:

$$EC_{CreditPortfolio} = EC_{Bank} \frac{\sum [Loss_{Credit}|Loss_{Bank} > EC_{Bank}]}{\sum [Loss_{Bank}|Loss_{Bank} > EC_{Bank}]}$$

With this definition, the capital allocated to a transaction is the capital for the portfolio multiplied by the percentage contribution of the transaction:

$$EC_{Loan} = EC_{CreditPortfolio} \frac{\sqrt{\rho_{Loan,Portfolio}} \, UL_{Loan}}{UL_{Portfolio}}$$

This allocation process also has the property that the bank's capital equals the sum of the capital for the individual transactions, but it also directly incorporates the capital multiplier for each type of risk.

APPENDIX C: SETTING THE HURDLE RATE RETURN ON ECONOMIC CAPITAL

The hurdle rate determines how much the shareholders expect to be compensated for taking risk. If a transaction is expected to pay back less than the hurdle rate, it is not attractive to the bank, and the bank would not do the transaction because it would be risking shareholders' funds without sufficient compensation.

The usual practice in banking is that the hurdle rate is determined at the beginning of the year by the CFO's office and then set as the minimum required expected rate of return for all uses of the bank's capital. This approach is practical in that the single hurdle rate can be easily communicated, and adherence to pricing discipline can be monitored.

The setting of the hurdle rate significantly affects the bank's measured profitability and determines the price that loan officers and traders must charge to their customers. It is therefore highly political. There are several methods for calculating the hurdle rate, each with its own set of assumptions. Given the sensitive nature of setting the rate, it is best to use all available methods and then take an average.

One approach to setting the hurdle rate is to calculate the rate of return implied by the bank's forecasted earnings and its current equity price. This assumes that shareholders believe the bank's earnings estimate.

A similar approach would be to look at historical data on the returns that the bank has made on its equity, and assume that investors expect the same return in the future.

Another approach is to look at the total amount of capital that the bank has and compare it with all the different investments that it can make, starting with the most profitable, until the capital is exhausted. The least profitable investment using the last piece of capital sets the minimum hurdle rate. Given the diversification between risks, such a selection must be iterative to find the best combination of businesses. This optimization approach assumes that the bank must use all its capital. In reality, if there are investments that give poor returns, it would be better for the bank not to take the risk and instead increase its credit rating, or give the excess capital back to the shareholders (as dividends or share buy-back schemes).

The most theoretically pure approach is to set the hurdle rate based on the capital asset pricing model (CAPM). The CAPM requires the following rate of return (r_i) for an investment:

$$r_i = r_f + \beta_i \left(r_f - r_m \right)$$

Here, r_f is the risk-free rate of return, r_m is the average return expected on the overall market, and β_i is the correlation between the return on the investment and the return on the market, weighted by the respective volatilities:

$$\beta_i = \rho_{i,m} \frac{\sigma_i}{\sigma_m}$$

σ_i is the volatility of the investment, σ_m is the volatility of the market, and $\rho_{i,m}$ is the correlation. When a shareholder applies this equation to investing money in a bank, σ_i is the volatility of the bank's share price, $\rho_{i,m}$ is the correlation between the share price and the market, and the required return, r_i, is the hurdle rate, H:

$$H = r_f + \beta_{bank} \left(r_f - r_m \right)$$

$$\beta_{bank} = \rho_{bank,m} \frac{\sigma_{bank}}{\sigma_m}$$

Glossary

Actuarial credit model: An approach used to estimate the loss distribution for a portfolio of loans. It is called "actuarial" because it uses the statistics of historical losses rather than defining an underlying mechanism for the cause of losses.

American depository receipts (ADR):   American depository receipts mirror shares of foreign companies that have been put on deposit in a U.S. bank. This allows Americans to buy securities easily that give the same return as foreign shares.

Arbitrage: The construction of a portfolio of instruments to mimic the characteristics of another instrument.

Ask price: The price at which a party suggests selling an asset.

Asset-backed securities: Asset-backed securities are comprised of the payments from many uniform assets, which are bundled together to form a pool. The pool is then used to make payments to several sets (or tranches) of bonds. Typically, asset-backed securities are used with retail assets, such as credit cards and mortgages.

Assets: Assets are any security or transaction for which the bank is owed money by another party.

Asset/liability management (ALM):   ALM deals with the management of the market risks that arise from a bank's structural position. This is a particular branch of market risk that is not directly part of trading risk. The two primary risks are interest-rate and liquidity risks. For further information, see the definition of "structural position."

Available capital: The current value of the assets minus the current value of the liabilities. If the assets and liabilities are traded, their value is simply the price. If the assets and liabilities are not traded, their value is estimated according to accounting principles.

Back office: A general term to describe the bank's support functions, such as the accounting, auditing, and settlements groups.

Basel Committee: The Basel Committee on Banking Supervision was established in the mid-1980s. It is a committee of national banking regulators, such as the Federal Reserve and the Bank of England. It has representatives from 12 industrial countries, including Belgium, Canada, France, Germany, Italy, Japan, Luxembourg, the Netherlands, Sweden, Switzerland, the United Kingdom, and the United States. The committee meets in the offices of the Bank for International Settlements in Basel, Switzerland, and is therefore often referred to as the "BIS Committee." Strictly speaking, however, the BIS and the Basel Committees are separate entities.

Basis point: A basis point is $1/100$ of a percent, e.g., 1 basis point of $1 million is $100.

Beta: Beta is a measure of the correlation between an individual asset's returns and the returns on the stock market in general. A Beta of 2 would mean that if the market increases by 1%, the asset price would tend to increase by 2%. Beta is the correlation between the asset and the market ($\rho_{a,m}$), multiplied by the standard deviation of the asset's returns (σ_a), divided by the standard deviation of the market's returns (σ_m): $\beta = \rho_{a,m}\sigma_a/\sigma_m$.

Bid price: The price at which a party suggests buying an asset.

Black-Scholes equation: The Black-Scholes equation calculates the current value of holding an option to buy or sell a stock.

Book capital: The book capital is the net value of the bank as measured by accounting methods.

Call option: A call option gives the holder the right to buy an underlying security by paying a predetermined strike price.

Capital: The difference in value between the bank's assets and liabilities. It can be viewed as the current net worth of the bank.

Capital asset pricing model: The capital asset pricing model (CAPM) specifies that the expected return on an asset as a simple linear function of the risk-free rate (r_f), the average market return (r_m), and Beta (β): $r_a = r_f + \beta(r_m - r_f)$.

Capital at Risk (CaR): Capital at Risk is a measure of the "worst-case" losses from credit risks. Typically, it is the 99% confidence level for annual losses. It is similar to Value at Risk, except that it generally applies to credit risk and uses the losses over 1 year.

Cash flow: A cash flow is a payment in cash made from one party to another.

Central limit theorem: This is a statistical concept which states that if a large number of independent, identically distributed (*iid*), random numbers are added together, the result will tend to have a Normal distribution.

Chief risk officer (CRO): A bank's risk-management function is typically headed by the CRO. Those reporting to the CRO include the chief credit officer, the chief market-risk officer, and the chief operating-risk officer.

Commercial loans: Loans that banks offer to commercial enterprises.

Confidence interval: A confidence interval is a specified range for a random variable with an associated probability of the variable's falling within the range. For example, if the 95% confidence interval for x is 2 to 10, there is a 95% chance that x will fall between 2 and 10.

Correlation: The correlation is a measure of the tendency for two variables to change together. The correlation is the covariance between the two variables, divided by the standard deviation of each of the variables:

$$\rho_{xy} \equiv \frac{\sigma_{xy}^2}{\sigma_x \sigma_y}$$

Counterparty risk: The risk of a credit loss due to a trading counterparty's not honoring an agreement.

Covariance: The expected average value of the product of the deviation of two variables. It is a measure of how much two variables tend to move together:

$$\sigma_{xy}^2 \equiv E[(x - \bar{x})(y - \bar{y})] \equiv \int_x \int_y [xypr(x,y)]dxdy$$

Convexity: The nonlinear relationship between the price of a bond and its yield.

Credit derivatives: Highly tailored, over-the-counter instruments whose values are linked to credit events, such as a default or downgrade.

Credit rating: An assessment of the likelihood that an individual, company, or government will honor its commitment to make future payments. Credit ratings are made by banks and by independent agencies.

Credit risk: Credit risk arises from defaults when an individual, company, or government fails to honor a promise to make a payment.

Creditworthiness: An entity's creditworthiness is its probability of honoring its promises to debt holders. For banks, it is determined by the amount of risk it takes compared with the amount of capital held. Creditworthiness is reflected by the credit rating given to the entity.

Cumulative probability distribution (CPF):   The CPF shows the probability of a variable's falling below a given level.

Daily earnings at risk (DEaR):   DEaR is the same as VaR, but specifically for a one-day loss horizon. The typical assumption is that $VaR = DEaR \times \sqrt{T}$, where T is the number of days for the quotation of VaR.

Debt: Debt is a liability or an obligation on a company, individual, or government agency to make specified payments.

Debt instruments: Debt instruments are securities that provide interest payments but no ownership claim on the issuer, unless a default occurs.

Debt rating: Debt rating is a measure of an entity's creditworthiness, and corresponds to the entity's probability of default.

Default: Failure by an entity to make a promised payment.

Delta: Delta is the linear approximation of how much the value of an option will change if the value of the underlying stock changes by 1 unit. For example, if the Delta is 0.5, the value of the option will change by $50 if the value of the underlying changes by $100.

Derivative: A derivative is a security or contract whose value is determined by the value of another security or external variable. For example, a stock option is a contract whose value depends the value of the stock. A weather derivative's value can depend on temperatures and precipitation.

Discriminant analysis: This analysis technique attempts to classify customers into two groups: those that will default, and those that will not.

Duration: Duration is a measure of the interest-rate sensitivity of an instrument or portfolio. It is typically used for bonds.

Economic capital: The required economic capital is the capital needed to support a given risk and maintain a given debt rating. The available economic capital is the value of assets minus the value of liabilities.

Equities: Equities are known as shares or stocks. Equities represent ownership in a company, and a right to the profits once all of the debts have been paid.

Expected exposure: The expected exposure is used to measure the counterparty credit risk for derivatives. It is the average credit exposure across all possible market movements, weighted by the probability of the movement.

Expected loss: The expected loss is the average loss expected from a portfolio or loan. It is the mean of a distribution or possible losses. Over several years, the average losses from a portfolio should equal the expected loss.

Exposure at default (EAD): The exposure at default is the outstanding amount at the time of default. The EAD is also known as the loan equivalence (LEQ).

Facility: A facility is an agreement between a bank and a company allowing the company to withdraw money from the bank with prespecified conditions. A line of credit is an example of a facility.

FASB 133: The full title of FASB 133 is the "Financial Accounting Standards Board, Statement No. 133: Accounting for Derivative Instruments and Hedging Activities, issued 6/98." These accounting rules stipulate that the value of derivatives should be reported on the balance sheet at their fair value. Furthermore, if the derivative hedges another asset or liability, changes in the fair value of that instrument may also be recorded.

Fair value: The fair value is the best assessment of the price at which an instrument could be sold in the market. If the instrument is traded, the fair value simply equals the market price. If the instrument is not traded, its value may be estimated using models.

FICO score: The FICO score rates the creditworthiness of retail customers. It is created by Fair, Issac, and Company based on credit-bureau information.

Fixed rate: An agreement to fix interest payments from the outset.

Floating rate: An agreement to reset interest payments periodically, according to a floating market rate such as the London interbank offered rate (LIBOR).

Foreign exchange (FX): FX trading is the same as currency trading.

Front office: The trading and sales desks in a trading operation, who talk directly to the customers or the market.

Funds-transfer pricing: Funds-transfer pricing is a set of rules used within a bank to determine how much each business unit should be charged when it receives funds from another business unit.

Generally accepted accounting principles (GAAP): A broad body of principles that govern and guide the accounting for financial transactions. They are created based on various sources, including the Financial Accounting Standard Board, and the American Institute of Certified Public Accountants.

Gamma: Gamma is the second derivative of an option's value with respect to the underlying. It describes how much more the price of the option will change beyond the linear approximation of Delta.

Gap report: In measuring ALM risk, gap reports characterize the bank's balance sheet as a fixed series of cash flows. The "gap" is the difference between the cash flows from assets and liabilities.

Global depository receipts (GDR): GDRs are negotiable certificates that typically represent an entity's publicly traded equity or debt.

Greeks: The Greeks describe the change in the value of an option if a market variable changes. They are called "Greeks" because they are symbolized by the Greek letters delta, gamma, vega, theta, and rho.

Hedging: A technique employed to minimize risk by matching one security with another security such that when the value of one security increases, the value of the other security falls.

Hurdle rate: The hurdle rate is the minimum rate of return required by an investor per unit of risk. The investment is only attractive if the expected return is greater than the hurdle.

Instrument: A contract for payments to be made between two parties.

Internal rate of return (IRR):   The IRR is closely related to NPV. It is the single interest rate (y) that would make the NPV of a series of cash flows from an instrument equal to the current trading price of the instrument:

$$Price = \sum \frac{Cashflow_t}{(1+y)^t}$$

Intrinsic value: The intrinsic value of an option is the value that would be realized if the option was exercised immediately. For a call option, it is the greater of zero, or the current value of the underlying, minus the strike price. For a put option, it is the greater of zero, or the strike price, minus the current value of the underlying.

Issuer risk: Credit risk due to the possibility that the issuer of a bond will fail to make the required payments on the bond.

Key risk indicator (KRI):   A set of indicators used for monitoring operating risk.

Key performance indicators (KPI):   A set of indicators used for monitoring operating risk. Very similar to KRIs, but more oriented to monitoring the level of activity rather than the probability of a loss event.

Kurtosis: Kurtosis is the fourth moment of a probability distribution. It is a measure of the "fatness" of the tails. Distributions with fat tails have more "crises" days than expected by a Normal distribution. The kurtosis of a Normal distribution equals three.

Leases: Leases are a form of collateralized loan. In lease arrangements, the bank formally owns the leased equipment until the customer has made all required payments. The agreement may or may not expect the customer to return the equipment at the end of the payment period.

Liabilities: In general, the term "liability" refers to all transactions for which the bank owes money to another party. The liability (or debt) may be in the form of bonds that the bank issues for itself. It may also be in the form of loans given to the bank by other banks, or it may be deposits taken from corporations and retail customers.

Liquidity risk: There are two primary types of liquidity risk. Funding liquidity risk is the risk that the bank will not have enough cash readily available to meet the demand for payments to customers. Trading liquidity risk is the possibility of losses in trading operations due to the inability to buy or sell at close to the midprice.

Log-Normal distribution: The log-Normal probability distribution is useful for describing variables that cannot have a negative value, such as interest rates and stock prices. If the variable has a log-Normal distribution, then the log of the variable will have a Normal distribution.

Long position: Owning a security or expecting future delivery of a security, and therefore benefiting if the security's value increases.

Loss in the event of default (LIED):   LIED is the loss of a percentage of the exposure at default. It is also known as loss given default (LGD) or severity (S). It can be considered to be one minus the recovery rate.

Lowest of cost or market (LOCOM):   LOCOM is a conservative accounting measure of the value of an instrument. The value is taken to be the original cost of buying the instrument, or the current market value, whichever is lower.

Margin account: A margin account is a form of collateralized loan. With a margin account, a customer takes a loan from the bank and then buys a security with the loan supplemented by his own funds. The security is then held by the bank as collateral against the loan.

Mark to market: Valuation of a portfolio according to market quotes, as opposed to using face value, purchase value, or LOCOM.

Mark to model: If liquid quotes are not available, the value of the portfolio may be estimated based on models and risk factors.

Market risk: Risk of losses due to changes in the perceived value of an asset, without any contractual failures.

Matched-funds-transfer pricing: Matched-funds-transfer pricing is a form of transfer pricing in which each transaction is matched with an internal transaction with the same interest-rate characteristics. (See also funds transfer pricing.)

Matrices: Matrices are representations of the parameters in a system of linear equations. They are an alternative way of writing normal algebraic expressions.

Maximum probable loss (MPL):   The MPL is a confidence level for the loss distribution. It is the loss that could occur with a given level of probability. For example, if the 99.9% MPL is $100 million, there is a 0.1% chance that the loss could be greater than $100 million.

Maximum likely exposure (MLE):   The MLE is used to measure counterparty credit risk for derivatives. It is a confidence level in the possible credit exposure across all possible market movements. Typically, the 95% confidence interval is used. For example, if the 95% MPL is $10 million, there is a 5% chance that the exposure could exceed $10 million.

Mean: The mean is commonly called the average. It is the expectation or expected value of a variable. The mean is the first moment of the probability-density function defined by $E[x] \equiv \bar{x} \equiv \int_x [x pr(x)] dx$ where $pr(x)$ is the probability-density function.

Merton-based models: The Merton model links the volatility of a company's equity value with the probability of defaulting on its debt.

Middle office: The risk management and legal groups.

Midprice: Midway between the bid and ask prices.

Monte Carlo simulation: Also known as Monte Carlo evaluation (MCE). It is a numerical technique for integrating probability distributions. In risk measurement, it is used to create future scenarios randomly and value the losses under each scenario.

Net present value (NPV):   The NPV is the sum of discounted future cash flows from a security or contract:

$$NPV = \sum \frac{Cashflow_t}{(1 + r_t)^t}$$

r_t is the current interest rate required by the market for a cash flow at time t.

Normal probability distribution: The Normal probability distribution is also known as the bell curve or Gaussian distribution.

Operating risk: There are many definitions for operating risk. The most general is that it is the risk of losses due to factors other than market risk and credit risk.

Option: An option is a contract that gives the holder the right to buy or sell a specific stock at a preset price by a given date.

Over the counter (OTC):   An OTC contract is one that is written specifically for one customer rather than being exchange traded.

Parametric value at risk: Parametric VaR is one of the three most common approaches to calculating the value at risk. It is also known as linear VaR, variance-covariance VaR, Greek-Normal VaR, Delta-Normal VaR, or Delta-Gamma-Normal VaR.

Probability-density function: A probability-density function is an equation that describes the probability of a random variable's falling in a specific range.

Probability of default (PD):   The probability of default is also known as the default rate or the expected default frequency (EDF).

Put option: A put option gives the holder the right to sell an underlying security and receive a predetermined strike price.

Regulatory capital: Regulatory capital is the minimum amount of capital that must be held by the bank according to regulators such as the Federal Reserve and the Bank of England.

Repurchase agreements (Repos):   In a repo, a security is sold by the bank with a guarantee that it will repurchase the security at a fixed price and date. In essence, it is a short-term collateralized loan.

Rho: Rho is the first derivative of an option's price in relation to interest rates. It is one of five "Greeks" used to measure the sensitivity of options to changes in the value of the underlying, interest rates, and volatility.

Risk-adjusted return on capital (RAROC):   RAROC is the expected return divided by the economic capital that is required to support the transaction.

Risk factors: Risk factors are fundamental market factors that can be used to determine the values of most securities. Typical risk factors include interest rates, exchange rates, bond spreads, equity indices, and implied volatilities.

Scenario analysis: Scenario analysis shows how the value of a portfolio would change in different scenarios, such as a war or the default of a major country.

Securities: Typically, a security is a transferrable contract that gives the owner the rights to payments from the issuer of the security.

Sensitivity analysis: Sensitivity analysis shows how the value of a portfolio would change if risk factors change by a small amount.

Shareholder value added (SVA):   Shareholder value added gives a dollar-based measure of bank performance. It is simply the expected profitability, minus the required profitability to meet the hurdle rate.

Short position: Owing future delivery of a security, and therefore losing if the security's value increases.

Skew: Skew is the third moment of a probability distribution. It is a measure of the asymmetry of the distribution.

Special-purpose vehicles (SPV):   Special-purpose vehicles are legal entities, separate from the parent bank. Transactions carried out by the SPV may benefit from improved tax status or may be more creditworthy than the same transaction carried out by the parent bank.

Spread: The spread is the difference between two rates. For example, the difference between the risk-free rate and the rate charged on a loan to a customer.

Standard deviation: Standard deviation is a measure of how much variation from the mean can be expected. It is the square root of variance. Standard deviation is commonly referred to as the "Sigma" of a distribution.

Stress testing: Stress testing uses specified changes in the market risk factors to reprice a trading portfolio with full, nonlinear pricing models.

Strike price: The strike price of an option is the cash amount to be paid for the underlying security.

Structural position: The structural position of a bank is the interest-rate position that is created by the bank's core business of intermediating between depositors and borrowers. Deposits generally have shorter maturities than loans, so if interest rates increase, the bank must immediately pay more to its deposit customers, but the income from the loans only increases slowly as the old loans expire and new loans are taken out. These are generally illiquid positions and cannot be quickly changed.

Swaps: A swaps contract is an agreement between two counterparties to exchange payments at specified points in the future. The amount of the payments is determined by a formula in the contract. The formula will typically specify the payments as a function of market factors, such as short-term interest rates, FX rates, or commodity prices. Swaps are derivatives because their value is derived from the current and future values of underlying securities.

Theta: Theta is the first derivative of the option in relation to time. It represents how much the option's value changes as it moves toward maturity. It is one of five "Greeks."

Time value of an option: The time value of an option is defined as the actual option value minus the intrinsic value.

Unexpected loss (UL): The UL is used to describe the credit risks. It is the standard deviation of a distribution of possible losses.

Unexpected loss contribution (ULC): The ULC for a loan is the amount of the portfolio's overall UL that is said to be caused by that loan.

Value at risk (VaR): Value at risk is primarily used to measure market risks in trading operations. It is the level that losses may exceed with a given probability. For example, a 99% VaR of $10 million means that there is a 1% chance that losses will exceed $10 million. VaR approximately equals 2 standard deviations of the change in the value of the portfolio. VaR is typically quoted for a 1-day loss horizon, but in some cases is for a multiday horizon.

Value at risk contribution (VaRC): The VaRC for a given desk or transaction is similar to ULC in that it describes the amount of the portfolio's overall VaR that is attributed to the individual desk or transaction.

Variance: See the statistics chapter. Variance is equal to standard deviation squared, and is a measure of the amount by which results vary from the mean. It is the mean square deviation of the variable; i.e., it is the expected value of the square of the difference between a random number and its mean:

$$\sigma_{xx}^2 \equiv E[(x - \bar{x})(x - \bar{x})] \equiv \int_x [(x - \bar{x})^2 pr(x)] dx$$

Vega: Vega describes an option value's sensitivity to changes in the volatility. It is the first derivative of the option price in regard to implied volatility. It represents how much the option value will change if the volatility of the stock price changes by 100% per year. It is one of five "Greeks."

Volatility: Volatility is the standard deviation of a variable as percentage of the mean.

Yield curve: The yield curve is the set of interest rates that is applied to payments with different maturities. The yield curve is generally shown as a graph, with the time until the payment along the x-axis, and the annualized discount rate up the y-axis.

Yield to maturity: The yield to maturity is the internal rate of return for a bond given the current market price and the future cash flows.

Zero coupon bonds: Zero coupon bonds are bonds that do not pay interest coupons. They have only a single "bullet" payment. The bond is sold at a discount to its face value, with the difference between the face value and the sale price implicitly being the interest payment.

INDEX

Note: Boldface numbers indicate illustrations.

ABOUT THE AUTHOR

Chris Marrison, Ph.D., is a veteran risk management consultant with experience in trading risk, credit risk, business control, asset/liability management, emerging markets, and project finance. A former managing principal with The Capital Markets Company and senior engagement officer with Oliver Wyman & Co., Dr. Marrison has been a Royal Air Force officer and a technical consultant on major engineering projects in the United States, Bulgaria, and Brazil, and has given risk management advice to banks and governments throughout North America, Europe, Asia, and Africa.